women's health matters

The Influence of Gender on Disease

Most medical protocols for treating women are based on clinical studies done on men. As a woman, do you want to be medically treated like a man? In this book, Dr. Karen Jensen and other practising physicians share their experiences in treating women's health conditions.

DR. KAREN JENSEN, ND

with Dr. Marita Schauch, ND

Foreword by Dr. Carolyn DeMarco, MD

Women's Health Matters:
The Influence of Gender on Disease

FOR INFORMATION CONTACT:

Mind Publishing Inc.
PO Box 57559,
1031 Brunette Avenue
Coquitlam, BC Canada V3K 1E0
Tel: 604-777-4330 Toll free: 1-877-477-4904
Fax: 1-866-367-5508
Email: info@mindpublishing.com
mindpublishing.com

ISBN: 978-1-927017-27-2
Printed in Canada

Design: FWH Creative
Editor: Janice Dyer
Editorial assistant: Brinda Navjee
Illustrations: Celia Bowes

Table of Contents

SECTION 4 – More Gender Differences in Common Diseases 207

Contributing Author

 Marita Schauch, ND is a graduate of the Canadian College of Naturopathic Medicine. Through her passion for education, she leads by example and hopes to empower others to choose positive lifestyle choices in order to live optimally. She actively lectures across North America and has a special interest in women's health. Dr. Schauch is the coauthor of *The Adrenal Stress Connection* and author of *Making Sense of Women's Health* and *Collagen: Myths & Misconceptions.* Dr. Schauch has a clinical practice in Victoria, BC.

Foreword

Dr. Karen Jensen's career exemplifies the true role of a doctor: to teach patients and doctors alike about the causes and remedies for women's health problems. She is a remarkable woman who put herself through medical school while she was a single parent raising three young children. She completed naturopathic school, and in the process won a prestigious award for proficiency in naturopathic medicine.

We are fortunate that at this stage in her career she is producing her most important and comprehensive book to date on women's health. In this book, you will find the synthesis of her experiences as a woman and a mother, her many years of clinical practice in Calgary, Vancouver, and Victoria, and her years of lecturing and teaching about the natural multifaceted approach to women's health and well-being.

For me, Dr. Jensen's groundbreaking work on the role of the thyroid and adrenal glands in women's health made a major difference to my approach to PMS, perimenopause, and menopause, as well as other hormonally related disorders. Her lectures on these topics have inspired me, along with many other alternative physicians.

In this book, she compiles the latest information on all aspects of women's health: the "hormonic" symphony and women's natural life cycles, as well as the role of the liver, the gut, the adrenal, and the thyroid glands. She provides detail on estrogen-dominant conditions in women, as well as comprehensive information about other women's health conditions. But this book goes much further by also addressing other important health conditions affecting women throughout their whole life spectrum, such as depression, anxiety, insomnia, dementia, heart disease, diabetes, and metabolic syndrome.

According to the latest research, inflammation has been shown to be the underlying cause of many illnesses, from heart disease to dementia to cancer. Dr. Jensen elucidates the most recent information on inflammation, and its role in osteoarthritis, irritable bowel syndrome, and celiac disease.

For many years, Dr. Jensen has provided practical solutions to women's health problems in the form of cutting-edge nutritional and herbal supplements. She is one of the top formulators of supplements designed to address the specific health needs of women at a time when few such supplements were available. Her effective and trustworthy formulations have withstood the test of time. In this book, she outlines the rationale for her recommendations and the ingredients contained in the supplements suggested for every stage of a woman's life.

Although we have made progress in women's health, there is still a long way to go. More women are entering the field of medicine, and women's health is being taught in medical school. However, young doctors seem hesitant to consider the differences that gender can make in health care. Some bias and discrimination has gone underground, but much still remains and is still very relevant to the practice of modern medicine.

This bias in women's health became evident when I recently listened to a radio program on women and migraines. As usual, it showed that women are still not being listened to and their valid concerns are being dismissed and discounted. Ageism in women's health care is also very much alive, which is alarming as women have longer lifespans than men. It is thus a welcome relief to read Dr. Jensen's chapter on dementia, which predominantly affects women. This chapter deals in depth with causes, prevention, and helpful remedies for dementia.

Of course, huge gaps and deficiencies still remain in medical research where women are concerned. Women are more susceptible to the side effects of medication. As Dr. Jensen says, there is no consideration of body size or differences in absorption, gut transfer times, and persistence of drugs in women's bodies, which is two to three times longer than in men's bodies!

Similarly, the action of many common drugs in women is completely unknown. And women are too often carelessly prescribed antidepressants and sedatives as a panacea for whatever ails them. Their life situation and stresses are not taken into account, and neither are important factors such as low thyroid, adrenal functioning, or hormonal imbalance.

As Dr. Jensen says in her introduction, "Gender remains an independent and important risk factor, and sex and gender differences in common diseases must be considered in order to improve health and quality of health care for both women and men."

It is a pleasure to recommend this book to women as the latest indispensable tool to help women to take charge of their health and bodies. I would like to see women enjoy and savour each and every part of the various and rich cycles of their lives. As I said in my first book, a healthy positive woman is an unstoppable force for change on this planet.

Dr. Carolyn DeMarco, MD

Author of *Take Charge of Your Body: Women's Health Advisor*

Dedication

I dedicate this book to my three sons and my grandchildren who teach me every day to know and understand the meaning of unconditional love.

Preface

Many different books about women's health are available on the market. *Women's Health Matters: The Influence of Gender on Disease* is different in that it provides in-depth information and solutions for the treatment of a range of gender-specific conditions as well as diseases that are more common in women. The book is a resource for women to refer to at various stages of life, as well as providing natural solutions to common diseases and conditions.

This new women's book is a culmination of my life's work. The knowledge and experience to write this book was gleaned from my 25 years in practice, as well as from many doctors who were my mentors and inspiration over the years. My patients have been the fuel for the fire that has kept my passion alive in the field of medicine. It has been an honour to be part of their healing journey. Empathetic listening with my patients kept me in touch with the art of medicine and the reality of medical practice, providing a link between the patient experience and scientific evidence.

I particularly want to give thanks to the many people in my field who strive with passion and knowledge to keep the information in the natural health field current, accurate, and reliable. Roland Gahler has been the inspiration behind the rallying of these practising physicians, by inviting and encouraging their knowledge and support. I have had the privilege of knowing and working with many of these doctors who, combined, share over 300 years in clinical practice:

Carolyn DeMarco, MD	Joe Pizzorno, ND
Jennifer Dyck, ND	Ronald Reichert, ND
Joyce Johnson, ND	Julie Reil, MD
Sara Kinnon, ND	Kate Rhéaume, ND
Michael Lyon, MD	Stephanie Rubino, ND
Gaetano Morello, ND	Marita Schauch, ND
Bryn Nyndman, ND, MD	Wendy Tao, ND
Sol Pilar, MD	Ken Walker (aka Gifford Jones), MD

Real Women's Health Solutions from Real Physicians

Dr. Karen Jensen along with other practising physicians, with many decades of cumulative clinical experience, share in this book what they have found to be the most effective health solutions for women.

Dr. Gaetano Morello, ND

Since 1991, Dr. Morello has been training and educating physicians, pharmacists, and health experts on the scientific use of natural medicines in the fields of cardiology, immunology, gastroenterology, anti-aging, and detoxification. He is the contributing author to the authoritative text on *Alternative Medicine, A Textbook of Natural Medicine* and lecturer and regular contributor to a number of magazines, journals, and publications.

Dr. Julie Reil, MD

Dr. Julie Reil is a medical doctor with 20 years' experience in family practice, obstetrics, women's health, and laser medicine. She is a mother of two, a nutrition advocate, educational speaker, and WomenSense® author. Her clinical focus is on educating and improving the lives of women with her innovative and results-driven procedures. Dr. Reil is the founder and director of Shiloh Medical Clinic in Billings, Montana.

Dr. Kate Rhéaume, ND

Author and naturopathic doctor, Kate Rhéaume is a graduate and former faculty member of the Canadian College of Naturopathic Medicine. Dr. Kate lectures internationally on many topics related to health and wellness, and is a frequent guest on radio and television across North America. She is the author of the best-selling book *Vitamin K₂ and the Calcium Paradox: How a Little-Known Vitamin Could Save Your Life.*

Introduction

Over the centuries, scientists have argued that men's brains must be more powerful because they are larger than women's brains. But, does size matter? Newer studies have found that the differences between men and women are much more complicated than the size of the brain. Sex is not related to a particular type of brain, and we are not born with brains stamped male or female, containing little pink or blue – or grey – cells. Although expert opinion varies in terms of what makes male and female brains different – not better or worse, just different – the overall consensus is that the brain contains a mix of both male and female characteristics as unique as our individual fingerprints.

The differences between men and women are determined by very complex interactions at the cellular level, including differences in brain structure, gene expression on X and Y chromosomes, a higher percentage of body fat in women, hormones, gut physiology, social experiences, and more. According to the Institute of Medicine, every cell in the body has a sex, which means that women and men are different even down to the cellular level. This also means that diseases, treatments, and chemicals will affect the sexes differently.

These differences not only influence personality traits, but also the prevalence and response to treatment of particular diseases that are likely to ail men and women. For instance, sex and gender differences in cardiovascular diseases are well-investigated, and there is strong evidence that men and women face different risk factors and have different treatment outcomes. According to the American Heart Association's journal *Circulation*, women's heart attacks may have different underlying causes, symptoms, and outcomes than men's. Despite some improvements in the rate of cardiovascular deaths over the last decade, women still fare worse than men after a heart attack, and heart disease in women remains underdiagnosed and undertreated.

Of course, cardiovascular diseases are by no means the only area in which men and women differ in their susceptibility to and survival of disease. Because gender affects a wide range of physiological functions, it has an impact on a wide range of diseases and conditions. In addition to "women only" health conditions, three times as many women suffer from autoimmune diseases as men, and women are more susceptible to Alzheimer's disease, chronic fatigue syndrome, osteoporosis, diabetes, anxiety and depression, urinary tract disorders, irritable bowel syndrome, and eating disorders. However, despite the wealth of data on differences, medical practice does not sufficiently take gender into account in diagnosis, treatment, or disease management.

Also contributing to the disease gender gap is the medical research gender gap. Excluding women from clinical trials is negatively affecting women's health. Today, even with mounting evidence of the gender differences in disease, women are still being ignored when it comes to health research. In a 2014 report, researchers at the Brigham and Women's Hospital in Boston stated:

"The science that informs medicine – including the prevention, diagnosis, and treatment of disease – routinely fails to consider the crucial impact of sex and gender. This happens in the earliest stages of research, when females are excluded from animal and human studies, or the sex of the animals isn't stated in the published results. Once clinical trials begin, researchers frequently do not enroll adequate numbers of women or, when they do, fail to analyze or report data separately by sex. This hampers our ability to identify important differences that could benefit the health of all."

Clinical trials designed to study the safety and effectiveness of drugs and other medical treatments are primarily done with men, and historically women have been treated as "small men". Even in diseases typical to women, generally the research is done with men. Can we apply what we learn from male rats or humans to a women's physiology? No, we cannot. So why, even today, are men the primary test subjects in clinical trials?

The answer is both practical and political, without malicious intent. The practical reason is that men are easier to study because they do not have menstrual cycles and they do not get pregnant. As a result, research data are easier to analyze. The political reason for excluding women from clinical trials is also historical. In the 1950s, the drug thalidomide caused pregnant women to give birth to babies with missing limbs, and in the 1970s, DES, an estrogen-like drug prescribed to prevent miscarriages, increased the risk that female babies would develop rare vaginal cancers later in life. As a result, the Food and Drug Administration (FDA) in the United States banned all women who could become pregnant from participating in early-stage clinical trials. However, the ban ended up also including all women who were not sexually active, who used contraception, or who were homosexual, as well as other minority groups. This law was upheld until 1993, even though in 1987 the National Institutes of Health (NIH) encouraged scientists seeking funding to include women and minorities in their clinical research.

Researchers surveyed papers published between 2011 and 2012 in five major surgical journals and found that in studies involving animals, 80% included only male subjects. In cell research, male cells were used 71% of the time, and in pre-clinical studies the disparity was even more pronounced and skewed overwhelmingly male.

Millions of women and men are prescribed the same drugs every day, yet women are more likely than men to experience adverse drug reactions. In fact, 80% of prescription drugs pulled from the US market from 1997 to 2001 caused more side effects in women. Metabolic differences determine how drugs are released and excreted, leading to additional risk factors for women. Women are not just men with "boobs and tubes". Lower body surface in women, as well as differences in kidney function, drug resorption, and metabolism, cause significant differences in how the body uses and excretes drugs. In addition, the gut transit time of medications, food, or anything else women ingest takes two times longer than men, and as a result these substances stay in the body for longer periods of time.

Major sex and gender differences have been reported for the efficacy and adverse effects of heart drugs, analgesics, psychiatric drugs, anticancer and cardiovascular drugs, as well as antidepressants, anti-inflammatory, and antiviral drugs. These differences are related to the appropriate dosage for each gender. It would seem obvious, therefore, that many drugs require different dosing to achieve optimal effects. However, a 2005 analysis of 300 new drug applications between 1995 and 2000 found that even the drugs that showed substantial differences in how they were absorbed, metabolized, and excreted by men and women had no sex-specific dosage recommendations on their labels. This might be one reason why women are 1.5–2 times more likely to develop an adverse reaction to prescription drugs than men.

In 1993, the US Congress passed an act requiring that all NIH-funded Phase 3 clinical trials include women, however the male-centric tendency still exists. According to a 2006 study in the *Journal of Women's Health,* women made up less than one-quarter of all patients enrolled in 46 examined clinical trials completed in 2004. And although heart disease kills more women than all cancers combined, a 2008 study published in the *Journal of the American College of Cardiology* reported that women comprised only 10–47% of each subject pool in 19 heart-related clinical trials.

As a result, the question is: If you are only studying males, how do you know the therapy will work or have the same effects or risk factors on women? Simple answer: You don't! Dr. Jerilynn Prior, a professor of endocrinology at the University of British Columbia, says men are not adequate replacements for women in research. "It is not scientifically correct. Period. Full stop." Women deserve to be studied to the same intensity and standards.

Many health care practitioners are not aware of the gender bias in clinical studies and the implications for women's health. As a result, it becomes a bottom-up situation, requiring education of the public, and women in particular.

In health care, as in any area of life, it is crucial to understand what it is we are trying to achieve – the best level of health with the least degree of harm. Armed with a greater level of knowledge, a person is in a better position to more readily assess the ability of different medical approaches, based as they are on distinct philosophies, to meet individual needs. It also allows for greater participation in discussions with health care practitioners when making informed choices regarding health promotion and disease prevention, treatment, and management.

It is always important to address the underlying causes of any condition when possible. There are times when treating symptoms of a disease with drugs or surgery is absolutely necessary, so it is important to be informed about the gender differences in treatment outcomes.

Medicine is both a science and an art. It is a science as it presents facts and involves principles; it is an art as it applies these principles to suit the needs of individual patients. Practising the art of medicine requires active and careful listening. Unfortunately, we live in a world where studies and statistics take priority, and many doctors have lost the art of listening to their patients. Gender remains an independent and important risk factor, and sex and gender differences in common diseases must be considered in order to improve health and quality of health care for both women and men.

As an individual, you have choices. You can take the proactive approach by making health care choices that promote greater health and vitality, and that are specifically intended to prevent disease from occurring. Should symptoms of disease strike, you can be prepared with a basic knowledge of what treatments are available to you, which ones are the safest and most effective. Ask questions and learn to listen to your own body.

The purpose of this book is to offer safe and effective ways to prevent and help treat health problems that are specific or more common in women. We hope you become inspired to begin taking more responsibility for your health. You won't be alone. Today, more and more people are becoming increasingly aware of the various health care choices available to them, and they want more information on how to achieve and maintain optimal health with appropriate natural supplement support, along with diet and lifestyle choices.

" I think women are foolish to pretend they are equal to men. They are far superior and always have been. Whatever you give a woman, she will make greater. If you give her sperm, she will give you a baby. If you give her a house, she will give you a home. If you give her groceries, she will give you a meal. If you give her a smile, she will give you her heart. She multiplies and enlarges what is given to her. So, if you give her any crap, be ready to receive a ton of shit! "

– **William Golding** (1911–1993),
British novelist and playwright

THE HORMONIC ORCHESTRA

"We're going on a journey through a remarkable kingdom, a place in which miracles and magic are everyday occurrences. In no other place in this world are more wondrous things happening than inside each of us."

– Tom Monte, author and natural healer

The "Hormonic" Symphony

The endocrine system is made up of a number of organs that powerfully influence the health of the hormonal system during the reproductive years and throughout the menopausal and postmenopausal years. In women, the endocrine organs that most influence hormonal balance are the adrenal glands, pituitary, hypothalamus, thyroid, and ovaries. In addition, although they are not endocrine organs, the liver and the large intestine play important roles in hormonal health. Together, these many organs can be thought of as an orchestra playing a complex, beautiful, and ever-changing musical work – a "hormonic" symphony.

Chapter  1

Hormones and the Endocrine System

Hormone Fluctuations

The amount of hormone released by an endocrine gland is determined by the body's need for the hormone at any given time. Through complex feedback mechanisms involving many body systems, hormone production is regulated so that there is no over- or underproduction of particular hormones. However, there are times when the regulating mechanisms do not function properly and hormonal imbalances occur. Stress factors and transitional hormonal times such as puberty and menopause have a tremendous effect on the endocrine system's ability to maintain balance.

The pituitary regulates so many hormones that it can be considered the "concert master" of the hormonal orchestra, taking its orders from the conductor, the hypothalamus, to release hormones. The pituitary sends out its instructions to the other endocrine organs via various stimulating hormones. It is through the leadership of the hypothalamus and pituitary that the hormonal symphony orchestra is able to continue playing tuneful music.

However, during times when hormonal levels fluctuate more dramatically, such as after ovulation and through the perimenopausal years, the orchestra may go out of tune. Players such as the thyroid or adrenal glands may not be able to adjust to the new notes the body wants to play. The adrenals may be exhausted from prolonged stress before menopause, and are then unable to meet the demand for more hormones. In addition, sometimes the concert master, the pituitary, cannot stimulate the glandular orchestra to play loud enough or in proper harmony.

The Menstrual Cycle

In order to have a greater understanding of hormonal fluctuations, it is important to know what happens during the menstrual cycle. The cycle is divided into the follicular phase and the luteal phase, and it is regulated by complex interactions between the hypothalamus, pituitary, and ovaries.

The hypothalamus directs the pituitary to secrete two hormones that are directly involved in the menstrual cycle: follicle-stimulating hormone (FSH) and luteinizing hormone (LH). These, in turn, stimulate the ovaries to produce estrogens, progesterone, and androgens. The hypothalamus is affected by these sex hormones and adjusts its instructions to the pituitary accordingly. When there is clear communication between the glands, the hormones are in balance. Normally all hormones are released in short bursts every 1–3 hours to maintain constant levels in the blood.

Days 1–5: Menstruation

In a normal cycle, the first five days are the time of menstruation (see Figure 1.1). This monthly bleeding takes place because of the sharp decline in estrogen and progesterone levels at the end of the luteal phase if pregnancy did not occur. These hormones maintain the womb's endometrial lining, the capillary-rich tissue in which a fertilized embryo implants itself. If there is no embryo implant, estrogen and progesterone levels fall, and as a result the endometrium sloughs off, tearing capillaries and causing bleeding. FSH secretion then rises because of the low estrogen levels, thus stimulating structures in the ovaries called follicles to begin secreting larger amounts of estrogen. In addition, LH stimulates the growth to maturity of new ova at this time.

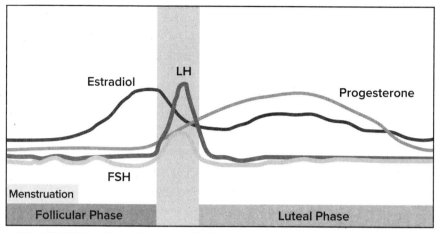

Figure 1.1 The menstrual cycle

Days 6–14: Follicular stage

The ova continue to mature during the follicular stage. After the menstrual period and until ovulation, FSH (primarily) and LH stimulate the ovarian follicles to produce estrogen in order to support the growth of the endometrium. The rising estrogen levels trigger a mid-cycle LH surge, which causes ovulation sometime between days 12 and 14 of the cycle. In ovulation, the follicle that has been nurturing the growing egg ruptures. The egg is released into the abdominal cavity and is swept up by special structures at the ends of the fallopian tubes, canals that lead into the womb.

Days 14–28: Luteal stage

The luteal stage occurs after ovulation and lasts approximately 12 days. Progesterone levels are higher relative to estrogen, as the ruptured ovarian follicle (corpus luteum) secretes large amounts of progesterone, needed to prepare the endometrial lining for implantation of a fertilized egg. If the egg is not fertilized, both estrogen and progesterone levels drop. When the uterus begins to shed the endometrial lining, menstruation begins.

The menstrual cycle continues for roughly 30 years, from puberty to menopause, unless pregnancy or hormonal problems interrupt it. Any extreme ups and downs in the estrogen/progesterone ratio, when either hormone is excessive or deficient, results in symptoms.

The Hormones – An Overview

Our bodies make a number of hormones, day in and day out. Steroid hormones are derived from cholesterol and include the sex hormones as well as the adrenal hormones. Cholesterol is the precursor substance needed for the synthesis, or creation, of all steroid hormones, and in essence it can be called the "mother" hormone. Both high-density lipoprotein (HDL) cholesterol ("good" cholesterol) and low-density lipoprotein (LDL) cholesterol (so-called "bad" cholesterol) are substrates (raw material) for hormones. LDL is used for hormone synthesis by steroid-producing cells in the ovaries, liver, fatty tissues, and brain, while HDL is used in the adrenal glands.

Types of hormones

The main female hormones are progesterone and estrogens; the main male hormones are testosterone and androstenedione. Women also require testosterone, in lower levels than men, however, and men also require progesterone and estrogen, but in lower levels than women. All steroid hormones are converted into more soluble excretion products in the liver.

Of all the hormones, three in particular are of great concern to women: the estrogens – estradiol, estrone, and estriol – and testosterone and progesterone.

The estrogens

Estrogen is produced in the ovaries (in the testes in men) and in smaller amounts in the adrenal glands. There are at least two dozen identified estrogens, and they have a multitude of functions.

The estrogenic hormones are uniquely responsible for the growth and development of female sexual characteristics and reproduction. In women, estrogen circulates in the bloodstream and binds to estrogen receptors on cells in targeted tissues. These affect the breasts and uterus, and also the brain, bone, liver, heart, and other tissues.

Estrogen plays a number of roles, including:

- Controlling growth of the uterine lining during the first part of the menstrual cycle
- Causing changes in the breasts during adolescence and pregnancy
- Establishing body fat deposition and body hair patterns
- Regulating various other metabolic processes, including bone growth and cholesterol levels

The three main naturally occurring estrogens in women are estrone, estradiol, and estriol:

- **Estrone (E1)** is produced in the ovaries, fat cells, and adrenal glands. During menopause, the adrenal glands take over steroid hormone production and they produce testosterone and androstenedione, which are then converted to estradiol and estrone in the fat cells. Estrone is the predominant form of circulating estrogen after menopause.

- **Estradiol (E2)** is primarily produced by the ovary and is the predominant form of estrogen found during the reproductive years.

- **Estriol (E3)** is a breakdown product of estradiol and estrone; it is not secreted by the ovary and is thought to be the weakest of all the estrogens. Estriol has protective effects when it binds to the receptors and prevents the stronger estrogens such as estradiol, estrone, or xenoestrogens (environmental estrogen imposters) from binding and creating unwanted symptoms of estrogen dominance.

Approximately six months prior to menopause, estrogen levels decline rapidly in most women as ovarian secretion of estrogen and progesterone ends. In contrast, the postmenopausal ovary retains the capacity to produce other steroids, specifically the androgens testosterone and androstenedione. Testosterone is converted to E2 in the body fat. Androstenedione, produced by both the ovaries and adrenals in postmenopausal women, is converted to E1 and E2. The total estrogen produced after menopause is, however, far less than that produced during a woman's reproductive years.

Progesterone

Progesterone is produced in the ovaries during and after ovulation, and during pregnancy in the placenta. A small amount is also made by the adrenal glands. Younger women with regular cycles should make adequate progesterone. However, with the added influence of diet and lifestyle factors, adrenal insufficiency, and environmental toxins, more women are experiencing symptoms of hormone imbalance related to progesterone deficiency at a younger age. Progesterone is important in maintaining normal menstrual cycles, breast development, maintaining pregnancy, facilitating the action of thyroid hormone, relaxing blood vessels, and influencing neurotransmitters in the brain.

Testosterone

Testosterone is made primarily by the ovaries in women and testes in men, and to a lesser degree, the adrenal glands. Testosterone is considered primarily a male hormone, but it also plays an important part in the overall hormonal health of women. Testosterone is a step on the way to estrogen, since testosterone converts to estradiol. Testosterone enhances libido, muscle strength and mass, moods, energy, and immune function. Elevated levels are associated with polycystic ovary syndrome (PCOS), acne, premenstrual syndrome (PMS), and facial hair.

Cortisol

Cortisol is synthesized in the adrenal cortex in response to chronic stress. The effects of cortisol are felt throughout the entire body. It is needed for nearly all dynamic processes, from blood pressure regulation and kidney function, to glucose levels and fat building, muscle building, protein synthesis, thyroid function, and immune function.

Thyroid hormones

The pituitary secretes thyroid-stimulating hormone (TSH) that causes the thyroid to release thyroid hormones (T3 and T4). These hormones regulate the body's metabolic rate, as well as heart and digestive function, muscle control, brain development, and bone maintenance. (Refer to *Chapter 4* for more information on the role of thyroid hormones.)

Aldosterone

Aldosterone, a steroid hormone like cortisol, is produced in the outer cortex of the adrenals. It helps regulate levels of sodium and potassium, which in turn helps control blood pressure, the distribution of fluids in the body, and the balance of electrolytes.

Prolactin

Prolactin, a hormone secreted by the pituitary gland, is involved in lactation. High levels of prolactin can interfere with ovulation and decrease fertility, delay puberty, and cause polycystic ovary syndrome.

Insulin

Insulin, produced by the pancreas, regulates carbohydrate and fat metabolism. Diets high in refined carbohydrates and sugars can cause increased levels of sugar (glucose), signalling the release of insulin. Chronically elevated levels of glucose cause the insulin receptors in the body to become resistant to the regulating effects of insulin, leading to insulin resistance. Some of the conditions associated with insulin resistance (metabolic syndrome) include diabetes, cardiovascular disease, thyroid problems, PCOS, and other hormone imbalances.

Dehydroepiandrosterone

Dehydroepiandrosterone (DHEA) is produced in the adrenal glands, gonads, fat cells, and brain. It is a precursor to male and female steroid hormones (androgens and estrogens). Low levels of DHEA can cause memory problems, low libido, elevated blood pressure, anxiety, elevated cholesterol, and poor stress recovery.

Melatonin

Melatonin is released by the pineal gland and helps regulate the sleep/wake cycles. Melatonin increases during darkness and decreases in light. Low levels are associated with insomnia, early morning fatigue, anxiety, and estrogen dominance.

Vitamin D, 25-hydroxyvitamin D – the hormone

What makes vitamin D unique compared to other vitamins is that the body converts vitamin D into a hormone. This hormone is sometimes called "activate vitamin D" or calcitriol, which functions as a steroid hormone in the body. Recent research is beginning to show just how far-reaching the role of vitamin D is in preventing several common diseases and conditions.

Vitamin D deficiency has been shown to cause mild depressive symptoms. Several studies have evaluated how vitamin D may be related to seasonal affective disorder (SAD), premenstrual syndrome (PMS), and fibromyalgia.

Testing and diagnosing hormonal problems

Hormone health during the reproductive years, as well as the transition into menopause, will be symptomatic or relatively symptom free depending largely on the health of the adrenal glands, liver, thyroid, and gut microbiome. Women who are having hormonal difficulties, particularly during the perimenopausal and menopausal years, may want to consider having a series of lab work.

Lab tests

Blood tests and saliva hormone tests are the two common lab tests used to assess hormonal levels.

Blood tests can be used to check the following hormones:

- TSH, free T3, reverse T3, free T4, thyroid antibodies
- Estradiol
- Progesterone
- Free and bioavailable testosterone
- LH
- FSH – the standard blood test for determining a diagnosis of menopause
- Prolactin
- DHT

Saliva hormone tests are much more sensitive than blood tests. Saliva can be tested for the following hormones:

- Estradiol
- Progesterone
- Testosterone
- DHEA
- Cortisol

Chapter 2

The Liver and Gut Microbiome in Hormonal Balance

Health problems can arise when we put things into our body, both consciously and unconsciously, that are either toxic or that build up an excess of toxicity over time, such as bad fat, processed foods, excess hormones, man-made chemicals, and excess alcohol and drugs (therapeutic or otherwise). The liver takes on the burden of breaking down and detoxifying these chemicals so the harmful substances do not get into the cells of the body.

The Liver – An Overview

The liver plays a number of roles, including:

- Detoxification, inactivation, and excretion of toxic chemicals, drugs, and hormones

- Acting as a hormone processor, manufacturing and regulating some hormone levels

- Directing various hormones to perform their proper function in other parts of the body
- Metabolizing more than 50% of estrogens
- Forming approximately 50% of the estrogen "couples", which are excreted via the bile into the intestines; the successful journey of these couples through the intestine depends on healthy microflora
- Breaking down hormones into "good" and "bad" estrogens

Healthy liver function is necessary to prevent many hormone imbalances, and in particular those related to estrogen dominance. If the hormone surplus exceeds the regulatory capacities of the liver, hormone levels in the blood increase, creating conditions related to estrogen dominance and other hormone imbalances.

Signs and Symptoms of Liver Dysfunction

Naturopathic doctors recognize a condition called "sluggish" or "congested" liver. A person with a congested liver has liver dysfunction, but the dysfunction is not yet at a level that is detectable through standard laboratory tests. The common symptoms of liver congestion include:

- Allergies
- Aggression, anger
- Chemical and environmental sensitivities
- Indigestion or distended abdomen
- Depression, moodiness
- Constipation
- Irritability
- Headaches and migraines
- Eye problems – red, itchy, watery eyes
- Fatigue
- Insomnia or inability to sleep deeply
- Hormonal problems such as PMS
- Muscular pain and tendon problems
- Neck and back tension and stiffness

Possible Causes of Liver Dysfunction

In premenopausal women, the ovaries produce primarily estradiol, most of which is converted to estrone, and eventually to estriol. The liver then metabolizes the remaining estradiol and estrone, breaking it down further, and excreting the excess from the body.

During the first phase of metabolism, estrone is converted into various metabolites, including 2-hydroxyestrone (2-OH estrone), a very weak estrogen, and 16-alpha-hydroxyestrone (16-OH estrone), a very potent estrogen (see Figure 2.1). If the conversion process favours the stronger form, then tissue that has an abundance of estrogen receptors, such as the breasts and uterus, may be more vulnerable to excessive estrogen activity, potentially leading to the formation of fibroids or the stimulation of estrogen-sensitive cancers.

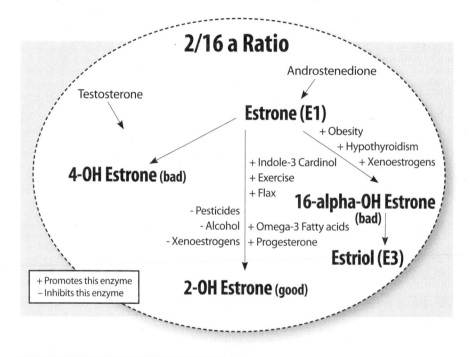

Figure 2.1 Estrogen metabolism: good and bad estrogens

During the second phase of liver metabolism, a process known as conjugation begins where nutrients are combined with hormones and other substances and converted to water-soluble compounds that can be excreted. Problems occur if the nutrients required by the liver to process toxins or hormone excesses are not available.

Testing and Diagnosis

Liver tests are used to assess the general state of the liver. In liver congestion or preclinical symptoms as discussed in this chapter, the lab tests will fall within the normal range.

Liver enzymes

Alanine aminotransferase (ALT) and aspartate aminotransferase (AST) are the most commonly used indicators of liver damage. These enzymes are normally found in liver cells, however they leak out of these cells and make their way to the blood when liver cells are injured. ALT is felt to be a more specific indicator of liver inflammation as AST is also found in other organs such as the heart and skeletal muscle. However, in chronic liver disease, these enzymes may be entirely within the normal range, even in the presence of cirrhosis.

Alkaline phosphatase

The alkaline phosphatase is the most frequently used test to detect obstruction in the biliary system. Elevation of this enzyme may be found in a large number of disorders as common as gallstone disease, alcohol abuse, and drug-induced hepatitis, or in less common disorders such as primary biliary cirrhosis (PBC) or biliary tumours.

Liver function tests

Bilirubin

Bilirubin is formed primarily from the breakdown of a substance called heme, which is found in red blood cells. It is taken up from the blood, processed, and then secreted into the bile by the liver. Since bilirubin may be elevated in many forms of liver or biliary disease, it is relatively non-specific. It is, however, generally useful as a true liver "function test" since it reflects the liver's ability to take up, process, and secrete bilirubin into the bile.

Albumin

Albumin is a major protein that is formed by the liver. Although many factors can affect the level of albumin circulating in the blood, chronic liver disease causes a decrease in the amount of albumin produced.

Prothrombin time and INR

The prothrombin time and the INR are tests used to assess blood clotting. When the liver is significantly injured, these proteins are not produced normally.

What is ISURA™?

Not all supplements are created equal. Natural health products that have passed the most rigorous testing in the world are granted the ISURA seal of approval. This seal guarantees that the products are safe, clean, effective, GMO-free, and properly labelled. When purchasing supplements, look for the Isura seal of approval on product labels. For more information, go to **isura.ca**

what we know works

Support for Liver and Environmental Toxin Detoxification

EstroSense® gently supports the body's natural detoxification processes to help with healthy estrogen metabolism, as well as prevent and treat estrogen dominant conditions and other hormonal imbalances. EstroSense contains milk thistle and turmeric, as well as powerful detoxification nutrients and antioxidants such as indole-3-carbinol (I-3-C), diindolylmethane (DIM), calcium-D-glucarate, sulforaphane, green tea extract, lycopene, and rosemary extract. Refer below for more information on individual ingredients.

Dosage: 3 capsules daily with food.

> **Milk thistle** *(Silybum marianum)* contains a group of flavonoids that promote liver health and also support the body's natural detoxification processes. The most impressive research showing support of liver function has been done on the extract of milk thistle. This powerful herb supports the liver by acting as an antioxidant, as well as preventing the depletion of glutathione. The antioxidant glutathione supports the liver and aids in the detoxification of harmful chemicals and toxins. (Refer to *Chapter 8* for information on the benefits of milk thistle for preventing breast cancer.)
>
> **I-3-C** is a compound found in vegetables of the Brassica family, including broccoli, cauliflower, cabbage, and kale. I-3-C supports liver detoxification and healthy estrogen metabolism by increasing the ratio of 2-hydroxyestrone (good estrogens) to 16-hydroxyestrone (bad estrogens).

Diindolylmethane (DIM) is synthesized from I-3-C which is found in cruciferous vegetables. It promotes beneficial estrogen metabolism and healthy hormonal balance and is especially helpful for managing estrogen-dominant conditions.

Calcium-D-glucarate has detoxifying and anticarcinogenic properties that are attributed to its ability to increase the excretion of potentially toxic compounds. During Phase II liver detoxification, chemical carcinogens such as xenoestrogens, steroid hormones, and other fat-soluble toxins are conjugated in the liver and excreted through the biliary tract.

Liver MD® is a comprehensive detoxification formula that supports your body in the processing and elimination of environmental toxins such as heavy metals and pesticides. Liver MD contains alpha-lipoic acid (ALA) and N-acetyl-L-cysteine (NAC), vitamin C, selenomethionine, zinc, broccoli powder as well as vitamin B12, milk thistle, and curcumin. Refer below for more information on the ingredients.

Dosage: 2 capsules twice daily.

Curcumin *(Curcuma longa)* is a well-researched herb shown to have potent antioxidant and liver supportive properties. It also promotes healthy inflammatory responses.

Dandelion root *(Taraxacum officinale)* is considered the ideal liver remedy during times of liver detoxification. It provides gentle liver support, but more importantly it has diuretic properties that aid in the removal of toxins from liver and kidneys during cleansing and detoxification.

NAC increases cellular levels of glutathione, a powerful antioxidant involved in protecting the body from environmental toxic damage. It has also been found to reduce toxicity and protect organs from the damage of heavy metals.

ALA stimulates glutathione synthesis and has been shown to protect against liver and nervous system damage from heavy metals and other environmental toxicity.

Chlorella is a single-celled fresh water algae that is a potent detox agent for mercury and other heavy metals. Chlorella also has liver-protective properties, is a potent antioxidant, and is immune supportive.

Vitamin C is a potent antioxidant and may also decrease lead levels. It is required for the synthesis of glutathione, which helps support our antioxidant defences and prevent free radical damage from environmental toxins.

Diet and Lifestyle Tips for Liver and Environmental Toxin Detoxification

- Start your morning with fresh lemon juice in water to help flush and decongest the liver.

- Eat beets or drink beet and vegetable juice regularly. Beets are an excellent liver cleanser. Organic beet juices are readily available at your local health food store.

- Consume green drinks regularly, such as Whole Earth & Sea™, to aid in liver cleansing.

- Eat high-quality protein foods, such as free-range eggs, fish, raw nuts, and seeds, to restore and sustain the liver.

- Get lots of fresh air, exercise, rest, natural foods, and good water.

- Eat foods and herbs rich in nutrients that help protect the liver from damage and improve liver function, including high-sulphur foods such as garlic, legumes, onions, and eggs; excellent sources of soluble fibre, such as pears, oat bran, apples, and legumes; cruciferous vegetables, especially broccoli, Brussels sprouts, and kale; artichokes; and spices such as turmeric, cinnamon, and ginger.

The Importance of the Vagina and Gut Microbiome

The microbial communities of the vagina, along with the acidic pH, serve as the "guard dogs" to regulate microbial growth and transmission to protect against entry of harmful bacteria and other pathogens into the uterus and fallopian tubes. The cervix serves as a physical barrier to prevent the entry of pathogens. Infections occur when microbial communities of the vagina are altered to permit the overgrowth of harmful microorganisms that are able to breach the immune protection and negatively impact the healthy bacteria. This breach results in reproductive disorders including infertility, preterm birth, pelvic inflammation, sexual transmitted diseases, gynecological cancers, and other diseases. Understanding, and more importantly, maintaining a healthy vaginal microbial environment is critical to preventing many reproductive disorders associated with various pathogens.

The gut microbiome influences the vaginal microbiome as well as hormone balance. As mentioned earlier, approximately 50% of the estrogen "couples" formed in the liver are excreted via the bile into the intestines. The successful journey of these couples through the intestine depends on healthy microflora. Specific gut bacteria produce an enzyme that helps metabolize estrogen and eliminate it from the body. If the microbiome is not functioning properly, estrogen metabolites are not carried out of the body efficiently and this can lead to symptoms and conditions associated with estrogen dominance. A very common condition that causes imbalances in the gut microbiome is called dysbiosis, also known as "leaky gut".

The Leaky Gut Factor

Stress can directly affect microbiota by altering intestinal permeability, allowing bacterial antigens and other toxic substances to penetrate the gut barrier. The mucosal gut barrier is said to be the body's second skin, which serves as the first line of defence against pathogens. Increased intestinal permeability, often called leaky gut, occurs when this protective barrier fails to prevent potentially harmful molecules from entering the bloodstream. These molecules can cause an inflammatory response, leading to brain degeneration and mood changes.

A healthy microbiome works to boost mood by generating healthy levels of brain-derived neurotrophic factor (BDNF) and the neurotransmitter gamma-aminobutyric acid (GABA), and by enhancing brain receptors for GABA. GABA is known to calm areas of the brain that are overactive in anxiety and mood disorders such as depression. Many women with hormone imbalances experience symptoms of anxiety and depression. (Refer to *Chapter 14* for more information on leaky gut.)

In addition, double-blind trials have shown that people treated with the probiotics lactobacilli and bifidobacteria experienced improvements in psychological distress, anxiety, and depression, and had decreased anger and hostility. This research verifies the two-way communication between the digestive tract and the brain.

Dysbiosis

Dysbiosis, an imbalance in gut bacteria, can result from anything that alters gut microbiota. The most common causes are antibiotics, oral contraceptives, hormone replacement therapy, acid-suppressing medications, corticosteroids, gastrointestinal infections, surgery, poor digestion, chronic constipation, chronic mental/emotional stress, a high-sugar and refined carbohydrate diet, and food allergies.

Dysbiosis can manifest in many ways, and may have a number of causes. The following questionnaire, adapted from the work of William Crook, MD, will help you determine what degree of dysbiosis you may have.

Dysbiosis Questionnaire

General History

10	Have you taken tetracyclines (e.g., Minocin) for acne for one month or longer?
10	Have you taken, or do you take, antibiotics for infections more than four times per year?
10	Have you taken birth control pills for more than two years?
5	Have you taken birth control pills for six months to two years?
10	Have you taken prednisone or other cortisone-like drugs (e.g., asthma medication)?
10	Does the smell of perfume, tobacco, or other odours or chemicals make you sick?
5	Do you crave sugars and breads?
_____	**Total score**

Symptoms

Enter **(1)** if symptom is mild; **(2)** if moderate or frequent; **(3)** if severe or constant

_____ Experience vaginal discharge or irritation

_____ Experience frequent bladder infections or incontinence

_____ Experience premenstrual syndrome or fluid retention

_____ Have difficulty getting pregnant

_____ Have frequent infections (sinus, lung, colds, etc.)

_____ Have allergies to foods or environmental substances

_____ Feel worse on rainy and snowy days, around molds or musty basements

_____ Experience feelings of anxiety and/or irritability

_____ Have insomnia

_____ Experience gas and bloating

_____ Experience constipation or diarrhea

_____ Have bad breath

_____ Have a difficult time concentrating (feel "spacey")

_____ Experience muscle weakness or painful joints

_____ Have nasal congestion

_____ Feel pressure behind or irritation of the eyes

_____ Have frequent headaches

_____ Generally "don't feel well" without an explanation or diagnosis

_____ Have thyroid problems

_____ Have muscle aches or weakness

_____ **Total score from all sections**

If you scored: Under 50 – You are considered to have mild dysbiosis. **50–90** – You are considered to have moderate dysbiosis. **90–120** – You are considered to have severe dysbiosis.

Diet and Lifestyle Tips for Dysbiosis

The four components of the treatment for cleansing the bowel and decreasing the toxic overload are:

- Make dietary changes to starve out candida and harmful bacteria
- Cleanse the bowel of harmful microflora and accumulated toxins
- Restore beneficial microflora
- Follow the moderate dysbiosis diet (see below)

The dysbiosis diet

The objective of the dysbiosis diet is to reduce the intake of foods that encourage the growth of harmful yeast and bacteria. Carefully follow this diet for a 10-week period.

Foods to avoid

- Sugars of all types, and foods that contain refined or simple sugars
- Dried fruit (e.g., raisins, prunes, dates)
- Fruit juices, both fresh and frozen
- Yeasted breads, pastries, and other baked goods (alternatives include corn tortillas and burritos, unyeasted crackers or rice cakes, sprouted breads, and yeast-free and sugar-free breads)
- Alcoholic beverages and malt products
- Peanuts and cashews
- Cow's milk (use in moderation on cereal or in coffee; alternatives include almond milk and goat's milk)
- Ice cream
- Antibiotics

Foods that can be eaten freely

- Fresh, unprocessed meats, poultry, and fish
- Eggs
- Raw nuts (except peanuts and cashews) and seeds
- Flaxseed and olive oil

- Low-carbohydrate vegetables such as all green leafy vegetables (chard, kale, celery, lettuce, spinach), broccoli, cabbage, and Brussels sprouts
- Butter and yogourt (in the absence of allergies to dairy products)

Foods that can be eaten cautiously

- Fruit (no more than two daily)
- Cereals and other whole grain products (ensure they are yeast free and sugar free)
- High-carbohydrate vegetables (e.g., squash, potatoes, carrots, beets)
- Cheese (small amounts, 2–3 times per week)

Monitor your intake of foods in the "eat with caution" category day by day. For example, if you have a high-carbohydrate vegetable for lunch (such as sweet potatoes), then have only a small serving of grains or pasta for dinner.

Additional support for dysbiosis

In addition to the dysbiosis diet, it is very important to kill off unfriendly microbes, and to take a probiotic to restore the beneficial microflora.

Various products decrease the load of toxic microbes, such as the following:

- **Berberine** is perhaps the most effective supplement for dysbiosis and leaky gut. It closes the tight junctions in leaky gut, preventing leakage of large food particles and bacteria into circulation. Berberine also has antimicrobial properties to help with dysbiosis.
- **Garlic supplements, grapefruit seed extract, peppermint oregano oil,** and **olive leaf extract** all kill off unfriendly microbes.
- **Psyllium seed** is a bulking agent that helps eliminate toxins by encouraging regular bowel movements and by binding with stored waste products that normally are not eliminated.
- The herbs **buckthorn** *(Rhamnus cathartica, Rhamnus frangula)* and **cascara sagrada** *(Rhamnus purshiana)* encourage efficient bowel elimination, which is important for microbial balance. These herbs increase peristalsis (the muscular contractions of the bowel), thereby assisting with the removal of toxins.

If you suspect dysbiosis, take immediate steps to bring your intestinal flora back into balance by following these recommendations:

- Eat unprocessed foods – whole grains, beans, vegetables, fruit, nuts – that are high in natural fibre. Plant fibres found in natural foods absorb harmful compounds and encourage regular evacuation.

- Avoid antibiotics whenever possible; instead, seek safer, naturally immune-enhancing treatments for infections. Antibiotics kill beneficial bacteria in the colon, allowing yeast and other harmful organisms to flourish.

- Avoid simple sugars and other refined foods that stress the digestive and immune systems and encourage microbiota imbalance.

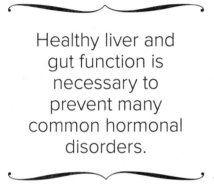

Healthy liver and gut function is necessary to prevent many common hormonal disorders.

- Avoid hormone replacement therapy, birth control pills, and steroid medications such as cortisone whenever possible, and investigate natural alternatives. These drugs encourage yeast overgrowth since they increase blood sugar levels.

- Take steps to reduce the various stressors in your life. Unrelieved stress lowers immunity, enhancing the possibility of dysbiosis.

Stress and the Gut

The Role of Microbiota

The gut-brain axis is a two-way communication system between the central nervous system (CNS) (brain and spinal cord) and the gastrointestinal tract, as shown in Figure 2.2. Gut microbiota are the microorganisms living in the gut; collectively these microbes are called the microbiome. This two-way communication network between the brain and the gut also involves the hypothalamic-pituitary-adrenal (HPA) axis. The HPA axis is considered the core stress axis responsible for the adaptive responses to stressors of any kind (refer to *Chapter 3* for more information on stress).

Studies demonstrate that gut microbiota influence stress reactions by directly affecting the HPA activity and the release of stress hormones, namely cortisol. The overproduction of stress hormones decreases the production of steroid hormones, causing hormonal imbalance. Research has found that when the gut is recolonized with healthy bacteria in the form of probiotics, it leads to a normalization of the HPA axis and a reversal of the exaggerated stress hormone response.

Stress and the Microbiota-Gut-Brain Axis in Health and Disease

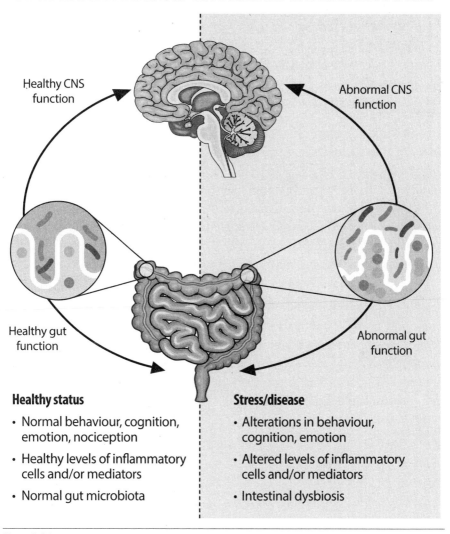

Figure 2.2 Stress and the microbiota-gut-brain axis in health and disease

Microbial communities within the gut are relatively resistant to change. However, it is recognized that factors such as alterations in diet, stress factors, inflammation, and the administration of antibiotics can cause modifications to the microbial balance. Studies have demonstrated that psychosocial stressors can also cause alterations in the gut microbial community. The role of the gut-brain axis is to monitor and integrate gut functions, as well as to link the emotional and cognitive centres of the brain. What is not commonly recognized is that it works both ways. Alterations in the balance of gut microbiota have been linked to a broad range of diseases, including autoimmune, metabolic, and gastrointestinal disorders, and brain disorders such as depression, mood disorders, hormonal imbalance, and learning disorders.

Support for Restoring Beneficial Microflora

Probiotics

The two most important friendly bacteria in our bodies are *Lactobacillus acidophilus* and *Bifidobacterium bifidum*. Lactobacilli and bifidobacteria in the intestines inhibit the growth of unfriendly organisms by producing antimicrobial factors. These bacteria are found in the fermented foods that most cultures use, such as yogourt, miso, tempeh, keifer, sauerkraut, and fermented juices. These foods, as well as probiotic supplements containing beneficial bacteria, benefit human health. A high-quality lactobacilli and bifidobacteria supplement provides greater colonization of the friendly bacteria.

Daily use of probiotics while following the dysbiosis diet and cleansing protocols, and regular use thereafter, is recommended. If you eat foods that are high in friendly bacteria, then you do not need to take a daily supplement, though you may wish to use one at least two days a week to maintain adequate levels of the friendly microbes. The dysbiosis cleanse program should be considered as part of your general health program to maintain a healthy hormone balance as well as mental emotional balance.

Chapter **3**

The Adrenal Glands and the Hormone Connection

The Adrenal Glands – An Overview

It is interesting that many people have never heard of the adrenal glands, considering they command the most powerful hormones that affect your body and, in fact, your life. They are no bigger than a walnut and sit on top of each kidney. You cannot live without your adrenal hormones and how well you live – your quality of life – depends a great deal on how well your adrenal glands function.

If there is a central command post for the body's stress response, it is the hypothalamus, a primitive area of the brain. Through an intricate array of hormonal signals, the hypothalamus connects to the pituitary gland and the main stress-reactive glands in the body, the adrenal glands. During a normal stress response, these hormones are carefully regulated to control everything from our immune, cardiovascular, gastrointestinal, behavioural, and hormonal systems. Even minute changes can have a significant effect on our health.

This hypothalamus-pituitary-adrenal (HPA) axis triggers the production and release of stress hormones during acute stress reactions (fight or flight), namely epinephrine and norepinephrine. The HPA axis also stimulates the release of cortisol, the main stress hormone during times of chronic stress.

How Does Stress Affect the Adrenals?

People experience stress when they perceive that there is an imbalance between demands made of them and the resources they have available to cope with those demands. Stressors are events or situations that require the body to adapt and respond in order to maintain balance or homeostasis. They include:

- **Physical** – chronic infection, illness, and pain
- **Mental and emotional** – money, work, the economy, personal relationships, family responsibilities, and family health problems
- **Lifestyle** – lack of exercise, too much sitting
- **Diet and nutrition** – depletion of the nutritional content of most foods due to modern agricultural and food processing practices; prevalence of junk food and highly processed foods in supermarkets; and contamination of the soil and water supply by pollutants
- **Electromagnetic fields (EMFs)** – cell and cordless phones, microwaves, baby monitors, cell phone towers, computers, etc.
- **Environmental toxins** – heavy metals such as mercury, lead, and aluminum; pesticides and herbicides; and plastic by-products like bisphenol A and phthalates, to name a few

Some stress is absolutely normal and necessary in living creatures. We all have a built-in gauge that helps us control our reaction to various stressors. However, in today's fast-paced society, the vast majority of individuals are under a barrage of constant stressors. While some of the initial fight-or-flight stress responses may be beneficial to survival (acute stress), there is an increased risk of various physical and psychological health challenges when the stressors are prolonged (chronic stress).

Stress is not something new, and it is not going away. We all benefit from reducing the stressors in our lives, but the obvious benefits vary depending on our overall stress resistance capabilities. Often the stressors can be nonspecific and less obvious, and we may not be aware of the effects on our bodies and minds.

Acute stress

Acute stress is the reaction to an immediate threat, commonly known as the "fight-or-flight" response. The threat can be any situation that is perceived, even subconsciously or falsely, as a danger. Common acute stressors include loud noises, hunger, public speaking, danger, isolation, sleep deprivation, technology (video games or constant ringing of phones), and imagining or remembering a fearful event from the recent or distant past. Under most circumstances, once the acute threat has passed, levels of stress hormones return to normal.

Chronic stress

Frequently, modern life exposes people to long-term stressful situations leading to more serious health conditions. Some common chronic stressors include ongoing work pressure or job uncertainty, long-term relationship problems, loneliness, persistent financial worries, chronic illness, or being the primary caregiver for an ill loved one. If stress is prolonged and severe, many people develop adrenal insufficiency, often leading to many kinds of hormone imbalances and other disorders.

General Adaptation Syndrome

All individuals subjected to chronic and severe stress go through stages of adapting to these stressors. The stages of stress-induced damage were first studied by a Canadian doctor, Hans Selye. He gave us a greater understanding of how stress affects the entire body.

Dr. Selye calls the body's mechanism for dealing with stress the general adaptation syndrome (GAS), which consists of three stages:

- **Stage 1:** Alarm reaction
- **Stage 2:** Resistance
- **Stage 3:** Exhaustion

Stage 1: Alarm reaction

The body has an initial reaction to a stressor through a complex chain of physical and biochemical responses brought about by the interaction of the brain, nervous system, and a variety of different hormones released through the main stress organs, the adrenal glands. During the initial fight-or-flight reaction to stress, the body goes on full alert and the adrenals produce extra stress hormones primarily dopamine, epinephrine, and norepinephrine. After the initial alarm reaction is over, the body goes into a recovery stage that can last 24–48 hours and the stress hormone levels return to normal.

Stage 2: Resistance

At this point, the adrenal glands are on constant alert and overreact to prolonged stress. The main adrenal hormone at this stage is cortisol, the hallmark of long-term stress. The resistance stage can last anywhere from months to as long as 20 years. If the stress is unrelenting, eventually the adrenal glands will no longer be able to rebuild and adapt. As a result, the body's ability to cope with stress and fight disease has been compromised. By this time the adrenals will start alternating between hypersecretion and hyposecretion of cortisol, and people can be exhausted one day and feel hyper the next. People push through the fatigue, overstimulate the release of stress hormones, and then find it hard to turn off. They feel "tired but wired", and symptoms such as feeling easily overwhelmed, insomnia, anxiety, and depression may start to appear. As well, stress hormones will start interfering with other hormones, leading to many kinds of hormone imbalances in both men and women.

Stage 3: Exhaustion

In this phase, the state of hypoadrenia is to the point where the ability to respond to stress is severely limited. There are no reserves left, resulting in fatigue, malaise, and lack of will. People who started in Stage 1 and managed to push through Stage 2 are now completely exhausted mentally, emotionally, and physically. Reserves are so depleted that their symptoms of disease become chronic and more degenerative. They experience extreme fatigue, may develop chronic fatigue syndrome (CFS), feel "burned out", and are more susceptible to infections with poor recovery from illness. At this point cortisol deficiency is a possibility, and in extreme cases some patients may be diagnosed with Addison's. If the person continues to push forward or to suppress the symptoms, it may finally result in failure of the whole system.

It is the relationship between the stressors and the body's stress resistance that decides when, and to what extent, ill health will result.

Gender Differences in Stress

"Medical research suggests that up to 90% of all illness and disease is stress-related."– Center for Disease Control and Prevention

According to a recent survey by the American Psychological Association, stress is on the rise for women. Women are more likely to report having stress, and almost 50% of the women who participated in the survey reported that their stress had increased over the past five years, compared to 39% of the men.

How Do the Adrenals Affect the Hormones?

The adrenals play an important role during the more dramatic hormonal changes during perimenopause or menopause. This time in a woman's life causes a roller coaster effect of hormone activity, with the rising and falling of estrogen and progesterone triggering a variety of symptoms.

When the adrenal glands are working properly, they produce adequate amounts of precursor hormones that are further synthesized into estrogens and testosterone to balance the diminished production from the ovaries. However, many women today have adrenal insufficiency due to chronic stress, and the adrenal glands are unable to respond to these additional demands.

In chronic stress, the precursor hormones (specifically pregnenolone and progesterone) are shunted into the stress hormone pathway to make more cortisol. This can cause a deficiency in steroid hormones such as estrogens, dehydroepiandrosterone (DHEA), progesterone, and testosterone. Stress-related diseases occur because of excessive activation of the stress response in the brain and endocrine systems to various sources of physical and psychological stress.

Adrenal Steroid Hormone Synthesis

Cholesterol is the precursor substance needed for the synthesis of all steroid hormones and in essence can be called the "mother" hormone. Other hormones have also been called the mother hormone, but the reality is that without cholesterol, no hormones can be made.

Cholesterol is either obtained from the diet or synthesized in the body: approximately 300 mg of cholesterol is absorbed from the diet and 600 mg is synthesized each day. About 80% of cholesterol required for steroid synthesis is low-density lipoprotein (LDL), although recent evidence has shown that high-density lipoprotein (HDL), the so-called "good" cholesterol, can also be used. LDL is used for hormone synthesis by steroid-producing cells in the ovaries, liver, fatty tissues, and brain. So is LDL really the bad guy?

When the adrenals are working normally, which in this day and age is seldom the case, the two steroids produced in greatest quantities by the adrenal cortex are DHEA and its sulfate, DHEA-S. Together with androstenedione, they are generally termed "weak androgens" and are converted peripherally to the more active testosterone in men or to estradiol in women (see Figure 3.1).

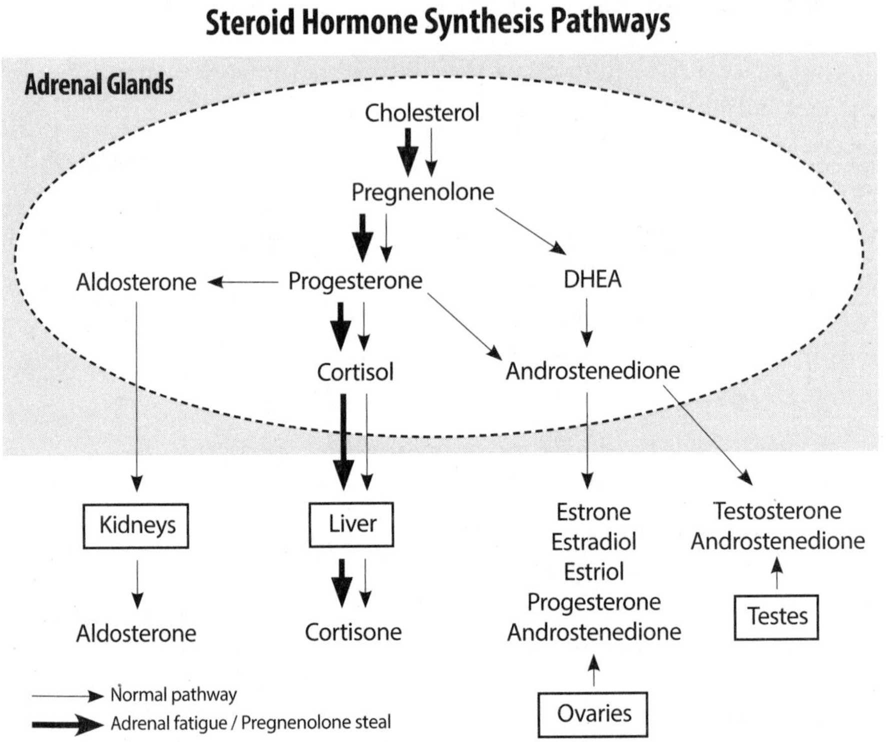

Steroid Hormone Synthesis Pathways

Figure 3.1 Adrenal hormone synthesis pathways

Adrenal Fatigue

Signs and Symptoms of Adrenal Fatigue

Adrenal fatigue symptoms for both hypo- and hyperfunction are very similar. They include:

- Fatigue/chronic fatigue
- Muscle weakness
- Anxiety, depression, mood swings
- Sleep disorders
- Irregular menses
- Hypoglycemia
- Inflammation

- Memory problems
- Difficulty losing weight
- Decreased immunity
- Low or high blood pressure
- Hair loss
- Low libido
- Dizziness on standing

Many people alternate between the two stages for years, some in a more hyper state and others more hypo. If left unchecked, these patients will eventually end up with severe adrenal exhaustion.

Many early symptoms can indicate changes in the normal cortisol rhythm, reflecting preclinical adrenal problems. See how you score on the Adrenal Stress Indicator provided in Table 3.1.

Table 3.1 Adrenal Stress Indicator

Write the number **1** beside symptoms you have had in the past; **2** beside symptoms that occur occasionally; **3** beside symptoms that occur often; **4** beside symptoms that occur frequently. Add up the total score.

_____ Blurred vision, spots in front of eyes

_____ Insomnia, frequent waking

_____ Hormonal imbalances (e.g., thyroid problems)

_____ History of asthma, bronchitis

_____ Prolonged exposure to stress (e.g., job, family, illness, caregiving)

_____ Headaches

_____ Environmental or chemical exposure or sensitivities

_____ Hypoglycemia, blood sugar problems (e.g., mood swings)

_____ Food allergies

_____ Poor concentration, memory problems (e.g., Alzheimer's)

_____ Low energy, excessive fatigue

_____ Easily overwhelmed, inability to handle stress

_____ Post-exertion fatigue

_____ Cold hands or feet

_____ Inflammatory conditions (e.g., arthritis, bursitis)

_____ Dizziness or fainting upon standing

_____ Nervousness, anxiety, depression, irritability, anger

_____ Air hunger (e.g., shortness of breath, yawning)

_____ Low back pain, knee problems, sore muscles

_____ Excessive urination

_____ Excessive perspiration or no perspiration

_____ Heart palpitations

_____ Edema of extremities or general edema

_____ Eyes light-sensitive

_____ Cravings for sugar, salt, coffee, or other stimulants

_____ Alcohol intolerance

_____ Recurrent colds or infections

_____ Digestive problems, ulcers

_____ Weight gain or weight loss

_____ High or low blood pressure

_____ **Total score**

If you scored: 30–50: You have received an early-warning indicator that your adrenals are starting to weaken. **50–80:** Start with adrenal support. **80–100:** Your adrenals are taxed; you may want to add an adrenal glandular product. **Over 100:** You are suffering from adrenal exhaustion and will require long-term adrenal support.

Possible Causes of Adrenal Fatigue

"To understand the mechanism of stress gives physicians a new approach to treatment of illness, but it can also give us all a new way of life, a new philosophy to guide our actions in conformity with natural laws." – Hans Selye, MD

Adrenal dysregulation is one of the most prevalent conditions in our time, yet it is rarely diagnosed in Western medicine. Unfortunately, the milder forms of hypo- or hyper-adrenal symptoms are often missed or misdiagnosed in health care practitioners' offices every day, even though all of the symptoms are present.

The diseases and conditions associated with stress and cortisol dysregulation include:

- Metabolic syndrome and diabetes
- Obesity
- Cardiovascular disease
- Anxiety disorders and depression
- Immune compromise and some cancers
- Thyroid disease

- Allergies and chemical sensitivities
- Inflammatory disorders (arthritis)
- Hormonal imbalances (e.g., PMS, polycystic ovary syndrome)
- Osteoporosis
- Insomnia

- Chronic fatigue syndrome/ fibromyalgia

- Asthma and bronchitis

- Gastrointestinal disorders

- Dementias (including Alzheimer's disease), concentration problems, and memory loss

Testing and Diagnosis

Although lab tests are a necessary part of the diagnosis, the narrow parameters often miss people in the earlier stages of a disease, called the preclinical range. The preclinical stage of a disease can have debilitating symptoms associated with it, but at this stage, most people are told there is nothing wrong because the lab test is within the "normal" range. As a result, many people suffer needlessly for years. This is no surprise considering lab tests are standardized according to statistical norms based on math instead of physiologically optimal norms, which are based on signs and symptoms.

The so-called normal lab values for cortisol include all, but the most extreme values, as shown in Figure 3.2. Addison's disease is at the extreme low end of adrenal function and is life threatening if left untreated. People suffering from Addison's usually need to take corticosteroid hormones for the rest of their lives. This rare and extreme form of adrenal exhaustion affects approximately four out of every 100,000 people. Cushing's syndrome is the extreme high end of adrenal function, and is caused by prolonged exposure to the stress hormone cortisol. This condition is relatively rare.

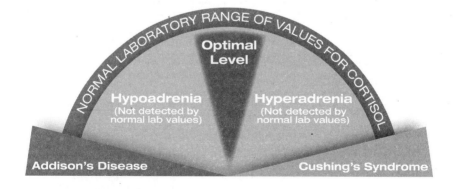

Figure 3.2 The range of values for cortisol

A number of lab tests are available for assessing adrenal fatigue.

Lab tests

24-hour urine cortisol test

This test is a helpful indicator of several adrenal steroid hormones, although the lab range considered normal is too broad to be of much value in diagnosing all, but the most severe cases of hypoadrenia (see Figure 3.1).

ACTH challenge test

This test helps evaluate the adrenal reserves and is usually only done if cortisol levels are abnormal. Specialists use other standard blood and urine tests to test for adrenal disease, but these tests are usually done only in the most severe cases, and are beyond the scope of this book.

Saliva adrenal profile – cortisol rhythm

Saliva hormone testing measures the amounts of various stress hormones in your saliva instead of blood or urine. Saliva testing measures the free (bioavailable) portion of hormones. This method is preferred for measuring adrenal health through testing levels of the adrenal hormone cortisol. Saliva testing usually requires collection either in the morning and evening (two point), or morning, noon, evening, and bedtime (four point). These tests are done through a naturopathic physician or a complementary medical doctor.

Ragland effect – postural hypotension

Normally, when a person goes from the lying position to standing, the systolic blood pressure should elevate 4–10 mm Hg (millimetres of mercury). In adrenal fatigue, the systolic blood pressure from lying to standing will either drop or stay the same. The level of drop in the blood pressure can help determine the level of adrenal fatigue.

Pupillary response

Adrenal fatigue causes an imbalance with sodium and potassium. One of the signs of this electrolyte imbalance is the pupillary reflex. Normally, shining a light into a person's eye will cause the pupil to constrict and it should maintain itself for 30 seconds. In the adrenal-fatigued person (especially in the later stages), the pupil fluctuates in size in response to the light, or the pupil initially constricts, but dilates even with continued light in less than 30 seconds.

In addition, health care practitioners need to do a thorough history, looking at various stressful events, including:

- Surgeries and hospital stays
- Illnesses such as flu, colds, and pneumonia
- Long-term pain
- Dental work such as root canals or implants
- Emotional stress such as job loss, moving, death of friend or relative, divorce, financial problems
- Other stressful incidents

A thorough patient history – coupled with the patient's signs and symptoms – is probably the most important assessment tool.

what we know works

Support for Adrenal Fatigue

AdrenaSense® includes several adaptogenic herbs that have been studied extensively and have proven very effective during times of increased demands and stress. Refer below for more information on individual ingredients.

Dosage: 1 capsule twice daily with food or as directed by a health care practitioner.

Rhodiola *(Rhodiola rosea)* modulates the release of cortisol and other stress hormones and supports the cardiopulmonary system during times of stress.

Ashwagandha *(Withania somnifera)* is considered the main adaptogen in Ayurvedic medicine. Studies show that ashwagandha prevents many of the biological changes that accompany the stress response, such as an increase in blood sugar and cortisol levels. Studies also indicate that ashwagandha supports emotional well-being and immune health.

Siberian ginseng *(Eleutherococcus senticosus)* (known as eleuthero in the US) is well studied in Russian athletes and has been shown to support the body's ability to adapt to adverse physical conditions, promote mental performance, regulate heart rate, and promote mental performance under stress. It helps regulate the HPA axis during stress.

Schisandra *(Schisandra chinensis)* is another adaptogen shown to decrease the effects of stress by supporting energy, reducing fatigue, and promoting mental endurance. In combination with rhodiola and Siberian ginseng, schisandra has also been shown to help support immune function and recovery from illness.

Suma *(Pfaffia paniculata)* has been used traditionally in Brazil for its energizing and rejuvenating effects. It provides excellent support for the cardiovascular system, central nervous, reproductive, digestive, and immune systems.

Karen Jensen, ND

When I started practice in 1988, there were very few good adrenal support products on the market. I formulated this product so my patients and other health food store consumers could rely on a safe and effective product that would balance and regulate their adrenal glands. Today there are many different adrenal support products available, but AdrenaSense has passed the test of time and has helped many people over the years recover from adrenal fatigue.

Additional support for adrenal fatigue

The term "adaptogen" refers to a category of plants that improve the body's response to stress. These herbs have many important properties, but the most important is their normalizing effect. Regardless of the condition, they help the body maintain homeostasis, which is the constant internal state necessary for health and life itself. Some of the common health-enhancing and adrenal-supporting properties of adaptogens include:

- Improving blood sugar metabolism
- Supporting the endocrine (hormonal) system
- Protecting and supporting the immune system
- Providing liver protection and support
- Increasing stamina and endurance
- Strengthening the cardiovascular and respiratory systems
- Strengthening the brain and central nervous system
- Protecting cells from antioxidant damage

B-Complex helps support the nervous system.

Dosage: all multi-B vitamins have different dosages. Follow the manufacturer's instructions.

Pantothenic acid (B5) can downregulate hypersecretion of cortisol from secondary to high-stress conditions, and is important for energy production, helping convert glucose into energy.

Dosage: 500 mg 3 times daily.

Vitamin B12 is thought to have an effect on helping to reset healthy secretion of cortisol during periods of stress, thus improving the stress response and quality of sleep.

Dosage: 1000–5000 mcg daily in the form of methylcobalamin.

Vitamin C is very important because it is used in the formation of adrenal hormones such as cortisol. During times of stress, the body's requirement for vitamin C can increase 10–20 fold.

Dosage: 2000–4000 mg daily (or until you begin to experience loose stools).

GABA (gamma-aminobutyric acid) is a neurotransmitter that works like a "brake" during times of runaway stress. Stress excites the nervous system, causing irritability, restlessness, anxiety, insomnia, seizures, and movement disorders. GABA helps regulate brain excitability.

Dosage: 100–600 mg daily.

L-theanine, an amino acid, is found in green tea and helps calm and relax the body when under stress.

Dosage: 200 mg 2–3 times daily.

CalmBiotic™ contains the gut bacteria *Bifidobacterium longum* and *Lactobacillus helveticus,* which have been proven to reduce symptoms of stress including sadness, anxiety, anger, and gastrointestinal symptoms such as nausea.

Dosage: 1 capsule daily.

Diet and Lifestyle Tips for Adrenal Fatigue

Exercise

Everyone knows that exercise can benefit overall health, but it also has direct stress-reducing benefits. Virtually any form of exercise can relieve stress. For example, exercise that gets the blood pumping, such as running, hiking, or racquetball, can increase the production of endorphins, the feel-good brain chemicals. As tensions and stress are released through exercise, sleep will improve, worries and anxieties will decrease, and you will feel more relaxed.

It doesn't take much; only two hours a week of moderate exercise or approximately an hour of vigorous exercise have been shown to provide anti-stress benefits. Choose an exercise you like to do. Any form of exercise of movement can help increase fitness and reduce stress, such as walking, climbing stairs, jogging, cycling, yoga, tai chi, gardening, swimming, or weight lifting, at least twice a week.

Perception

Perception is what we think about a given situation, and it plays a very important role in our body's reaction to stress. The stress reaction is the result of many complex interacting factors, such as the influence of the actual stressor as well as our perception of the stressor. How we perceive the event is part of what determines whether or not the fight-or-flight response is triggered. For example, if our perception is influenced by a negative and pessimistic attitude, then the stressor will be perceived as more of a threat than it would be if we had a more optimistic and positive outlook.

Can changing how you perceive stress make you healthier? The answer is "Yes". A 2012 study used data from a stress questionnaire that tracked over 28,000 adults. The first question was about how much stress they experienced, and the next question was if they felt that their stress was harmful to their health. Over the next eight years, researchers tracked public death records of the participants to see who among them had died. The results showed that worrying and believing that stress was harmful to their health predicted an early death. Shockingly, those who were under high levels of stress, but who did not believe that it caused them harm, had much better health and longevity. They even had a lower risk of dying compared to those who had less stress, but who held the belief that their stress was harmful.

Once we fully understand that we have choices in our lives, we come to realize that the majority of the limitations placed upon us are those we create with our own belief systems and ideologies. If our thought formations help create our reality, we can use and manipulate them to contribute to the creation of good health (or conversely, of disease). Listen carefully to your spoken and unspoken thoughts and observe where they are leading you. As evidence has shown, in many cases you are your own master.

The attitude of gratitude: remember to say thank you!

New research conducted by Robert A. Emmons, PhD, of the University of California, and Michael E. McCullough, of the University of Miami, shows that the "attitude of gratitude" has been linked to better health, sounder sleep, less anxiety and depression, higher long-term satisfaction with life, and kinder behaviour toward others. In the study, people kept a brief "gratitude journal" – just one sentence for each of five things that they were grateful for, done once a week. There were significant effects after only two months. Compared with a control group, the people keeping the gratitude journal were more optimistic and felt happier. They reported fewer physical problems and spent more time working out.

> "The greatest weapon against stress is our ability to choose one thought over another."
> — William James

"If you want to sleep more soundly, count blessings, not sheep", Dr. Emmons advises in *Thanks!,* his book on gratitude research.

For more information on stress, refer to the following:

Stress and the Disease Connection: A Complete Guide, by Karen Jensen, ND and Marita Schauch, ND

Chapter 4

The Thyroid and the Hormone Connection

It is estimated that 200 million people in the world have some form of thyroid disease. In Canada, a staggering number of people are affected with a thyroid condition: Recent studies indicate that one in every ten Canadians has a thyroid disorder. Of those, as many as 50% are undiagnosed.

The Thyroid – An Overview

The thyroid gland is a small, butterfly-shaped gland located in the base of the neck. The thyroid produces hormones called thyroxine (T4) and triiodothyronine (T3). T4 is the most abundant thyroid hormone produced (about 93%) and at one time was thought to be the active hormone. However, we now know that T3 is 3–5 times more active biologically, and that it is the active hormone in target cells. About 80% of T4 is converted to T3 in the liver, kidneys, and body cells, and the thyroid is responsible for the rest.

Thyroid-stimulating hormone (TSH) is secreted by the pituitary in response to levels of thyroid hormones in the blood. TSH stimulates the production of thyroid hormones, primarily T3 and T4. As the thyroid hormones in the blood increase, the pituitary gland slows the production of TSH and vice versa.

For example, if TSH levels are elevated and T4 and T3 are decreased, this would indicate hypothyroidism.

The thyroid's job is to increase the body's metabolic rate, maintain body temperature, stimulate protein synthesis, increase the use of glucose, break down fats for energy production, and speed up the elimination of cholesterol into bile from the liver. Because the thyroid hormones have such broad effects, keeping the thyroid healthy is another key to optimal health. An important influence on thyroid health is adrenal health.

Adrenal Stress and the Thyroid Connection

One of cortisol's more important functions is to act in concert with thyroid hormones. Cortisol makes the thyroid work more efficiently – not too low and not too high. It is very important for normal thyroid function, and this is why many people who have an imbalance in adrenal cortisol levels usually have thyroid symptoms.

Both cortisol and thyroid hormones have to be in the cells, bound to their respective receptors, for optimal thyroid function. When cortisol levels are low, caused by adrenal exhaustion, the thyroid is less efficient at doing its job. When cortisol levels are too high, again due to adrenal response to stressors, the tissues no longer respond to the thyroid hormone signal, creating a condition of thyroid resistance. This means that although thyroid hormone levels can be normal, the tissues fail to respond to the thyroid signal.

Resistance to the thyroid hormone caused by elevated cortisol levels also applies to all other hormones, such as insulin, progesterone, estrogens, testosterone, and cortisol itself. When cortisol is too high, you get resistance from the hormone receptor sites, requiring more of the hormone to create the same effect. Every cell in the body has receptors for both cortisol and thyroid, and nearly every cellular process requires optimal functioning of the thyroid. That is why people feel so terrible with chronic stress, which elevates cortisol levels – none of the hormones are able to work at optimal levels.

Thyroid Disorders and the Gut Microbiome

Hippocrates said "All disease begins in the gut". Today, we are just beginning to understand how right he was. Poor gut health can suppress thyroid function and trigger Hashimoto's disease, an autoimmune thyroid disorder. Low thyroid function can also lead to an inflamed and leaky gut.

The thyroid influences the gut in several ways:

- When the intestinal barrier becomes permeable, called leaky gut, large protein molecules escape into the bloodstream, triggering an immune response. The immune response plays a role in the development of autoimmune diseases such as Hashimoto's thyroiditis.

- Thyroid hormones strongly influence the tight junctions that form the gut barrier that protects the gut mucosal lining from stress-induced cellular damage. During examination of people with gastric ulcers, researchers found low T3 and T4, and abnormal levels of reverse T3.

- One very important role of the gut bacteria is to assist in converting T4 into the active form of thyroid hormone, T3. This conversion requires healthy gut bacteria. Intestinal dysbiosis, discussed in *Chapter 2*, significantly reduces the conversion of T4 to T3.

- Inflammation is commonly caused by stress-induced elevated cortisol, which decreases T3.

- Hypochlorhydria, or low stomach acid, also increases intestinal permeability, causing inflammation.

Gender Differences in Thyroid Disorders

Thyroid diseases are generally more prevalent in females, affecting 20–25% of the female population in North America. In contrast, only about 10% of the male population experience hypothyroidism.

The relationship between gender and thyroid disease is becoming more recognized, particularly in the aging population. There is increased prevalence of hypothyroidism in women of all ages, and studies report a higher prevalence for autoimmune thyroiditis (Hashimoto's disease) and overt or subclinical hypothyroidism in women with advancing age.

Hypothyroidism

Signs and Symptoms of Hypothyroidism

Hypothyroidism (underactive or low thyroid function) is the most common thyroid disorder. It occurs when the thyroid gland fails to produce sufficient amounts of the thyroid hormones T4 and T3, or if there is a failure in the conversion of T4 to T3. As a result, TSH becomes elevated.

The signs and symptoms of hypothyroidism vary widely, depending on the severity of the hormone deficiency. But in general, any problems that arise tend to develop slowly, often over a number of years. Some of the common signs and symptoms of hypothyroidism include:

- Fatigue and lethargy
- Cold intolerance, and cold hands and feet
- High cholesterol
- Hair loss; dry, coarse hair; loss of lateral one-third of eyebrow
- Constipation
- Depression, memory loss, poor concentration
- Infertility or miscarriage
- Low libido
- Puffy face, especially around the eyes
- Swelling of the hands and feet
- Weight gain or difficulty losing weight
- Muscle aches and swelling in joints (fibromyalgia)
- Hormonal imbalances
- Goitre

A number of conditions are associated with hypothyroidism, including:

- Arthritis
- Adrenal fatigue
- Anemia
- Cardiovascular disease

Depression and fatigue are the most common thyroid symptoms in menopausal women. Women are frequently given antidepressants or hormone replacement to treat these problems commonly related to hypothyroidism. When it is treated, the emotional cloud is lifted.

Hashimoto's thyroiditis

In Hashimoto's thyroiditis, the immune cells mistakenly attack healthy thyroid tissue. Antibodies bind to the thyroid and prevent the production of sufficient levels of thyroid hormone. In addition to binding to thyroid tissue, these antibodies may also bind to the adrenal glands, pancreas, and acid-producing cells of the stomach. Serum antibodies against thyroid proteins, such as thyroglobulin or thyroperoxidase, are often present in blood tests. When this occurs, the thyroid becomes inflamed and enlarged to the point of developing a goitre. It is possible to have Hashimoto's thyroiditis for years without experiencing symptoms.

The primary sign of a goitre is visible swelling in the front of the neck. At first, the bulge may be painless, but if left untreated, it can put pressure on the lower neck. In advanced stages, a goitre can interfere with proper breathing and swallowing. Goitres are estimated to affect more than 200 million people worldwide.

Wilson's syndrome

Wilson's syndrome (WS) is a thyroid disorder that occurs when there is a low temperature and an excess of reverse T3 (RT3) because the liver is unable to convert T4 to T3. The enzyme responsible for this conversion is dependent on selenium and zinc, vitamin B12, and the amino acid cysteine. Heavy metals such as mercury, cadmium, and lead will also block this conversion in the liver. Adrenal stress and adrenal fatigue are also culprits in WS, and therefore adrenal function should be assessed if levels of RT3 are high.

Possible Causes of Hypothyroidism

The most common cause of thyroid disorders worldwide is iodine deficiency, leading to goitre formation and hypothyroidism. Almost one-third of the world's population lives in areas of iodine deficiency. In iodine-replete areas, most people with thyroid disorders have autoimmune diseases. Some individuals may actually be getting enough iodine in the diet, but it may be that the uptake of iodine is not as efficient. As we discuss below, the theory of goitrogens suggests that certain foods block iodine use. These include vegetables in the Brassica family (turnips, cabbage, broccoli, Brussels sprouts, mustard, kale, and cauliflower), as well as soybeans, peanuts, and millet. However, cooking these foods will inactivate the goitrogens.

The gut-thyroid connection

Hypothyroidism is associated with altered gastrointestinal (GI) motility, and reduced motility poses a significant risk of developing bacterial imbalance (dysbiosis) in the gut. Dysbiosis can trigger an inflammatory response by the immune system. Did you know that your gut is home to over 80% of your immune system? The gut–thyroid connection is a two-way street. Inflammation in the gut, which can be caused by several factors, also directly influences thyroid function. (See *Chapter 2* for more information on dysbiosis.)

Chronic inflammation can interfere with thyroid function in different ways:

- Inflammation in the gut causes inflammation in the brain as an up-stream mechanism. The inflammation can affect the way the pituitary gland in the brain sends messages to the thyroid; the result is less output of the thyroid hormone (T4) by the thyroid gland.

- Inflammation impairs the conversion of T4 to the active form of thyroid hormone T3 at the tissue level.

Other causes of thyroid disorders include:

- **Radiation** – Radiation used to treat cancers of the head and neck can affect the thyroid gland and may lead to hypothyroidism. Radiation exposure from X-rays and nuclear fallout can dramatically affect thyroid function.

- **Thyroid surgery** – Removing a large portion of or the whole thyroid can reduce or stop thyroid hormone production. A majority of these cases will require thyroid medication for life.

- **Medications** – A number of medications can contribute to hypothyroidism. Lithium, used to treat psychiatric disorders, is one such medication. Other medications such as phenobarbitol, benzodiazepines, calcium channel blockers, and steroids can increase the metabolism of thyroid hormones so that they are used up faster.

- **Heavy metals** – Lead, mercury, and cadmium can interfere with the liver's conversion of T4 to T3.

- **Times of hormonal transition** – Times of rapid hormone shifts, such as pregnancy, menopause, and childbirth, can affect thyroid function. During pregnancy, women can sometimes produce antibodies against their own thyroid gland. If left untreated, hypothyroidism increases the risk of miscarriage, premature delivery, and preeclampsia, a condition that causes a significant rise in blood pressure during the last three months of pregnancy. It can also seriously affect the developing fetus.

- **Estrogen dominance** – Hormone replacement therapy (synthetic or bio-identical), the birth control pill, and xenoestrogens (environmental estrogens) can affect thyroid function by blocking thyroid hormone receptors.

- **Iron and other vitamin deficiencies** – Low levels of zinc, selenium, copper, magnesium, manganese, or vitamins A, B2, B3, B6, B12, C, and E can cause or contribute to low thyroid function.

- **Food allergies** – Certain foods, such as gluten and dairy, cause stress on the immune system as well as adrenal and thyroid function.

- **Candida** – An overgrowth of candida and bowel toxicity can affect thyroid function.

- **Sluggish liver or liver disease** – The liver is one of the organs that aid in the conversion of T4 to T3.

- **Pituitary disorder** – A relatively rare cause of hypothyroidism is the failure of the pituitary gland to produce enough TSH, usually as a result of a benign tumour of the pituitary gland.

- **Other environmental toxins** – Perchlorate in synthetic fertilizers will inhibit the ability of the thyroid gland to trap iodine. PCBs can mimic thyroid hormone and contribute to Hashimoto's autoimmune thyroid disease.

Testing and Diagnosis

Lab tests

Blood tests

The diagnosis of thyroid disorders is most often based on symptoms along with the results of blood tests that measure the levels of TSH, free T3, free T4, reverse T3, thyroid antimicrosomal antibodies (TPO Abs), and antithyroglobulin antibodies (Tg Abs). Most medical doctors only order the TSH blood test, and thyroid function is considered normal if the TSH falls between 0.38 and 5.5 IU/mL. However, there is a difference between "normal" and "optimal" ranges. The TSH range for optimal thyroid function is between 1.0 and 2.0 IU/mL. In the case of hypothyroidism, naturopathic doctors and some medical doctors are now using a new "norm" for the TSH lab value and will treat for hypothyroidism if the TSH lab value is above 1.9 – especially if accompanied by low thyroid symptoms.

Although most medical doctors will only test TSH, it is important to measure the levels of actual thyroid hormones T4 and T3 to get a more accurate picture of the function of the thyroid. Remember that because T4 must be converted to the active form T3, tests that only measure T4 do not illustrate the whole thyroid picture. It is possible that although circulating T4 levels are in a healthy range, there may be a problem converting T4 to T3. Be sure to ask your health care practitioner to test levels of both hormones. TSH alone and the old lab reference range are often inadequate and many hypothyroid patients suffer needlessly for years.

Two terms that will repeatedly be used in reference to the thyroid are "clinical" and "preclinical":

- When the results of a medical test are of clinical significance, they lie outside normal parameters as defined by conventional medicine. For example, a diagnosis of clinical hypothyroidism (underactive thyroid) is made by most doctors only when TSH levels are higher than 5.5 UI/mL. This level allows for a very broad definition of what is normal.

- In preclinical thyroidism, the TSH is slightly elevated, T4 and T3 are within normal ranges, and people may experience mild symptoms of hypothyroidism. In addition, anti-thyroid antibodies can be detected in 80% of patients with SHT, indicating an autoimmune factor.

- Lowering the upper limit of normal for TSH from 5.5 to 2.5 UI/mL has been proposed, and some health care practitioners are already following that guideline.

Basal body temperature

The basal body temperature (BBT) is an easy way to test thyroid function and reflects metabolic rate, which is determined by the levels of thyroid hormones secreted. The basal body temperature should be taken first thing in the morning before getting out of bed. Normal basal body temperature should be 36.6–36.8 °C. Normal fluctuations occur during the menstrual period, and BBT will rise just after ovulation. If the BBT is consistently lower than this, there may be a diagnosis of low thyroid. There are many other causes for low BBT and these should be ruled out before the diagnosis of hypothyroidism can be made.

Other causes for low BBT include:

- Low progesterone
- Low cortisol (adrenal fatigue)
- Low iron
- Depression
- Poor circulation

what we know works

Support for Hypothyroidism

ThyroSense® contains the following ingredients: tyrosine, iodine, ashwagandha, guggal extract, panthothenic acid, copper, manganese, and selenium. It is an excellent product for supporting symptoms of hypothyroidism by maintaining healthy levels of T4 and T3 thyroid hormones. ThyroSense may be used with medication prescribed to increase thyroid function (e.g., Synthroid) but NOT in hyperthyroid cases (overactive thyroid). Refer below for more information on individual ingredients.

Dosage: 2 capsules daily with breakfast and 2 capsules with lunch.

Tyrosine is an important amino acid precursor for the synthesis of thyroid hormones T4 and T3, melanin, and the brain neurotransmitters dopamine, epinephrine, and norepinephrine. During the stress response, these neurotransmitters are produced by the adrenal glands. If tyrosine levels are drained, the adrenal glands cannot respond to stress adequately and there is less available to help with the synthesis of thyroid hormones.

Iodine is essential for the synthesis of thyroid hormones. Bladderwrack and other types of seaweed contain variable levels of iodine. Iodine should not be consumed in supplement form if diagnosed with hyperthyroidism (an overactive thyroid).

Ashwagandha *(Withania somnifera)* is an important herb in Ayurvedic medicine. It serves as an adaptogen, helping the adrenal glands combat stress. As well, the herb supports healthy thyroid function by supporting the synthesis of thyroid hormones.

Guggul extract *(Commiphora wightii)* has been shown to impact thyroid hormone conversion by increasing levels of the thyroid hormone T3 peripherally in the body.

Pantothenic acid, or vitamin B5, is needed for adrenal function and is involved in the stress response. Recall that adrenal function and thyroid function are closely linked. Ensuring that the adrenal glands are functioning optimally is key to supporting healthy thyroid function.

Copper plays an important role in thyroid metabolism, especially in hormone production and absorption. Copper stimulates the production of thyroxine hormone (T4) and prevents overabsorption of T4 in the blood cells by controlling the body's calcium levels. (Calcium is required for the stabilization of cell membranes and reduces cell permeability.)

Manganese plays a vital role of manganese in liver function, fat metabolism, and liver antioxidant status. This relates to thyroid hormone activation as most activation occurs on cell membranes in the liver. Manganese also serves as an antioxidant protector of the thyroid hormones. By doing so, manganese helps support increased metabolic rate and healthy thyroid function.

Selenium deficiency reduces the conversion of T4 into active T3 and increases the production of rT3. It is important to ensure that selenium levels are adequate for healthy thyroid function.

AdrenaSense® provides adrenal support in any thyroid disorder, which is often one of the root causes of thyroid dysfunction.

Dosage: 1 capsule twice daily with food.

Vitamin D is a cofactor for the synthesis of thyroid hormones.
Dosage: 3000–5000 IU daily.

Julie Reil, MD

Dr. Julie Reil is a medical doctor with 20 years' experience in family practice, obstetrics, women's health, and laser medicine. She is a mother of two, a nutrition advocate, educational speaker, and WomenSense® author. Her clinical focus is on educating and improving the lives of women with her innovative and results-driven procedures. Dr. Reil is the founder and director of Shiloh Medical Clinic in Billings, Montana. Go to **shilohmedicalclinic.com** for more information.

"Supplements cannot take the place of prescription medication in most people diagnosed with clinical hypothyroidism. But ThyroSense enhances the beneficial action of your thyroid hormone medication, reducing fatigue and other thyroid-related symptoms. Compounded with L-tyrosine, ashwagandha, guggul, pantothenic acid, iodine, selenium, copper, and manganese, ThyroSense provides proper thyroid nutrition. My patients report improved energy, weight loss, and reduced sensitivity to cold. In fact, it has proven to be so beneficial that I recommend it to any patient who has a family history of hypothyroidism or a diagnosis of subclinical hypothyroidism."

Conventional treatment for hypothyroidism

The most commonly prescribed conventional medication for hypothyroidism is levothyroxine (Synthroid), which is a synthetic form of T4. In some cases, Synthroid works well, but individuals who are unable to convert T4 into T3 will still experience symptoms of low thyroid while on this medication. These individuals may respond better to Armour (desiccated thyroid). Dosages for desiccated thyroid range from 60–120 mg and because it contains both T4 and T3, some individuals may respond to it better than synthetic Synthroid medication.

Calcium and iron supplements will interfere with thyroid medication or thyroid hormone supplements. Always take them at least an hour apart from any thyroid supplements, including prescribed medication. Studies also show that drinking coffee or espresso within an hour of taking low thyroid medication may affect how it works in the body for optimizing T4 hormone levels. So make sure you drink your coffee apart from any thyroid support.

Diet and Lifestyle Tips for Hypothyroidism

Iodine

You will recall that iodine is an essential nutrient for the production of thyroid hormones. While there are many benefits to reducing salt intake, doing so might contribute to the current epidemic of hypothyroidism. Iodized salt was a major source of dietary iodine for many North Americans – by eliminating salt, we have eliminated the source of this important nutrient. If you have subclinical or clinical hypothyroidism, be sure to boost your intake of iodine-rich foods, including

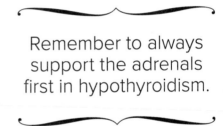

Remember to always support the adrenals first in hypothyroidism.

seafood and sea vegetables (e.g., dulse, kelp, nori, hiziki, wakame). Other food sources of iodine include fish, asparagus, garlic, sea salt, sesame seeds, soybeans, spinach, summer squash, and turnip greens.

Tyrosine

Tyrosine is a building block for thyroid hormones T4 and T3. Try to include food sources of tyrosine in the diet such as sunflower seeds, pumpkin seeds, lima beans, eggs, poultry, fish, spirulina, soy, and aduki beans.

Selenium

The antioxidant selenium protects the thyroid gland from stressors and helps the body recycle its stores of iodine. Shiitake mushrooms, salmon, oats, Brazil nuts, and garlic are all sources of selenium. Be sure that you have plenty of B vitamins on the menu, too, as these are involved in the manufacture of T4. You will find B vitamins in brewer's yeast, wheat germ, sunflower seeds, and legumes.

Environmental toxins

Many environmental toxins can inhibit optimal thyroid function. Be sure to consume hormone and antibiotic-free meat, choose low mercury content fish, and if consuming dairy, always buy organic. Many autoimmune thyroid conditions are affected by certain food allergens. If an autoimmune thyroid disease is suspected, try to avoid wheat and other gluten-containing grains as well as all dairy products.

Goitrogens

Goitrogens are a group of foods that can interfere with the thyroid gland's ability to use iodine when dietary iodine is deficient. To review, goitrogens include the Brassica family of vegetables (e.g., cabbage, broccoli, Brussels sprouts, cauliflower, kale, turnips, kohlrabi, rutabaga), as well as mustard seeds, peanuts, pine nuts, millet, spinach, peaches, pears, and soy. As mentioned earlier, cooking these foods usually inactivates goitrogens and their effect is minimized if iodine-rich foods are consumed with them. It is important to note that goitrogens do not cause thyroid disease; they may only worsen an already-diagnosed hypothyroid condition.

Hyperthyroidism

Since low thyroid disease is the most common thyroid disorder, we will only briefly discuss hyperthyroidism (hyperactive thyroid). Hyperthyroidism is a condition whereby the thyroid produces increased levels of the thyroid hormones T4 and T3. Graves' disease, which is another autoimmune disease, accounts for up to 85% of all cases of hyperthyroidism. Graves' disease is eight times more common in women than in men and typically begins between the ages of 20 and 40.

Signs and Symptoms of Hyperthyroidism

Symptoms of hyperthyroidism include:

- Weakness
- Sweating
- Weight loss
- Nervousness
- Insomnia
- Loose stools

- Heat intolerance
- Irritability
- Fatigue
- Racing heartbeat
- Warm, moist skin

Often there is diffuse enlargement of the thyroid (goitre) and increased blood levels of the thyroid hormones (T4 and T3). Some individuals will exhibit mild protrusion of the eyes with lid retraction, as well as pigment changes such as vitiligo.

An overactive thyroid may result in the following findings at the doctor's office:

- Fast pulse
- Irregular heartbeat
- Tremors
- Low TSH and elevated T3 or T4
- Brisk Achilles reflex
- High basal temperature
- Osteoporosis

what we know works

Support for Hyperthyroidism

Astragalus *(Astragalus membranaceus)* is a Chinese herb that strengthens the body's natural defences. Astragalus root tones the immune system, cardiovascular system, and the liver and adrenal glands. Research reported in Chinese journals demonstrates that it effectively inhibits chronic active hepatitis, hyperthyroidism, insomnia, and other conditions.

Dosage: 250–500 mg solid extract (4:1) 2–3 times daily.

Passionflower *(Passiflora incarnata)* is a tonic herb with sedative action that helps decrease many of the symptoms of an overactive thyroid: anxiety, tension, irritability, insomnia, and nervousness. It also relaxes the muscles. Its sedative effects are not strong enough to interfere with the alertness of people who need to remain active and awake.

Dosage: 150–200 mg solid extract (4:1) twice daily.

Carnitine is manufactured within the body where it is important in energy metabolism. Carnitine has been shown to be an antagonist of thyroid hormone in peripheral tissues.

Dosage: 2000–4000 mg daily.

Conventional treatment for hyperthyroidism

When a patient is medically diagnosed with hyperthyroidism, the symptoms are usually severe enough to warrant immediate attention. In some cases, conventional treatment focuses on destroying the thyroid gland with radioactive iodine (radioactive iodine ablation, RIA). Advantages include a high rate of response, but disadvantages include the progression to hypothyroidism.

Depending on the severity of the case, prior to RIA most doctors will begin antithyroid prescribed medications, such as methimazole or propylthiouracil. These drugs work by entering the thyroid and blocking the formation of thyroid hormones by specifically inhibiting the binding of iodine to tyrosine. In many parts of the world, antithyroid drugs are the first-line treatment for hyperthyroidism, and many cases will resolve within 18 months. Others develop hypothyroidism after treatment, and still others go on to require RIA.

Diet and Lifestyle Tips for Hyperthyroidism

Stress control is important to normalize the thyroid (both hypo and hyper), and counselling can prevent a return to that stressful incident or trauma. Patients with autoimmune thyroid disease are more likely to suffer from celiac disease and/or gluten sensitivity. It is important to identify any other food allergies such as dairy, soy, eggs, etc. It is also important to avoid caffeine as well as dietary sources of iodine (especially iodized salt, kelp and other seaweeds, and nutritional supplements that contain more than 300 mcg of iodine).

Goitrogens

Goitrogens (foods that prevent the use of iodine) may also be helpful for controlling hyperthyroidism as these compounds are similar in action and structure to antithyroid drugs such as propylthiouracil. However, these foods cannot reliably be used to treat hyperthyroidism on their own because their goitrogen content is quite low compared with the dosing of the antithyroid medications. On another note, there does not seem to be substantial literature that proves that these naturally occurring goitrogens interfere with thyroid function when dietary iodine levels are adequate.

FOR WOMEN AND THE MEN IN YOUR LIFE

"Feminine wisdom is the intelligence at the heart of creation. It is holistic, intuitive, contextual, and functions as a field of infinite correlation."

– Deepak Chopra, MD

Chapter 5

Perimenopause and Menopause

Natural Life Cycles

The natural cycles of life bring change and growth to all living things – change and growth that we must learn to embrace if we are to enjoy life's full potential. The hormonally driven transition to menopause is one of the significant times of change and growth in every woman's life.

Many women have a difficult time with the decline of their youthfulness (such as their perky body, smooth skin, and youthful hair) and they associate aging with unbearable loss. These women have totally "bought into" the standards of appearance set by advertising and the media and will do anything to stop or delay the process – hormone replacement and/or anti-aging hormones, along with other treatments. When women accept the false images propagated by the media, changes in their physical appearance can spark severe emotional difficulties. Consider Figure 5.1. Do you see an old woman or a young woman?

Figure 5.1 Old woman/young woman

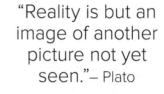

"Reality is but an image of another picture not yet seen." – Plato

THE SEASONS OF SEXUALITY

Just as the seasons in nature bring change, so do the seasons of sexuality:

- **Spring** represents the beginning of a new cycle. It corresponds to puberty and its hormonal fluctuations prepare women for the reproductive years and new birth.

- **Summer** represents a highly energetic, vital time: the reproductive years.

- **Autumn** is rich in colour and texture, and carries a hint of sadness as we leave the hot, vibrant days of summer. Autumn corresponds to the menopausal years. The autumn years then prepare women for the quieter, more introspective months of winter.

- **Winter** represents the postmenopausal years. Winter's snow and ice is white, which corresponds to our own experience of greying hair. It is a time to prepare for the start of another cycle: helping prepare grandchildren for adult life, and you do not have a family or grandchildren, finding someone to share your life with. Your many years of experience are invaluable to those who choose to listen.

Men and women alike go through these seasons of sexuality. The transitions need not be threatening to changes in sexuality if we remember that sexual expression is simply a way in which two people share love and affection – and the ways we choose to express ourselves sexually can change. Lovemaking that includes intercourse is a means of reproduction which also involves a very high degree of intimacy. However, intimacy does not have to mean intercourse. Sexual expression can be accomplished in many ways, and the right way for each person will vary throughout life. When you see an older couple walking down the street holding hands, observe the way they look at each other with love, complete acceptance, and respect – you see deep intimate expression.

When the changes of the sexual seasons reverberate in our lives and that of our partners, the most important thing is to learn to accept the changes and then find new ways to express the love that was once given voice in the heat of passion. Learn to embrace the seasons of sexuality, and as you find yourself in the autumn – or even the winter – seek out new and creative ways to express yourself sexually, ways that authentically reflect who you are at this time in your life. The most important aspect of sexual intimacy is that both partners are content with the way intimacy is expressed. If the sexual expression is good in a relationship, it is 10% of the relationship; if the sexual expression is not good or the partners feel differently about the level of satisfaction, it becomes 90% of the relationship.

Perimenopause and Menopause

Many women are not aware that hormones can start to shift from as early as 35 years of age. Usually, however, the hormonal shift starts 3–6 years before the last period, as the body approaches menopause. The relatively consistent up-and-down rhythm your hormones followed during your reproductive years is now shifting as wildly as it did during puberty. Sometimes estrogen will be high and progesterone low, while at other times progesterone will be high and estrogen low, and at still other times deficiencies or excesses of both will be present. "Oh fun!" you say – but enjoy the ride, and know that there are things you can do to make the transition smoother for yourself.

Some women start to notice hormonal changes through such symptoms as menstrual irregularities, breast tenderness, brain fog, insomnia, weight gain, hot flashes or intermittent sweats, mood changes, fatigue, or changes in vaginal secretions. For some the changes may be subtle, while others may experience full-blown perimenopausal symptoms by the time they are 40. However, if the process is this advanced at such a relatively young age, diet and lifestyle history, stress levels experienced to date, and the number of years hormones were manipulated with birth control pills will probably all have played a role.

Menstrual irregularity is one of the more common perimenopausal symptoms. The periods start to become erratic, some starting earlier, some later – the odd one may even be missed. Sounds like puberty, when things are just starting up, doesn't it? In fact, one older study found that the symptoms of perimenopause are closer to those of pubescent girls than to those of postmenopausal women. Well, you survived puberty didn't you? This too shall pass.

The ups and downs of perimenopause are often mistakenly called menopausal symptoms, but don't get hung up on semantics. The bottom line is that most women will probably experience symptoms to varying degrees for a few years before menstruation stops completely, and for a few years after. For some postmenopausal women, the symptoms go on for many years.

At the physical level, menopause is defined as total cessation of the menses for six months or more, generally accompanied by other symptoms. The hormonal fluctuations during menopause are not as dramatic as during perimenopause – the orchestra has become more familiar with the new melody that it is expected to play. Most women will experience some difficulty:

- Only 10–15% of women have no discernible symptoms at menopause
- 10–15% of women have very severe symptoms at this time, sometimes severe enough that they require hospitalization
- 70–80% of women have mild-to-severe symptoms

Signs and Symptoms of Perimenopause and Menopause

The major sign of menopause, of course, is the cessation of the monthly menstrual period. In many traditional societies, this is considered the time in which a woman comes into her full power and wisdom.

Menopause can cause a range of symptoms. Many of these symptoms, while commonly attributed to perimenopause or menopause, are actually associated (from the naturopathic perspective) with adrenal dysfunction (A), thyroid dysfunction (T), liver congestion (L), and dysbiosis (D), as indicated below. (Note that beside each symptom we have included the organs which, when imbalanced, may cause these symptoms.)

- Acceleration of the aging process – wrinkles appear overnight (T, A)
- Anxiety or panic attacks (A, D)
- Bloating and indigestion, gas (T, D)
- Increase in blood pressure or cholesterol (A, T, L)
- Bone pain (often associated with osteoporosis/osteopenia) (A)
- Inability to breathe deeply (air hunger) (A)
- "Crawly" skin sensations, especially of the lower limbs (restless leg syndrome)
- Low energy (A, T, L, D)
- Increased facial hair, particularly around the chin and upper lip
- Heart palpitations (T, A)
- Hot feet, worse in bed (L)
- Hot flashes and/or night sweats (L, D)
- Insomnia or interrupted sleep (A, T, D, L)
- Itching around the vaginal area, with or without discharge
- Joint and muscle aches and pains (L, T)
- Diminished libido or painful intercourse (A, T)
- Lightheadedness, dizzy spells, vertigo (A)
- Memory problems or brain fog (A, D)
- Mood change, depression, irritability, or anger (L, A)
- Migraine headaches (L, D)
- New food or environmental sensitivities or allergies (D, L, A)
- Urinary incontinence (worse with coughing or laughing)
- Vaginal or urinary tract infections (D)
- Weight gain, usually around or on the abdomen, hips, and breasts (T)

At this point you are probably saying, "I'm outta here! I won't accept that these things have to happen in my life." Take heart: They don't have to, and there is life during and after the menopausal years! Women spend one-third of their lives in the post-menopausal years. Let's embrace the wisdom and power our hormonal transitions have given us and accept that menopause is not a disease that needs to be treated with drugs for years on end.

It is difficult not to get caught up in the attitudes fostered by the medical profession and the media, which claim that women in this stage of life are drying up, wrinkling, and shrinking away. The menopausal transition is seen as a pathology, a disease of the endocrine system that needs to be treated.

Certainly, symptoms are more common nowadays. The quality of our food is extremely compromised, being deficient in nutrients and containing added hormones and antibiotics. This, coupled with stress and environmental toxins, has a profound effect on the hormonal system. The problem, however, is with stress, toxins in our food supply, and the environment, not with the menopausal years.

Hot flashes and night sweats

Hot flashes affect about 85% of women during the years immediately before and after menopause. Every woman's menopausal symptoms are different. Some women have night sweats, which are hot flashes that occur while sleeping. They can be disruptive to sleep, not to mention the need to get up and change nightclothes or sheets. Some women may get back to sleep, while others spend most of the night tossing and turning.

Hot flashes typically last 1–5 minutes. The hot flash is described as a hot sensation that radiates through the body, particularly the upper body. There is an increase in heart rate, sweating, and peripheral vasodilation (flushing). Hot flash frequency increases during perimenopause and continues for an unknown length of time. All hot flashes involve the vasomotor system. The intensity of the flashes and the areas of the body most affected vary from woman to woman due to the unique manifestations of the changes in the hormonic symphony.

Vasomotor hot flashes

Vasomotor symptoms (VMS) are the most common symptoms and cause the most disruption in menopausal women. VMS include:

- Hot flashes
- Dry skin
- Itchy, crawling sensation on skin
- Sleep issues
- A sudden feeling of warmth spreading through the upper body and face
- A flushed appearance with red, blotchy skin
- Rapid heartbeat
- Perspiration, mostly on the upper body
- Feeling chilled as the hot flash subsides

Hormone balance questionnaire

The following questionnaire is designed to provide a basic overview of the possible causes of symptoms you may be experiencing based on hormone levels. Often symptoms can be due to a combination of the various hormone imbalances. Saliva hormone testing can provide more definitive information.

Hormone Balance Questionnaire

If you experience three or more symptoms in the different groups, your symptoms could be related to an excess or deficiency of the specific hormone.

Progesterone Deficiency

○ PMS	○ Early miscarriage
○ Anxiety/depression	○ Unexplained weight gain
○ Premenstrual acne	○ Insomnia
○ Painful or lumpy breasts	○ Memory lapses

Total boxes checked [   ]

Estrogen Deficiency

○ Vaginal dryness   ○ Low libido
○ Night sweats   ○ Hot flashes
○ Brain fog   ○ Insomnia
○ Incontinence   ○ Bladder infections

Total boxes checked [   ]

Estrogen Excess

○ Water retention   ○ Weight gain
○ Tender breasts   ○ Fibrocystic breasts
○ Uterine fibroids   ○ Endometriosis
○ Mood swings   ○ Hormonal headaches
○ Anxious and irritable

Total boxes checked [   ]

Androgen (testosterone) Excess

○ Acne   ○ Increased facial hair
○ Thinning hair on head   ○ Hypoglycemia (low blood sugar)
○ PCOS (polycystic ovary)   ○ Infertility

Total boxes checked [   ]

Androgen Deficiency

○ Loss of muscle mass   ○ Low libido
○ Depression   ○ Sleep disturbances
○ Fatigue

Total boxes checked [   ]

Progesterone deficiency – This is the most common hormone imbalance among women of all ages. Progesterone deficiency is primarily caused by diet, environmental factors (see *Chapter 6*), and long-term use of birth control pills. EstroSense® can help balance excess estrogen and Chastetree can be helpful in regulating progesterone levels. If tests show more severe levels of progesterone deficiency, some women may require USP progesterone, as discussed later in this chapter.

Estrogen deficiency – This hormone imbalance is most common in menopausal women. Follow the recommendations provided later in this chapter to help with estrogen deficiency symptoms.

Excess estrogen or estrogen dominance – This is a very common condition today due to diet, environmental factors, gut microbe imbalances, or long-term use of birth control pills. EstroSense helps balance estrogen in the body. (Refer to *Chapter 6* for more information on estrogen dominance symptoms and solutions.)

Excess androgens – This imbalance is often caused by a diet high in refined sugars and carbohydrates, elevated insulin levels, or imbalances in adrenal stress hormones. Ovarian tumours can also cause elevated androgens and must be ruled out. Dietary chances, probiotics, adrenal support, and regulating blood sugar can help to balance testosterone levels.

Androgen deficiency – This is often caused by elevated stress hormones. Chronic stress causes the precursor hormones to androgens and estrogens to be used up by the cortisol pathway, as discussed later in this chapter. AdrenaSense® and Ultimate Libido™ can be helpful in this case.

Note: The information contained in this questionnaire is not intended to replace the advice provided by your health care practitioner. Rather, it is a guideline to help determine the cause of your symptoms.

Testing and Diagnosis

Neuro-endocrine-immune connection

The human body consists of multiple systems that communicate to maintain homeostasis and health. Neurotransmitters, hormones, and cytokines are essential chemical signals that are involved when hot flashes occur. Collectively, these systems form the neurological, endocrine, and immune system. The interactions primarily occur in three axes:

- Hypothalamic-pituitary-adrenal (HPA) axis
- Hypothalamic-pituitary-thyroid (HPT) axis
- Hypothalamic-pituitary-gonadal (HPG) axis

Lab testing can be done to determine which systems may be out of balance. The results of the tests can help develop a specific supplement protocol to control the imbalances causing the hot flashes.

Hormone Replacement Therapy – To Do or Not to Do?

The medicalization of menopause – A history lesson

Estrogen enthusiasm around menopause dates back to the early 1960s. Before then, the aura around estrogen was one of caution. One estrogen enthusiast, A. Walsh, ignored the cautions, and in 1965 she introduced the book *Now! The Pills to Keep Women Young! ERT: The First Complete Account of the Miracle Hormone Treatment That May Revolutionize the Lives of Millions of Women!* She was definitely right about that last statement.

Hot on the heels of Walsh came Dr. Robert A. Wilson, who wrote an article for *Newsweek* magazine in January 1964 entitled "No More Menopause". With financial backing from Ayerst Laboratories, he also wrote a book entitled *Feminine Forever* that did wonders for the sale of Premarin, an estrogen replacement drug derived from pregnant horses' urine. The basic attitude underpinning the promotion of estrogen in Walsh's writing is summed up in the following words from *Feminine Forever:* "The unpalatable truth must be faced that all postmenopausal women are castrates... From a practical point of view, a man remains a man until the very end."

Walsh's book and its effect on Premarin sales were the beginning of the billion-dollar relationship between estrogen and menopause. Premarin historically was the most widely sold drug in North America, with over $2 billion in sales in 2001. However, major health concerns were raised by the Women's Health Initiative (WHI) study (discussed below) and sales dropped to $880 million in 2004.

Menopause is NOT a disease

Many doctors still believe that menopause is essentially a disease of the endocrine system that needs to be treated with drugs, and that all women need hormone replacement for optimal health during and after the menopausal transition. There is something fundamentally disturbing about turning a natural event such as menopause into a disease that demands decades of drug treatment. Today, estrogen is sold in a variety of forms – pills, patches, creams, and injections – you can choose your flavour of the month!

Hormone replacement therapy

Hormone replacement therapy (HRT) has been a popular course of treatment for many women with menopausal symptoms, but the decision to use HRT is a difficult one. HRT was originally developed to halt the symptoms of menopause, although doctors primarily used it to prevent cardiovascular disease and to prevent bone loss, and also in the treatment of depression, urinary incontinence, Alzheimer's disease, and libido problems. However, no randomized, controlled clinical trial had ever been conducted to verify if HRT could be used safely for these conditions.

Finally, in 1991 the first randomized, controlled clinical trial, the WHI study, was launched to study the long-term effects of HRT on women. The study was scheduled to run until 2005, but was halted in 2002 due to significant health risks. The researchers studied women between the ages of 50 and 79 who were using Premarin (estrogen from pregnant horses' urine) and synthetic progesterone called progestins. The majority of the women using Premarin were between the ages of 60 and 69.

According to the study's findings, over the course of one year, **for every 10,000 women** taking estrogen plus progestin, there were:

- 7 more women with heart attacks (compared to those who took a placebo)
- 8 more women with strokes
- 8 more women with breast cancer
- 18 more women with blood clots

The WHI study's overall conclusions included the following:

- The estrogen plus progestin combination does not prevent heart disease in older, postmenopausal women several years post-menopause.
- For women taking estrogen plus progestin, the risks (i.e., increased breast cancer, heart attack, stroke, and blood clots in the lungs and legs) outweigh the benefits (i.e., fewer hip fractures and colon cancer) for women who do not have other reasons besides prevention to take hormone therapy.

WHI revisited

A reanalysis of the results of the WHI showed that the risks HRT and breast cancer, stroke, and heart disease were **not increased in the fifth decade, but rose in the sixth and seventh.** The new analysis also showed that If HRT is started early in postmenopausal women, the cardiac endothelium is still responsive to estrogens, and the procoagulant effects may be buffered. Although women still have relatively healthy arteries at the onset of menopause, arterial disease increases with age. So, is it the HRT that is providing the possible benefits in younger menopausal women, or the fact that most younger menopausal women still have a healthy cardiovascular system? In elderly postmenopausal women, HRT has no beneficial effect and in fact has a detrimental effect because of the predominance of the procoagulant effects that increase the risk for stroke and venous thromboembolic events.

The potential risks of HRT

- **Breast cancer** – While studies have been inconsistent, an emerging consensus appears to suggest that HRT may slightly increase the risk for breast cancer. This risk is similar to that associated with natural late menopause, and it comes into effect after at least 5 years of continuous

HRT. The lifetime risk of developing breast cancer significantly increases with long-term HRT use. This observation indicates that it is the duration of lifetime sex hormone exposure that is relevant.

- **Ulcerative colitis** – Another study of 108,844 postmenopausal US women found an association between hormone therapy and increased risk of ulcerative colitis (UC). The risk of UC increased with longer duration of hormone use and decreased with time since continuation.

- **Cholelithiasis (gallstones)** – Cholelithiasis is common among postmenopausal women and the incidence increases with age and obesity. In various studies, including the WHI, the risk further increased in postmenopausal women receiving HRT. The annual incidence for any gallbladder event was 78 events per 10,000 person-years for women taking estrogen-only preparations versus 47 events for placebo. Rates were 55 per 10,000 person-years for combined estrogen and progestogen versus 35 events for placebo.

- **Ovarian cancer** – In women who have undergone a hysterectomy, the use of estrogen alone for more than 10 years was linked to an increased risk of ovarian cancer. This increase in risk was not observed in women who took HRT for less than 10 years. In women with an intact uterus, 5 or more years of estrogen plus progestogen was positively associated with ovarian cancer.

- **Dementia and cognition** – Increasing age is the most important risk factor for dementia, and most of the risk is attributed to Alzheimer disease, cerebrovascular disease, or a combination of both. In theory, HRT in postmenopausal women should prevent and help treat dementia and related disorders. However, various studies have failed to provide a consensus on this aspect. A memory substudy of the WHI showed that older women taking combination hormone therapy had twice the rate of dementia, including Alzheimer disease, compared with women who did not. At present, no definite evidence supports the use of HRT to prevent or improve cognitive deterioration.

Evaluation criteria for prescribing HRT

All women considering HRT should be thoroughly evaluated with a detailed history and complete physical examination for a proper diagnosis and identification of any contraindications. Baseline laboratory and imaging studies that are considered a requirement prior to administering HRT include the following:

- Urinalysis
- Fasting lipid profile
- Blood sugar levels
- Serum estradiol levels
- Serum follicle-stimulating hormone (FSH) levels
- Electrocardiography
- Ultrasonography (to measure endometrial thickness and ovarian volume)
- Pap test
- Mammography (performed once every 2–3 years and annually after the age of 50 years)

Endometrial sampling is not required in routine practice. However, the presence of abnormal bleeding before or during HRT should prompt consideration of ultrasound to check endometrial thickness.

The increased risks of HRT only started to receive some attention from the medical community after the WHI study reported the increased breast cancer and cardiovascular risk factors. Even then, there was great resistance from the medical world in accepting the results of the study. After 10 years of litigation, more than 1,000 Canadian women who claimed they were not properly warned of breast cancer risks by the manufacturers of Premarin and other popular menopause drugs requested compensation from a $13.6-million settlement fund in 2015.

Karen Jensen, ND

When I wrote my first book on menopause in 1999, *Menopause: A Naturopathic Approach to the Transitional Years,* I blew the whistle on the use of synthetic estrogens and progestins, based on earlier studies from the 1990s that reported the increased risk for breast cancer and cardiovascular disease. Even though these and other early studies reported risks with the use of synthetic hormone replacement, I received nothing but criticism from the medical establishment.

Oral contraceptives – "the pill" – another form of hormone replacement

The oral contraceptive, commonly referred to as "the pill", is a form of hormonal contraception taken by millions of women to prevent pregnancy. Many women start taking the pill at a very early age. Some women also take the pill for non-contraceptive purposes such as irregular, painful, or heavy periods, PMS, acne, or breast and ovarian cysts.

The two types of contraceptive pills both contain synthetic forms of the hormones estrogen and progesterone (progestin). Combination pills contain both of these hormones, whereas the "mini pill" contains only the hormone progestin.

> In my 25 years in practice, I have never seen a female patient screened according to the guidelines outlined on the previous page prior to the medical doctor prescribing HRT.

Many women experience common side effects when taking the pill, such as intermenstrual spotting, nausea, breast tenderness, headaches, weight gain, mood changes, missed periods, decreased libido, vaginal discharge, and visual changes with contact lenses. Depression is also very common in women who take the pill, and this is getting medical attention more recently.

Combination pills pose an increased risk of cardiovascular side effects such as heart attack, stroke, and blood clots, which can be fatal. Combination pills with the synthetic progesterone drospirenone also have a slightly higher risk of blood clots, including deep vein thrombosis and pulmonary embolism.

> *People with a history of blood clots, heart attacks, or stroke are advised not to take the combination birth control pill.*

Additional factors that increase the risk of blood clots include obesity and a family history of heart disease. It is not recommended to take hormonal contraceptives if there is a personal history of liver or heart disease, uterine or breast cancer, uncontrolled blood pressure, or migraines with an aura.

Natural Alternatives

Natural alternatives, including herbal products, nutrition, and lifestyle changes, are quickly becoming the preferred choice over the controversial HRT. This awareness and education of HRT alternatives needs to be promoted in order for women to make educated decisions about their treatment options.

However, many women experience severe symptoms, especially if the onset of menopause has been sudden. These women may require prescription HRT until their body is able to rebalance itself, with the help of stress reduction, diet and lifestyle changes, and natural remedies. Such short-term use (less than 4–5 years) of HRT raises few concerns, especially if the form of HRT chosen is among the safer ones. But every woman needs to remember that HRT is not a miracle treatment or a fountain of youth. As is the case with any drug, it should be used with caution, and only when the less invasive, non-toxic methods are not as immediately effective.

It is advised that women who are undergoing surgery stop taking the pill for at least 4–6 weeks prior to surgery. Most doctors do not inform women of this. If this holds true for the pill, which has lower doses of synthetic hormones, one would logically assume that it is even more important for menopausal women who are taking higher doses of synthetic hormones with HRT.

The medical world tends to agree that it is number of years that women take hormones, along with their age, that increase risk factors for many conditions, including breast cancer, heart disease, stroke, and ovarian cancer. Many women start taking the pill at a very young age. Some may take breaks in order to have children, but then move right into prescription HRT at the onset of menopause. Wouldn't it be wise to consider the total number of years that women are taking synthetic hormones in the pill as well as the number years on HRT?

Bio-identical Hormones

Bio-identical hormones have an identical molecular structure to the hormones that are made by the body and are synthesized from soy and yams. The more common synthetic HRT prescribed is molecularly altered so a pharmaceutical company is able to obtain a patent. No substance identical to that produced by the body is patentable.

The body does not recognize synthetic hormones the same way as bio-identical hormones. This difference is why, according to many health care practitioners, synthetic hormones produce so many unhealthy side effects. For instance, Premarin, an estrogen derived from horse urine, may be natural to horses, but it contains two additional estrogens not made by women.

> Start by treating the adrenals, and addressing liver and gut health. Then add bio-identical hormones if necessary. As these organs become more balanced, it may no longer be necessary to take hormones. Always start with the lowest dose of bio-identical hormones and increase if necessary.

As mentioned, HRT drugs do not resemble the respective hormones produced by the body, with the exception of United States Pharmacopeia (USP) progesterone found in Prometrium, as well as some estrogen products such as Estrace and Estraderm, which have unique delivery systems allowing them to be patented. Compounding pharmacies make bio-identical hormones such as Bi-Est, Tri-Est, or USP progesterone cream.

Bio-identical hormones vs. patentable hormones

It costs approximately $3 million to get a new drug approved for use – money that is spent mainly on researching the compound's efficacy and safety. Thus, if a company cannot expect to make a profit on a drug because it cannot patent it – that is, cannot claim it as its property alone and thereby shield itself from competition – then it makes little economic sense to do the necessary studies. It is simply a matter of economics. As a result, companies focus on patentable hormones rather than bio-identical hormones.

Bio-identical Hormone Therapy

The bio-identical hormones include estrone, estradiol, estriol, progesterone, testosterone, and dehydroepiandrosterone (DHEA). The bio-identical hormones most commonly prescribed for hot flashes and other menopausal symptoms include Bi-Est (80% estriol and 20% estradiol), Tri-Est (80% estriol, 10% estradiol, and 10% estrone), and progesterone.

The general rule for taking hormone replacement is to always start with the lowest dose of hormones and increase if necessary, and take for shortest duration possible.

Estriol cream for vaginal dryness

Estriol is considered safe and is the weakest of all three estrogens. It has been shown to be protective against breast cancer and other potential estrogen-dominant conditions. It can be helpful for vaginal dryness and in preventing bladder infections. It can be used as a cream or suppository. To determine your dosages of bio-identical hormones, consult with a naturopathic or complementary medical doctor.

what we know works

Support for Perimenopause and Menopause

Today, many women are seeking safer alternatives to HRT for perimenopausal and menopausal symptoms. The natural approach encompasses much more than treatment with the hormonal drugs currently offered. Once you begin to work toward achieving optimal health and become healthier, you will likely find that any unwanted symptoms of hormonal imbalance can be handled safely and effectively with nutrition, exercise, and natural remedies.

MenoSense® contains black cohosh, dong quai, chasteberry, hesperidin, and gamma-oryzanol to support and balance hormones, and reduce hot flashes and night sweats. Refer below for more information on individual ingredients.

Dosage: 1–2 capsules twice daily.

Black cohosh *(Cimicifuga racemosa)* is one of the most popular herbs used today to treat a variety of female health problems experienced during perimenopause and menopause.

Dong quai *(Angelica sinensis)* helps relieve hot flashes and vaginal dryness, and is traditionally used as a uterine tonic in Chinese medicine.

Chasteberry *(Vitex agnus-castus)* is the most commonly used botanical in Europe to treat hormonal imbalances. Its action in the body helps balance progesterone levels relative to estrogen levels.

Hesperidin is a naturally occurring bioflavonoid, has been shown to reduce hot flashes by up to 53% when combined with vitamin C.

Gamma-oryzanol *(Oryza sativa)* is isolated from rice bran oil. It was first shown to be effective for menopausal symptoms, including hot flashes, in the early 1960s. Subsequent studies have further documented its safety and effectiveness. In one study, 85% of the subjects who took 300 mg daily reported improvement in menopausal symptoms.

Ultimate™ Probiotic plays an important role in the maintenance of normal microflora in the gut. Probiotics also help with the detoxification and binding of harmful estrogens and in eliminating them from the digestive tract.

Dosage: 1–3 capsules daily.

AdrenaSense® helps keep the adrenal glands well supported and strong before you reach menopause, making this time much easier on you and your body. In addition to carrying the burden of stress, our adrenal glands are also responsible for taking over hormone production when the ovaries shut down during menopause. The adrenal glands are truly the foundation of hormone health.

Dosage: 2 capsules daily in the morning and 1 at noon.

EstroSense® contains essential nutrients for the removal of excess and harmful estrogens in the body. Healthy liver function is important for hormonal balance.

Dosage: 1 capsule 3 times daily with food.

SomniSense™ contains the important herbs passion flower, California poppy, skullcap, and linden flower to help ensure a good night's sleep.

Dosage: 2–4 capsules 1 hour before bed.

Additional support for perimenopause and menopause

Ultimate Maca Energy™ has been used in Peru for thousands of years. It has proven to be useful for boosting energy levels, supporting the production of both estrogen and testosterone, improving libido, and providing relief of some menopausal symptoms. Maca seems to act on the hypothalamus and pituitary, two key players in hormone balance.

Dosage: 2–4 capsules daily.

Red clover *(Trifolium pratense)* has been shown to significantly reduce hot flashes in menopausal women.

Dosage: 300–500 mg extract daily.

* Caution in women diagnosed with breast cancer or at high risk for breast cancer due to isoflavone content in red clover.

Menopause support: Step-by-step

Step 1 – Perimenopausal and asymptomatic menopausal women

Women with few or no symptoms of hormonal changes who want to maintain hormonal balance can use the following protocol:

- Follow the general guidelines for creating optimal health in *Chapter 19*.
- Support your adrenal glands with AdrenaSense.
- Support your liver and estrogen balance for 10–12 days a month with EstroSense.
- Take a probiotic such as CalmBiotic or Ultimate Probiotic regularly.
- Add essential fatty acids to your diet if you aren't taking them already.

Step 2 – Mildly symptomatic women

Perimenopausal, menopausal, or postmenopausal women with mild-to-moderate symptoms will benefit from the following protocol:

- Take all steps outlined above, and add MenoSense (standardized botanical products are discussed earlier in this chapter).

Step 3 – Severely symptomatic women

Perimenopausal, menopausal, or postmenopausal women with severe symptoms such as debilitating hot flashes or chronic insomnia will benefit from the following treatment:

- Take all steps outlined above; however, do not take MenoSense at this point.
- Add bioidentical hormones such as Tri-Est and USP progesterone as directed by your health care practitioner for 3–6 months until symptoms are stable. At this point, you may want to start to wean off hormone replacement.

Weaning off estrogen

The following chart provides a guide to help you wean from supplemental estrogen.

Women on HRT (Bioidentical or Other)

WEEKS	ESTROGEN (Tri-Est or Other)	BOTANICAL (e.g., MenoSense)	PROGESTERONE (USP or oral)
1 and 2	4 days per week	3 days per week	as directed
3 and 4	3 days per week	4 days per week	as directed
5 and 6	2 days per week	5 days per week	as directed
7 and 8	0 – 1 day per week	7 days per week	as directed

Weaning off progesterone

To begin decreasing progesterone use, remember that the least amount possible of any hormone is ideal. Try decreasing your progesterone use by one-half. Then try using this halved dosage every other day. Let your sense of well-being, your symptom frequency, and salivary tests guide the process.

Most women will find that once they have made the necessary lifestyle and dietary changes and begin giving support to the adrenal glands, intestines, and liver, they will require only botanical support to maintain hormonal balance. Both for its effects on yourself and your environment, it is a worthy goal to work toward – and getting there can be a whole new adventure.

Diet and Lifestyle Tips for Perimenopause and Menopause

Phytoestrogen food sources

Nutrition and diet can greatly influence menopause and menopausal symptoms. One of the most important dietary recommendations for all menopausal women may be to increase foods that are high in phytoestrogens. Phytoestrogens are plant versions of the human hormone estrogen. They are considered to be very weak estrogenic compounds with an average of about 2% of the strength of estrogens. They can be beneficial when estrogen levels are either too high or too low. When metabolized, they bind on the same receptor sites as estrogens, altering estrogenic effects.

There are several types of phytoestrogens including the following:

- Coumestans are found in red clover, alfalfa, garden peas, and Brussels sprouts. They are the least commonly ingested phytoestrogens and are thought to have the most estrogenic effect of all the phytoestrogens.
- Stilbenoids are being studied for their chemopreventive effects, lipid lowering and vascular activities, and as agents to increase lifespan in general.
- Flavonoids have several subgroups including isoflavones and flavones, many of which are reported to have estrogenic activity. The isoflavones from legumes, including genistein and daidzein, are the most studied phytoestrogens. Soy products are the major source in the diet.
- Geistein is the most active and well-studied of the isoflavones. Numerous studies have noted a biphasic effect where genistein reduces

the stimulation of estrogen receptors at low dosages but stimulates them at higher doses, suggesting caution in regard to active cancers.

A study published in 2009 in the *Journal of the American Medical Association* concluded that among women with breast cancer, soy food consumption was significantly associated with decreased risk of death and recurrence. However, some doctors still recommend that women with breast cancer eliminate soy products and other foods such as flaxseed due to the phytoestrogen content.

Commonly consumed foods containing phytoestrogens include: nuts and seeds; grains such as wheat, oats, and barley; legumes such as peas, beans, and lentils; yam; rice; alfalfa; fruits and vegetables such as apples, carrots, and pomegranates; and coffee and beer. As you can see, in order to avoid consuming phytoestrogens, we pretty much have to give up most foods.

The topic of phytoestrogens is far too complex to address fully in this book. However, it is important to understand that simply because a plant or food has estrogenic activity does not mean it is contraindicated for women or men with hormone-sensitive conditions.

Treating hot flashes and night sweats

To treat hot flashes and night sweats, start off by following simple changes, and see whether they bring some relief:

- **Avoid alcohol.** Many women become very alcohol-sensitive during the transitional years. Alcohol increases heat in the body and for some, even very small amounts, will cause night sweats.

- **Avoid highly spiced foods.** Garlic, peppers, and the like, especially during the evening meal, may exacerbate symptoms.

- **Exercise regularly.** A study of 900 menopausal women showed that those who exercised regularly (a minimum of 3.5 hours per week) had milder and less frequent hot flashes.

- **Avoid red wine and coffee.** Many women find that drinking red wine and/or coffee causes hot flashes. Try eliminating them for a few days and see if things improve.

- **Make time for stress-relieving exercise** like massage, yoga, hiking, painting, and jogging – whatever helps you relax and unwind.

- **Eliminate food sensitivities.**

- **Support your adrenal glands.**

- **Detoxify and support the liver.** (Refer to *Chapter 2* for more information.)
- **Avoid polyester fabrics.** Polyester fabrics make you perspire more easily even if you are not going through hormonal changes. Use only natural fabrics for clothing, and cotton sheets, cotton or wool blankets, and cotton nightclothes.

The Later Years – 65 and Older

For some women the symptoms of the hormone transition in the menopausal years can last throughout their sixties. But for most, by the time women their reach late sixties, the symptoms are gone. However, other symptoms can occur for many women at this stage of life. Women over the age of 65 should pay attention to the following:

- **Exercise** – It becomes even more important to continue with an exercise regime as you get older. Even if you haven't incorporated exercise into your life prior to this stage, it is NEVER too late to start. It is vital to keep the muscles strong in order to prevent falls and fractures.
- **Vitamin D** – Vitamin D is one of the most important supplements you can take as you age. Aging, even in healthy people, is accompanied by a reduction in muscle mass and muscle strength. The gradual loss of muscle strength results in functional impairment, the need for assistance in the performance of daily activities, and an increased risk of falling fractures. Therefore, the preservation of muscle strength is of utmost importance. Vitamin D deficiency is associated with muscle weakness, and approximately 50% of aging women are deficient.

> Personally, I was shocked a few years ago when I had my vitamin D levels checked and discovered I was at low normal levels. Now I make sure to take 5000 IU of vitamin D daily.

- **Water** – The importance of water cannot be emphasized enough. Our body becomes more dehydrated as we get older, for several different reasons. With age, our body doesn't hold as much water because we lose muscle mass. By the age of 80, we have 15% less water than when we were 20, making our bodies more vulnerable to dehydration. Starting around age 50, and becoming more serious around age 70, the kidneys begin to lose some of their ability to remove toxins from the blood. Because kidneys are less able to concentrate urine, we expel water more quickly as we age. Older people also lose the sensation of being thirsty, much as our taste buds decrease as we age. Some seniors may drink less because they fear incontinence. In addition, drugs such as diuretics, laxatives, and some blood pressure medications can cause more frequent urination or perspiration, which interferes with fluid balance. Drink at least 1.5–2 litres of water a day. Yes, you will have to make frequent trips to the bathroom as your body starts to flush toxins, but this will settle down.

- **Energy** – It is common to notice changes in energy levels once you reach your sixth or seventh decade of life. The organs just aren't as vital as they were in your younger years. Taking added supplement support such as an essential fatty acid, probiotics, multivitamin, mineral, and adrenal support such as AdrenaSense can be very helpful. Following the dietary and lifestyle guidelines in Section 5 is also important to stay healthy as you age.

- **Sleep** – Sleep can come less easily as you age. Refer to *Chapter 12* for helpful tips for getting a good night's sleep.

- **Cardiovascular disease** – As women age, they become at greater risk for cardiovascular disease. Eating well, drinking more water, and exercising are very important to help prevent CVD. In addition, a cardio support product such as CardioSense could be considered to prevent heart disease. (Refer to *Chapter 17* for more information.)

Andropause – For the Men in Your Life

The following section provides information to help women understand the hormone changes and symptoms men experience during andropause. Men may find it difficult to talk about the changes they are noticing and it may become the elephant in the room.

You are not alone when it comes to the hormone transitions. However, the men in your life may not know that they also go through these physical changes – or perhaps they are in denial. Men are less likely to seek preventative care, visit the doctor, pay attention to health information, seek timely treatment, and follow recommendations suggested by health care practitioners. So why do men resist seeking support for personal health problems? Even in this time of growing gender-equality and mixing of stereotypical roles and traits, masculinity is strongly associated with physical strength and virility, emotional stoicism, assertiveness,

> Men don't understand women, but at least they know it. Women don't understand men, but most women don't know it.

and control. Many men still hold this idealized vision of masculinity. The idea of declining hormones shows vulnerability or weakness and poses a threat to this stereotypical view of masculinity.

Like women, men experience changes in their body when they reach their late forties to early fifties. Symptoms may vary and include erectile dysfunction, depression, weight gain, fatigue, and other physical and emotional symptoms similar to those experienced by women during the transitional years. This cycle of life is sometimes referred to as the male menopause, now commonly called "andropause". The symptoms in men emerge more slowly and subtly compared to women and are therefore often overlooked or misdiagnosed. Symptoms are caused primarily by declining levels of the hormone testosterone and, to a lesser degree, variations in estrogen levels. Yes, men have estrogen too.

Testosterone – The "man maker"

Testosterone is a powerful androgen, a steroid hormone manufactured primarily in the testes and also in the adrenal glands. The name is derived from the Greek words for "man-maker" and the term is appropriate, since androgens are responsible for the large muscles, strong bones, deep voice, and pattern of hair growth that characterize the gender. In addition, testosterone is responsible for sperm production, sex drive, and sexual performance, and has effects on emotional behaviour.

After peaking in his 20s, a man's testosterone level tends to gradually decrease and continues to further decline throughout the remainder of his life, resulting in a number of symptoms. Total testosterone levels fall by about 1% a year starting around age 40, while bioavailable testosterone, the form that does the hormone's work, falls about 2% a year. Despite declining levels, most men stay in the normal range throughout their life.

Signs and Symptoms of Andropause

- Erratic moods, irritability, depression
- Fatigue, lack of endurance and/or stamina
- Low libido, erectile dysfunction
- Prostate and urinary disorders
- Weight gain (around mid-section)

- Increase in blood pressure or other cardiovascular problems
- Decreased ambition and work performance
- Restlessness and insomnia
- Increased insulin resistance and blood sugar
- Cognitive decline (memory and concentration)

In addition, testosterone deficiency can lead to cognitive impairment, osteoporosis, cardiovascular disease, benign prostate hypertrophy (BPH), and prostate cancer.

Testing and Diagnosis

When assessing a man's hormone status, clinicians frequently measure "total testosterone", which includes free testosterone and testosterone bound to serum hormone-binding globulin (SHBG). It is free testosterone, however, that is the most relevant measure of a man's testosterone status. It is also recommended that men have a prostate-specific antigen (PSA) test done around age 40 to establish a baseline.

Recommended lab tests include the following:

- **Male hormone analysis** – free and total testosterone, DHT (dihyrotestosterone), SHBG, PSA, and prostate exam
- **Thyroid** – TSH, T3, T4, thyroid antibodies, and reverse T3
- **Naturopathic assessment** – lifestyle, diet, nutrition, stress levels, organ health, toxic burden, and mental/emotional health
- **Saliva hormones** – estradiol, progesterone, testosterone, DHEA, and cortisol

what we know works

Support for Andropause

A recurring theme throughout this book is that when it comes to treatment for a health condition, the first step is to address the cause of the symptoms and support the body with natural remedies, diet, and lifestyle whenever possible. The following recommendations have proven helpful for many men who are experiencing symptoms of declining testosterone.

AdrenaSense® helps regulate the stress response in the body. Prolonged stress can result in high levels of cortisol, which leads to a low testosterone-to-cortisol ratio. The ashwagandha in AdrenaSense has also been shown to increase testosterone levels.

Dosage: 2–3 capsules daily.

Ultimate™ Probiotic helps balance the intestinal microbiome. Recent studies show that male mice that consumed the probiotic *Lactobacillus acidophilus* had larger testicles and increased serum testosterone levels compared to their age-matched controls.

Dosage: 1 capsule 2–3 times daily.

Ultimate Libido™ helps support and increase testosterone levels.

Dosage: 3 capsules 1–2 times daily.

Ultimate Maca Energy™ *(Lepidium meyenii)* has been shown to improve erectile dysfunction and libido, both common symptoms in andropause.

Dosage: 2–4 capsules daily or 1 tablespoon powder daily.

Testosterone replacement therapy – Is it an option?

If andropause symptoms are severe and are not being helped by natural therapies, some men may consider testosterone replacement. Please keep in mind the following information before making a decision and discuss the pros and cons with your health care practitioner.

The medicalization of male menopause – A cautionary tale

Male menopause was a much-discussed topic from the late 1930s to the mid-1950s, but it virtually disappeared for the next 40 years until the late 1990s. Along with the renewed interest in male menopause came the concept of medicalization of the life-cycle because people have come to expect medicine to provide a cure for any ailment. The medicalized model has also been effectively marketed for treating menopause in women, a parallel, if not identical, stage in the life-course of women. However we need to remember the story of hormone replacement in women as a cautionary tale.

Doctors once widely prescribed estrogen and progesterone to women as a way to ward off heart disease – until a large US trial found that older women given the hormones actually faced increased risks of blood clots, heart attack, stroke, and breast cancer. As a result, many doctors are worried that testosterone therapy in turn may not be safe, and testosterone therapy for older men remains controversial.

The role of testosterone in prostate disease, both benign prostatic hyperplasia (BPH) and prostate cancer, is one unresolved issue. Other possible side effects include polycythemia (an excessive number of red blood cells), sleep apnea (respiratory pauses during sleep that can increase the risk of hypertension, heart attack, and stroke), gynecomastia (benign breast enlargement), acne, and liver disease.

Researchers reviewed more than 200 clinical trials and concluded that the prescription of testosterone supplementation for cardiovascular health, sexual function, physical function, mood, or cognitive function in men with low testosterone is not supported by clinical trial data. More research is needed to learn if these concerns about the safety of testosterone are justified in order to avoid repeating the same mistake that was made in hormone replacement in women.

Some men may choose to take testosterone replacement in addition to natural supplement support for a time until the main hormone shifts are over and symptoms improve. If the general guideline for hormone replacement in women is followed in men – "the smallest does for the shortest time" – the side effects and risks are decreased. Conventional treatment is provided by synthetic testosterone in different forms including transdermal, oral, or injections.

Bioidentical testosterone cream may provide a safer form of treatment and it is available on prescription from a compounding pharmacy. (Refer to the section on bioidentical hormones earlier in this chapter.)

Low Libido in Women

Changes in libido are quite common for women throughout their lifetime due to many influences, but changes tend to increase with aging, especially in menopause. As many as 30% of women have low sexual desire, and about 50% of these feel distressed about it.

Possible Causes of Low Libido in Women

Numerous variables affect sexual function, including emotional and psychological factors, medical problems causing fatigue and/or pain, certain medications (e.g., antidepressants, birth control pill, antihistamines, and high blood pressure medications), and hormonal influences. Testosterone is also a key player and is necessary for a normal sex drive in women and men, helping to determine desire, arousal, and sexual sensation.

During perimenopause, estrogen levels are fluctuating but ultimately declining, as is the production of the hormone testosterone. Fluctuating and declining testosterone levels seem to be associated with a decrease in libido. Loss of estrogen is also responsible for most of the changes, and a decrease in lubrication during sexual arousal, vaginal tone, and vaginal elasticity also occur. Vaginal dryness is not only associated with painful intercourse, but also with a decrease in sexual desire.

Increased cortisol from chronic stress can block the effects of testosterone, which can suppress libido. Scientists know that high cortisol inhibits the body's main sex hormone, gonadotropin-releasing hormone (GnRH), and subsequently suppresses not only libido, but also ovulation and sperm count. However new research from the University of California, Berkeley shows that stress also increases brain levels of a reproductive hormone named gonadotropin-inhibitory hormone (GnIH). This small protein hormone puts the brakes on reproduction by directly inhibiting GnRH.

what we know works

Support for Low Libido in Women

Sex Essentials® contains L-arginine, gingko biloba, and Korean ginseng. Refer below for more information on individual ingredients.

Dosage: 3 capsules daily taken together.

Ginseng has been shown to help improve sexual function in both men and women. A randomized, placebo-controlled, double-blind crossover trial evaluated the efficacy of Korean red ginseng for improving sexual function in menopausal women. The results of the study found that supplementation with ginseng improved sexual arousal, satisfaction, and frequency in menopausal women. Studies have also shown clear benefits in men with reported improvements in libido, erectile function, and testosterone levels.

Ginkgo biloba is well known for its ability to enhance blood circulation and oxygen flow throughout the body. This improved circulation also includes the sex organs. By increasing blood flow to this area of the body, ginkgo can help improve sensitivity and sexual response. In an open trial, gingko biloba was found to be 84% effective in treating antidepressant-induced sexual dysfunction, with women showing a 91% response rate to the sexually enhancing effects of ginkgo, compared to an equally impressive 76% of men.

L-arginine is a precursor of nitric oxide (NO) in the human body. Studies have shown that nitric oxide is an essential compound that enhances blood circulation. Insufficient NO levels are thought to be involved in both male and female sexual dysfunction. Higher levels of NO result in increased blood flow, which makes the penile, clitoral, and vaginal tissues more sensitive and responsive to sexual stimulation, and helps increase the possibility of having a satisfactory erection and reaching orgasm. One study found that postmenopausal women who took L-arginine experienced heightened sexual response. Another study involving 77 women of all ages found that after four weeks, 73.5% of the women who took a supplement including L-arginine experienced greater sexual satisfaction, including heightened desire and clitoral sensation, increased frequency of intercourse and orgasm, and less vaginal dryness.

AdrenaSense® works to counteract chronic stress, which can suppress the libido-boosting hormone testosterone. Ashwagandha in AdrenaSense has been shown to increase testosterone levels.

Dosage: 2–3 capsules daily (2 with breakfast and 1 midday).

Additional support for low libido

Ultimate Maca Energy® contains maca, which has been used in Peru for 5000 years. Alkaloids from the root of the plant act on the hypothalamus as well as the pituitary, supporting and boosting energy levels, and encouraging the modulation of the hormones estrogen and testosterone.

Dosage: 2–4 capsules daily.

Vitamin E can be used topically as a lubricant to improve vaginal dryness and pain.

Dosage: insert a vitamin E capsule nightly for 5–7 nights.

Low Libido – For the Men in Your Life

Many women experience a dramatic shift in libido when the hormones start to change, which is both frustrating and concerning. Men, on the other hand, may not lose their desire for sexual relations but rather their performance ability commonly changes. It is important that couples try to understand the physiological changes that each partner is experiencing during these years of hormone transition.

Erectile Dysfunction

A Canadian study has shown that approximately half (49.4%) of men aged 40 and over are affected by erectile dysfunction (ED) to some degree, and close to half (44.3%) have a severe condition. Many men do not see their doctors about treatment because they believe ED is a normal part of aging, or they are just too embarrassed.

Possible Causes of ED

As in any condition, it is important to identify and treat the underlying cause of ED.

- **Head injury** – Research indicates that 15–25% of people with severe head injury experience ED.
- **Cardiovascular disease** – Cardiovascular disease, such as atherosclerosis, affects blood flow and can cause ED.
- **Diabetes** – 35–75% of men with diabetes experience ED. Diabetes can lead to unhealthy blood vessels and nerve damage –both of which may cause ED.
- **Obesity** – Excess weight, especially excess belly fat, can interfere with the body's ability to supply blood to the penis, and decrease testosterone production.
- **Medications** – Certain medications such as diuretics, anti-hypertensives (betablockers), cholesterol-lowering medications (statins), antihistamines, and antidepressants are just some of the medications that can have an effect on sexual function.

Undoubtedly there will be varying degrees of psychological stress in men who experience ED, which can then become emotionally self-perpetuating. The more failures a man has, the more worried or anxious he becomes, and the worse it gets. This can often lead to depression and anxiety, which can contribute to the vicious cycle or be direct a cause of ED.

In addition to addressing some of the causes of ED, there are natural supplements that can provide support.

what we know works

Support for ED

AdrenaSense® helps regulate the stress response, which can help and prevent the decrease in testosterone associated with elevated cortisol, the main stress hormone.

Dosage: 2–3 capsules daily (2 with breakfast and 1 midday).

Ultimate Libido™ helps support and increase testosterone levels.

Dosage: 3 capsules 1–2 times daily.

Ultimate Maca Energy™ *(Lepidium meyenii)* has been shown to improve erectile dysfunction and libido, both common symptoms in andropause.

Dosage: 2–4 capsules daily or 1 tablespoon powder daily.

Chapter  6

Estrogen-Dominant Conditions

"States of health or disease are, at the heart, the organism's success or failure at adapting to environmental challenges." **– René Dubos (1901–1982), microbiologist**

Our bodies are becoming increasingly more toxic from the air we breathe, the food we eat, and the water we drink, as well as from the harmful electromagnetic frequencies (EMFs) we are exposed to. All of us are living with some degree of environmental toxins in our bodies. These toxins are causing illness and contribute to many common hormonal disorders, as well as chronic disease.

The Tale of Lake Apopka: Are We Listening?

Come with me to the sea, the sea of... gender-bending chemicals.

In the early 1970s, scientists began counting alligators in Lake Apopka, Florida, an ideal place to hatch baby alligators. In the early 1980s they would often see up to 2,000 alligators a night on the lake. Then something began to happen. By the late 1980s they were finding at most only 150 per night. What could be going on? It was also found that the poor alligators had some big (or small) worries. The males' penises were only one-quarter the normal size, and their testosterone levels were so low they were sterile and unable to do their part in making baby alligators. The researchers eventually found that some poisonous substances (DDT metabolites) had similar effects on mice, and lo and behold, it turned out that thousands of litres of these same poisons (DDT-containing pesticides) had spilled into Lake Apopka in the 1980s. The alligators were living in a sea of gender-bending chemicals – but then, so are we.

The chemicals the alligators had to deal with were similar enough in structure to estrogen hormones that they were able to trick the alligators' bodies into using the imposters as they would estrogen molecules. And yes, human men also have receptor sites for estrogen. Surrounded by these chemicals, the male alligators started becoming more and more female-like; they were becoming hermaphrodites, creatures that could not be classified as male or female because they had sex characteristics of both. The estrogen imposters not only created serious problems in the sexual development of the male alligators, they also interfered with the healthy development of the female alligators. The result? No more baby alligators.

Florida panthers that eat high on the food chain now contaminated with estrogen-like pesticides have their own reproductive problems: more infertile females and sterile males, lower sperm counts, and high estrogen levels. In March 1994, toxicologist C. Facemire of the United States Fish and Wildlife Service said that male panthers had estrogen levels higher than most females. And if the estrogen impostors are good enough to trick the alligators (and panthers), they can sure fool us too.

Hormone Imposters – Xenoestrogens

Literally hundreds of chemicals found in the environment – PCBs, pesticides, polycarbons used in many plastics, chlorine-containing compounds, and synthetic estrogens and estrogen metabolites that enter the water supply via the urine of women taking synthetic estrogens – all resemble the human hormone estrogen. And yes, chlorine is added to our drinking water. These hormone imposters are called xenoestrogens. The word xeno comes from the Greek word meaning "foreign". The molecules of these chemicals are similar enough to human estrogens to fit into the same cell receptor sites, the estrogen parking spots, that the body's naturally produced hormones would use. There is plenty of evidence that these environmental estrogen-like chemicals affect the human hormonal system.

In November 1995, an international conference was held in the United States to study the xenoestrogens, or as they are otherwise known, endocrine-disrupting chemicals. The conference report stated that many endocrine-disrupting contaminants, even if less potent than natural hormones, are present in living tissue in most creatures at concentrations millions of times higher than the normal levels of natural hormones. Note that these studies were done over 20 years ago – gender-bending chemicals were a problem even then, so what it is like now with the billions of chemicals dumped into the environment each year?

How Xenoestrogens Affect Us

When chemicals are not removed efficiently by the detoxification pathways of liver and/or imbalances in the gut microbiome, they accumulate in the body; those that are fat soluble accumulate in fat stores. The majority of the hormones made by the body are bound by sex hormone-binding substances in the blood, thereby reducing their availability for initiating responses. It has been found that xenoestrogens, however, bind far less to the hormone-binding substances than do internally produced hormones, leaving more available to bind with estrogen receptor sites on the cells. If several of these chemicals are added together, their effects are additive, so exposure to even small quantities of a range of xenoestrogens can add up to a large impact.

A recent study published in *The Envionmental Health Perspectives Journal* (October 2016), states that the combined estrogenic activity of mixtures of xenoestrogens in serum samples was positively associated with breast cancer risk, even though no single compound showed a significant effect when analyzed individually. The increase in risk was strong and progressive across all detected estrogenic levels.

If we continue to ignore the warning signs, and if we do not change the way we are headed, our ability to reproduce will be drastically affected. The present-day plight of alligators and panthers, along with the human health effects documented to date, strongly indicate that rapid change is necessary. The media are finally beginning to report the negative health effects of estrogen-mimicking or xenoestrogenic chemicals. The first step to reducing the load of toxic buildup in our body is awareness and avoidance.

The Top Six Environmental Toxins and How to Avoid Them

The top six environmental toxins are bisphenol A (BPA), dioxin, atrazine, phtalates, perchlorate, and glyphostate.

Bisphenol A (BPA) is a common chemical found in plastics, food and beverage can linings, thermal receipts, and other consumer products. BPA is known to mimic estrogen, and studies have linked developmental exposure of BPA to reproductive harm, increased cancer susceptibility, abnormalities in brain development, and fat metabolism. In addition, research also suggests that BPA can promote a range of other health issues, including heart disease, diabetes, obesity, and infertility.

Tips to avoid BPA:

• Replace plastic sippy cups with glass or stainless.

• Do not microwave or store food or drink in plastic.

• Rinse canned fruit or vegetables to reduce the amount of BPA you ingest.

• When possible, avoid polycarbonate, especially in children's food and drinks. This plastic may be marked with the recycling code number 7 or the letters "PC". Choose plastics with the recycling label numbers 1, 2, and 4 on the bottom.

• Avoid plastic reusable water bottles (unless clearly marked BPA-free), as well as metal food and beverage cans, including beer and soft drink cans.

Dioxins are formed during waste burning, pulp and paper bleaching, and pesticide manufacturing. They can disrupt the delicate balance of both male and female sex hormone signals in the body. Exposure to low levels of dioxins in the womb and early in life can both permanently affect sperm quality and lower the sperm count in men during their prime reproductive years.

Tips to avoid dioxin:

• Try to eat less animal fat, and buy lean meats and poultry.

• Purchase food products that have been grass fed.

• Reduce dairy consumption.

Atrazine is a pesticide used on crops (such as corn and sugar cane) and on turf (such as golf courses and residential lawns). This widespread use has also lead to runoff, which can end up in lakes, streams, and even drinking water. Atrazine is "immunotoxic", disrupting the function of the immune system. It decreases the production of interferon, a molecule that fights viral infection. Atrazine disrupts hormone systems, and it also affects testosterone, prolactin, progesterone, luteinizing hormone, estrogen, and a thyroid hormone. Some studies suggest a possible association between atrazine and ovarian, breast, and prostate cancers, as well as birth defects.

Tips to avoid atrazine:

- Try to buy organic produce.
- Avoid tracking pesticides into the house by having everyone remove their shoes at the door.
- Vacuum carpets, mop floors, and damp-wipe dusty surfaces weekly.
- Filter your drinking water!

Phthalates are commonly found in plastics in order to make them more flexible, and are used as lubricants in cosmetics. Phthalates are known hormone disruptors and mimickers, contributing to abnormal sexual development, obesity, and diabetes and thyroid irregularities.

Tips to avoid phthalates:

- Avoid plastic food containers and plastic wrap made from PVC (recycling label #3).
- Avoid older plastic toys that may still contain phthalates.
- Stay away from fragrances. Instead, use products that are scented with only essential oils.
- Find phthalate-free personal care products with EWG's Skin Deep database at **ewg.org/skindeep**.

Perchlorate is both a naturally occurring and man-made chemical used in the production of rocket fuel, missiles, fireworks, flares, and explosives. It contaminates a good portion of our produce, water, and milk. It can disrupt the thyroid's ability to produce hormones needed for normal growth and development.

Tips to avoid perchlorate:

- Filter your water!
- Improve thyroid function by ensuring enough iodine in your diet.
- Try to buy organic as often as possible.

Glyphosate herbicides (one common brand name is Roundup) are the mostly commonly used herbicides in the United States and the world. Exposure is linked with increased risks of non-Hodgkin's lymphoma, miscarriages, and attention deficit disorder.

There is also evidence that suggests glyphosate herbicides can reduce production of sex hormones and that glyphosate exposure causes a rapid increase in and a disruption in cell division. The type of disruption found in this study is "a hallmark of tumour cells and human cancers".

Tips to avoid glyphosate:

- Choose organic foods – most are GMO free.
- Avoid food containing genetically modified glyphosate-tolerant foods.
- Demand labelling of GMO ingredients on all foods.
- Do not use glyphostate chemicals on your lawns or gardens.

WomenSense® Clean Body Care products include shampoo, conditioner, body wash, lotion, and facial cleanser. These body care products are vegan, GMO and gluten free, and made with coconut oil, grapeseed oil, and essential oils. They are free of parabens, sulphates, silicones, phthalates, propylene glycol, PVPs, petro chemicals, synthetic fragrances, colours/fillers, and xenoestrogens. These products are also free of ethanolamines, such as diethanolamine (DEA) and triethanolamine (TEA), which are carcinogenic.

Estrogen Dominance

Endometriosis

Endometriosis is one of the most common, yet misunderstood, gynecological diseases in women, affecting more than 5.5 million women in North America alone. It commonly occurs between the ages of 25 and 40 in menstruating women, but it can occur at younger ages. Symptoms can begin with the onset of menstruation and progressively increase as women enter the menopausal years. In endometriosis, the endometrial lining of the uterus that normally grows inside the organ begins to grow in other areas of the pelvic cavity and often on the bowel. Diagnosis is possible only through a surgical procedure called laparoscopy, unless the endometrial lesions are present on the cervix or vagina, which is rare.

Endometriosis is often associated with pelvic pain during menstruation or intercourse, abnormal menstrual cycles, and may or may not be accompanied with infertility. For those women who experience pain as a symptom, it can be so debilitating that it can affect their quality of life.

Signs and symptoms of endometriosis

- Extremely painful or disabling menstrual cramps (dysmenorrhea)
- Chronic pelvic pain including low back and pelvic area
- Pain during or after intercourse
- Painful bowel movements or urination during menstrual periods
- Intestinal pain
- Heavy menstrual period
- Heavy clotting during menstruation
- Infertility

Other symptoms may include fatigue, diarrhea, or constipation, and bloating and/or nausea, especially during menstrual periods. Abdominal and bowel symptoms linked to endometriosis are commonly misdiagnosed as irritable bowel syndrome (IBS).

Uterine Fibroids

Uterine fibroids are non-cancerous tumours that grow within the wall of the uterus. Fibroids, known as leiomyomata, can vary in size and number and may be accompanied by infertility, miscarriage, and early onset of labour. A large number of women, 50–75%, have or will suffer from uterine fibroids.

While the majority of women usually have no symptoms, one in four end up with symptoms severe enough to require treatment. Because little is known about how to treat them, most women end up with a surgical procedure to remove the uterus – a hysterectomy. More than 200,000 hysterectomies are performed each year to treat uterine fibroids, making it the second-most-frequently performed surgery (after cesarean section) for women. More than 90% of patients with fibroids who seek a second opinion are only given the option of abdominal hysterectomy, whereas in reality only half of these women require traditional surgery. The others are treated with less invasive alternatives such as laparoscopic myomectomy; uterine fibroid embolization; non-invasive, MRI- guided, focused ultrasound; or even holistic techniques.

The fibroid is a hard mass of fibrous tissue rich in blood vessels, growing on the inside wall of the uterus, on the outside of the uterus, or within the uterine muscle itself. Fibroids vary in size; some grow very large and come to weigh several kilograms. Although fibroids themselves are not fatal or detrimental to health, they can give rise to complications that can be annoyingly painful.

Signs and symptoms of uterine fibroids

One of the most common symptoms of fibroids, particularly large ones, is profuse menstruation. Blood may flow to such an extent that the affected woman becomes anemic and extremely fatigued. Fibroids can also cause pressure on the organs surrounding the uterus, such as the bladder and bowels, causing serious problems with urination and bowel movements. As a result, digestion is compromised, and pain with or without intercourse is often present.

Fibroids are, in part, caused by an estrogen excess that, from a naturopathic perspective, is due to bowel toxicity, liver congestion, and exposure to environmental xenoestrogens. Another common finding in naturopathic assessments of women with fibroids is undiagnosed clinical or subclinical hypothyroidism. Many health care practitioners recommend removing fibroids, even small ones, but thousands of women go through life with fibroids without suffering any major symptoms, even when large fibroid tumours are present.

A Little More on Hysterectomy

Canada's hysterectomy rate is one of the highest in the world, and is double that of Britain, Sweden, the Netherlands, and Norway. Approximately 40% of all Canadian women will have had a hysterectomy by the age of 60. Canada's high rate suggests that hysterectomies may be overused when less invasive alternatives exist and may be more preferred for most women. However, the hysterectomy rate has steadily decreased since 1997. This decrease may be explained in part by the development of alternative procedures such as endometrial ablation, myomectomy, colporrhaphy, laparoscopic or vaginal suspension, uterine artery embolization, uterine balloon therapy, or pharmacological treatments and natural supplements.

In 1945, an eminent surgeon, Dr. N. Miller, delivered a paper, now a classic, to his peers: "Hysterectomy: Therapeutic Necessity or Surgical Racket", published in the *American Journal of Obstetrics and Gynecology*. Dr. Miller stated that the "uterus in the non-pregnant state is one of the more important revelations of our age", meaning that the organ's importance above and beyond the gestation of children has been highly underestimated. He asserted that hysterectomy in the absence of disease cannot be justified any more than can the removal of a normal breast or gallbladder. He also stated that in his research, he found that one-third of all hysterectomies performed were done despite a complete absence of disease, or else disease that would not benefit from hysterectomy.

Today almost half of all hysterectomies are done to remove healthy uteri and ovaries, in which no disease whatsoever is present. Indications for bilateral removal of the ovaries and fallopian tubes (salpingo-oophorectom) include the following:

- Elective – removal of normal appearing ovaries and tubes at the time of a concurrent surgery, commonly a hysterectomy for benign disease, to decrease the risk of development of ovarian pathology, and decrease the need for future procedures
- Risk reducing – removal of ovaries and tubes in women genetically susceptible to ovarian cancer
- Malignancy – ovarian cancer, uterine cancer, or metastases to ovaries from a distant primary malignancy (gastrointestinal, breast, lung carcinoma)
- Benign adnexal mass
- Ectopic pregnancy
- Endometriosis

Removal of normal ovaries and fallopian tubes (critical parts of the anatomy) in case one day the woman might get some disease represents a warped form of preventive medicine. Think of the reaction if the same were recommended for men: the routine removal of the testicles because the risk of testicular cancer rises with age. The fact is that ovarian cancer is rare: Only 4% of women get ovarian cancer. One out of every eight women, however, will get breast cancer – this disease is the leading cause of death in North American women between 40 and 45 years of age. But no one would suggest routine removal of the breasts to prevent breast cancer... Or would they?

The allopathic profession typically views the uterus as useless once women are past childbearing age – hence the exceedingly high numbers of so-called harmless, if unnecessary, hysterectomies. This viewpoint misses a great deal, including a growing body of research that totally refutes the idea of a "useless" uterus. A hysterectomy seriously interferes with sexual fulfillment – which may be a surprise to those who think that the sensations of intercourse are limited to the clitoris and vagina. Sexual desire is usually completely lost or severely diminished after a hysterectomy. In fact, for most women, libido and sex life after a hysterectomy, even if the ovaries have been left intact, are worse than after menopause. During menopause the libido gradually slows down and the change is usually manageable, but after the trauma of a hysterectomy, sexual desire can stop abruptly. Hysterectomy results in shortening, narrowing, and drying of the vagina, loss of sensitivity, decreased blood flow to the ovaries, as well as damage to the nerves that enter the ovaries, and frequent pain caused by pressure from any source on the scar tissue that develops after the operation.

The uterus is also vital for immunity. Evidence indicates that it produces a variety of prostaglandins that regulate the female immune system, even after menopause. Prostaglandins are hormone-like compounds that function as regulators of a variety of physiological responses, including inflammation, muscle contraction, vascular dilation, and platelet aggregation. They are made in every cell of the body, and in the female they influence the shedding of the endometrium. They may also affect luteinizing hormone levels and ovulation. In addition, the uterus produces prostacyclin, a compound that prevents blood from clumping and forming clots, thereby helping prevent cardiovascular disease.

> Keep in mind that nature never makes an organ that loses its usefulness at a particular stage of life.

Many women also lose most of their ovarian function when the uterus is removed, even when the ovaries are conserved. Women who have had a hysterectomy, even those who retain their ovaries, have a much higher risk of cardiovascular disease and depression than women who have never had a hysterectomy. They also are more prone to osteoporosis at an earlier age, and develop osteoarthritis more frequently than women who go through menopause with all their parts intact. Hysterectomy is unnecessary for almost everything except cancer of the genital tract.

For those women who have had a complete hysterectomy (uterus and ovaries removed), refer to the section on bio-identical hormones in *Chapter 1*. Most women require hormone replacement as a result of radical hysterectomies.

Going through menopause can have one of two effects on fibroids: some begin to shrink, or atrophy, because of decreased estrogen levels, while others grow larger and in rare cases become malignant. If you have fibroids and your symptoms are so severe that surgery is required to remove them, find a gynecologist who will remove the fibroids only (this operation is called a myomectomy), keeping the uterus and ovaries intact. If this is impossible because of the large size of the fibroids, then insist that the cervix is kept intact. Most women who have the cervix removed are no longer capable of experiencing orgasm, and their sexual desire is generally considerably diminished or eliminated completely with the surgeon's knife. Finally, of course, keep your ovaries! It is common for women to be talked into having their ovaries removed along with the uterus (radical hysterectomy) as a preventive measure against ovarian cancer. Removing a healthy, needed organ because of possible disease is a poor health care strategy. Work toward optimal health instead to significantly lower your risk of cancer.

Possible Causes of Endometriosis and Uterine Fibroids

According to naturopathic medicine, endometriosis and uterine fibroids are related to diet, liver congestion, bowel toxicity, possible thyroid dysfunction, and estrogen dominance. From a medical perspective, the cause is not entirely understood; in essence these conditions are simply thought to be the result of a hormonal imbalance.

Risk factors for endometriosis and uterine fibroids include:

- A mother or sister with endometriosis or uterine fibroids
- Not having given birth
- A history of pelvic infection
- Hypothyroidism (clinical and subclinical)
- Estrogen dominance
- Exposure to environmental estrogens – dioxin, PCBs, BPA, and phthalates
- Increased body fat (fat stores estrogens and xenoestrogens)
- A diet high in animal fat (increases arachidonic acid, increasing pain and inflammation
- Lack of exercise from an early age
- High stress and increased levels of cortisol (hormone disruption and inflammation)
- Poor liver function
- Bowel toxicity and constipation
- Gut microbial imbalances (dysbiosis)

The role of estrogen

Estrogen appears to promote the growth of endometriosis, uterine fibroids, and other estrogen-dominant conditions. Research points to the effect of xenoestrogens due to the disruption of hormone metabolism.

Retrograde flow in endometriosis

One theory is the process of retrograde flow during menstruation. In retrograde menstruation, menstrual blood containing endometrial cells flows back through the fallopian tubes into the pelvic cavity instead of out of the body. These displaced cells stick to the pelvic walls and surfaces of the pelvic organs, where they grow and continue to thicken and bleed over the course of the menstrual cycle. The problem with this theory is that 90% of women have some degree of retrograde flow without endometriosis.

The role of the liver

The liver is one of the most important organs because it is involved in the removal of harmful toxins. Because of its key role in the detoxification, the liver has an enormous task of breaking down estrogen and other hormones and eliminating the harmful metabolites through the bowel and large intestine. If the liver is not functioning optimally, poor metabolism of estrogen can cause liver damage and the continual recycling of estrogens throughout the body.

The role of the gut

A delicate balance between the "good" and "bad" microbial bacteria in the gut is very important for hormone regulation and estrogen metabolism. Many people have disruptions in the microbial balance. Taking probiotics on a regular basis can help rebalance the gut microflora. This will ensure that the higher amount of estrogen metabolites will be eliminated through the large intestine, preventing and recycling of stronger "bad" estrogen throughout the body. Following a dysbiosis program (candida) can be helpful for many women with endometriosis. (Refer to *Chapter 2* for more information.)

The role of the immune system

Women with low immune function may be more susceptible to tissue implants and growth in endometriosis due to inflammation and free radical production. Natural killer (NK) cells in the immune system help keep abnormal cell growth in check. Studies suggest a correlation between high levels of estrogen and decreased NK cell activity in women with endometriosis. Women with endometriosis also have higher levels of antibodies, specifically immuno-globulins IgM and IgG. Immunoglobulins are part of the immune system and provide protection from foreign toxins. A higher level of immunoglobulins can cause the body to attack its own tissues, such as the ovaries and endometrial cells. Some of these women also have autoimmune disease.

The role of inflammation

In addition to problems with estrogen metabolism, inflammation is a factor with both uterine fibroids and endometriosis. Studies indicate that women with endometriosis and fibroid tumours have elevated levels of key proinflammatory cytokine.

what we know works

Support for Endometriosis and Uterine Fibroids

Endometriosis and uterine fibroids can be stubborn conditions to treat. Follow the recommended diet, lifestyle, and natural treatment suggestions, and if you are still having difficulties, consider working with a naturopathic doctor. You may require an individualized program that addresses dietary and lifestyle factors that are weakening overall health, possible dysbiosis, liver and bowel congestion, and assessment for thyroid function.

EstroSense® for liver health and hormone balance contains essential nutrients for the removal of excess and harmful estrogens in the body. Healthy liver function is absolutely critical for the treatment of uterine fibroids and other estrogen-dependent conditions. EstroSense contains the herbs milk thistle, indole-3-carbinol (I-3-C), diindolylmethane (DIM), and calcium-D-glucarate, which help with the breakdown of these harmful estrogens. As well, it provides antioxidant support with lycopene, rosemary, and green tea extract for removal of any toxic by-products.

Dosage: 3 capsules daily.

Liver MD® contains N-acetyl-cysteine (NAC) is a precursor of glutathione (GSH), an important antioxidant produced in the liver. NAC serves as a detoxification promoter, helping with the metabolism and elimination of toxic substances from the body, including harmful estrogens. Liver MD also contains vitamin B6, DL-alpha-lipoic acid, zinc picolinate, selenium, magnesium malate, milk thistle extract, vitamin C, vitamin B12, chlorella, and broccoli powder.

Dosage: 2 capsules twice daily with food.

MagSense™ contains magnesium, which helps relax muscles and cramping that may be associated with endometriosis.

Dosage: 1–2 scoops daily mixed with water.

Ultimate Probiotic is known to play an important role in the maintenance of normal flora in the gastrointestinal tract. Probiotics also help with the detoxification and binding of harmful estrogens in the digestive tract, and eliminate them from the body through the colon.

Dosage: 2 capsules daily.

Chasteberry *(Vitex agnus-castus)* is one of the single most important herbs for supporting hormonal imbalance in women. It affects the hypothalamus/hypophysis axis, where it increases luteinizing hormone and favours progesterone. This action prevents excess estrogen from stimulating endometrial tissue.

Dosage: up to 250 mg daily.

Note: It may take up to three months to see results.

Omega-3 fatty acids in the form of uncontaminated pure fish oil block the formation of PGE2, which is a messenger molecule that helps increase inflammatory pathways in the body. They are very helpful in reducing pain and inflammation and help prevent additional endometrial growth.

Dosage: 3000 mg fish oil daily.

Natural bio-identical progesterone cream may be helpful in reducing painful cramping and uterine contractions in women who are deficient in progesterone and who often have estrogen excess.

Dosage: 1.5–3 mL twice daily.

Diet and Lifestyle Tips for Endometriosis and Uterine Fibroids

- Pay particular attention to restoring the full health of the liver and bowel (refer to *Chapter 2*). Add a liver support formula such as EstroSense for estrogen-dominant conditions.

- Detect and remove the inflammatory trigger. This perhaps is the biggest challenge when it comes to eliminating the inflammation.

Some of the common factors that cause inflammation include food allergens, infections, environmental toxins, and trauma. It is also important to understand that while healthy levels of estrogen can have a positive effect on the immune system, high levels of estrogen can have a pro-inflammatory effect.

- Eat an anti-inflammatory diet. Eating a healthy diet consisting of whole foods, while avoiding refined foods, fried foods, bad fats, and sugars, will greatly help reduce inflammation. Dairy and gluten can be primary sources of inflammation.

- Eat organic foods as much as possible to help minimize exposure to endocrine-disrupting chemicals.

- Try not to drink regularly out of plastic water bottles, as the xenoestrogens from the plastic can also be a factor. There is some evidence that BPA and phthalates can promote the growth of uterine fibroids and endometriosis.

- It is also important to use toxin-free skin and body care products, such as the WomenSense body care line, to avoid harmful chemicals and xenoestrogens.

- Decrease insulin resistance and obesity. Because insulin resistance and obesity are associated with high-estrogen levels, it makes sense that improving insulin resistance and decreasing body fat can greatly help with the reduction of estrogens. (Refer to *Chapter 16* for more information on insulin resistance.)

Estrogen Dominance – For the Men in Your Life

Men do not escape the influence of our environment and the effect these environmental stressors have on hormones. As discussed previously, xenoestrogens are foreign estrogens that mimic the body's natural estrogen and interfere with normal hormone pathways, resulting in excess estrogen.

Signs and Symptoms of Estrogen Dominance in Men

In men, estrogen dominance can contribute to prostate problems, impotency, male pattern baldness, weight gain, and low libido. Excess estrogen also promotes abnormal blood clots. A recent study found that men with the highest levels of estradiol had a greater risk of stroke. Sex hormones were measured in patients with acute heart attack, patients with old heart attack, and patients with normal coronary arteries. The results showed significantly higher levels of estradiol in both groups of heart attack patients compared with those without coronary disease. As would be expected from numerous prior studies, heart attack victims also had decreased testosterone levels. This imbalance of estrogen overload and testosterone insufficiency is an often overlooked cause of cardiovascular disease.

what we know works

Support for Estrogen Dominance in Men

EstroSense® for liver health and hormone balance contains essential nutrients for the removal of harmful estrogens in the body and can help prevent estrogen-dominant conditions in both men and women.

Dosage: 3 capsules daily.

Chapter 7

Common Hormone Imbalances

Premenstrual Syndrome

Premenstrual syndrome (PMS) is very common, with roughly 50% of women – some reports claim 70% – experiencing some form of PMS during the premenstrual time. It is so common, in fact, that many women think that PMS is normal. However, just because so many women experience PMS symptoms does not make the condition normal.

Signs and Symptoms of PMS

Women experience the various symptoms of PMS at different times during the cycle and to varying degrees. Some suffer to such an extent that they may experience only a few days during the month when they feel normal.

Recurrent signs and symptoms that many women develop during the 7–14 days before menstruation include the following:

- **Female organs** – tender and enlarged breasts, uterine cramping, altered libido

- **Gastrointestinal** – abdominal bloating, constipation or diarrhea, change in appetite with increased cravings, usually for carbohydrates, chocolate, and sugar

- **General** – fatigue, migraines and headaches, backaches, skin problems, water retention with edema of fingers, face, and ankles, heart palpitations, dizziness with or without fainting insomnia, herpes and decreased immunity

- **Mental/emotional** – nervousness, anxiety, irritability, mood swings, depression

A severe form of PMS called premenstrual dysphoric disorder (PMDD) was added to the list of psychiatric depressive disorders in the *Diagnostic and Statistical Manual of Mental Disorders V* in 2013. The disorder is characterized by significant emotional and behavioural symptoms occurring during the luteal phase of the menstrual cycle. The treatment of PMDD in conventional medical circles relies largely on antidepressants that modulate serotonin levels in the brain, as well as ovulation suppression using contraception.

Possible Causes of PMS

Premenstrual tension was known as a type of hysteria by the herbalists of earlier days, and was treated as a nervous condition associated with loss of emotional control and functional disturbances. The term "hysteria" was taken from the Greek word for uterus, hystera, because this condition was more commonly recognized in women.

From a naturopathic perspective, the main causes of PMS are poor diet, lack of exercise, liver and bowel congestion, estrogen dominance, and general toxicity. Once these factors are addressed, along with short-term botanical or nutritional supplements, most women no longer experience symptoms.

Types of PMS

Dr. Guy Abraham, a leading researcher in the field, has identified four distinct types of PMS, each with specific symptoms, hormonal patterns, and metabolic mechanisms. Some women will find that their symptoms fit almost perfectly into one of the PMS types described below; others will have symptoms that fit into one or more PMS types.

PMS-A (Anxiety): 65–75% of PMS sufferers

Symptoms:

- Anxiety
- Irritability, anger
- Mood swings, depression
- Nervous tension
- Feeling overwhelmed

The estrogen excess in PMS-A is due to decreased breakdown of estrogen by the liver. It creates a relative progesterone deficiency. In other words, not enough progesterone is normally produced to balance the excess estrogen. Again, we see the importance of a healthy liver for hormonal balance.

PMS-C (Cravings): 24–35% of PMS sufferers

Symptoms:

- Increased appetite
- Increased carbohydrate tolerance
- Heart palpitations
- Craving for sugar, carbohydrates, salt
- Fatigue, dizziness, fainting
- Headaches

Imbalances in the production and balance of prostaglandins can lead to lowered blood glucose levels (hypoglycemia) and sugar cravings, as well as increased inflammation and pain.

PMS-D (Depression): 23–37% of PMS sufferers

Symptoms:

- Depression
- Lethargy, lack of interest in normal activities
- Insomnia
- Forgetfulness and confusion

The increase in estrogen results from a stress-induced increase in adrenal androgens or progesterone. Low levels of thyroid hormones and serotonin can also be contributing factors. Vitamin B6 has been proven effective for treating symptoms of PMS, especially those experiencing depression. Vitamin B6 is important in the synthesis of neurotransmitters such as serotonin and dopamine.

PMS-H (Hyperhydration/water retention): 60% of PMS sufferers

Symptoms:

- Weight gain
- Breast tenderness and congestion
- Abdominal bloating
- Fluid retention, with swelling face, fingers, hands, or ankles

Increased levels of aldosterone (adrenal hormone) due to stress, estrogen excess, and dopamine deficiency cause sodium and water retention.

Other causes of PMS include:

- Serotonin or tryptophan deficiency or excess
- Hypothyroidism
- Adrenal insufficiency
- Magnesium deficiency
- Essential fatty acid deficiency resulting in abnormal prostaglandin synthesis
- Stress
- Vitamin B6 deficiency

what we know works

Support for PMS

To treat PMS, implement the general protocols in combination with the specific remedies and diet as well as lifestyle changes given for the PMS types. If you do not obtain full relief, further consultation with a health care practitioner may be necessary.

EstroSense® supports the liver in hormonal imbalances to aid with detoxification and elimination of harmful estrogens and symptoms of estrogen dominance in PMS. EstroSense contains milk thistle, curcumin, indole-3-carbinol (I-3-C), diindolylmethane (DIM), sulforaphane, calcium-D-glutarate, green tea extract, lycopene, and rosemary extract to help support estrogen metabolism and bind harmful by-products and promoting their elimination from the body.

Dosage: 1 capsule 3 times daily with food.

AdrenaSense® helps normalize cortisol, the main stress hormone, as well as aldosterone levels, and reduce symptoms of fatigue, sugar cravings, anxiety, and water retention. (Refer to *Chapter 3* for more information on stress.)

Dosage: 1–3 capsules daily.

ThyroSense® supports low thyroid function, which contributes to many conditions related to hormone imbalances including PMS, especially moods and depression. Start with adrenal support unless you have been diagnosed with hypothyroidism. ThyroSense can be taken with synthyroid and other thyroid medications. (Refer to *Chapter 4* for more information on thyroid.)

Dosage: 2 capsules twice daily.

Additional support for PMS

Vitamin B6 (pyridoxal-5-phosphate) can be very helpful for the relief of PMS symptoms. In addition to reducing some of the adverse effects of estrogen excess, B6 may increase the concentration of neurotransmitters serotonin and dopamine. Research has found B6 is helpful for relieving edema, bloating, headaches, breast pain, depression, and irritability.

Dosage: 50–250 mg day with food throughout the menstrual cycle.

Some women find that increasing to 150–250 mg/day one week prior to menstruation helps with symptoms.

MagSense™ can be very helpful for PMS symptoms such as anxiety, depression, irritability, and headaches. Some studies show lower levels of magnesium in women who experience PMS.

Dosage: 1–2 scoops daily.

Black cohosh *(Cimicifuga racemosa)* can address an estrogen excess and inhibit prostaglandin production. Traditionally, it has also been used to treat "hysterical" PMS symptoms such as restlessness and nervous excitement. It is also beneficial in the treatment of breast tenderness and headaches associated with menstruation.

Dosage: 250–500 mg solid extract (4:1) twice daily; 40 mg solid extract standardized to contain 2.5% triterpene glycosides once or twice daily.

Chasteberry *(Vitex agnus-castus)* is the number one botanical remedy used in Europe to treat PMS symptoms. Its action in the body increases progesterone levels relative to estrogen levels. It has also been shown to reduce prostaglandin levels.

Dosage: 250 mg extract standardized to contain 0.5% agnuside twice daily. It may take up to three months to see results.

Flaxseed oil and/or fish oil (omega-3 fatty acids) block the formation of prostaglandin PGE2, which promotes the inflammatory pathways and causes inflammation and pain. Fish oil is also effective in controlling cravings.

Dosage: up to 30 mL flaxseed oil daily and/or up to 3000 mg of fish oil daily, minimum of 800 mg of eicosapentaenoic acid (EPA) and 400 mg of docosahexaenoic acid (DHA).

Diet and Lifestyle Tips for PMS

Diet plays a very important role in PMS. Generally it has been found that PMS sufferers consume more refined sugars and carbohydrates, salt, dairy products, and meats than women who do not have PMS. Diet recommendations include the following:

- Minimize dairy products such as milk, cheese, and butter. Organic yogourt and goat or sheep's cheese in moderation is acceptable.

- Consume at least 3–4 servings of fruit and vegetables daily.

- Keep sugar in the form of refined products (cookies, pastry, white bread, pastas, white rice) to an absolute minimum. Reduce the intake of fruit juice, which contains a highly concentrated form of sugar, fructose. Read labels carefully and avoid added sugars in the form of glucose, sucrose, fructose, and corn syrup.

- Increase intake of high-fibre foods such as barley, brown rice, quinoa, millet, and buckwheat.

- Include free-range hormone and antibiotic-free protein sources such as chicken, lamb, turkey, non-GMO tofu, beans, nuts, and seeds. Red meat is fine in moderation as long as it is hormone free.

- Avoid caffeine, especially if PMS symptoms involve anxiety, depression, breast tenderness, or fibrocystic conditions. Replace caffeine with herbal teas.

- Minimize alcohol intake to once or twice weekly.

- Avoid saturated fats (animal source) and hydrogenated vegetable oils.

- Use extra-virgin olive oil when cooking on low heat or coconut or avocado oil for higher temperature.

- Avoid excess salt if you suffer from water retention.

Lifestyle factor recommendations include the following:

- Due to the association of hormonal imbalances with hypothyroidism, be sure to have your thyroid hormones checked. (Refer to *Chapter 4* for more information.)

- Be aware of the different sources of PCBs, dioxins, BPA, and heavy metals in foods and in the environment, and minimize exposure.

- Exercise regularly. Several studies show that women who exercise regularly do not suffer from PMS as often as those who lead a sedentary lifestyle.

- Drink at least two litres of water daily.

In addition, support the liver and treat the dysbiosis. (Refer to *Chapter 2* for more information.)

Polycystic Ovary Syndrome

It is estimated that 10–20% of women have polycystic ovary syndrome (PCOS), and androgen excess is the most common disorder in women of reproductive age. It is also known as Stein-Leventhal syndrome or polycystic ovary disease.

Signs and Symptoms of PCOS

The most common characteristics associated with PCOS are obesity hirsutism (increased facial hair) and problems with ovulation, such as irregular or absent menses often leading to fertility problems. However, not all women have these classic symptoms. In fact, less than 50% of women with PCOS are obese. Many women diagnosed with PCOS are of normal weight or underweight, have no excess hair growth on the face, and may even have normal menstrual cycles.

PCOS symptoms vary from person to person. Some common signs and symptoms include:

- Infrequent or absent menstrual periods

- Excessive bleeding during menses

- Skin tags, typically in armpits or neck area
- Excess facial hair
- Acne
- Elevated blood sugar
- Weight gain, obesity (especially around the abdomen)
- Elevated cortisol
- Elevated luteinizing hormone (LH) causing excess androgens
- Elevated total cholesterol and triglycerides, low HDL and high LDL
- Hypothyroidism
- Infertility
- Recurrent miscarriage
- High prolactin
- Excess estrogen
- Ovarian cysts
- Skin hyper-pigmentation

Possible Causes of PCOS

Historically PCOS was thought to be caused by the excess production of androgens, but more recent research shows that metabolic abnormalities are very common in women with PCOS, particularly insulin resistance and obesity. Insulin resistance means that the cells do not respond to insulin and sugar is denied entry into the cells. Excess blood sugar is dangerous, so the pancreas reacts by secreting more insulin. Too much insulin then causes excess production of androgens. It is a vicious cycle between elevated insulin and insulin resistance, and androgen excess.

Elevated levels of androgens and insulin resistance disrupt the production of female hormones including luteinizing hormone (LH) and follicle-stimulating hormone (FSH), which control the menstrual cycle and ovulation. This leads to irregular menstrual cycles and missed ovulation cycles for women with PCOS. Inflammation caused by poor diet, environmental toxins, and stress can lead to insulin resistance and cholesterol accumulation in the blood vessels (atherosclerosis). Research has shown that women with PCOS have low-grade inflammation.

Testing and Diagnosis

Diagnosis of PCOS is difficult as there is no specific test to definitively diagnose it – it therefore becomes a diagnosis of exclusion. The current diagnostic criteria from the 2003 Rotterdam PCOS consensus is that at least two of the following three features must exist:

- Chronic anovulation (lack of ovulation, irregular periods)
- Clinical signs (acne, excess hair, oily hair, thickened skin, male pattern balding) or biochemical signs of hyperandrogenism (elevated levels of male hormones or androgens)
- Polycystic ovaries on ultrasound

Some important blood tests to help assist in the diagnosis of PCOS include:

- Free testosterone
- DHEA
- LH/FSH
- Prolactin
- HDL, LDL, triglycerides, C-reactive protein (CRP)

- TSH, T3, T4, anti-microsomal antibodies, anti-thyroglobulin antibodies
- 17-hydroxyprogesterone
- Fasting insulin and glucose, glucose tolerance test

what we know works

Support for PCOS

Natural supplements are a safe and effective way to balance hormones for many with PCOS.

Saw Palmetto Plus for Women with Vitex® contains saw palmetto, chasteberry, zinc, and copper. Refer below for more information on individual ingredients.

Dosage: 2 capsules daily.

Saw palmetto inhibits the activity of the enzyme 5-alpha-reductase, thereby reducing the conversion of testosterone to dihydrotestosterone (DHT), which is commonly elevated in women with PCOS. This action also helps reduce acne, excess facial and body hair, as well as hair loss from the scalp.

Chasteberry, also commonly referred to as vitex, is used to treat menstrual irregularities and to improve fertility. It is thought to exert hormonal activity through action on the pituitary gland, specifically on the production of luteinizing hormone (LH). LH stimulates progesterone release after ovulation.

Zinc and copper are two minerals needed for the normal production of hormones.

EstroSense® contains milk thistle, curcumin, indole-3-carbinol (I-3-C), diindolylmethane (DIM), sulforaphane, calcium-D-glutarate, green tea extract, lycopene, and rosemary extract to help support estrogen metabolism, bind harmful by-products, and promote their elimination from the body. Supporting the liver's ability to break down hormones and fats is essential for treating PCOS by reducing excess androgens and estrogens and promoting healthy ovulation.

Dosage: 3 capsules once daily.

AdrenaSense® is proven effective during times of increased stress. Chronic stress increases excess androgens in the body and affects how the liver can efficiently eliminate and metabolize excess estrogens. Stress also affects blood sugar regulation, and insulin resistance is a common problem in PCOS.

Dosage: 2 capsules in the morning, 1 at noon.

Vitamin D is deficient in 67–85% of women with PCOS. Vitamin D deficiency has been associated with insulin resistance, ovulatory and menstrual irregularities, fertility problems, hirsutism, hyperandrogenism, obesity, and elevated cardiovascular disease risk factors.

Dosage: 3000–5000 IU daily.

PolyGlycopleX® (PGX®) is a unique complex of naturally occurring, water-soluble polysaccharides (dietary fibres). Regulating blood sugar is a key factor in many health conditions, including PCOS. Research has shown that PGX controls and balances blood sugar levels, helps promote weight loss, lowers the glycemic index of meals by 50%, reduces food cravings, and lowers cholesterol and triglyceride levels.

Dosage: powder: start with 2.5 g at every meal; capsules: 1–2 capsules with each meal.

GlucoSense® contains the following ingredients: chromium picolinate, Chinese cinnamon, bitter melon, alpha-lipoic acid, as well as berberine, mission cactus, and bilberry. It is an excellent product for balancing blood sugar, preventing insulin resistance and diabetes, and the associated complications. Refer below for more information on individual ingredients.

Dosage: 1 capsule daily.

Chromium is well researched in the treatment of glucose and insulin imbalances such as insulin resistance and diabetes.

Chinese cinnamon increases glucose metabolism, which significantly improves blood sugar regulation. It is also been found to have insulin-like effects.

Bitter melon has been used traditionally as a remedy for diabetes.

Alpha-lipoic acid is a potent antioxidant that has the potential to regulate blood glucose and to prevent diabetes and its complications.

••

Additional support for PCOS

Flaxseed oil and/or omega-3 fish oils support healthy cell membranes, thereby improving glucose metabolism. These healthy fats also promote the anti-inflammatory pathways in the body, which protect the heart, breasts, and uterus. Fish oils have also been shown to decrease body fat deposition.

Dosage: up to 30 mL flaxseed oil daily or up to 4000 mg fish oil daily with a minimum of 1000 mg of EPA and 600 mg of DHA.

Maitake mushroom *(Grifola frondosa)* has been compared to the prescription drug clomiphene citrate for its ability to induce ovulation in women with PCOS. A randomized trial was conducted with half the participants receiving maitake mushroom extract and the other half receiving clomiphene citrate for up to 12 weeks. The study found that maitake extract induced ovulation in patients with PCOS with a success rate of 76.9%.

Dosage: 35–70 mg daily of maitake extract.

Probiotics (such as *Lactobacillus acidophilus* and *bifidobacterium*) and prebiotics (such as the digestible fibre PGX) play an important role in the maintenance of normal microflora in the gut. A healthy gut microbiome is very important for the detoxification and removal of excess estrogens and androgens.

Dosage: at least 10 billion CFU daily.

Diet and Lifestyle Tips for PCOS

- Aim to normalize weight, blood sugar, and insulin through healthy lifestyle changes such as the low glycemic diet. (Refer to *Chapter 16* for more information.)

- Eat 5–6 smaller meals throughout the day rather than three larger ones. This will help keep the blood sugar levels more balanced.

- Try to follow a regular exercise program, including weight resistance and aerobic activity. Exercising 4–6 times a week will help increase muscle mass, burn fat, balance hormones, and help with blood sugar and insulin levels.

- Reduce stress. Stress is a factor in increasing androgen levels. (Refer to *Chapter 3* for more information.)

- Reduce exposure to xenoestrogens chemicals in fertilizers, pesticides, and herbicides by consuming organic produce whenever possible.

- Use ingredients free of other sources of xenoestrogens, such as parabens and phthalates in personal care products. (Refer to *Chapter 6* for more information.)

- Reduce or stop cigarette smoking. In women with PCOS, smoking increases free testosterone and fasting insulin levels, resulting in increased insulin resistance.

Chapter 8

Breast Disease

Fibrocystic Breasts

Formerly referred to as fibrocystic breast disease (FBD), fibrocystic breasts are characterized by lumpiness and discomfort in one or both breasts. Affecting more than 60% of women, this condition tends to be an issue for women primarily between the ages of 30 and 50, with impact diminishing after menopause. Monthly hormone fluctuations are the most significant contributing factor to fibrocystic breasts, as a woman's body prepares each month for a possible pregnancy. The hormones estrogen and progesterone directly affect breast tissue by causing cells to grow and multiply. Prolactin, growth factor, insulin, and thyroid hormone are also involved.

During the monthly cycle, hormones stimulate the growth of breast glandular tissues and increase the activity of blood vessels, cell metabolism, and supporting tissue in anticipation of pregnancy. If pregnancy does not occur, breast cells undergo programmed cell death (apoptosis). Cells are devoured by enzymes and inflammatory scavenger cells. The efficiency of this cleanup process can vary from one woman to another, and can even be different within a breast. Over time, from puberty to menopause, the repeated monthly hormonal cycles, along with the accumulation of fluid, cells, and cellular debris within the breast, can lead to fibrocystic breasts. Although benign, fibrocystic breasts can confound the detection of breast cancer.

Signs and Symptoms of Fibrocystic Breasts

The signs and symptoms of fibrocystic breasts include:

- Breast tenderness or pain
- Nipple itching
- Lumpiness in one or both breasts
- A feeling of heaviness

Symptoms vary among women and can be intermittent, coming and going with the monthly cycle or persistent throughout the month.

Possible Causes of Fibrocystic Breasts

Women with irregular menstrual cycles seem to suffer more severe symptoms of fibrocystic breasts, likely due to the prolonged and irregular hormonal stimulation of the breasts. Symptoms also tend to be most severe right before the menstrual period due to the increased estrogen to progesterone ratio.

Other causes include:

- An underactive thyroid (hypothyroidism)
- Iodine deficiency that would cause cells to be more sensitive to the effects of estrogen
- Increased estrogen, decreased progesterone
- Nutritional deficiencies such as vitamin E, vitamin B6, CoQ10, and essential fatty acids
- Overconsumption of animal products, such as meat and dairy
- Accumulations of xenoestrogens in the breast tissue
- Bowel toxicity/constipation
- Liver congestion
- Poor lymphatic drainage possibly due to lack of exercise or ill-fitting bra
- Overconsumption of methylxanthine found in coffee, black tea, cola, and chocolate

Testing and Diagnosis

Breast self-examination

Monthly breast self-exams are important to detect any changes that occur in the breasts. (Refer to the Breast Cancer section below for more information.) Medical doctors will often perform breast exams as a part of an annual physical check-up.

During the exam, the doctor visually and manually examines breasts and lymph nodes in the lower neck and underarm area for any changes. The lumps in fibrocystic breast disease are typically not attached to overlying or underlying tissue and are easy to locate on the upper breast toward the underarm. Lumps have round, smooth borders, feel pliable, and are moveable. Sometimes fibrocystic breasts feel irregular or like small beads.

Ultrasound

Ultrasound exams are helpful in assessing breast lumps. Women under the age of 30 might undergo this test instead of a mammography because it can better evaluate dense breast tissue. Ultrasound is also particularly helpful in distinguishing between fluid-filled breast cysts and solid masses.

Did you know?

Wearing a bra that is too tight or has underwire can affect breast health by compressing lymphatic vessels causing congestion and inflammation in the breast tissue. Choose a bra that fits properly, is not too tight, and preferably without underwire that when removed, does not leave any red marks on the skin.

If a lump appears suspicious, further testing such as mammogram and/or tissue biopsy will be done. (Refer to the *Breast Cancer* section later in this chapter for more information.)

what we know works

Support for Fibrocystic Breasts

EstroSense® is an excellent product for supporting healthy liver detoxification and reducing symptoms of estrogen dominance such as fibrocystic breasts. Since the liver is the primary site for healthy estrogen metabolism and clearance, supporting the liver and its pathways is essential for preventing estrogen dominance in the body as well as the breast tissue. Adequate levels of B vitamins are necessary for estrogen clearance from the body, especially vitamin B6 and folic acid. EstroSense contains calcium D-glutarate, indole-3-carbinol (I-3-C), diindolylmethane (DIM), milk thistle extract, sulphoraphane, and turmeric. (Refer to *Chapter 2* for more information on individual ingredients.)

Dosage: 3 capsules daily.

Liver MD® contains N-acetyl-cysteine (NAC), which is a precursor of gluta-thione and is an important antioxidant produced in the liver. NAC serves as a detoxification promoter, helping with the metabolism and elimination of toxic substances from the body, including harmful estrogens. Liver MD also contains milk thistle, vitamin B6, selenium, curcumin, and other ingredients necessary for healthy liver detoxification.

Dosage: 2 capsules twice daily with food.

Evening primrose oil and other omega-6s can be used to alleviate fibrocystic breast pain. It contains linoleic acid (LA) and gamma-linolenic acid (GLA). The body uses LA to produce GLA to help create beneficial prostaglandins that regulate inflammation, pain, blood pressure, fluid balance, and blood clotting. Researchers have investigated the benefits of evening primrose oil for premenstrual breast pain as well as fibrocystic breasts.

Dosage: 1500 mg twice daily.

Flaxseed oil and/or **pure fish oil** blocks the formation of PGE2, which is a messenger molecule that promotes inflammatory pathways in the body. These oils may be beneficial in reducing breast pain and inflammation, as well as preventing abnormal changes in the breast tissue.

Dosage: up to 30 mL of flaxseed oil daily and/or up to 3000 mg fish oil daily with a minimum of 800 mg EPA and 400 mg DHA.

Chasteberry *(Vitex vinifera)* is used to alleviate many gynecological symptoms such as PMS, fibrocystic breasts, endometriosis, PCOS, and fibroids, to name a few. It seems to work in favour of progesterone, reducing symptoms of estrogen dominance.

Dosage: 80 mg 1–3 times daily.

Additional support for fibrocystic breasts

Vitamin E has been shown to relieve many PMS symptoms, particularly fibrocystic breasts.

Dosage: 400–800 IU daily.

Iodine supplementation to support an underactive thyroid results in decreased breast pain and breast nodules, and therefore helps with the symptoms of fibrocystic breast disease. When iodine is deficient, the breast tissue becomes more sensitive to estrogenic stimulation, creating estrogen dominance in the breast.

Iodine supplementation is also known to have significant anti-inflammatory and antifibrotic effects.

Dosage: 150–500 mcg of potassium iodide daily.

Probiotics are known to play an important role in the maintenance of normal flora in the gastrointestinal tract. They also help with the detoxification and binding of harmful estrogens in the digestive tract and the elimination of them from the body through the colon.

Dosage: at least 10 billion CFUs daily with food.

Natural progesterone cream helps reduce symptoms of a high-estrogen/low-progesterone imbalance, which often leads to fibrocystic breasts.

Dosage: apply 1.5 mL twice daily on days 15–27 of the menstrual cycle.

Diet and Lifestyle Tips for Fibrocystic Breasts

The key to relieving symptoms of fibrocystic breasts and preventing breast cancer (discussed in the next section) is to balance the hormones. Diet recommendations include the following:

- Increase intake of vegetables from the Brassica family, which contain compounds that help metabolize "bad" estrogens and convert them into friendlier ones. Include foods such as kale, broccoli, cabbage, cauliflower, and Brussels sprouts. (Refer to *Chapter 2* for information on supporting healthy bowel and intestinal function to help eliminate harmful hormone metabolites from the body.)

- Eat a diet rich in fibre. Excellent sources of fibre include ground flax, oat bran, psyllium, chia or hemp seeds, legumes, and plenty of fruits and vegetables.

- Reduce inflammatory foods in the diet by avoiding overconsumption of saturated fats such as red meat and dairy, trans fats and sugars.

- Consume lots of deep-water fatty fish like anchovies and wild salmon, as well as nuts and seeds for sources of anti-inflammatory omega-3 fats and omega-6 gamma-linoleic acid (GLA).

- Minimize or eliminate sources of methylxanthines found in coffee, tea, chocolate, and colas. These compounds promote the overproduction of fibrous tissue and cysts in the breast. One study reported a 97.5% improvement in breast tissue in women who eliminated consumption of foods containing methylxanthines, and a 75% improvement in those who limited consumption.

- Choose antibiotic- and hormone-free animal products and organic foods whenever possible to reduce exposure to xenoestrogenic pesticides, herbicides, and hormones.

Lifestyle factor recommendations include the following:

- Book yourself an appointment for a bra fitting. Most women are wearing the wrong size, which can affect circulation, cause breast and shoulder pain, or provide lack of support.
- Use warm heating pads or hot water bottles to help soothe aching breasts.
- Learn to read labels to avoid xenoestrogens in the home and beauty care products. (Refer to *Chapter 6* for more information.)
- Know your breasts – do monthly breast self-exams.
- Exercise regularly to help improve lymphatic circulation and removal of toxins.
- Use castor oil topically as an excellent anti-inflammatory.

CASTOR OIL PACK

A castor oil pack increases blood flow and lymphatic drainage to the area being treated. Castor oil can also improve indigestion and immune function, and reduce swelling of the joints and extremities. Castor oil packs can also be used in cases of menstrual irregularities, uterine fibroids, ovarian cysts, and anywhere in the body where there is reduced circulation. For fibrocystic breasts, apply castor oil packs to the liver and breasts.

Materials:
- Castor oil
- Hot water bottle or heating pad
- Plastic wrap
- Pure cotton flannel 3–4 layers thick, big enough to cover the area

Method:
- Saturate the flannel so that it is wet but not dripping.
- Place flannel over the area to be treated.
- Place a sheet of plastic wrap over the flannel (castor oil can stain linens and clothing).
- Place heating pad or hot water bottle on top of the plastic wrap.
- Leave castor oil pack in place for 20–30 minutes.
- Repeat this process three times a week.

Breast Cancer

About two in five Canadians will develop cancer in their lifetime. Although the vast majority (89%) of Canadians who develop cancer are over the age of 50, cancer can occur at any age. Of all cancers affecting women in developed nations, 8% are associated with obesity, compared to just 1.5% in developing countries. Similarly, 3% of all cancers in men in developed nations are associated with obesity, compared to a mere 0.3% in developing countries. The vast majority of the food eaten in developed countries is processed, whereas most developing countries still consume a more traditional diet. This finding, combined with results from other studies, confirms that diet plays a significant role in the development of cancer.

Did you know?

Castor oil is an excellent anti-inflammatory and can be used for improving lymph drainage and detoxification.

According to the Canadian Cancer Society, about 30–35% of all cancers can be prevented by eating well, being active, and maintaining a healthy body weight. Breast cancer is the most common cancer among Canadian women ages 35–54, with an estimated one in eight women developing breast cancer in their lifetime.

The diagnosis of breast cancer, or any form of cancer for that matter, is an extremely difficult and life-changing experience for most people. Although we no longer face high rates of infant mortality from infectious disease, we are experiencing a new range of diseases resulting from fundamental changes in our environment, lifestyles, nutritional habits, and chronic stress levels.

Signs and Symptoms of Breast Cancer

While the jury still appears to be out on the best form of detection, it is a good idea to be familiar with your own breasts in terms of how they look and feel throughout the month. The National Cancer Institute recommends that you immediately report the following to your doctor:

- Any breast lump or thickening that feels different from the surrounding tissue
- A change in the shape or size of a breast
- Puckering or dimpling of breast skin

- Inverted nipple – if the nipple turns inward into the breast
- Peeling, scaling, or flaking of the nipple or skin
- Discharge from the nipple, especially if it is bloody
- Redness or pitting of the skin over the breast (like skin of an orange)

Possible Causes of Breast Cancer

The role of stress

A study of breast cancer patients assessed their overall stress level and found that a high degree of stress predicted a decreased ability of natural killer (NK) cells to destroy cancer cells. As well, those with a high degree of stress and higher levels of cortisol showed a poorer response to interventions aimed at improving NK cell activity.

Emotional and social stressors also influence the nervous and hormonal systems, and have prognostic values due to the influence on the immune system. For years it has been known that a positive outlook on life and adopting stress-coping skills lead to a better immune function and lower cortisol levels. Recent studies confirm the positive benefits of guided imagery on psychological well-being and immune function in patients with breast cancer. Also, women with breast cancer who have a confidante – someone they trust implicitly and can tell their deepest feelings to – deal with the diagnosis and treatment better and have an overall health improvement compared with women who do not feel safe to express their emotions.

Oxidative stress

Cancer disrupts the entire balance of metabolism in the body. It all starts with the genetic material (DNA), followed by cellular mutation that begins due to oxidative stress on the DNA. Oxidative stress is essentially an imbalance between the production of free radicals and the ability of the body to counteract or detoxify their harmful effects. In cancer, the oxidation overrules the antioxidant capacity of the body. There is a constant production of free radicals in the normal course of metabolism, caused by the influence of stress hormones, natural and artificial radiation, toxins in air, food, and water, and other miscellaneous sources. The result is damage in the cellular respiration mechanism, causing mutation of the DNA. If there are enough mutations and the cell does not die, then the cell can be transformed into a renegade cancer cell.

Genetics

Inheriting the genes linked to breast cancer can account for approximately 5% of the cases. Having a mother or sister with breast cancer increases the risk 1.5–3 times above the average susceptibility risk of one in eight. There is also a greater chance of developing breast cancer if a first, second, or third degree relative has been diagnosed with ovarian or endometrial cancer. BRCA-1 and BRCA-2 gene mutations make women more susceptible to both breast and ovarian cancers. Some studies show a four-fold increased risk when a brother or father is diagnosed with prostate cancer. While family history and genetics play a role in determining risk, most women with breast cancer do not have a family history of the disease.

Food as a stressor

People often eat foods that cannot be easily assimilated and metabolized, putting added stress on the body to process and eliminate these food toxins. This in turn stresses the immune system and adds to increased inflammation. Food sensitivities are very common today, especially when it comes to dairy products, wheat and soy products, and foods with additives. In addition, the standard (North) American diet (SAD) is indeed very SAD! Most people eat too much sugar and refined carbohydrates, bad fats, not enough fresh fruit and vegetables, and the added insult of GMOs – all leading to metabolic stress, inflammation, and cancer.

Insulin resistance and the cancer connection

New evidence supports an association between insulin resistance and an increased incidence of many malignancies, including colorectal, hepatic, pancreatic, breast, endometrial, ovarian, lung, cervical, bladder, and urinary tract malignancies. Cancer cells have high metabolic requirements to maintain cell proliferation rates, and can use the "metabolic fuels" present in people with insulin resistance, diabetes, or obesity. (Refer to *Chapter 16* for more information on insulin resistance.)

Other known risk factors include:

- Aging (over 50 years of age)
- Starting menstruation early and going through menopause late (increased estrogen exposure)
- Having never given birth or having children after age 30
- Overweight or obesity after menopause
- Alcohol consumption

- Cigarette smoking
- Chronic inflammation
- High-fat diet
- Hormone replacement therapy
- Prolonged use of oral contraception
- Pre-menopausal mammography with repeated exposures
- Exposure to xenoestrogens (refer to *Chapter 6* for more information)
- Lack of exercise
- Stress – mental emotional, dietary, and environmental

Testing and Diagnosis

Breast cancer risk assessment

Take the following breast health test and discover if you are at risk for breast cancer.

1 Have not had children and are under 25 years of age

1 Have not had children and are 25–35 years of age

3 Have not had children and do not intend

2 Did not breastfeed

1 Had an abortion on the first pregnancy

3 Took birth control pills during teens or early 20s. (A few months of use may increase risk by 30%, and 10 years may double risk.)

3 Taking or have taken HRT (Premarin, Provera, Prempro)

2 Have had regular mammograms before menopause

2 Do not exercise three times a week

2 Have taken tricyclic antidepressants for depression

1 Have breast implants (breast trauma)

2 Had chest X-rays as teenager or during 20s

1 Are exposed to EMFs due to excessive computer use or other

2 Dye your hair with dark-coloured dyes (source of xenoestrogens)

1 Wear dry-cleaned clothing (source of xenoestrogens)

2 Use bleached sanitary products, such as tampons (xenoestrogens)

3 Eat pesticide- and herbicide-laden foods (xenoestrogen source)

1 Use nail polish remover containing toluene or phthalate

2 Menstruation started before age of 12

2 Late onset menopause after age of 54

3 Diet is high in animal fat, dairy, and meat (xenoestrogens source)

3	Smoke, started early with excessive use	2	Using tranquilizers (studies show increase in breast tumours)
3	Alcohol, started early with excessive use	2	Using ulcer medications which disrupt estrogen metabolism
3	Do not eat cruciferous vegetables (e.g., broccoli, cauliflower, kale)	3	Are overweight or obese (fat stores estrogens)
3	Take cholesterol-lowering drugs, which deplete CoQ10	2	Use Flagyl for yeast infections (increases mammary tumours)
3	Use anti-hypertensives for lowering blood pressure (decrease CoQ10)	1	Family history of breast cancer in mother, sister, or daughter

Total score: _____

If you scored: 0–18: You are at low risk for breast cancer. **19–35:** You are at moderate-to-high risk for breast cancer. **36–65:** You are at high risk for breast cancer.

Breast self-examination

Breast self-exam (BSE) should be practised once a month. If you menstruate, do it 2–3 days after the end of your period, when your breasts are least likely to be tender or swollen. If you are not menstruating, due to menopause, amenorrhea, or other causes, choose a day such as the first of the month and perform BSE each month on that day.

Visual exam:

1. Stand before the mirror and inspect both breasts for anything unusual, such as discharge from the nipples, rash or puckering, dimpling, or scaling of the skin.

2. Watching closely in the mirror, raise both arms over your head, stretching them high. Examine both breasts and the underarm area.

3. Next, press hands firmly on the hips and bow slightly toward the mirror as you pull your shoulders and elbows forward.

Palpation:

4. Raise your left arm. Use three or four fingers of your right hand to explore your left breast firmly, carefully and thoroughly feeling for any unusual lump or mass under the skin. Beginning at the outer edge, press the flat part of your fingers in small circles, moving the circles slowly around the breast. Pay attention to the area between the breast and armpit.

5. Gently squeeze the nipple of both breasts and look for discharge. See a health care practitioner if you have discharge during the month.

6. Repeat Steps 4 and 5 lying on our back with your arm over your head and a pillow or folded towel under the shoulder of the breast you are examining. Use the same circular motion described in Step 4. Do this for both breasts.

If you find anything suspicious, or have any concerns or questions, report it to your health care practitioner immediately.

Mammography

Sometimes if a woman or health care practitioner detects a breast lump or unusual thickening in the breast tissue, mammography may be suggested. Mammography is a structural imaging X-ray that is useful for detecting actual structural differences or suspicious lumps. It is followed up with a tissue biopsy, which is always the gold standard for the diagnosis of breast cancer.

Mammograms do not reduce breast cancer deaths in middle age women

Research involving nearly 90,000 women in Canada has found that mammography does not reduce breast cancer deaths and offers no survival advantage over physical breast examinations for middle-aged women. The study, published in 2014 in the *British Medical Journal*, has reignited the debate about the benefits and harms of breast X-rays. The 25-year long randomized controlled Canadian National Breast Screening Study was conducted with women aged 40–59. Researchers found that while breast X-rays detected more invasive cancers, the number of deaths from breast cancer was virtually the same in both groups. In addition, 22% of screen-detected cancers were "over-diagnosed", meaning the tumours would never have grown large enough to cause symptoms or death if they had not been found. The result is that women are being unnecessarily inflicted with therapy for cancers that would not have shortened their lives.

Women want to believe that finding cancer early has benefits, and this is something their doctors and radiologists will tell them. However, there is no evidence to support this claim according to the study. Dr. Anthony Miller, first author of the study, says that the overselling of mammography has led to the popularity paradox: "The more cancers found as a result of screening, and the more people who believe, wrongly, that screening has saved their lives, the more the number of cancer 'survivors' and advocates for screening grows."

In addition, the *Cochrane Review,* which is recognized as the highest standard in evidence-based health care resources, reviewed seven trials that involved 600,000 women 39–74 years of age. The studies, which provided the most reliable information, showed that mammography screening did not reduce breast cancer mortality.

"If we assume that screening reduces breast cancer mortality by 15% and that overdiagnosis and overtreatment is at 30%, it means that for every 2,000 women invited for screening throughout 10 years, **one** will avoid dying of breast cancer and **10 healthy women,** who would not have been diagnosed if there had not been screening, **will be treated unnecessarily**... we have written an evidence-based leaflet for lay people, that is available in several languages on **cochrane.dk**... Recent observational studies show more overdiagnosis than in the trials and very little or no reduction in the incidence of advanced cancers with screening." June 4, 2013: *Cochrane Review*

Thermography

Many women are choosing to monitor breast health using thermography, a screening tool that uses infrared images of the breast. Thermography goes not diagnose breast cancer, but rather helps determine the risk of developing breast cancer. The sensors detect heat and increased vascularity in the breast tissue, which would indicate an increase in metabolic activity. Typically, in most cancerous tumours, there is an increased need for nutrients and the tumours will increase the circulation to their cells by creating new blood vessels to feed the tumour. This process frequently results in a temperate increase in the breast tissue, allowing thermography to detect the change in heat patterns. Breast thermography can be used preventively and if something suspicious is discovered, follow-up tests such as ultrasound or tissue biopsy will be done.

Treatment Choices

If diagnosed with cancer, it is normal to experience fear and shock and to accept the first treatments that are offered, namely chemotherapy and radiation or surgery. Individuals have to make decisions that they feel are right for themselves and that they feel will provide the best possible results. We would encourage you to ask questions regarding all of the benefits and side effects before you make your decision. For example, patients are given statistics that may be misleading when they ask about the benefits and risks of chemotherapy. Most studies are presented with a positive bias.

Dr. Ralph Moss, author of *Questioning Chemotherapy*, documents the ineffectiveness of chemotherapy in treating most cancers:

- Researchers conducting a large study in Australia found that the contribution of chemotherapy to five-year survival in adults was 2.3% in Australia, and 2.1% in the United States. The Australian authors wrote: "...in lung cancer, the median survival has increased by only two months during the past 20 years, and an overall survival benefit of less than 5% has been achieved in the adjuvant treatment of breast, colon, and head and neck cancers".

- When a drug company gives physicians the "relative risk reduction" figures for a chemotherapy regimen, they are more likely to recommend it to their patients than when they are given the mathematically identical information expressed as an "absolute risk reduction". For example, if receiving a treatment causes a patient's risk to drop from 4% to 2%, this can be expressed as a decrease in relative risk of 50%. But another, equally valid way of expressing this is to say that it offers a 2% reduction in absolute risk, which is less likely to convince patients to take the treatment.

- Since 80% of patients choose what their oncologist recommends, the way in which the oncologist perceives and conveys the benefits of treatment is of vital importance. As admitted in a study published in the journal *Clinical Oncology* back in 2004, chemotherapy is really only effective about 2% of the time for all cancers based on the standard five-year survival rate criteria, which is not technically indicative of a cure.

- In a letter to the editor of the journal *American Family Physician*, Dr. James McCormack, PharmD, Faculty of Pharmaceutical Sciences, University of British Columbia used the example of the prescription of bisphosphonate drugs in the treatment and prevention of osteoporosis, but identical issues apply to the use of anticancer drugs. Consider the following statement: "Mrs. Jones, your risk of developing a fracture over the next three years is approximately 8%. If you take a drug daily for the next three years, that risk can be reduced from 8% to around 5%, or a difference of just over 3%." Of course that sounds far less impressive than saying that taking the drug will decrease the risk of fracture by almost half, even though technically both are mathematically accurate ways of expressing the benefit to be gained by the therapy.

Support for Breast Cancer

Melatonin and protection from cancer

Many studies have shown that melatonin inhibits the growth of breast, cervical, and ovarian cancer cells. Melatonin is a new member of a group of regulatory factors controlling cell multiplication and death. In physiologic and pharmacologic concentrations in some cancer cells, melatonin reduces the infiltrative and metastatic potential. In other types of cancer cells, melatonin induces cancer cell death. Researchers found that simultaneous administration of melatonin and tamoxifen may contribute to the regression of cancer in women with metastatic breast cancer who had not responded to tamoxifen alone. For cancer management, higher doses of melatonin are required.

Many of the risk factors associated with breast cancer can be addressed with dietary and lifestyle changes, with a focus on strengthening the immune system and adopting a health promotion lifestyle. In addition, certain natural supplements can help reduce the risk of developing breast cancer or provide adjunctive support to those who have breast cancer.

what we know works

Support for Breast Cancer

EstroSense® contains indole-3-carbinol, diindolylmethane (DIM), calcium-D-glutarate, curcumin, lycopene, and milk thistle. It is an excellent product to support the liver and aid in the removal of cancer causing estrogens. If you have been diagnosed with breast cancer, you can add additional curcumin and green tea extract to reach the recommended dosage. Refer below for more information on individual ingredients.

Dosage: 3 capsules daily with food.

> **Milk thistle** *(Silybum marianum)* has been used for centuries as a medicinal plant. The active component in milk thistle, silibinin (silybin), is usually derived from the seeds of the plant. According to the *German Commission E* monograph, milk thistle is commonly used as a liver protectant and for the treatment of dyspepsia, cirrhosis, and liver damage due to toxins. Milk thistle has been shown to help protect the liver from the toxic effects of chemotherapy.

> **Indole-3 carbinol (I-3-C)** is a phytonutrient found in cruciferous vegetables. Research has shown that I-3-C helps break down cancer-causing

estrogens to a non-toxic form. Research featured in the *British Journal of Cancer* found that I-3-C may help to prevent development of cancer in women with mutations of the BRCA1 and BRCA2 genes.

Curcumin *(Curcuma longa)* is a type of curcuminoid that is a beneficial compound within turmeric. Curcumin is considered to be the most potent, medicinally powerful component of turmeric. More specific to cancer, it increases antioxidant capacity, induces apoptosis (cell death) in cancer cells, inhibits inflammation, inhibits COX-2 and PGE2 promoters of tumour growth, and in general has been shown to inhibit cancer initiation, promotion, and progression.

AdrenaSense® supports the system during times of stress, and can therefore help prevent breast cancer due to stress.

Dosage: 2–3 capsules daily (2 with breakfast and 1 midday).

Melatonin induces apoptosis and reduces breast cancer invasiveness and metastasis. Studies show that higher melatonin levels are associated with a lower risk of breast cancer. Melatonin may be used as an adjuvant in cancer therapy.

Dosage: 3–20 mg daily.

Milk thistle – Stands falsely accused

Silibinin, a constituent of milk thistle with cancer chemopreventive activity, has been shown in preclinical trials to be effective treatment in models of prostate and colorectal cancer. Other beneficial effects noted in the many scientific investigations of milk thistle include the following:

- Prevention of the expression of genes and enzymes pivotal in breast cancer development
- Inhibition of breast cancer cell growth and the key pathways that cancer cells use to grow
- Promotion of apoptosis (programmed cell death) in breast cancer cells
- Protection of the liver from chemical damage and recommended for people undergoing chemotherapy

In more recent years, however, there has been some controversy and misguided information disseminated regarding milk thistle and its effect on breast cancer. This bias was based on one rodent study that suggested milk thistle stimulated the growth of mammary tumours in women with established breast cancer.

The study, published in *Carcinogenesis* in 2006, failed to show dose dependence. In many cases, the doses used in animals are far in excess of human doses and this may have masked the beneficial effect of the silibinin.

Further studies support the benefits of silibinin for use in breast cancer:

- In 2008, the journal *Cancer Chemotherapy and Pharmacology* tested the hypothesis that silibinin contributed to breast cancer development in the mouse model. The conclusion was that intervention with silibinin or other milk thistle constituents neither promoted, nor interfered with, tumour development. The result suggests that "promotion of carcinogenesis is not a feature of silibinin consistent across rodent models of mammary carcinogenesis" as suggested in a previous rodent study in *Carcinogenesis* in 2006.

- A study published in 2009 in the *Journal of Molecular Cancer Therapy* shows the ability of silibinin to inhibit the growth of cancerous cells via a very specific molecular mechanism involving protein synthesis. Unregulated protein synthesis is a key event in the development of breast cancer. Regulation of protein synthesis is required for cell growth, proliferation, differentiation, and cellular homeostasis. Loss of this regulation leads to excessive growth in cancer cells – the greater the loss, the more aggressive the cancer.

- In 2011, the *Journal of Breast Cancer* published another study confirming the benefits of milk thistle in the treatment of breast cancer. Silibinin strongly induced cancer cell death and the results suggest that it is an important agent for treating patients with breast cancer.

- In 2014, the journal *Cancer Medicine* published a study showing that silibinin inhibits breast tumour growth and there was a significant prolongation in survival rates of rodents given silibinin versus controls.

This unsubstantiated attack on milk thistle's safety is surprising because the herb has been very safely used for over 2000 years. It is one of the most extensively studied herbs and has an exceptional safety record. Based on current research, milk thistle has a range of benefits. So what's the problem? **That's the problem, there isn't one.**

Additional support for prevention/treatment of breast cancer

Vitamin D has been studied primarily for its role in preventing breast cancer, but new research indicates that prognosis may also be improved with vitamin D therapy. Studies indicate that women with low levels of vitamin D tend to have more advanced breast cancer, while women with higher levels of vitamin D tend to have less advanced cancers.

Dosage: 5000 IU daily or consult your ND or MD for guidance on higher dosages.

Boswellia *(Boswellia serrata)* is a chemical compound found in the gum resin frankincense. Boswellic acid has the potential to kill cancer cells, and it may be a viable treatment for breast, prostate, brain, and ovarian cancer. It is very important to stop the inflammatory cascade, and boswellia is a powerful anti-inflammatory herb.

Dosage: 300–500 mg 2–3 times daily of an extract standardized to 30–40% boswellic acids.

Grapeseed extract is a very powerful antioxidant, 50 times that of vitamin C and 20 times that of vitamin E. Grape seed extract is toxic to breast, lung, and gastric cancers, while at the same time enhancing the viability of normal cells.

Dosage: 50 mg standardized to 5% polyphenols and 80% proanthocyanidins, 1–3 capsules daily.

Ashwagandha *(Withania somnifera)* has been shown to reduce cell proliferation and increase apoptosis in ER+ and ER– human breast cancer cells.

Dosage: 1–3 g daily of dried herb. (This dose will change depending on the standardized active ingredients.)

Diet and Lifestyle Tips for Breast Cancer

Refer to the diet and lifestyle tips provided for fibrocystic breasts earlier in this chapter.

What else can you do?

It is not uncommon for women to put themselves last, taking care of everyone else's needs while sacrificing their own. What is more symbolic of the ability to nurture life than a woman's breast?

We have provided some overall nutritional suggestions for prevention and support treatment of breast cancer. However, for those who have been diagnosed with breast cancer, we strongly recommend you seek the care of a naturopathic doctor or complementary medical practitioner to help with dietary and nutritional needs, along with stress assessment and modification. Also, start working with a counsellor to help you heal the mental and emotional stresses that may be underlying the disease.

Karen Jensen, ND

Approximately 20–30% of the female patients I saw in clinical practice had, or previously had, breast cancer. Almost 100% of these women did not feel that their feminine nature was being nurtured. It is up to each one of us to ensure that our own needs are met, to learn to communicate these needs to others, and to make time in our lives to nurture ourselves. If not you, who?

Additional resources:

- The work of Ralph Moss, PhD, who provides a different viewpoint on the various cancer therapies through his monthly newsletters or one of his many books, such as *Customized Cancer Treatment.*

- *Naturally, There Is Always Hope,* by Neil McKinney, ND, who specializes in oncology.

- *The Definitive Guide to Cancer* by Lise Alschuler, ND, FABNO and Karolyn Gazella, which provides more information on the treatments available for specific forms of cancer.

GENDER DIFFERENCES IN COMMON DISEASES

"Rarely ever are half of the participants in trials women, so how can you apply information that relates only to men, to women whose physiology is different? Men are not adequate replacements for women in research. Not scientifically correct. Period. Full stop."

"Excluding women from drug trials creates an imbalance. Millions of women and men are prescribed the same drugs every day. Yet some of those drugs were tested only on men. There are metabolic differences. How the drug is complexed [released] or excreted may vary a lot in women versus men. So then you have new risk factors that you didn't even know were a possible risk."

– Dr. Jerilynn Prior, Professor of Endocrinology, University of British Columbia

Chapter 9

Urinary Tract Infections, Interstitial Cystitis, and Urinary Incontinence

The Urinary System – An Overview

The urinary system consists of the kidneys, ureters, bladder, and urethra. This system plays a role in removing waste from the body: the kidneys filter waste from the blood and regulate the concentration of many substances, and the tubes called ureters carry urine from the kidneys to the bladder, where it is stored.

When the kidneys secrete urine, it is sterile until it reaches the urethra, which transports it from the bladder to the urethral opening for excretion. Urinary tract infections (UTIs) typically occur when bacteria outside the body enters the urinary tract through the urethra.

The urinary tract is designed to stop the microscopic invaders through the following defences:

- Urine flow tends to wash away bacteria.
- The bladder secretes a protective coating that prevents bacteria from attaching to its walls.
- The pH of the urine has antibacterial properties that inhibit the growth of bacteria.
- In men, the prostatic fluid has many antimicrobial substances.
- The body quickly secretes white blood cells to control the bacteria invasion.

Although bacterial infections are the most common causes of UTIs, a number of non-infectious factors may cause the bladder to become inflamed. Some of these factors include different forms of cystitis caused by drugs, radiation, chemicals, or complications of other disorders such as pelvic inflammatory disorders, Crohn's disease, gynecological cancers, or diverticulitis.

Gender Differences in UTIs

In general, UTIs are more common in postmenopausal women and the elderly. There is also a high incidence in younger women during pregnancy and at onset of sexual activity. One key reason why women are more likely than men to develop recurrent UTIs is physical anatomy. Women have shorter urethra, which shortens the distance bacteria must travel to reach the bladder.

Citing data for 1997, researchers noted that in the United States, urinary tract infections accounted for fewer than one million emergency department visits resulting in 100,000 hospitalizations. Ten years later, the average was 2.7 million emergency department visits each year for UTIs, leading to 450,136 admissions. In 2007 alone, there were more than 8.6 million outpatient visits for UTIs, with 84% of them made by women. Even though the incidence of UTIs is higher for women, men were most likely to be admitted for inpatient care, especially elderly men.

Signs and Symptoms of UTIs

Although some UTIs can be asymptomatic, most present with the following symptoms:

- Strong, persistent urge to urinate
- Blood in the urine

- Burning sensation when urinating
- Low-grade fever

- Passing frequent, small amounts of urine

- Discomfort in the pelvic area, even when not urinating

- Passing milky, cloudy, or strong-smelling urine

- Feeling of pressure in the lower abdomen

In addition to the classic UTI symptoms listed, symptoms of kidney infection can include the following:

- Pain in the back or side, below the ribs

- Nausea and vomiting

- Fever and chills

Possible Causes of UTIs

The rise in the incidence and hospitalizations UTIs can be attributed, in part, to the aging population. However, researchers have found that the increasing levels of diabetes and other illnesses, and rising resistance to antibiotics, are also factors.

Risk factors

Other factors associated with an increased risk of bladder infection include the following:

- Sexual intercourse can result in bacteria being pushed into the urethra.

- Birth control methods such as the use of diaphragms can increase the risk.

- Using condoms with spermicidal foam have been found to have an increased risk when compared to other forms of birth control.

- Pregnancy can double the incidence of UTIs due to hormonal changes.

- Menopause women lose the protective effects of estrogen that can decrease the likelihood of UTIs.

- A large number of bacteria live in the rectal area and on the skin, leading to contamination from the rectum. Bacteria may get into the urine from the urethra and travel to the bladder. Always remember to wipe from front to back.

- Irritable bowel syndrome (IBS) or constipation have been shown to increase urinary urgency and frequency, as well as incontinence.

- Prolonged use of bladder catheters that may be required in people with chronic disease or in older adults can increase the risk of UTIs.

- Depressed immune system can put people at higher risk for UTIs due to a reduced ability to fight off infections. This can occur with conditions such as diabetes, HIV, infections, cancer treatment, and others.

- Certain foods can aggravate the bladder and contribute to a depressed immune system as well as inflammation, both of which can increase the risk for bladder infection.

- Interference with the flow of urine can occur in conditions such as a stone or tumour in the bladder, strictures, or in men, an enlarged prostate.

Testing and Diagnosis

In general, diagnosis is made based on signs and symptoms as well as urinary findings. Microscopic examination of the infected urine will show high levels of white blood cells and bacteria. Culturing the urine will indicate the quantity and type of bacteria involved. The *Escherichia coli (E. coli)* bacteria is responsible for 90% of bladder infections. Normally, a UTI does not cause a fever if it is in the bladder or urethra, however a fever may indicate the infection has spread to the kidneys.

what we know works

....
Support for UTIs

UriSense® combines probiotics with a very concentrated form of cranberries. It takes 36 pounds of cranberries – fruit, seeds, skin, and juice – to produce just one pound of CranRich, the cranberry concentrate in UriSense. Women have used cranberry for decades as a treatment for conditions in the urinary tract. Several studies have shown that cranberries and cranberry juice are effective in prevention and treatment of UTIs.

Dosage: 2–4 capsules daily.

CranSense® contains the cranberry concentrate CranRich (refer to UriSense above for more information).

Dosage: 500 mg 1–3 times daily.

ReliefBiotic™ is a probiotic formula developed to address symptoms of an irritable bowel. The connection between bladder and bowel function is apparent in interstitial cystitis, urinary incontinence, and overactive bladder. Probiotics help restore the gut microflora and normalize bowel function. A number of probiotics have been studied for effectiveness in the prevention of recurrent UTIs. *E. coli*, the primary pathogen involved in UTIs, travels from the intestines and/or vagina to inhabit the normally sterile urinary tract, so improving the gut or vaginal flora benefits the overall health of the urinary tract. Each capsule contains the four unique clinically researched strains: *Lactobacillus helveticus, Lactobacillus rhamnosus, Bacillus subtilis,* and *Enterococcus faecium.*

Dosage: 1 capsule daily.

Uva ursi *(Arctostaphylos uva ursi)* is a very useful herb in most cases of UTIs. Much of the research has focus on its antiseptic and antibacterial component, arbutin. Uva ursi has been reported to be especially active against *E. coli* as well as having diuretic properties.

Dosage: 250–300 mg up to 3 times daily.

Julie Reil, MD

"Choose unsweetened cranberry juice, or if that's too tart, consider adding a supportive dietary supplement that is made from whole fruit, not fruit juice concentrate. The one I recommend to all my patients who are experiencing urinary issues of any kind is UriSense®. UriSense contains CranRich®, an exceptional, patented, cranberry concentrate. It is so concentrated, in fact, that it takes 36 pounds of cranberries – fruit, seeds, skin, and juice – to produce just one pound of CranRich. Most other cranberry supplements are made from sweetened dehydrated juice, with none of the other parts of the fruit. UriSense also contains BB536®, a shelf-stable probiotic to keep your gut, vagina, and urinary tract flora in balance with any candida that may be present. With UriSense my patients get the nutritional support they need to avoid repeated urinary tract infections, and they report feeling healthier and more comfortable with their urinary routine. So, to fight back against chronic or recurring UTIs, do not choose just one weapon – antibiotics. Choose also wise supplementation, make necessary changes in your habits and routine, and in these ways beat recurrent UTIs for good!

Additional support for UTIs

Berberine is present in many plants, including goldenseal, Oregon grape, and barberry. Berberine extracts have demonstrated significant antimicrobial activity against a variety of organism, including bacteria, viruses, and fungi.

Dosage: 500 mg 2–3 times daily.

Vitamin C is well known for its immune-enhancing properties. A small study of 100 pregnant women showed the occurrence of UTIs was significantly lower in the group receiving vitamin C compared to placebo.

Dosage: 1000 mg 1–4 times daily (or until you begin to experience loose stools).

Estriol cream can greatly reduce the incidence of UTIs. Hormonal changes, particularly reduced estrogen levels in postmenopausal women, result in thinning of the vaginal and urethral tissue, disruption of the flora, and an increased risk for UTIs. In fact, 10–15% of women over the age of 60 suffer from recurrent UTIs.

Dosage: as per doctor's prescription.

Antibiotics are typically the first choice in conventional medicine for the treatment of UTIs. The type of antibiotic prescribed depends on health history and the type of bacteria cultured in the urine. There are times when antibiotics will be necessary if the UTI is not responding to natural treatments as there is a risk of the bacteria spreading to the kidneys.

Diet and Lifestyle Tips for UTIs

A natural approach can be the best treatment for most UTIs, with the infection usually resolving without recurrence or complications. There is some concern that antibiotic treatment actually promotes recurrent infections by disturbing healthy bacterial flora and increases the risk of antibiotic-resistant strains of *E. coli*. One of the primary goals in the natural approach to prevention and treatment of UTIs is to enhance the internal defences by supporting the immune system.

Diet recommendations include the following:

- Drink adequate amounts of liquids such as water and herbal teas to help flush the urinary tract, thus preventing the colonization of the bacteria. During a bladder infection, 1.5–2.0 L or more of fluids should be consumed.
- Avoid concentrated fruit juices with high-sugar content, coffee, and soft drinks.

- Avoid a diet high in refined carbohydrates including breads, pasta, pastries, and foods containing sugars in all forms (glucose, fructose corn syrup, and sucrose), which can significantly reduce the ability of white blood cells to fight infection.

- Increase the intake of fruit and vegetables. Consume at least eight servings daily, especially those from the Brassica family (cabbage, kale, and broccoli), as well as onions, garlic, Brussels sprouts, and sea vegetables.

- Consume an adequate amount of protein to support the function of the immune system. Choose both vegetarian and lean animal protein sources. Vegetarian sources include organic non-GMO soy foods (e.g., tempeh, tofu, miso), legumes, nuts, and seeds. Animal sources include fish, eggs, and organic and antibiotic-/hormone-free chicken, turkey, lamb, and beef.

- Avoid known allergic foods completely. For those who are unaware of a specific allergen, limit common allergenic foods such as dairy, gluten, eggs, and corn. Consider allergy testing with your naturopathic health care practitioner.

CRANBERRY –
A NATURAL CHOICE FOR UTIs

It is helpful to incorporate cranberry into your diet. Women have used cranberry for decades as a treatment for conditions in the urinary tract. Most cranberry juices sold in the grocery store contain one-third cranberry juice mixed with water and sugar. Sugar has a detrimental effect on the immune function and sweetened cranberry juice is not recommended.

Not all current human studies support the use of cranberry extracts as a primary treatment in UTIs. However, cranberry concentrate is a good first choice. In many cases it will prevent the use of antibiotics, especially if the product uses a highly concentrated form of cranberry such as CranRich, which is contained in both CranSense and UriSense.

Lifestyle recommendations include the following:

- Support the adrenal glands. Stress and the release of stress hormones inhibit the immune system and the production of white blood cells thereby increasing the susceptibility to infection.

- Wipe from front to back to prevent bacteria around the anus from entering the vagina or urethra. Use unscented and unbleached toilet papers as many women react to the dyes and chemicals in other toilet paper products.

- Do not delay urinating. Holding in the urine and not emptying your bladder completely can increase the risk of UTIs.

- Urinate before and after sexual intercourse to help decrease the risk of UTIs by flushing out any bacteria that are introduced during intercourse.

- Wear cotton underwear.

- Avoid feminine hygiene deodorants, douches, and powders that can lead to irritation of the urethra.

- Only use natural cotton sanitary napkins and tampons.

- Take showers instead of baths.

> Water is extremely important! Make sure you drink enough water to prevent bacteria from gaining a foothold in your urinary tract. A good rule of thumb is that your urine should be pale yellow, never darker.

Interstitial Cystitis

Interstitial cystitis (IC), also known as painful bladder, is a chronic multifactorial syndrome characterized by a combination of pelvic pain, pressure, or discomfort in the bladder and pelvic region, often associated with frequency and urgency. IC is frequently misdiagnosed as a UTI and patients may go years without a correct diagnosis. IC often occurs around 30–40 years of age, and 90% of people with the condition are women.

Inflammatory bowel disorders such as IBS, colitis, and Crohn's disease are commonly associated with IC. Rheumatoid arthritis, fibromyalgia, hysterectomy, or allergies to food or medications are also associated with IC.

Signs and Symptoms of IC

Signs and symptoms can vary from person to person and can be triggered by menstruation, prolonged sitting, stress, exercise, or sexual activity. Some of the more common symptoms include:

- Pain in the pelvis or between the vagina and anus in women or between the scrotum and anus in men
- Chronic pelvic pain
- A persistent urgent need to urinate
- Frequent urination, often in small amounts throughout the day and night
- Pain during intercourse

Although many of the signs and symptoms resemble those of chronic UTIs, urine cultures are usually free of bacteria.

Possible Causes of IC

Several theories have been proposed as causes of IC, including the following:

- **Bladder permeability** – The lining of the bladder contains glycosamino-glycans (GAGs) that normally protect it from toxins, microorganisms, and carcinogens, which may damage the bladder wall. It has been suggested that individuals with IC have a breakdown of this protective layer leading to changes in permeability, stimulation of pain receptors, and inflammation.

- **Neurological** – Substance "P" is an inflammatory mediator released by the peripheral nerves that has been found in higher levels in the urine of women with IC. Injury to the peripheral nerves from previous infections, hysterectomy, or childbirth can cause inflammation or bladder ulceration, which can also lead to an increase in pain impulses.

- **Mast cell activation** – Mast cells play a key role in the inflammatory process and release of histamine, inflammatory prostaglandins, and other substances that can affect the bladder.

- **Estrogen** – Estrogen levels seem to play a role in determining the intensity of inflammation within the bladder. It has been reported that 40% of IC patients experience an exacerbation of symptoms particularly around the time of ovulation.

- **Inflammation** – Inflammation is most commonly thought to be a cause of IC since significant levels of inflammatory mediators are found in the bladder.

- **Infection** – The symptoms of IC are very similar to bacterial cystitis, but urine samples often demonstrate no evidence of an infection. The possibility that there is an infectious cause is up for debate, but the overall thought is that very small amounts of microorganisms may be able to persist in the bladder wall.

Testing and Diagnosis

An initial evaluation of IC includes a patient history, physical exam, and review of symptoms. Key diagnostic symptoms include:

- Bladder and pelvic pain or discomfort
- Urinary urgency or frequency
- Symptoms that persist for more than six weeks
- Negative results of lab tests for UTI or other infections

People with IC often have overlapping symptoms related to other pelvic diseases. As a result, it is important to rule out other urinary and genital tract infections or tumours of the urinary or gastrointestinal tract, as well as endometriosis. A pelvic exam and urinalysis are often done first, followed by a cystoscopy where the doctor looks for inflammation or ulcerations in the bladder wall.

Sometimes a test called a potassium sensitivity test, also referred to as Parson's test, will be used. It involves inserting two solutions – water and potassium chloride – into the bladder one at a time. The patient's pain and urgency is recorded. Typically those who have IC will report more pain when the potassium is inserted.

what we know works
....

Support for IC

EstroSense® helps maintain healthy hormone levels by targeting estrogen metabolism. Estrogen may be a trigger for individuals with IC, and balancing estrogen levels can help reduce potential flare-ups.

Dosage: 3 capsules daily.

GISense™ works to decrease stress-induced inflammation, one of the main causes of IC. GISense contains the following herbs: boswellia, chamomile, curcumin, ashwagandha, and bacopa. Refer below for more information about individual ingredients.

Dosage: 3 capsules daily.

Bacopa has been proven to facilitate adaptation responses and to normalize plasma cortisol in acute and chronic stress models. Stress is a major cause of inflammation and cognitive disorders.

Ashwagandha has remarkable stress-relieving properties in addition to its excellent protective effects on the nervous system. In one of the most complete human clinical trials to date, participants showed up to a 26% reduction of the stress hormone cortisol, which is a major cause of inflammation.

Curcumin has potent anti-inflammatory and antioxidant properties that can help prevent and support inflammatory conditions. Research has shown that curcumin is comparable to common prescription medications like hydrocortisone and over-the-counter medications such as ibuprofen in the treatment of inflammation.

Chamomile *(Chamomilla recutita)* has traditionally been used as a calming and anti-inflammatory herb. It is sometimes called "herbal aspirin".

Boswellia *(Boswellia serrata)* contains boswellic acids and has been used as a major anti-inflammatory agent for centuries. Many studies have shown that boswellia is just as effective as nonsteroidal anti-inflammatory drugs (NSAIDs), which are the most commonly used treatment for inflammation.

Quercetin and **bromelain** help reduce allergic inflammation and promote tissue healing inside the bladder. A high concentration of mast cells has been found in the bladder of those individuals with IC. Quercetin stabilizes mast cells and reduces histamine secretion. Preliminary studies have found that it significantly reduces IC-related pain. A supplement combining quercetin with bromelain is recommended.

Dosage: 500–1000 mg twice daily.

Flaxseed oil and/or **pure fish oil** decrease the formation of inflammatory prostaglandins and increase the anti-inflammatory prostaglandins, thereby preventing and reducing inflammation in the bladder tissue.

Dosage: 30 mL of flaxseed oil daily or up to 3000 mg fish oil daily.

Vitamin D3 studies show that it reduces the production of mast cells and may be a successful anti-inflammatory agent.

Dosage: 3000–5000 IU daily.

··

Diet and Lifestyle Tips for IC

Many individuals with IC find avoiding certain foods and beverages helpful in preventing flare-ups. Refer to the information below on urinary incontinence as many of the foods that aggravate symptoms are the same for both conditions. Further information can also be found through the IC Association.

In addition to removing foods that may irritate symptoms, consider the following:

- Avoid all processed, refined foods and food that contains artificial sweeteners.
- Try to wear loose clothing to minimize pressure on the abdomen and pelvic regions.
- Reduce stress by practising meditation, yoga, or deep breathing, or have regular massages. A regular exercise program also helps reduce stress.
- Do pelvic floor exercises to help gently stretch and strengthen the pelvic floor muscles, and help with muscle spasms.
- If you smoke, try to quit.

Urinary Incontinence

Due to an increasing aging society, the number of people suffering from urinary dysfunction, including incontinence, has reached an all-time high.

Urinary incontinence is the inability to hold urine in the bladder due to loss of voluntary control over the urinary sphincters, resulting in the involuntary passage of urine – urinating when you do not want to. Severity and impact on quality of life vary greatly, and incontinence varies in degree of severity from several drops to complete bladder emptying. It may occur daily, or many times a day, or only occasionally, perhaps once a month.

Gender Differences in Urinary Incontinence

In young women, the prevalence of incontinence is usually low, but prevalence peaks around menopause, with a steady rise thereafter into later life, especially between the ages of 70 and 80. By the age of 60, over 30% of women will have experienced urinary incontinence and 15% bowel incontinence. About 48% of women and 17% of men over age 70 suffer from urinary incontinence. Elderly women differ from their younger counterparts because of various physiological changes in the urinary tract, as well as the presence of polypharmacy and incidence of other disease conditions such as diabetes, joint disease, or dementias, which contribute to urinary incontinence difficulties.

Types of Urinary Incontinence

Types of urinary incontinence include the following:

- Stress incontinence occurs as a result of pressure on the bladder by coughing, sneezing, laughing, exercising, or lifting something heavy.

- Urge incontinence is caused by a sudden, intense urge to urinate followed by an involuntary loss of urine, and in some a need to urinate often including throughout the night. Urge incontinence may be caused by an infection, neurologic disorder, or diabetes.

- Overflow incontinence results in frequent or constant dribbling of urine due to a bladder that does not empty completely.

- Functional incontinence is a physical or mental impairment that keeps individuals from making it to the toilet in time. For example, if a person has severe arthritis, they may not be able to unbutton their pants quickly enough.

- Mixed incontinence occurs when people experience more than one type of urinary incontinence.

Typically people either suffer from urge or from stress incontinence, and sometimes both. Stress incontinence is highest among postmenopausal women and is not as bothersome as compared to urge incontinence. Although urge incontinence is less prevalent, it is more bothersome and more likely to require treatment.

Possible Causes of Urinary Incontinence

Urinary incontinence can be caused by underlying physical problems or other conditions, including the following:

- **Pregnancy** – Hormonal changes and the increased weight of the uterus can lead to stress incontinence.

- **Childbirth** – Vaginal delivery can weaken the muscles needed for bladder control and also damage bladder nerves and supportive tissue, leading to a dropped (prolapsed) pelvic floor. With prolapse, the bladder, uterus, rectum, or small intestine can get pushed down from the usual position and protrude into the vagina. Such protrusions can be associated with incontinence.

- **Changes with age** – Aging of the bladder muscle can decrease the bladder's capacity to store urine.

- **Menopause** – After menopause women produce less estrogen, a hormone that helps keep the lining of the bladder and urethra healthy. Deterioration of these tissues can aggravate incontinence.

- **Hysterectomy** – In women, the bladder and uterus are supported by many of the same muscles and ligaments. Any surgery that involves a woman's reproductive system, including removal of the uterus, may damage the supporting pelvic floor muscles, which can lead to incontinence.

- **Enlarged prostate** – Especially in older men, incontinence often stems from enlargement of the prostate gland, a condition known as benign prostatic hyperplasia.

- **Prostate cancer** – In men, stress incontinence or urge incontinence can be associated with untreated prostate cancer. But more often, incontinence is a side effect of treatments for prostate cancer.

- **Obstruction** – A tumour or urinary stone anywhere along the urinary tract can block the normal flow of urine, leading to overflow incontinence.

- **Stress** – Stress activates the fight-or-flight response. Together with panic and other sympathetic nervous system responses, it can make the muscles that control the "urge feeling" stronger. Try to stay calm if you have a sudden urge; close your eyes, hold your breath for a few seconds, and let the urge pass.

- **Neurological disorders** – Multiple sclerosis, Parkinson's disease, stroke, brain tumour, or spinal injury can interfere with nerve signals involved in bladder control, causing urinary incontinence.

- **Being overweight** – Extra weight increases pressure on your bladder and surrounding muscles, which weakens them and allows urine to leak out when you cough or sneeze.

- **UTIs** – Urinary tract infections can irritate the bladder, causing strong urges to urinate and sometimes incontinence.

- **Constipation** – The rectum is located near the bladder and shares many of the same nerves. Hard, compacted stool causes these nerves to be overactive, resulting in increased urinary frequency.

- **Diet** – Certain drinks, foods, and medications can act as diuretics, and can temporarily increase the volume and frequency of urination. They can also increase symptoms of both IC and urinary incontinence. Examples include alcohol, coffee, carbonated drinks, artificial sweeteners, corn syrup and sugar, spicy foods, citrus fruits, foods that contain nitrites such as processed meats, MSG, high doses of vitamin B and C, medications such as heart and blood pressure medications, sedatives, muscle relaxants, and large doses of vitamins B or C.

Not all individuals with urinary incontinence or IC are sensitive to the same foods. It may be helpful to test for allergies using the enzyme-linked immunosorbent assay (ELISA), which detects and measures antibodies in the blood to determine if there are antibodies related to certain infectious conditions. The ELISA testing method can be done through a complementary health care practitioner. An elimination/challenge diet can also be tried to determine food sensitivities.

The bladder-bowel connection

The connection between bladder and bowel function is apparent in several clinical disorders, including IC, urinary incontinence, colon and bowel disorders, and overactive bladder (OAB). OAB is urinary urgency, usually accompanied by frequency and nighttime urination, with or without urgency or urinary incontinence. It affects one in six adults over the age of 40. People with OAB are significantly more likely to experience chronic constipation or fecal incontinence compared to those without OAB.

Studies have demonstrated that treating the constipation may improve lower urinary tract symptoms, including urgency and frequency. Non-pharmacological approaches to managing primary constipation include increasing fluids, fibre intake, and physical activity. If this treatment is not sufficient to eliminate the constipation, laxatives may be needed, especially for severe or chronic constipation.

what we know works

Support for Urinary Incontinence and Overactive Bladder

PolyGlycopleX® (PGX®) is a form of dietary fibre that contains non-digestible carbohydrates that can improve digestion and bowel movements. As a consequence of the type of diet that many people in the Western world now consume, our digestive system has altered, making it difficult to digest and absorb fibre in its whole or natural form. This leads to slow fibre intake and dietary fibre can displace calories as well as other nutrients. Bowel problems such as constipation are very common in people who have urinary incontinence, and often improving bowel movements is all that is required to provide relief from the urinary incontinence symptoms. PGX also restores the blood sugar to proper levels, decreases appetite, and prevents weight gain.

Dosage: 750–1500 mg before each meal.

BladderSense® contains water-soluble pumpkin seed extract, shown to be highly effective in addressing urinary urgency and frequency for both men and women.

Dosage: 1 capsule 3 times daily for the first 2 weeks. After 2 weeks, reduce to 2 capsules daily or as recommended by a health care practitioner.

ReliefBiotic™ is a probiotic formula developed to address irritable bowel symptoms. The connection between bladder and bowel function is apparent in interstitial cystitis, urinary incontinence, and overactive bladder. Probiotics help restore the gut microflora and normalize bowel function. A number of probiotics have been studied for effectiveness in the prevention of recurrent UTIs. *E. coli,* the primary pathogen involved in UTIs, travels from the intestines and/or vagina to inhabit the normally sterile urinary tract, so improving the gut or vaginal flora benefits the overall health of the urinary tract. Each capsule contains the four unique clinically researched strains: *Lactobacillus helveticus, Lactobacillus rhamnosus, Bacillus subtilis,* and *Enterococcus faecium.*

Dosage: 1 capsule daily.

Soy isoflavone extract provides standardized phytoestrogens that have been shown to help with symptoms relating to estrogen deficiency in women. (Refer to *Chapter 5* for more information on phytoestrogens.) Soy extract is thought to decrease the atrophy of tissues in the bladder and urethra, thereby helping with symptoms of urges and urinary incontinence.

Dosage: 125 mg twice daily.

Saw palmetto can inhibit the formation of DHT and prevent DHT from binding to the prostate in men, which can result in a reduction of symptoms. This is even more effective when combined with antioxidants, polyphenols, and anti-inflammatories such as grapeseed extract and white willow bark.

Dosage: 2 160-mg capsules daily.

Genityte® is a 100% non-invasive procedure that returns the urethra to a normal position, and improves both inner and outer urethral support: no surgery, no injections, and no recovery time. It also treats vaginal wall prolapse as well as rectal incontinence. Without strong urethral tone and support, simple daily events such as walking, lifting, coughing, sneezing, laughing, or exercising can cause involuntary leaking of urine, or incontinence. It uses infrared light to gently heat the skin to treat the skin laxity in the genital region. Infrared light helps stimulate the formation of collagen and elastin, giving skin improved tone. For more information, go to **shilohmedicalclinic.com**.

Julie Reil, MD

"Prescription drugs can help by relaxing the muscle that empties the bladder, or by blocking the nerve impulses that tell the bladder to contract. But pharmaceutical solutions can cause unwanted side effects such as: dry mouth, constipation, blurred vision, dizziness, and even interference with mental clarity. I find the higher the dose and the older the patient, the more likely these side effects are to be reported.

I recommend that patients try natural solutions first. Try BladderSense®, which is a water-soluble pumpkin seed extract – a natural option. It has been shown to be highly effective in addressing urinary urgency and frequency, including the "need to go" that wakes you from sleep. Much safer than the prescription drugs on the market, BladderSense has impressed me with its ability to reduce the symptoms of those who use it daily. So, don't be embarrassed by your symptoms and don't assume you're alone in dealing with them, either – because you aren't, not by a long shot! If you've been limiting your life and avoiding activities you love, please know that there is help available. See a trusted health care practitioner or naturopath, or try BladderSense as a starting point!

Many women are embarrassed to admit they experience incontinence and probably don't realize that approximately 30% of women up to the age of 60 have urinary leakage and 15% have bowel leakage. I have over 15 years of experience in women's healthcare and I recommend PGX® at my clinic. I've seen amazing results with incontinence and PGX."

Diet and Lifestyle Tips for Urinary Incontinence and Overactive Bladder

Pumpkin seeds

As previously mentioned, urinary incontinence worsens after menopause and is usually associated with low levels of estrogen, testosterone, and progesterone. Pumpkin seed extracts affect the pelvic floor muscles through different mechanisms that essentially make more testosterone available to strengthen these muscles. By promoting androgen activity, pumpkin seeds have been found to play a very important role in structural integrity and urinary tract disorders.

In the first human study, water-soluble pumpkin seed extract was combined with soy isoflavone to evaluate the frequency of nighttime urination and the number of incontinent episodes. The extract combination was shown, on average, to reduce incontinent episodes by up to 79%, daytime urination by up to 39%, and nighttime urination by up to 68%. Subsequent studies have shown equally impressive results. The combination of water-soluble pumpkin seed and soy extract can significantly improve urinary incontinence in postmenopausal women and thereby improve mobility and quality of life in affected individuals.

Kegel exercises

Kegel exercises for women can provide benefit in some cases.

- Try stopping your urine mid-stream when going. The muscles you use are pelvic floor muscles.
- Focus on tightening those muscles when you have an empty bladder.
- Breathe normally when doing these exercises.
- Avoid squeezing your stomach, thighs, or buttocks instead of your pelvic floor muscles.

Or try the Beyond Kegels® program, a new set of exercises for the pelvic floor. These techniques provide statistically improved results over the usual Kegel squeezes, and they are especially good for mothers and women who have developed uterine prolapse.

Urinary Conditions – For the Men in Your Life

Women are not alone in suffering from age-related urinary complaints. About 60% of men over age 50 suffer from benign prostate enlargement. The most common complaint is the need to urinate frequently at night, which can interfere with sleep. Chronic sleep deprivation significantly increases the risk in women and men of common diseases including heart attack, cancer, depression, and various inflammatory syndromes. Water-soluble pumpkin seed extract reduces prostate-induced urinary symptoms and has been clinically shown to help improve sleep. One study of men 66–88 years if age showed that after six weeks, there was a 39% reduction in nighttime urinary frequency.

Chapter 10

Fertility Problems

Perhaps the most basic measure of a civilization is the ability to reproduce successfully in order to continue its achievements and to meet the demands of the future. Although reproduction is fundamental to civilization's future, it is also the factor that makes it most vulnerable. The reproductive system, the fetus, and the infant are extremely susceptible to disruptions, whether from lack of nutrients or the ever-increasing exposure to toxins in our foods and environment.

Infertility

Infertility refers to an inability to conceive after 12 months of having regular unprotected sexual intercourse. Infertility can also refer to the biological inability of an individual to contribute to conception, or to a female who cannot carry a pregnancy to full term.

Gender Differences in the Rates of Infertility

Infertility is on the rise in Canada, according to the first study conducted in nearly two decades. The Canadian study, published in the *Journal of Human Reproduction* in March 2012, estimated that in 1984 the incidence of infertility in couples where the woman was 18–44 years of age was 5.4%. By 2009–2010, that figure for the same age group was as high as 16% – a near doubling of the rate since 1992. Not surprisingly, the older the woman, the higher the prevalence of infertility.

These new statistics focus on female infertility, yet according to the Mayo Clinic in the United States, approximately 20% of infertility is attributed to the male, 40% attributed to the female, and 30–40% due to problems in both (or unexplained). According to a study published in the *British Medical Journal* in 2012, only one in four men have optimal semen quality; and by some accounts, sperm counts may have dropped by 50% since the 1930s.

Possible Causes of Infertility

No one knows for sure what is causing this disturbing decline, but it is clear that some of the factors that plague our modern world are partly to blame. For example, stress hormones and toxic chemicals that act as endocrine disruptors (such as insecticides, flame retardants, and phthalates from plastics) all affect the hormones responsible for sperm production. In addition, excessive oxidant stress can damage the vulnerable reproductive organs and have negative effects on sperm and egg production. The obesity epidemic is another factor.

In some cases, infertility may have a single cause in one of the partners, or it could be a network of predisposing factors. Some common causes of infertility in men and women include the following:

- **Hormone imbalances** – In men, infertility can result from disorders of the testicles, and in women the ovaries themselves. Or there may be an abnormality affecting other hormonal systems, including the hypothalamus, pituitary, thyroid, and adrenal glands.

- **Intolerance to wheat and gluten** – A digestive disorder caused by a sensitivity to gluten can cause defective gonad development and/or infertility in men and women. Fertility may improve after adopting a gluten-free diet.

- **Environmental stressors** – Environmental chemicals with estrogenic activity (xenoestrogens) are responsible for much of the decrease in quantity and quality of human sperm over the past 40 years. Overexposure to certain environmental toxins and chemicals can cause estrogen dominant conditions in women, such as polycystic ovary syndrome, endometriosis, amenorrhea (lack of menstruation), and other common disorders that affect fertility. (Refer to *Chapter 6* for more information)

- **Emotional stress** – Severe or prolonged emotional stress can interfere with the hormones needed to produce sperm. In women, stress can cause symptoms of estrogen dominance as more progesterone is used to make cortisol. Studies indicate that female ovulation and sperm production may be affected by mental emotional stress.

- **Frequency of intercourse** – If this is a potential issue, the couple may be advised to have sexual intercourse more often. Sex 2–3 times per week may improve fertility.

- **Smoking, alcohol, and caffeine** – Smoking significantly increases the risk of infertility in both men and women. Smoking may also undermine the effects of fertility treatment. A woman's pregnancy can be seriously affected by any amount of alcohol consumption, and alcohol abuse may also lower male fertility. Couples trying to conceive may also want to avoid caffeine, as frequent consumption has been shown to increase time for conception.

- **Being obese or overweight** – Along with a sedentary lifestyle, being overweight is often found to be the principal cause of female infertility. An overweight man has a higher risk of having abnormal sperm.

- **Infections** – Some infections can interfere with sperm production or cause scarring that blocks the passage of sperm. Infections include some sexually transmitted diseases such as chlamydia and gonorrhea, inflammation of the prostate (prostatitis), or inflamed testicles due to mumps. Chlamydia can damage the fallopian tubes, as well as making the man's scrotum become inflamed. In most cases infections do not cause permanent damage.

- **High cholesterol** – Prospective parents with high cholesterol levels could be in for a long wait to become pregnant, according to a new study published in the *Journal of Clinical Endocrinology & Metabolism*.

- **Radiotherapy** – If radiation therapy was aimed near the man's or the woman's reproductive organs, it may affect fertility.

Common causes associated with infertility in women

- **Thyroid disorders** – Common problems caused by thyroid dysfunction are anovulation (i.e., no ovulation, or release of an egg), a shortened luteal phase, and menstrual irregularities.

- **Luteal phase syndrome** – The luteal phase is critical since this is when the fertilized egg implants in the uterus. A short luteal phase usually means that the uterine lining starts to shed before the fertilized egg has had a chance to implant. A luteal phase under 10 days is considered to be a problem.

- **Premature ovarian failure** – Premature ovarian failure (POF) can occur when women stop producing eggs much earlier than normal menopause. Standard tests for POF are done to test FSH and estrogen on Day 3 of the cycle. POF sometimes can occur after a woman has been on the birth control pill for many years.

- **Polycystic ovary syndrome** – Polycystic ovary syndrome (PCOS) is one of the main causes of infertility in women due to hormonal imbalances: progesterone deficiency as a result of estrogen excess and androgen excess as a result of insulin resistance. It is estimated that 10–20% of women today have PCOS. Androgen excess is the most common disorder in women of reproductive age. (Refer to *Chapter 7* for more information on PCOS.)

- **Autoimmune infertility** – Diseases such as lupus, autoimmune thyroiditis, and diabetes are linked to decreased fertility. Even causes of infertility such as POF, endometriosis, and PCOS include autoimmune factors. Many unexplained cases of infertility contain inflammatory processes that can be directed against hormones and reproductive tissues such as the ovaries and testes. Autoimmune thyroiditis has also been correlated to infertility and miscarriage, even in the absence of hypothyroidism.

- **Problems in the uterus or fallopian tubes** – The egg travels from the ovary to the uterus (womb) where the fertilized egg grows. If there is something wrong in the fallopian tubes or in the uterus, such as fibroids or endometriosis, a woman may not be able to conceive naturally.

- **Ovulation disorders** – Problems with ovulation are the most common cause of infertility in women. Ovulation is the monthly release of an egg. In some cases the woman never releases eggs, while in others the woman does not release eggs during regular monthly cycles. Premature ovarian failure occurs when the woman's ovaries stop working before she is 40 years of age.

- **Surgery** – Pelvic surgery can sometimes cause scarring or damage to the fallopian tubes. Cervical surgery can sometimes cause scarring or shortening of the cervix.

- **Hyperprolactinemia** – If prolactin levels are high and the woman is not pregnant or breastfeeding, it may affect ovulation and fertility.

- **Chemotherapy** – Some medications used in chemotherapy can result in ovarian failure. In some cases, this side effect of chemotherapy may be permanent.

Common causes associated with infertility in men

- **Sperm production, quality, and motility** – At least one of the testicles must be functioning correctly, and there must be adequate testosterone and other hormones to trigger and maintain sperm production. Sperm production is also affected when one (or both) testicle fails to descend from the abdomen into the scrotum during fetal development. When this occurs, the testicle is at a higher temperature, and healthy sperm need to exist in a slightly lower-than-body temperature. Abnormal semen is responsible for about 75% of all cases of male infertility, and in many cases the reason is not known. There could also be a problem with low sperm mobility (motility) or more commonly, "slow swimmers". Sperm concentration should be 20 million sperm per millilitre of semen. If the count is under 10 million, there is a low sperm concentration. Low sperm counts or motility problems can be due to multiple causes, including cell phones, which may reduce sperm quality through exposure to radio-frequency electromagnetic radiation.

- **Varicocele** – A varicocele is a swelling of the veins that drain the testicle. It is the most common reversible cause of male infertility and it is found in 35% of men with primary infertility and in 75–81% of men with secondary infertility. This may prevent normal cooling of the testicle, leading to reduced sperm count. The increased temperature creates "lazy swimmers". Varicocele is often diagnosable with palpation and in most cases can be corrected by a minimally invasive surgical procedure.

- **Problems with sexual intercourse** – These can include trouble keeping or maintaining an erection sufficient for sex (erectile dysfunction), premature ejaculation, painful intercourse, anatomical abnormalities such as having a urethral opening beneath the penis (hypospadias), or psychological or relationship problems that interfere with sex.

- **Certain medications** – Testosterone replacement therapy, long-term anabolic steroid use, cancer medications (chemotherapy), certain anti-fungal medications, some ulcer drugs, and certain other medications can impair sperm production and decrease male fertility.

- **Overheating of the testicles** – Prolonged bicycling is another possible cause of reduced fertility, due to overheating of the testicles. Erectile dysfunction occurs due to pressure from the bicycle seat. Frequent use of saunas or hot tubs may temporarily lower sperm count. Sitting for long periods or working on a laptop computer for long stretches of time may also increase the temperature in the scrotum and slightly reduce sperm production.

Testing and Diagnosis for Women

General physical exam

A general physical exam involves taking a medical history, including medications, menstruation cycle, and sexual habits, along with a gynecological examination.

Blood tests

Blood tests can aid in determining causes of infertility. Some include:

- Thyroid (TSH, T3, rT3, and T4 and antibodies) (Refer to *Chapter 4* for ideal reference ranges.)
- Luteinizing hormone (LH), follicle-stimulating hormone (FSH), prolactin (PRL), estradiol, and progesterone
- Testosterone and DHEA-S – to make sure pituitary function is healthy, (changes in pituitary function can cause menstrual cycle and ovulation problems; steroid hormones should also be checked)
- Adrenal function tests – to make sure adrenal response is healthy
- Blood sugars and insulin levels – to rule out diabetes and PCOS
- Iron deficiency

At-home methods to predict ovulation

There are three types of at-home methods useful for predicting ovulation:

- Basal body temperature (BBT) can be measured at home using a special thermometer (to help predict the most fertile days in a woman's monthly menstrual cycle when ovulation occurs. Normal BBT is 35.5–37.7 °C. BBT (taken before getting out of bed) decreases just before ovulation and rises at ovulation, remaining elevated for up to three days. If the cycle is charted for 3–4 months, a pattern can be recognized and intercourse can be timed accordingly. Though sperm have been shown to remain functional in the female genital tract up to five days, the most fertile period is 48 hours prior to ovulation. This method is not 100% reliable, but it is simple and inexpensive.
- Self-examination of vaginal discharge is another method to predict ovulation, but is also more subject to error. Prior to ovulation, the mucus is stretchy, clear, thin, and slippery, a necessary environment

for the survival and transport of sperm. When mucus can be stretched between the thumb and index finger into a thin strand 5–7.5 cm long, ovulation is about to occur and a woman is entering her most fertile period. If a thin layer is placed on a glass slide, a fern-like appearance is present during ovulation. Post ovulation, no fern-like appearance will be present because the mucus becomes too thick and less conducive to sperm survival.

- Ovulation predictor kits are the most accurate method. The test detects an increased level of LH present in an early morning urine sample 1–2 days before ovulation.

Additional tests

A number of other tests can be done to help determine the cause of infertility in women, including the following:

- **Chlamydia test** – If the woman is found to have chlamydia, which can affect fertility, she will be prescribed antibiotics to treat it.

- **Pelvic ultrasound** – High-frequency sound waves create an image of an organ in the body, which in this case is the woman's uterus, fallopian tubes, and ovaries.

- **Laparoscopy** – A thin, flexible tube with a camera at the end is inserted into the abdomen and pelvis to look at the fallopian tubes, uterus, and ovaries, and to detect endometriosis, scarring, blockages, and some irregularities of the uterus and fallopian tubes.

- **Ovarian reserve testing** – This testing is done to find out how effective the eggs are after ovulation.

- **Genetic testing** – This testing is done to find out whether a genetic abnormality is interfering with the woman's fertility.

- **Hysterosalpingography** – Fluid is injected into the woman's uterus, which shows up in X-ray pictures. X-rays are taken to determine whether the fluid travels properly out of the uterus and into the fallopian tubes. If the doctor identifies any problems, such as a blockage, surgery may need to be performed.

- **25-hydroxy vitamin D status** – Due to the influence on infertility and the increasing number of people who have vitamin D deficiency, it would be beneficial to have testing done.

Testing and Diagnosis for Men

A general physical exam involves taking a medical history, including infections (STDs), medications, sexual habits, and examination of the genitals to rule out any abnormalities such as varicocele.

A number of tests can be done to help determine the cause of infertility in men, including the following:

- **Semen analysis** – This test involves analyzing a sperm sample in a lab for sperm concentration, motility, colour, quality, and infections. Since sperm counts can fluctuate, the man may have to produce more samples.

- **Blood tests** – Blood tests can aid in determining causes of infertility, including tests for thyroid (TSH) and bioavailable and free testosterone, which may be more accurate than total testosterone.

- **Saliva hormone test** – This test measures estradiol (E2), progesterone, testosterone (T), DHEA, and cortisol.

- **Ultrasound test** – This test identifies whether there is any ejaculatory duct obstruction, retrograde ejaculation, or other abnormality.

- **Chlamydia test** – Chlamydia affects fertility, and if positive then antibiotics will be prescribed to treat it.

- **25-hydroxy vitamin D status** – Due to the influence on infertility and the increasing number of people who have vitamin D deficiency, it would be beneficial to have testing done.

what we know works

Support for Infertility in Men and Women

AdrenaSense® contains adaptogenic herbs and is a base for both men and women with infertility problems. Adaptogens help regulate the HPA-axis and prevent the negative effects of stress hormones on the production of hormones needed for fertility. Ashwagandha *(Withania somnifera)* is an ingredient in AdrenaSense. Studies show that it can treat stress-related infertility. Men who took ashwagandha had increased testosterone, less stress, and improved overall sperm quality, and by the end of a three-month trial, 14% of their partners had conceived.

Dosage: 1 capsule twice daily with food or as directed by a health care practitioner.

Saw Palmetto Plus for Women® is proven to be beneficial in cases of androgen excess. PCOS is a common cause of infertility in women, saw palmetto works as an alpha reductase inhibitor, blocking the conversion of testosterone into too much DHT, the more potent form of testosterone.

Dosage: 2 160-mg capsules daily.

EstroSense® helps maintain healthy hormone levels by targeting estrogen metabolism. It may be helpful for women who are experiencing irregular menstruation, no menstruation, PMS, or heavy periods. It may also be beneficial for men who are experiencing an imbalance of estrogen to testosterone where they are converting more testosterone to estrogen.

Dosage: 3 capsules daily.

Omega-3 (EPA and DHA) are directly correlated with improved sperm motility, concentration, and structure. The rate of successful pregnancies in previously infertile couples increased by 40% when the level of omega-3 fatty acids was increased. For women, albeit after pregnancy, studies show that omega-3 FA during pregnancy lowers the risk of premature birth, and taken during breastfeeding may facilitate the child's brain development. There is also some evidence that omega-3 FA can prevent preeclampsia and postpartum depression.

Dosage: 1500–3000 mg daily of combined EPA and DHA.

Vitamin D is positively correlated with sperm motility and normal structure. One study found men had vitamin D levels below 20 ng/mL, while optimal levels are 50 ng/mL. A receptor molecule for vitamin D was detected on the surface of sperm in all tissues of the male reproductive tract. Vitamin D deficiency reduces the ability of male lab animals to deposit sperm in female reproductive tracts, and the rate of successful pregnancies in females who received sperm from D-deficient males was decreased by 73%. Vitamin D is also an emerging factor influencing female fertility and IVF outcome.

Dosage: 2000 IU daily, though 5000 IU is safe and may be needed to achieve optimal vitamin D levels.

Ultimate Maca Energy® *(Lepidium meyenii)* has some of the same properties of adaptogen herbs and works to balance hormones in both men and women. It is rich in amino acids, iodine, iron, and magnesium. Traditionally, Maca root has been used for its fertility and libido-enhancing properties. Studies have shown improvements in seminal volume, sperm count, and sperm motility.

Maca also increases energy and may be useful for supporting the body's stress response and healthy adrenal function.

Dosage: 2–4 capsules daily.

....

Additional support for female infertility

Folic acid is an essential vitamin in pregnancy for the prevention of neural tube defects. Studies have shown that infertile women are deficient in this vitamin. Supplementation with folic acid has been known to reverse infertility.

Dosage: 1 mg daily.

Chasteberry *(Vitex agnus castus)* is a progesterone agonist, which can help minimize the risk of miscarriage. Although it does not contain progesterone, it affects the pituitary gland in such a way that it regulates the secretion of progesterone from the ovaries thereby stimulating ovulation. Vitex is also helpful in correcting hormone deficiency of either estrogen or progesterone and in PCOS-related infertility.

Dosage: 400–1000 mg daily.

Iron deficiency or borderline low iron may result in women having difficulty conceiving.

Dosage: 15–20 mg daily of iron bisglycinate.

Ultimate Probiotic® balances the microflora of the vagina. Changes in these microflora have been linked to reproductive failure and adverse pregnancy outcomes such as preterm labour, miscarriage, and spontaneous preterm birth.

Dosage: 1–2 capsules.

Additional support for male infertility

Zinc picolinate increases sperm counts, mobility and fertilizing capacity. Zinc deficiency is associated with poor sperm quality and the reduced volume of semen produced. Studies show an increase of 74% in total normal sperm count in previously sub-fertile men taking 66 mg daily of zinc, particularly when folic acid (5000 mcg daily) is added to the supplementation.

Dosage: 60 mg daily.

L-carnitine is a vital transporter molecule whose function is to carry high-energy fat compounds into mitochondria, where they are "burned" to release their energy. This helps give sperm the boost they need if they are going to have a chance at fertilizing an egg. When men were treated with carnitine, 22–31% of their partners achieved pregnancy. The pregnancy rates in the control groups were 1.7–3.8%.

Dosage: 2000–3000 mg daily.

Vitamin C improves sperm count and motility, and in combination with vitamin E improved pregnancy rate by 100%. Vitamin E enhances sperm binding to egg, and improved pregnancy rate by 21%.

Dosage: 1000 mg daily, 500 IU *d*-alpha-tocopherol.

N-acetyl-L-cysteine (NAC) is a modified amino acid with potent direct antioxidant effects that also boosts the natural cellular antioxidant glutathione. NAC has been shown improve sperm volume and motility. A dosage of 600 mg daily improved both volume and motility.

Dosage: 600 mg daily.

Diet and Lifestyle Factors for Infertility in Men and Women

Alcohol

According to some experts, even moderate consumption (1–2 glasses of wine per week) can increase prolactin levels and suppress ovulation. The elevation of prolactin also occurs with the usage of antidepressants and analgesics. Men apparently tolerate more alcohol without effect on fertility, but excessive alcohol conception can lead to poor sperm motility and activity, and can result in premature ejaculation.

Tobacco

Nicotine appears toxic to sperm, and thus smoking can interfere with fertility. This may also pose problems for women although the exact link is unknown. Female smokers generally have decreased estrogen levels, poor cervical mucus, a higher risk of pelvic infection, and an increased incidence of ectopic pregnancy and miscarriage.

Gluten and wheat intolerance

As mentioned previously, gluten intolerance can affect fertility in both men and women. The incidence of gluten intolerance or celiac disease is higher in women experiencing unexplained infertility than among the general population. Gluten intolerance is not only related to unexplained infertility, but also to recurrent miscarriage, and intolerance to gluten contributes to nutrient malabsorption.

Refined sugars and insulin intolerance

There is a strong connection between insulin resistance and infertility, even when there is no PCOS. Too much insulin in the blood promotes insulin growth factor, which causes cysts and fibroids to grow. Elevated insulin levels can also contribute to abnormalities in the HPA axis, which affects hormone levels. Insulin resistance is caused by eating too many sugars and carbohydrates, and not getting enough healthy nutrition – especially omega-3 fats – to balance it out. A low-glycemic diet that limits the consumption of refined sugars can improve fertility and pregnancy outcomes in many women. Sugar and refined carbohydrate consumption plays a particularly devastating role in PCOS, and women may see improvements in their fertility by increasing protein and restricting or eliminating simple, refined sugars.

Stress

Stress hormones in both men and women disrupt the HPA axis, causing imbalances in many of the reproductive hormones involved in fertility – such as diminished FSH and LH secretion, decreased progesterone and testosterone, and elevated or decreased estrogen. (Refer to *Chapter 3* for more information on stress.)

Chapter 11

Mood Disorders – Depression and Anxiety

Mood Disorders – An Overview

Depression and anxiety disorders are very common conditions and they are becoming more and more prevalent in people of all ages. One in five Canadians will experience a form of mental illness in their lifetime, with depression affecting up to 15% of people. However, a staggering 90% of people who are depressed never seek treatment. The World Health Organization lists depression as one of the leading causes of disability worldwide.

The most common anxiety disorders include obsessive control disorder (OCD), post-traumatic stress disorder (PTSD), social anxiety disorder, and general anxiety disorders (GAD). These are collectively the most common mental health disorders in North America, affecting about 40 million adults in a given year. The National Institute of Mental Health reports that by 2020, anxiety-related disorders will affect seven out of ten individuals in North America alone.

Sadly, those with the highest rate of depression are under 20 years of age, and those with the highest rate of anxiety symptoms are 20–29 years of age.

The Gut-Brain Axis: How the Microbiome Influences Anxiety and Depression

The human intestine harbours nearly 100 trillion bacteria that are essential for health. Based on recent discoveries, gut microbiota play a significant role in how the gut and brain communicate. They also influence the risk of disease and mental health disorders, including anxiety and depression. .

Stress influences the composition of the gut microbiota, and the gut microbiota affects the stress reactivity of the hypothalamic-pituitary-adrenal (HPA) axis. Stress-induced changes in the microbiota increase inflammation, contributing to depression, anxiety, dementias, and other mental health disorders. Stress hormones also known increase intestinal permeability, causing a leaky gut. This allows pathogens the opportunity to cross the gut barrier and directly affect immune cells and neurons of the gut-brain axis. A recent study has shown that pretreating rodents with the probiotic lactobacillus reduced the intestinal permeability typically resulting from stress and also prevented associated HPA hyper-reactivity.

Targeting microbiota and the gut-brain axis seems to have effective and safe therapeutic potential in mood and anxiety disorders. In general, people are looking for safe and effective treatments for their anxieties, tension, stress, and insomnia, and they are starting to turn to non-pharmaceuticals such as herbal products and other alternative remedies. Many safe options are available that can effectively treat people with depression, anxiety. Remember, it is most important to address an important underlying cause: the adrenal stress and stressors.

Brain Imbalances and Mood Disorders

Brain imbalances that cause anxiety and mood disorders such as depression are most often related to other factors that are seldom addressed in Western medicine. It is important to treat the cause of any condition. For example:

- Many people are diagnosed with depression when they really are not depressed – they are simply exhausted and do not have the energy for life. It is very common for people who are diagnosed with depression and anxiety to have adrenal fatigue and/or thyroid disorders. Chronic stress can cause adrenal fatigue, resulting in many symptoms similar to the classic depression diagnosis criteria. For example, low energy, sleep problems, mood swings, depression, anxiety, and weight loss or weight gain are common in people with adrenal fatigue. (Refer to *Chapter 3* for more information.)

- Symptoms of thyroid disorders include anxiety, emotional volatility, irritability, lack of focus and attention, depression, insomnia, changes in appetite, loss of interest and initiative, and poor memory. (Refer to *Chapter 4* for more information).

- Gut problems such as microbiota imbalance can also cause symptoms of depression. Evidence shows that bowel disorders are often correlated with poor mood. Almost one-third of patients with IBS have been found to have anxiety or depression.

- Inflammation is the cause of depression in many people. Major life stressors, especially those involving interpersonal stress and social rejection, and even people's mere perceptions of some of these stressors, are among the strongest proximal risk factors for depression. These stressors increase pro-inflammatory cytokines, which are involved in inflammation. Cytokines are associated with treatment-resistant depression and tend to decrease the function of serotonin. In one study, treatment-resistant patients taking antidepressants were supplemented with aspirin, an anti-inflammatory agent. More than 50% of the patients responded to this combined treatment, and at the end of the study more than 80% of the group responsive to the anti-inflammatory agent went into remission. Canadian researchers found that a protein known to be a marker of inflammation was up to one-third higher in the brains of depressed patients compared to healthy ones. Those with the most severe forms of depression also had the most inflammation.

- Depression is commonly present in patients with coronary heart disease (CHD) and is independently associated with increased cardiovascular morbidity and mortality.

- Vitamin D deficiency has been repeatedly observed in conditions involving inflammation, such as cardiovascular disease, diabetes, anxiety, and depression. New research shows that low serum levels of vitamin D are associated with clinically significant symptoms of depression in otherwise healthy individuals.

- Sugar consumption has been linked to depression, anxiety, suicide, irritability, anger outbursts, anxiety, fatigue, and lethargy. Sugar is a "mood-altering drug".

- Other causes of mood disorders include environmental toxins and heavy metals, hormonal imbalances, and food allergies or intolerances. Add this to the fact that other forms of stress also cause inflammation, it starts to look as if depression and anxiety are a kind of allergy to modern life – which might explain their ever-increasing prevalence all over the world as we systemically eat and stress ourselves into a state of chronic inflammation.

Gender Differences in Mood Disorders

Women are up to 40% more likely than men to develop mental health conditions, according to new analysis by a clinical psychologist at Oxford University. Women are approximately 75% more likely than men to report having recently suffered from depression, and around 60% more likely to report an anxiety disorder. Doctors need to be aware of these gender disparities.

Women outnumber men in each anxiety disorder category, except for OCD and social phobia, for which both sexes have an equal likelihood of being affected. GAD affects about twice as many women as men.

Depression

Signs and Symptoms of Depression

It is normal to feel down or out of sorts some of the time. However, it can become debilitating when depressive episodes last months, or sometimes years, and interfere with all aspects of life, such as social interactions and work functioning. According to the Diagnostic and Statistical Manual of Mental Disorders (DSM-5), to be considered depressed, you need to have at least five of the following symptoms:

- Depressed mood most of the day, nearly every day
- Markedly diminished interest or pleasure in all, or almost all activities
- Significant weight loss when not dieting or weight gain, or decrease or increase in appetite
- Insomnia or sleeping too much nearly every day
- Psychomotor agitation (unintentional motion caused from muscle tension)
- Fatigue or loss of energy almost daily
- Feeling of worthlessness, or excessive or inappropriate guilt
- Diminished ability to think or concentrate or indecisiveness
- Recurrent thoughts of death, suicidal thoughts or attempt

Possible Causes of Depression

One thing the conventional medical community agrees on, at least for the most part, is that neurotransmitters have an influence on mental health disorders and behaviour. It is also widely accepted that depression is influenced by genetic, environmental, developmental, and biochemical factors. However, what is not agreed upon is the role of nutrients like vitamins and minerals.

Neurotransmitter problems, in some cases, have a genetic component that involves absorption, metabolism, or storage of key nutrients, and some people benefit from medications. However, for many people, medications have too many negative side effects and/or they are ineffective. Moreover, the underlying cause of the mental health problem still remains. Nutrient therapy, diet, and lifestyle, along with addressing any other factors such as microbiota imbalances in the gut, food allergies, inflammation, and blood sugar imbalances, can be very potent and effective treatments for many people with brain disorders, without the risk of side effects.

The Pfeiffer Treatment Center has amassed a large database of biochemical information from more than 10,000 patients with mental health problems. Examination of this data shows that most of these persons have striking abnormalities in specific nutrients required for neurotransmitter production. Supplements that contain amino acids are converted to specific neurotransmitters that can alleviate symptoms of many mental health disorders. More recent scientific evidence has shown that nutritional supplementation has proven beneficial in helping to control symptoms of major depression, bipolar disorder, schizophrenia, anxiety disorders, eating disorders, attention deficit disorder/attention deficit hyperactivity disorder (ADD/ADHD), addiction, and autism.

> Whether you "fit" the depression diagnosis is not the most important thing. If you are feeling so down that you feel you need to do something about it, then that is the most important factor.

Support for Depression

"Hey, you know, breakdowns come and breakdowns go. So what are you going to do about it? That's what I'd like to know."– **Paul Simon, Gumboots**

The good news is that there are many things people can do through dietary changes, natural supplementation for inflammation, and adrenal support, as well as stress reduction techniques in order to prevent the inflammatory cascade.

The first step is a proper medical diagnosis that includes an outline of all the possible treatment options available to the individual. The final decision on whether or not to try nutritional supplements as a treatment must be the decision of the patient. New clinical studies are being published daily on the positive effects of nutritional and supplement therapies on all types of disorders and diseases. It may take time for health care practitioners to become educated and aware of the options available, however this option should not be ignored. Several natural supplements have proven effective in the treatment of mild-to-moderate depression.

what we know works

Support for Depression

MoodSense™ contains saffron, 5-hydroxytryptophan (5-HTP), vitamin B6, lavender, and magnesium. Refer below for more information on individual ingredients.

Dosage: 2 tablets 3 times daily.

Saffron *(Crocus sativus)* has been shown to be an effective natural antidepressant in several clinical trials. One study compared the effects of saffron with fluoxetine (generic form of Prozac). Both treatments resulted in significant improvements in depression symptoms and severity, with no difference in the amount of improvement between the two groups. Saffron's antidepressant properties seem to be related to serotonin metabolism. In another study, saffron was compared to the tricyclic antidepressant imipramine. The effects were found comparable in the treatment of mild-to-moderate depression without the common side effects of imipramine such as dry mouth and sedation.

5-HTP is a building block for serotonin and it also increases endorphin levels (the feel-good brain chemicals). Depression and anxiety have been linked to serotonin imbalances in the brain. Numerous studies have shown that 5-HTP is as effective as SSRIs and tricyclic antidepressants, with fewer side effects.

Vitamin B6 (pyridoxal 5-phosphate) is required as a coenzyme for the biosynthesis of several neurotransmitters, including gamma-aminobutyric acid (GABA), dopamine, norepinephrine, and serotonin. Vitamin B6 concentrations in the brain are about 100 times higher than levels in the blood, so it is not surprising that vitamin B6 deficiency has neurological effects including depression, insomnia, and mental confusion.

Lavender *(Lavandula angustifolia)* has neuroprotective properties and is an effective mood stabilizer, anxiolytic, and sedative. Clinical trials show that lavender is effective in the treatment of depressive symptoms, anxiety disorder, and generalized anxiety disorder, as well as restlessness, agitation, and disturbed sleep. It also has a beneficial influence on general well-being and quality of life.

Magnesium (glycinate) deficiency is very common today due to nutrient depletion of the soils. Magnesium has been shown to be effective in the treatment of nervous system disorders such as anxiety, insomnia, and depression.

CalmBiotic™ contains *Bifidobacterium longum* and *Lactobacillus helveticus*, which help balance gut microflora and reduce stress and dysbiosis. Stress and dysbiosis are associated with a number of brain disorders and symptoms, including mood swings, anxiety, depression, cognitive and learning disorders, and insomnia. Gut bacteria communicate with and influence brain function.

Dosage: 1 capsule daily.

It is important to address the inflammation factor in depression and the following supplements have proven helpful in preventing and treating inflammation.

GISense™ contains boswellia, bacopa, ashwagandha, curcumin, and chamomile to support the inflammatory and stress components of depression. (Refer to *Chapter 3* for more information on stress.)

Dosage: 2 capsules twice daily.

Omega-3 fatty acids found in fish oils and flax oils decrease the elevation of pro-inflammatory compounds known as cytokines, which are common in anxiety and depression. Mood disorders appear to be linked to lower levels of omega-3 fatty acids. Psychological stress can also cause an elevation of these cytokines. Studies suggest that the anti-inflammatory role of omega-3 fatty acids may influence brain-derived neurotrophic factor (BDNF) in depression. BDNF has been found to be negatively correlated with the severity of depressive symptoms.

Dosage: 1000–3000 mg daily.

St. John's wort *(Hypericum perforatum)* has been used in traditional medicine for centuries to treat a wide range of disorders and is licensed in Germany to treat anxiety, depression, and sleep disorders. It has proven to be as effective as standard antidepressants in many clinical trials for the treatment of mild-to-moderate depression. It also has fewer side effects.

Dosage: 300 mg 1–3 times daily, standardized to 0.3% hypericin.

Note: If you are taking an SSRI (serotonin reuptake inhibitor), do not take saffron or St. John's wort. You can safely take GISense to support the inflammatory aspect of depression.

Medication

Antidepressant medications are effective in severe cases and should be considered as first-line therapy in those patients who have severe forms of depression.

Anxiety Disorders

Signs and Symptoms of Anxiety Disorders

Although each anxiety disorder has different symptoms, all of the symptoms cluster around excessive, irrational fear and dread that compromise a person's life to one degree or another. General symptoms of anxiety include excessive worry about little things, increased startle reflex, fear of crowds, jumpiness, impaired concentration, ongoing irrational thoughts, restless sleep or insomnia, muscle tension, and irritability or edginess. Panic attacks include symptoms such as palpitations, pounding or rapid heart rate, sweating and body temperature changes, trembling, shortness of breath, chest pain and discomfort, nausea or digestive distress, dizziness and light-headedness, and fear of losing control or "going crazy".

Possible Causes of Anxiety Disorders

Like many other mental health conditions, anxiety disorders seem to be a result of a combination of biological, psychological, genetic, and other individual factors. The neurotransmitters (chemical messengers) in the brain involved in anxiety include serotonin, norepinephrine (NE), and GABA. In many cases, these neurotransmitter imbalances are caused by acute or chronic stress. Certain medical conditions, such as stress-induced adrenal fatigue, anemia, and thyroid problems, can also cause symptoms of anxiety.

Stress hormones and anxiety disorders

Along with glucocorticoids, the adrenal glands secrete another class of hormones called catecholamines. NE and epinephrine (E) are the main catecholamines often associated with the fight-or-flight response in acute stress. NE can increase heart rate and blood pressure, as well as create a sense of overwhelming fear. Most anxiety symptoms are due to elevated NE levels. The fight-or-flight response is a chemical reaction to a real or perceived life-threatening situation. Excess amounts of NE and E are produced, which provide extra strength and energy needed to run or to fight in survival situations. However, when these hormones become elevated during normal activity, they cause anxiety, and sudden increases cause full-blown panic attacks. In addition, cortisol and other stress hormones increase the permeability of the blood-brain barrier, a protective barrier that prevents toxic substances from entering the brain. As a result of the increased permeability, more chemicals and toxins can enter the brain, many of which are excitotoxins that cause overstimulation of the brain and anxiety.

what we know works

Support for Anxiety Disorders

In addition to stress support, other herbs and vitamins have been found to be effective in the treatment of anxiety.

AdrenaSense® contains most of the important adaptogenic herbs that help regulate stress hormones. Treat the cause, support the adrenal glands. Ashwagandha, an ingredient in AdrenaSense, reduces levels of cortisol, which becomes elevated in stressful conditions, and improves overall well-being. In an animal study assessing the anti-anxiety and anti-depressive actions of ashwagandha compared to commonly prescribed pharmaceuticals such as lorazepam for anxiety, both the ashwagandha group and the lorazepam group demonstrated reduced brain levels of a marker of clinical anxiety. (Refer to *Chapter 3* for more information on stress and the adrenals.)

Dosage: 1 capsule twice daily with food or as directed by a health care practitioner.

L-theanine has been shown to stimulate the brain's alpha waves, a state often related to meditation, suggesting that it has the ability to put users into a more relaxed mood. It also reduces beta waves, which are associated with hyperactivity, nervousness, and scattered mind chatter. Studies have shown that L-theanine reduces stress, helps with sleep, and increases mental alertness.

Dosage: 100–200 mg 1–3 times daily.

Kava kava *(Piper methysticum)* has been used for centuries by many cultures to relieve anxiety, restlessness, and insomnia. Kava has anti-anxiety effects without sedative or mentally impairing side effects commonly caused by benzodiazepines or antidepressants. Kava can be used for those people tapering off of benzodiazepines.

Dosage: 250 mg 1–2 times daily of an extract standardized to 30% kavalactones.

GABA is the most important inhibitory neurotransmitter in the brain. It acts like a brake in times of increased stress, eliciting a sense of calm. Low levels of GABA have been linked to anxiety, depression, and insomnia. GABA increases the production of alpha brainwaves characterized with being relaxed. It also increases mental focus and alertness and reduces beta waves associated with nervousness and hyperactivity. In addition, GABA has been shown to produce relaxation by reducing stress markers such as heart rate, cortisol levels, and pupil diameter.

Dosage: 100–200 mg 2–3 times daily. As a general guideline, it is recommended to take no more than 3000 mg within a 24-hour period.

••

Additional support for anxiety disorders

MagSense™ (magnesium bisglycinate) is an easy-to-take powder and provides an ideal dose in an efficiently absorbed and well-tolerated form of magnesium. MagSense also includes other important minerals, vitamins, and nutrients that are involved in the biochemical reactions and metabolism in the body. All of these are essential factors in the body and work with magnesium to promote optimal functioning of the heart, nerves, muscles, and other systems throughout the body. Magnesium has been found to be effective for the treatment of depression and anxiety, insomnia, short-term memory loss, irritability, agitation, and headaches.

Dosage: 1 scoop (18 mL) daily.

CalmBiotic™ contains *Bifidobacterium longum* and *Lactobacillus helveticus*. Studies shows these bacteria have a marked effect on GABA levels, lowering the stress-induced cortisol and resulting in reduced levels of anxiety and depressive behaviour.

Dosage: 1 capsule daily.

L-lysine and L-arginine combination effectively reduces anxiety scores with no reported side effects, as indicated in randomized controlled studies. Amino acid supplements may also help in balancing cortisol levels triggered by stress in both healthy individuals and those with high anxiety. It has long been postulated that the dysregulation of neurotransmitters, specifically GABA, serotonin, dopamine, and NE, may be a cause for anxiety. Recent studies show that L-lysine and L-arginine seem to influence the neurotransmitters involved in stress and anxiety. L-lysine has also been shown to decrease blood cortisol levels.

Dosage: 2500 mg daily of each.

Passionflower *(Passiflora incarata)* is known as a "calming" herb for anxiety or nervousness, insomnia, generalized anxiety disorder, and ADHD. Recent studies found passionflower to be comparable to benzodiazepine drugs such as lorazepam in the treatment of anxiety and insomnia, and it causes less drowsiness.

Dosage: 200–400 mg daily.

Echinacea *(Echinacea angustifolia)* is an effective herbal treatment for anxiety when administered at low dosages. Researchers found that some of the plants contain cannabinoid receptors, which are components affecting brain chemistry. Cannabinoid receptors are known to influence the way the brain experiences anxiety, and only *E. angustifolia* has high levels of beneficial compounds showing anti-anxiety effects. After one day of use, the participants with anxiety disorder experienced a significant reduction in anxiety and a 25% reduction by day seven. However, anxiety relief with echinacea occurs only at low dosages, and disappears when the dosage is greatly increased. It can be taken before a stressful event, such as public speaking, a presentation, or air travel.

Dosage: no more than 20 mg at a time, several times a day if necessary.

Diet and Lifestyle Tips for Mood Disorders

For many people, medications for mood disorders have too many negative side effects and/or they are ineffective. Moreover, the underlying cause of the mental health problem still remains. Nutrient therapy, diet, and lifestyle, along with addressing any other factors such as microbiota imbalances, food allergies, inflammation, and blood sugar imbalances, can be a very potent and effective treatment for many people with mood disorders, without the risk of side effects.

During the past decade, a mountain of evidence has been building indicating that dietary patterns are strongly correlated with risk for depression. The first-ever randomized controlled clinical trial to test a dietary intervention as a treatment for clinical depression was published in February 2017. In the SMILES Study (Supporting Modification of Lifestyle in Lower Emotional States), researchers recruited several hundred patients with moderate to severe depression and entered 67 into a 12-week parallel group trial. The treatment group received seven 60-minute sessions of dietary counselling. In these sessions, participants were asked to increase consumption of certain foods including whole grains, fruits, vegetables, nuts and legumes, lean meats, chicken, and seafood. Foods that correlated with a higher risk of depression were eliminated, including empty carbohydrates, refined starches, and highly processed foods. The researchers developed a dietary pattern called the Modified Mediterranean Diet, or the Modi-Medi Diet. The outcome was positively significant. In the treatment group, about 32% of patients achieved remission, compared with 8% in the control group. In terms of risk-benefit profiles, a dietary intervention is emerging as a very safe and effective way to treat depression.

Refer to *Chapter 19* for more information on optimal health guidelines, including the Mediterranean diet, other nutritional tips, and the spiritual side of optimal health.

THE ROLE OF BERRIES

Participants in a recent study (36 healthy adults, 18–35 years of age) consumed a 250 mL (9 oz) drink that was a placebo, an anthocyanin-rich drink made from berries, or a cold-pressed juice made from New Zealand blackcurrants. They then conducted a set of demanding mental performance assessments. The results showed that attention and mood were improved in the groups consuming the anthocyanin-rich drink and the blackcurrant drink, and mental fatigue was reduced. In addition, blood tests showed that the activity of the monoamine oxidase enzymes (MAOs) was strongly decreased. MAOs regulate serotonin and dopamine concentrations in the brain. These chemicals are known to affect mood and cognition, and are the focus for treatments of both the neurodegenerative symptoms associated with Parkinson's disease and mood disorders. This study strongly supports the potential for antioxidant compounds found in blackcurrants and other berries to support optimal health.

Chapter 12

Sleep Disorders

Insomnia

According to Statistics Canada, one in seven Canadians have insomnia, the inability to fall asleep, stay asleep, or experience restorative sleep. The World Association of Sleep Medicine states that sleep problems, including insomnia, sleep apnea, restless legs syndrome, and sleep deprivation in general, affect up to 45% of the world's population. It claims that 60% of Canadian adults feel tired most of the time and get, on average, 6.9 hours of sleep a night, despite the fact that experts recommend eight hours. Canadian research indicates that 30% of adults get fewer than six hours of sleep a night. Chronic sleep deprivation can contribute to obesity, diabetes, high blood pressure, heart attack, stroke, depression, decreased immunity, and inflammatory and other medical conditions.

Insomnia is one of the most common sleep disorders seen in medical practice, and treatment of this condition is challenging and often unsatisfactory for the patient. Severe insomnia is defined as the difficulty initiating or maintaining sleep at least three times a week for one month or longer, with the problem being bad enough to cause fatigue or impaired functioning during the day. Insomnia has always been and still is under-recognized. It is an under-treated problem since about 60% of the people suffering from insomnia never talk to their health care practitioners about their sleeping difficulties.

Gender Differences in Insomnia

Most but not all evidence suggests a female predisposition for insomnia. The trend of female predisposition is consistent and progressive across age, with more significance in the elderly. Distinct hormonal and physical changes at specific time in a woman's life, such as puberty, pregnancy, and menopause, can impact sleep health. Sleep disorders such as restless leg syndrome and obstructive sleep apnea are also more prevalent during these times. The insomnia risk generally emerges with the onset of menses, contributing to the gender differences.

Possible Causes of Insomnia

There are many possible causes of insomnia including the following:

- **Psychological conditions** – Sleep disturbance is a common feature of emotional disorders. For example, 90% of depressed people have insomnia. However, insomnia is also a major risk factor for depression. It is often unclear which condition triggers the other.

- **Gut-brain inflammation** – Anxiety and depression are common causes of insomnia, and new research shows a direct link between gut microbiota and mental health disorders such as anxiety and depression.

- **Alcohol** – An estimated 10–15% of chronic insomnia cases result from substance abuse, especially alcohol, cocaine, and sedatives. For most people, one or two drinks a day pose no problem and may even help initiate sleep.

- **Medical conditions** – Several conditions contribute to or cause insomnia, including chronic pain (e.g., arthritis, back pain), cardiovascular disease, respiratory diseases, gastrointestinal disorders, hormone conditions, and some neurological conditions. In one survey, 22% of adults reported that health conditions, pain, or discomfort impaired their sleep.

- **Medications** – Several medications cause insomnia. If your insomnia seems to be associated with when you started taking a medication, talk to your health care practitioner.

- **Nightly leg problems** – Leg disorders that occur at night, such as restless leg syndrome or leg cramps, are very common and are an important cause of insomnia.

- **Shift work** – Shift work throws off the body's circadian rhythm and may lead to chronic insomnia.

- **Blood sugar imbalances** – Blood sugar imbalances are a common – though less recognized – cause of insomnia. Adrenal compromised individuals commonly have blood sugar problems ranging from hypoglycemia (low blood sugar) to hyperglycemia (high blood sugar). Low blood sugar at night results in restless sleep, bizarre dreams, and poor sleep quality for the entire night. One of the mechanisms the body will call on to liberate more glucose is to increase cortisol and adrenaline, which will convert stored fats and carbohydrates into sugars for immediate use. The increase in blood sugar sends more sugar to the brain, causing a restless, light sleep during the night. Coffee and alcohol exacerbate the problem, while eating a small protein meal before bed can help regulate blood sugar levels.

- **Menopause** – Another type of insomnia very commonly seen is sleep disturbances as a result of the menopausal transition. Some women wake up due to hot flashes at night, sometimes followed by episodes of chilling. For others, insomnia is independent of hot flashes. Once hormones are regulated, sleeping problems will improve for most women.

- **Sleep apnea** – It is important to rule out sleep apnea in anyone suffering with insomnia. This disorder results in brief interruptions of breathing during sleep. Some individuals will experience snoring in-between these pauses, while others will describe a choking sensation. People with sleep apnea experience periods of anoxia (oxygen deprivation of the brain) with each episode. The most common treatment of sleep apnea is the continuous positive airway pressure (CPAP) machine. Testing is often done through a referral to a sleep clinic through your health care practitioner.

The stress-sleep connection

Stressful life events are closely associated with the onset of chronic insomnia. Stress plays a leading role in the hypothalamic-pituitary-adrenal (HPA) axis dysregulation and the associated increase in cortisol and norepinephrine (NE) play a primary role in some sleep disorders. In other cases, the HPA axis dysfunction is actually the result of a sleep disorder, as seen in obstructive sleep apnea.

The effect of sleep disorders on cortisol levels

The daily rhythm of cortisol secretion is influenced by the circadian clock. Sleep, particularly deep sleep, has an inhibitory effect on cortisol secretion, while sleep disruptions are accompanied by cortisol stimulation. Consistent research shows an elevation in cortisol levels following even partial sleep loss. After only one night of sleep restricted to four hours, plasma cortisol levels were 37% higher the following day. Even if sleep deprivation is modest, it causes a profound disruption in the daily cortisol rhythm, resulting in activation of the HPA axis, associated with sleep disturbances.

In the not too distant past, it was thought that sleep loss had no ill-health effects, apart from daytime sleepiness. More recent research has overturned this belief and has shown that sleep loss (less than seven hours per night) may have wide-ranging effects on the cardiovascular, endocrine, immune, and nervous systems. Some of the common conditions potentially caused by sleep problems include obesity in adults and children, chronic pain symptoms, diabetes and glucose intolerance, cardiovascular disease, hypertension, cognitive impairments, anxiety, and depression.

> Elevated cortisol due to stress and HPA dysregulation is a main cause of chronic insomnia. Insomnia worsens HPA dysregulation and increases cortisol, resulting in a vicious cycle that is difficult to control.

The effect of cortisol levels on sleep disorders

The main stress hormone cortisol has a natural rhythm – normally peaking between 6 am and 8 am. Then, between 8 am and 11 am, cortisol levels begin to drop and gradually decline throughout the day, reaching the lowest point about 2 am. The cyclical rise and fall of cortisol levels govern our level of wakefulness throughout the day and night. Cortisol is excitatory; it arouses us and wakes us up which is great in the morning. But, when cortisol levels get stuck at higher levels as a result of prolonged stress, it is bad news for a good night's sleep.

Stress is associated with the activation of the HPA axis, causing increased cortisol, and resulting in arousal and sleeplessness. Studies have shown that cortisol levels are significantly higher in insomniacs compared to normal sleepers. So we know that stress-induced dysfunction of the HPA axis and elevated cortisol play a significant role in sleep disorders, but in other cases, the HPA axis dysfunction may be a result of a sleep disorder. Which came first? Or does it matter? Either way, it is a vicious cycle for people suffering from chronic insomnia.

Other brain chemicals and hormones affecting chronic insomnia

Abnormal levels of certain brain chemicals have been observed in some people with chronic insomnia.

The cortisol-melatonin relationship

In adults, melatonin onset typically occurs during low cortisol secretion, which under normal circumstances would be at night. However, as mentioned previously, chronic stress causes an increase in cortisol in the evening, resulting in decreased secretion of melatonin, one of the body's sleep hormones. Also, with aging, the production of melatonin declines and is shifted to later hours, while the production of cortisol increases and its peak occurs earlier in the night. Perhaps this is where the mistaken belief that older people need less sleep comes from. It is not that the elderly need less sleep, it is simply that aging can cause dysregulation in cortisol and melatonin secretions.

> Unless you have experienced cycles of chronic insomnia, it is very difficult to understand just how utterly devastating it is!

Cortisol and gamma-aminobutyric acid (GABA)

GABA is synthesized in the brain and cortisol has a dual action on the GABA receptors. Lower levels of cortisol enhance concentrations of GABA, while higher levels of cortisol inhibit GABA. As is the most important inhibitory neurotransmitter in the brain, GABA acts like a "brake" during times of runaway stress. Decreased GABA function in the brain is associated with several neurological disorders, including anxiety, depression, insomnia, and epilepsy.

Thyroid disorders

It is common knowledge that hyperthyroidism (excess of thyroid hormone) is strongly associated with insomnia. The excess thyroid hormone causes anxiety, fast heart rate, and hyper-arousal of the nervous system. One study showed that after only six days of four-hour sleep time, thyroid-stimulating hormone (TSH) levels were strikingly decreased, and overall mean TSH levels were reduced by more than 30%. Therefore, if you have long-term chronic insomnia and have never been tested for thyroid problems, you might want to consider it. (Refer to *Chapter 4* for more information on thyroid disorders and thyroid testing.)

The mental-emotional-physical cycle

In addition to the sleep deprivation/HPA/cortisol cycle, many people experience emotional responses to chronic insomnia. The resulting cycle becomes even more self-perpetuating. The emotional response added to the physical cause (i.e., dysregulation of the HPA axis, chronic pain) is called psychophysiological insomnia. This occurs as follows:

- An episode of transient insomnia disrupts the person's circadian rhythm.

- The person begins to associate the bed not with rest and relaxation, but with a struggle to sleep, causing added stress. From here a deeper pattern of sleep failure emerges.

- Over time, this event repeats, and bedtime becomes a source of anxiety. The person is stressed about the inability to sleep, the consequences of sleep loss, the lack of mental control, and the overall debilitating effects. All attempts to sleep fail.

- Eventually excessive worry about sleep loss becomes persistent and provides an automatic nightly trigger for anxiety and arousal, and insomnia becomes self-perpetuating, lasting indefinitely.

what we know works

Support for Insomnia

AdrenaSense® provides stress reduction support to help prevent the overproduction of stress hormones that can keep you wired even though you are exhausted from lack of sleep. An effective way to manage sleep problems due to cortisol dysregulation is to ensure the adrenal glands are supported by proper nutrition. Adrenal regulation is necessary in order to stop the vicious cycle of stress and insomnia. Stress is a very real factor for many people with insomnia. Insomniacs and those who feel "tired but wired" should take most supplements – including adrenal support – in the morning. (Refer to *Chapter 3* for more information on stress and stress support.)

Dosage: 1 capsule twice daily with food or as directed by a health care practitioner.

SomniSense™ contains the important herbs passion flower, California poppy, hawthorn, skullcap, and linden flower to help ensure a good night's sleep. Refer below for more information about individual ingredients.

Dosage: 2–4 capsules daily 1 hour before bed.

Passion flower *(Passiflora incarnate)* has been used traditionally for anxiety disorders, general nervousness, attention deficit hyperactivity disorder (ADHD), and insomnia. Several controlled studies have demonstrated enhanced sleep benefits for adults with insomnia.

California poppy *(Eschscholzia californica)* is used to treat insomnia, mood disorders, and nervous agitation, and to promote relaxation. It is also effective for pain relief, specifically nerve pain.

Hawthorn *(Crataegus oxyacantha)* has been used traditionally as a cardiovascular tonic. New research indicates that hawthorn has antioxidant properties and is effective in treating stress-related disorders such as nervousness and anxiety that are often the underlying cause of insomnia. This herb is usually used in combination with other herbs in the treatment of insomnia.

Linden flowers *(Tillia cordata)* have traditionally been used to soothe nerves and to treat conditions associated with stress, including anxiety and insomnia.

Skullcap *(Scutellaria lateriflora)* has been used for centuries as a relaxant and as a therapy for anxiety, nervous tension, and insomnia. Studies show that American skullcap has significant antioxidant effects, and may help protect against disorders such as Alzheimer's disease, anxiety, and depression.

Melatonin helps maintain the body's circadian rhythm, an internal 24-hour clock that plays a critical role when we fall asleep and when we wake up. The body produces more melatonin when it is dark and less when it is light. Being exposed to bright lights too late in the evening can disrupt melatonin production. Older people typically exhibit poor sleep due to reduced melatonin levels. A double-blind placebo-controlled study examined the effects of melatonin in doses ranging from 1–3 mg in subjects over 50 years of age. Both doses improved sleep.

Dosage: start with 1–2 mg at bedtime and if necessary increase up to 5 mg.

Valerian *(Valeriana officinalis)* has been proven beneficial for sleep disorders, especially those associated with stress and anxiety. In a double-blind comparison study involving patients 18–73 years of age diagnosed with insomnia, two groups were treated with either 600 mg daily of valerian extract or 10 mg daily of oxazepam (benzodiazepine). Sleep quality after six weeks in those taking valerian extract was at least as effective as the oxazepam treatment. Both treatments markedly increased sleep quality compared with baseline. Adverse events occurred in 28.4% receiving valerian extract and 36.0% taking oxazepam, and were all rated mild to moderate. No serious adverse drug reactions were reported in either group. Most patients assessed their respective treatment as very good (82.8% in the valerian group, 73.4% in the oxazepam group).

Dosage: 400–700 mg daily of a solid root extract 1 hour before bed.

Pharma GABA™ contains GABA, the most important inhibitory neurotransmitter in the brain. It acts like a brake in times of increased stress, eliciting a sense of calm. Low levels of GABA have been linked to anxiety, depression, and insomnia. GABA increases the production of alpha brainwaves characterized by being relaxed, as well as greater mental focus and alertness. It also reduces beta waves associated with nervousness and hyperactivity. In addition, it has been shown to produce relaxation by reducing stress markers such as heart rate, cortisol levels, and pupil diameter.

Dosage: 100–200 mg 2–3 times daily. As a general guideline, it is recommended to take no more than 3000 mg within a 24-hour period.

Additional support for insomnia

Magnesium has been found to be effective for treating depression and anxiety, insomnia, short-term memory loss, irritability, and agitation. People suffering from headaches also benefit from magnesium supplementation.

Dosage: 200–400 mg daily for capsules. MagSense™ is a source of magnesium bisglycinate: 6–12 mL of powder daily.

5-hydroxytryptophan (5-HTP) may prove to be better than melatonin at treating insomnia. Several clinical studies have shown 5-HTP to produce good results in promoting and maintaining sleep in normal subjects as well as those experiencing insomnia. In many cases, insomnia has been associated with tryptophan deficiency in the tissues of the brain. Tryptophan is the precursor to 5-HTP, which is converted into serotonin and then into melatonin.

Dosage: 100–300 mg daily.

Medication

There is a time and a place for every medical philosophy. Sometimes pharmaceuticals are not only necessary, but lifesaving. This will depend on the individual. Once the sleep cycle begins to improve, it is time to try natural sleep remedies. Begin by taking less of the prescription medication along with a natural product. If prescription medications prove to be necessary, it is important to support the adrenal glands and address any accompanying anxiety with the supplements mentioned above. The underlying causes need to be addressed despite the medications providing relief from symptoms. Improvements in the adrenals can take months for some, depending on the level of ongoing stress.

Diet and Lifestyle Tips for Insomnia

Most people who have chronic insomnia have tried all of the "sleep tips" and will get frustrated and tired of hearing the most basic and logical of suggestions. For those who suffer from occasional insomnia, some of the following tips may be helpful:

- Cut out stimulants by avoiding caffeinated beverages (coffee, chocolate, tea, soft drinks) past noon.

- Do not exercise in the evening as this can cause cortisol levels to increase in people with adrenal fatigue.

> **Remember:**
> you are the most important item on your "to do" list.

- Do not eat a large meal late in the evening (after 7 pm). Try to avoid snacking after dinner.

- Keep your fluid intake high during the day and less at night to avoid having to get up in the night to urinate.

- Take a hot bath before bed (unless it aggravates hot flashes if you are a menopausal woman). Add calming essential oils such as lavender and chamomile.

- Take time for meditation, contemplation, or prayer before you retire.

In this stressful world, it is often hard to find time for yourself. When there is a window, the "brain chatter" often takes over with reminders of all the things on the "to do" list. Everyone has something that they find both physically and mentally calming, the inner quiet time where the brain is quiet and the body is more relaxed. Whether it is a walk in nature, yoga, meditation, being mesmerized by watching water, climbing a mountain, or listening to relaxing music, just do it! If you have a full schedule, make an appointment with yourself that you cannot cancel.

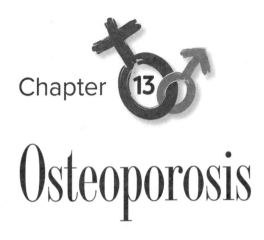

Chapter 13

Osteoporosis

Bones – An Overview

When we look at the skeleton in the chiropractor's office we might be led to think that bones are dead matter and do not count for much. Bones, however, are a living substance and one of the most active tissues in the body. They offer support for all the other body structures, as well as protect delicate structures such as the brain, spinal cord, lungs, heart, and major blood vessels. They are also the levers to which the muscles of the body are attached – without them the muscles would not be able to move us around. Finally, they are critical in blood cell production.

Despite their importance, it is often forgotten that the bones are more than just a collection of calcium crystals that simply require more calcium to remain healthy. In reality, bone is a composite: 30% of bone mass consists of osteoid, living tissue made up of connective tissue and proteins; 70% of bone is made of minerals; and 95% of the minerals are made up of mineral salts, primarily calcium phosphate and calcium carbonate called hydroxyapatite, along with small amounts of magnesium, sodium, potassium, chloride, and fluoride.

As complex structures, bones need complex nutritional support to stay strong and healthy. Bones also becomes stronger as a result of mechanical stress and other stresses involving the effects of gravity such as weight-bearing exercise, walking, and standing.

Bone Growth

Bones grow in length and density until the late teens after which time the bones increase in density, but at a slower state. At approximately 30 years of age, bones reach what is referred to as "peak mass", which means they stop forming density and natural bone loss occurs at rate of approximately 0.3–1% per year. Bone loss occurs at the same rate in both men and women until menopause, when bone loss in women will be 2–6 times faster.

Bone is constantly being broken down and rebuilt every year after peak mass. Osteoclasts are the bone cells responsible for breaking down old bone. They detect slightly damaged and older bone, and slowly dissolve it, leaving behind an empty space. Enter the osteoblasts, which build new bone to fill the space. When the osteoclast and osteoblast activity is balanced, bone mass remains stable. Bone loss occurs when there is increased osteoclast activity or decreased osteoblast activity. The result of increased bone loss is osteoporosis.

The Missing Link – Collagen

Bone strength depends not only on the quantity of bone tissue, but also on the quality. This is determined by the shape and architecture of bones, the turn-over rate between osteoblasts and osteoclasts, mineral content, and collagen.

The bone matrix is a system that involves two parts: a mineral phase (calcium and other minerals) that provides the stiffness, and the collagen fibres that provide the toughness and ability to absorb energy. The mineral portion (mainly calcium) comprises of 70% of the bone matrix, and collagen makes up 30%. This combination of collagen and calcium makes bone both flexible and strong, which in turn helps bone to withstand stress. Variations in collagen production or a deficiency in collagen can therefore affect the strength and mechanical properties of bone, and increase fracture risk.

Another important role collagen plays in the bone matrix is driving calcium into the bones. Each collagen fibre contains "calcium-binding sites", whereby the more collagen there is in the bone, the more calcium is absorbed. This provides a stronger framework and more bone toughness to withstand fractures.

Osteoporosis

Osteoporosis is a degenerative disease in which the bones become porous and easily broken. When bone is broken down faster than it can be rebuilt, this leads to increased bone fragility and risk of fractures, particularly the hip, spine, and wrist. It is one of the most debilitating and costly illnesses that may confront us as we age.

Fractures from osteoporosis are more common than heart attack, stroke, and breast cancer combined, and osteoporotic hip fractures consume more hospital bed days than stroke, diabetes, or heart attack. What is also alarming is that less than 20% of fracture patients in Canada currently undergo diagnosis or adequate treatment for osteoporosis.

Gender Differences in Osteoporosis

Osteoporosis is generally thought of as a "woman's disease" because the prevalence of osteoporosis and the rate of fractures are much higher in post-menopausal women than in older men. For example, one in four Canadian women and one in eight men over the age of 50 will be diagnosed with osteoporosis, and at least one in three women and one in five men will suffer from an osteoporotic fracture during their lifetime. Nationally, an estimated 13–18% of women and 1–4% of men age 50 and older have osteoporosis.

Although osteoporosis is more common in postmenopausal women, older men still suffer poor health outcomes related to osteoporosis and fractures. Additionally, a lower proportion of men at high risk of fracture are treated when compared to women at high risk. Men also tend to have worse outcomes after fracture than women – they are twice as likely to die after hip fracture than women.

Signs and Symptoms of Osteoporosis

Osteoporosis is referred to as a "silent disease" because often there are no signs or symptoms. However, some early warning signs that can indicate decreased bone density include:

- Chronic back pain; deep bone aches
- Oral bone loss – studies show a relationship between oral bone loss, tooth loss, and an increased risk for osteoporosis
- Extreme fatigue
- Loss of height – height normally decreases by approximately 4 cm every 10 years after menopause; if your height appears to be declining more quickly, you may have osteoporosis
- Kyphosis (dowager's hump)

- Night cramps in the legs and feet
- Poor nail growth or brittle nails
- Compression or stress fractures

Possible Causes of Osteoporosis

Osteoporosis is influenced by genetics, endocrine function, diet, and lifestyle, and environmental factors. Osteoporosis prevention and treatment therefore requires a fully integrated approach that addresses all possible contributing factors.

In addition to diet and lifestyle influences on optimal bone mass, there are several additional factors that can predispose a person to developing osteoporosis. Risk factors for osteoporosis include the following:

- Amenorrhea (lack of menses)
- Small bones and/or low peak bone mass
- Caucasian or Asian heritage
- Family history of osteoporosis
- Hyperthyroidism (overactive thyroid) or excess thyroid medication
- Hyperparathyroidism (overactive parathyroid)
- Complete hysterectomy or early menopause
- Sedentary lifestyle
- Anorexia or bulimia
- Age – postmenopause in particular
- Intestinal disorders (e.g., Crohn's disease, celiac disease)
- Heavy alcohol or tobacco use
- Excessive coffee or soft drink intake
- Medications such as long-term corticosteroid use (e.g., prednisone), acid-blocking drugs called proton pump inhibitors (PPIs), chemotherapeutic agents, diuretics, or antidepressant medications called SSRIs (selective serotonin reuptake inhibitors)
- Stress

No risk factor alone or in combination will accurately predict who will experience osteoporotic fracture. As a general rule, the more risk factors present, the greater the potential for osteoporosis.

Stress and bone metabolism

Throughout this book you have read how the hormone cortisol is secreted from the adrenal glands during periods of high stress. High levels of cortisol inhibit the cells that form bone (osteoblasts). This dramatically decreases bone-building capacity and lowers bone density. High cortisol also increases collagen breakdown, and collagen is an important component for strong and flexible bones as well as for reducing fracture risks. As long as the body remains under elevated stress levels, without adequate rest and repair, bone mineralization and collagenous formation will be reduced.

As an example, the use of corticosteroids (such as prednisone), which mimics the action of cortisol, has the same effect on bone health. These drugs also decrease the amount of calcium that is absorbed from food and increase the amount of calcium lost in the urine. An increased production of cortisol is also very acidic and corrosive to our bones, forcing the body to leach vital bone-building minerals from the bone to buffer the acidity in the blood, and thus excreting those minerals in the urine.

Testing and Diagnosis

Bone Densitometry Scan (DEXA) measures bone mineral density (BMD). DEXA is considered the "gold standard" because it exposes a person to considerably less radiation than other X-ray procedures. In the DEXA scan, measurements of both the hip and lumbar spine are taken. A baseline at 50 years of age should be encouraged, with re-tests done every 2–4 years. If any of the above risk factors apply, especially tobacco use, chemotherapy for breast cancer, amenorrhea (no period), prolonged Depo-Provera injections, menopause before age 45, or a history of fractures, DEXA scans are recommended earlier.

Limitations of BMD

BMD is a wonderful way to increase the awareness of early signs of bone loss and establish a diagnosis of osteoporosis. However, it is not a complete measure of bone health because it does not measure bone quality, only bone quantity. A bone's resistance to fracture is heavily dependent on its flexibility or "toughness" (its ability to bend rather than break). BMD testing is more an indication of the hardness or "stiffness" of bone and does not measure bone toughness, which is heavily dependent on adequate collagen formation in bone.

Bone density is not the only risk factor that contributes to future fractures. In fact, osteoporosis accounts for only about 15–30% of all hip fractures in postmenopausal women. Another important risk factor for hip fractures is an increased risk of falling due to poor balance and lack of muscle strength.

Bones markers – a better predictor of bone health?

Measuring enzymes and proteins released during bone formation and measuring degradation compounds produced during bone resorption can gauge bone health and how the disease (osteoporosis) has affected you. These "bone marker" tests are useful for monitoring bone loss and success (or failure) of treatment. Some of these tests include:

- Osteocalcin – a marker of bone formation
- Urinary N-telopeptide of type I collagen – a marker of bone resorption, or loss of bone
- Vitamin D – a deficiency of vitamin D may indicate your body is not absorbing calcium optimally

what we know works

Support for Bone Health

AdrenaSense® is one of the foundations of healthy bone metabolism and the prevention of osteoporosis and bone loss.

Dosage: 2–3 capsules daily (2 with breakfast and 1 midday).

BioSil™ is a highly bioavailable form of silicon. During bone growth and the early phases of bone calcification, silicon has an essential role in the formation of the cross-links between collagen. Remember that bone is actually made up of 30% collagen. The collagen in bone also helps accumulate more calcium deposition through its calcium-binding sites. Therefore, increasing collagen increases calcium and makes for strong bones. Accumulating evidence over the last 30 years strongly suggest that dietary silicon is beneficial to bone and connective tissue health, and there are strong positive associations between dietary silicon intake and BMD.

Dosage: 1 capsule daily or mix 6 drops in water or juice daily.

MagSense™ (magnesium bisglycinate) is an easy-to-take powder and provides an ideal dose in an efficiently absorbed and well-tolerated form of magnesium. MagSense also includes other important minerals, vitamins, and nutrients that are involved in the biochemical reactions and metabolism in the body. When it comes to strong bones, magnesium supplementation may turn out to be as important if not more important than calcium supplementation. Magnesium regulates the parathyroid hormone and is necessary for the absorption of vitamin D. It is also involved in bone mineralization, with magnesium deficiency leading to the cessation of bone growth, decreased osteoblastic and osteoclastic activity, osteopenia (early bone loss), and bone fragility.

Dosage: 1–2 scoops daily.

Calcium is a key component for the prevention of osteoporosis as well as for the maintenance of good bone health. However, remember that calcium alone may only have a slight protective effect for bone health, and that a combination of the key bone builders discussed below is fundamental in any healthy bone program. The requirements for calcium increase as women age because of reduced intestinal calcium absorption, due to low stomach acid. The most absorbable forms are often chelates that are bound to citrate, fumarate, or malate. It is also important to outline dietary calcium before deciding on how much calcium is needed in supplement form. Check out the calcium content of foods that you are consuming on a daily basis before taking large amounts of calcium supplements. You may be getting enough from diet alone.

Dosage: 500–1000 mg daily in divided doses.

Note: Calcium supplements should be taken at a different time during the day than thyroid supplements or thyroid medications and iron.

Vitamin D is well known for its role in building strong bones and teeth, as it promotes calcium absorption and utilization in the body. Vitamin D deficiency is quite common among women with osteoporosis. Vitamin D has proven to be useful for the reduction of fractures and the maintenance of bone health. A meta-analysis of five double-blind trials (including a total of 9,292 individuals at least 60 years of age) found that supplementation with 700–800 IU daily of vitamin D reduced the incidence of hip fractures by 26%.

Dosage: 2000–5000 IU daily.

Vitamin K2 is important for the maintenance of healthy bones. It is required for the production of osteocalcin, a protein found in large amounts in bone. Osteocalcin attracts calcium to bone tissue, enabling calcium crystal formation to occur and thus supporting bone mineralization. Vitamin K2 is an important component of bone formation and remodelling. Many studies have found that vitamin K2 levels are significantly lower in those patients diagnosed with osteoporosis, and that decreased vitamin K2 intake is associated with an increased incidence in hip fractures in both men and women.

MK7 (a specialized form of vitamin K2) has been found to be more potent, more bioavailable, and have a longer half-life than MK4.

Dosage: 100 mcg daily.

Kate Rhéaume, ND

"The long overlooked vitamin K2 is a key missing piece to the puzzle of bone health. It guides calcium into bones while making sure the mineral doesn't end up lining arteries. If you are taking vitamin D or calcium for bone health or any reason, vitamin K2 is critically important."

Kate Rhéaume is the author of *Vitamin K2 and the Calcium Paradox.*

Boron has been found in research studies to reduce urinary excretion of calcium by 44%. It can also reduce urinary magnesium excretion and increase serum 17 beta-estradiol and testosterone levels.

Dosage: 3 mg daily.

Additional support for osteoporosis

Ipriflavone is a synthetic flavonoid derived from the soy isoflavone, daidzein. It has been shown to slow down osteoclastic activity (bone breakdown) and increase bone-building activity. Research has found that treatment with ipriflavone for 1–2 years slowed bone loss in women during the first several years after the onset of menopause.

Dosage: 200 mg 3 times daily.

Note: Although rare, some women develop low white blood cell count while taking ipriflavone. Have your white blood cell count and lymphocytes checked before and every six months while taking ipriflavone.

Vitamin B12 helps protect collagen from the damaging effects of high homocysteine in the body. Bone formation markers (osteoblast activity) such as alkaline phosphatase and osteocalcin are dependent on vitamin B12 status.

Dosage: 1000 mcg daily.

Omega-3 fatty acids in the form of organic flaxseed or uncontaminated fish oil block the formation of PGE2, a messenger molecule that promotes inflammatory pathways in the body. Increased inflammation is associated with disrupting the acid/alkaline balance in the body and the destruction of collagen. Elevated levels of PGE2 also correlate with increased urinary calcium excretion from the body. Reducing urinary calcium excretion would help prevent osteoporosis and reduce the formation of kidney stones. Essential fatty acids also help increase absorption of calcium in the body.

Dosage: up to 35 mL of flaxseed oil daily and/or up to 3000 mg fish oil daily with a minimum of 800 mg EPA and 400 mg DHA.

Probiotics (e.g., *Lactobacillus acidophilus* and *Bifidobacterium* spp.) are known to have an important role in the maintenance of normal flora in the gastrointestinal tract. They are involved in the absorption and assimilation of important vitamins and minerals. A healthy digestive tract with adequate "good" bacteria will help maintain bone health by assimilation of crucial bone-building nutrients.

Dosage: at least 10 billion CFUs daily with food.

A word on bisphosphonates

The most widely prescribed medications for osteoporosis are bisphosphonates. These drugs include Alendronate (Fosomax), Risedronate (Actonel, Atelvia), Ibandronate (Boniva), and Zoledronic acid (Reclast, Zometa). Side effects include nausea, abdominal pain, difficulty swallowing, and the risk of an inflamed esophagus or esophageal ulcers. That is why it is very important that individuals taking oral bisphosphonates remain standing or seated upright for 45–60 minutes after taking the medication. Although rare, osteonecrosis of the jawbone can occur in some cases where a section of the jawbone dies and deteriorates. These medications reduce osteoclastic activity (bone breakdown) and increase mineralization of old bone tissue, which, in some cases, will actually cause bones to become more brittle. This risk for brittle bones may be associated with long-term use, and therefore bisphosphonate drugs are limited to five years at most.

Diet and Lifestyle Tips for Bone Health

The role of stomach acid

Something that many physicians do not address in regards to healthy bones is the digestive system's role in ensuring that adequate stomach acid is produced for vitamin and mineral (especially calcium) absorption.

As we age, our stomach acid and absorption capability decrease, making us very vulnerable to vitamin and mineral deficiencies. In fact, decreased stomach acid is seen in as many as 40% of postmenopausal women.

There is also an association between increased risk of hip fractures and long-term use of proton-pump-inhibiting, acid-blocking drugs (PPIs), such as Losec, Prevacid, Nexium, Pariet, and Panteloc. These PPI drugs rank as the third highest selling drug class in the United States and work by drastically reducing the amount of acid produced by the stomach, which unfortunately leads to a reduction of vitamin and mineral absorption.

Calcium supplements

When supplementing to increase calcium in the body and the bones, the form of calcium is critical. Avoid calcium carbonate, as it is the most difficult form to absorb. A common recommendation by many medical doctors is calcium in the form of the antacid medication such as TUMS. TUMS will actually slow down the absorption of calcium by blocking stomach acid and is therefore a very poor choice. Choose calcium citrate, fumarate, malate, or MCHC instead. Ossein Microcrystalline Hydroxyapatite Complex (MCHC) is a freeze-dried extract of bovine bone that retains the intact microcrystalline structure and micronutrient content of bone. It contains a unique calcium source that has been proven in over 30 years of clinical trials to be beneficial for bone building and maintenance.

If you choose to supplement with calcium, it is also important to include magnesium. Supplement with magnesium or eat foods rich in magnesium like kelp, millet, beet greens, Swiss chard, buckwheat, brown rice, walnuts, and kidney beans.

Dairy products

Milk and dairy products are often promoted as good for bone and for preventing osteoporosis because of their high-calcium content. However, the results from long-term studies may be surprising. These studies have shown conflicting results between milk consumption and strong, healthy bones. In other words, high-calcium intake from drinking milk does not actually appear to lower a person's risk for osteoporosis. For example, a large Harvard study of male health care practitioners and female nurses found that those individuals who drank one glass of milk (or less) per week were at no greater risk of breaking a hip or forearm than were those who drank two or more glasses per week. When researchers combined the data from the Harvard study with other large prospective studies, they still found no association between calcium and fracture risk. It was even suggested that calcium supplementation taken without vitamin D might increase the risk of hip fractures.

Calcium intake

An interesting trend exists around the globe with regards to calcium intake and fracture risk. Countries such as India, Japan, and Peru have an average daily calcium intake as low as 300 mg daily (less than a third of the US recommendation for adults), and the incidence of fractures in those countries is quite low. Other factors may come into play as well – such as physical activity and the amount of sunlight – but it is still indeed an interesting observation.

Another observation reported by many complementary health care practitioners is that their patients have allergies to casein, the milk protein. The chronic consumption of dairy can also cause intestinal inflammation, potentially leading to malabsorption and nutritional deficiencies that would negatively affect bone health. Luckily, there are plenty of non-dairy, calcium-rich foods, including:

- Greens (e.g., kale, collard greens, spinach, Swiss chard, turnip greens)
- Almonds
- Salmon and sardines
- Sesame seeds

- Navy beans
- Brazil nuts
- Seaweeds (e.g., kelp, nori, dulse)
- Goat's milk
- Tempeh (e.g., fermented tofu)

Studies have also shown that a diet high in animal protein may promote bone loss by causing calcium excretion through the urine. Certain animal proteins such as red meat and pork can acidify the blood, causing calcium and other minerals to be leached from the bones to buffer the acidity in the body. While meat is certainly not all bad, healthy protein sources should be encouraged, including chicken, turkey, fish, legumes, organic soy products, nuts and seeds, and eggs. Organic, hormone, and antibiotic-free lean animal meats should be eaten whenever possible.

Another offender in osteoporosis is the high phosphorus found in carbonated beverages such as soft drinks. Serum phosphates compete with calcium in the blood for cellular absorption.

Still other nutritional factors that speed up calcium loss from the bones and contribute to osteoporosis include the following:

- High salt
- Refined sugars
- Refined grains
- Excess alcohol

- Excess caffeine in coffee, black tea, and chocolate
- Smoking
- Dehydration (not enough water)

Exercise is not an option

When it comes to preventing osteoporosis, a regular exercise program is as important as a nutrient-dense diet and supplementation. Weight-bearing exercises stimulate osteoblasts (our bone builders) to deposit in stressed areas of the bone and increase the secretion of calcitonin, a thyroid hormone that inhibits osteoclasts (our bone breakers). An exercise program for bone building should include weight-bearing activities (jogging, walking, stair climbing, hiking) for at least 30–45 minutes 3–5 days a week, and strength-training activities (weight-training, yoga, or Pilates) at least three times per week.

MORE GENDER DIFFERENCES IN COMMON DISEASES

"Women are not just men with boobs and tubes. They have their own anatomy and physiology that deserves to be studied with the same intensity."

– Dr. Alyson McGregor, Associate Professor of Emergency Medicine, Brown University

Chapter 14

The Inflammation Factor in Osteoarthritis and Gastrointestinal Disorders

Inflammation – An Overview

Inflammation is a normal process of the human body. It is the first response of the immune system to infection, injury, or irritation from a foreign substance. Perhaps the most common type of inflammation is acute, the kind you experience when you burn your hand while cooking, sprain your ankle while playing a sport, or overuse your muscles while lifting heavy items. The body usually responds with redness, pain, swelling, and warmth in the area.

When the immune system is performing normally, inflammation helps initiate the healing process. The inflammatory process is mediated by the release of certain inflammatory mediators including histamine, prostaglandins, and cytokines such as C-reactive protein and interleukin-6 (IL-6), which cause redness, swelling, warmth, and pain. The purpose of the inflammatory response is to remove debris, attack foreign invaders, remove cellular waste, and encourage the healing process.

Chronic inflammation

Chronic inflammation is a pathological condition characterized by continued active inflammation and tissue destruction. The inflammatory process causes oxidative stress and reduces cellular antioxidant capacity. The free radicals generated then react with cell membrane fatty acids and proteins, impairing their function permanently. In addition, free radicals can lead to mutation and DNA damage that can be a predisposing factor for cancer and age-related disorders. Inflammation affects many body tissues, including blood vessels, organs, and nerves, with few or no obvious signs and symptoms until a serious health problem develops.

The body reveals increased levels of inflammation in various ways, including:

- Skin conditions (e.g., rashes, eczema, psoriasis, rosacea)
- Autoimmune conditions
- Cancers
- Cardiovascular disease
- Mental health disorders
- Chronic fatigue syndrome/fibromyalgia
- Inflammatory bowel diseases
- Arthritis

Stress Hormones and the Inflammatory Response

During periods of stress, the hormone cortisol is released as a coping mechanism. Cortisol has potent anti-inflammatory properties, which is particularly evident when it is administered pharmacologically as a drug (cortisone or prednisone) to treat inflammatory conditions such as arthritis, and as adjunctive therapy for conditions such as autoimmune diseases.

Cortisol blocks not only the initial inflammatory response, but also the later stages such as cellular proliferation resulting in chronic inflammation. In small quantities, cortisol is very useful and essential in tissue repair, and in controlling inflammation and excess immune cell production.

In chronic stress, elevated cortisol levels slow down the production of anti-inflammatory messengers, resulting in inflammation and immune suppression. Eventually, when cortisol levels are depleted due to chronic stress, adrenal fatigue will allow the immune system cells to circulate in excess. This leads to the immune system attacking itself, resulting in autoimmune diseases such as rheumatoid arthritis and lupus.

Osteoarthritis

The term arthritis ("arthro" meaning joint, "itis" meaning inflammation) is used to refer to more than 100 related conditions. The most common form of arthritis is osteoarthritis, which is also known as degenerative joint disease because it is characterized by joint degeneration and loss of cartilage, the shock-absorbing gel-like material between joints. One in five Canadians 15 years of age and older report having arthritis. It can strike anyone at any time, regardless of age, physical condition, or ethnic background.

Gender Differences in Osteoarthritis

Women face a higher risk of developing osteoarthritis than men based on biology, genetic predisposition, and hormones. Experts estimate that almost 40 million Americans have osteoarthritis and that about 60% of them are women. Before 45 years of age, more men tend to have osteoarthritis, but after age 45 the number of women with the condition far surpasses men. Joints affected by osteoarthritis also tend to vary by gender. Men are more prone to experience arthritis in their hips, while women tend to have it in the knees or hands. Because women's bodies are designed to give birth, the theory is that the tendons in their lower body are more elastic and mobile than men's. Also, because women's hips are wider than their knees, their knee joints are not aligned as straight as men's. The alignment of a women's body can lead to a higher rate of knee injuries, and injuries can lead to osteoarthritis later in life.

There also seems to be a strong genetic link of osteoarthritis among women. Women whose mothers developed osteoarthritis will probably find that they will develop it in the same joints at around the same age. Researchers have found that hand and knee osteoarthritis in particular have specific genetic links.

In addition, researchers believe that women's hormones have an effect on cartilage in various joints. Experts have found that the hormone estrogen protects cartilage from inflammation – and this inflammation can lead to osteoarthritis. Therefore, when women go through menopause and estrogen levels decrease, they lose that protection and may have a higher risk of developing osteoarthritis.

Signs and Symptoms of Osteoarthritis

Osteoarthritis usually causes the affected joints to become stiff in the morning, but the stiffness generally only lasts about 15–20 minutes. As the day progresses and joints are used, the pain and discomfort can get worse. Resting the joints tends to provide relief, but the joint may become inflamed with pain, warmth, and swelling. The pain and stiffness causes the joints to be used less often, and the muscles surrounding the joints weaken. Loss of flexibility and reduced range of motion can also occur.

As the cartilage wears down over time, the joints may slowly become bigger (bony) as the body tries to heal itself. With severe osteoarthritis, the cartilage may wear away entirely and the bones may rub together ("bone-on-bone"). When this happens, the joints can become extremely painful.

Possible Causes of Osteoarthritis

Factors that increase the risk of osteoarthritis include the following:
- Older age
- Genetic predisposition
- Fractures and mechanical damage
- Hormonal and sex factors
- Inflammation
- Obesity – carrying more body weight puts added stress on weight-bearing joints, such as the knees
- Other diseases – diabetes, low thyroid, gout, or Paget's disease can increase the risk of developing osteoarthritis

Testing and Diagnosis

During the physical exam, your health care practitioner will closely examine your affected joint, checking for tenderness, swelling, or redness, as well as checking the joint's range of motion. Your practitioner may also recommend imaging and lab tests.

Imaging tests

Pictures of the affected joint can be obtained during imaging tests such as the following:
- X-rays – Cartilage does not show up on X-ray images, but the loss of cartilage is revealed by a narrowing of the space between the bones in the joint. An X-ray may also show bone spurs around a joint. Many people have X-ray evidence of osteoarthritis before they experience any symptoms.

- Magnetic resonance imaging (MRI) – MRI uses radio waves and a strong magnetic field to produce detailed images of bone and soft tissues, including cartilage. This can be helpful in determining what exactly is causing the pain.

Lab tests

Analyzing blood or joint fluid can help pinpoint the diagnosis. Blood tests may help rule out other causes of joint pain, such as rheumatoid arthritis. Joint fluid analysis involves using a needle to draw fluid out of the affected joint. Examining and testing the fluid from the joint can determine if there is inflammation and if the pain is caused by gout or an infection.

what we know works

Support for Osteoarthritis

AdrenaSense® supports the adrenal glands and the stress response, which are key in all inflammatory diseases such as osteoarthritis, fibromyalgia, rheumatoid arthritis, and chronic fatigue syndrome.

Dosage: 1–3 capsules daily.

BioSil™ helps generate and preserve healthy collagen using the body's own DNA by stimulating collagen-producing cells (fibroblasts). Healthy joints are comprised of collagen-rich ligaments, tendons, and cartilage. Chronic inflammation results in the degradation of these important structures, and thus results in osteoarthritis, weakness, and painful joints. BioSil is a highly bioavailable form of silicon (choline-stabilized orthosilicic acid) that also helps promote proline, an important building block for collagen and healthy joints.

A recent double-blind, multi-centre, randomized, placebo-controlled study was conducted with 166 people with painful knee osteoarthritis. Participants scored a Grade 2 or 3 on the Kellgren-Lawrence Grading Scale for osteoarthritis (see below), and reported a pain score of moderate or moderately severe on a five-point Likert scale.

Dosage: 1 capsule twice daily or 5 drops twice daily.

Medi-C Plus™ contains vitamin C and lysine, which are key components for collagen synthesis and connective tissue repair. The Framingham Osteoarthritis Cohort Study concluded that a high intake of antioxidant nutrients, especially vitamin C, may reduce the risk of cartilage loss and disease progression with osteoarthritis.

Dosage: at least 1000 mg daily.

Note: 2000 mg of vitamin C and 1300 mg of lysine are found in 1 scoop of Medi-C Plus.

GISense™ contains the powerful anti-inflammatory herbs boswellia, chamomile, and curcumin, in addition to ashwagandha and bacopa, to support stress-induced inflammation. Inflammation is one of the main causes of osteoarthritis and the degeneration of joints throughout the body. Clinical studies using herbal formulas with boswellia have yielded good results in osteoarthritis of the knee, with patients experiencing decreased knee pain, decreased swelling, and increased knee flexion and walking distance.

Dosage: 3 capsules daily.

Omega-3s (EPA and DHA), the active constituents of fish oils, have anti-inflammatory effects. As a result, fish oil is used to help people with various inflammatory conditions. The EPA component holds especially potent anti-inflammatory properties useful for heart health and treating inflammatory conditions, while the DHA component is an important structural component of the brain, eyes, and nervous system.

Dosage: a minimum of 1000 mg EPA and 500 mg DHA daily. For extreme inflammatory conditions, 3000–5000 mg of EPA can be taken daily.

Vitamin D levels are associated with the progression of osteoarthritis. Specifically, several studies have shown that low serum levels of vitamin D appear to be associated with an increased risk for progression of osteoarthritis, especially in people under 60 years of age. Low serum levels of vitamin D also predict loss of cartilage as assessed by loss of joint space and increase in bony growths.

Dosage: 4000–8000 IU daily.

....

Additional support for osteoarthritis

Devil's claw *(Harpagophytum procumbens)* contains harpagosides, active compounds with potent anti-inflammatory, analgesic, and anti-arthritic actions. Devil's claw has been shown to significantly reduce the pain and stiffness associated with arthritis.

Dosage: 750–1000 mg 3 times daily standardized to contain 2.5% harpagosides.

Glucosamine, chondroitin, and methylsulfonylmethane (MSM) are all helpful in the treatment of inflammation. Glucosamine is produced naturally in the body to help maintain and build healthy joint tissue that seems to break down with the aging process. Chondroitin sulfate is vital to the structure and function of cartilage, providing it with shock absorption properties. MSM holds our basic connective tissues together, forming the elemental structure of proteins, and also has a powerful anti-inflammatory effect.

Dosage: glucosamine sulfate: 1500 mg; chondroitin sulfate: 1200 mg; MSM: 1000–4000 mg.

Serrapeptase *(Serratia peptidase)* is an enzyme derived from silk worms that may be beneficial in inflammatory conditions. Proteolytic enzymes digest protein and help the body break down immune and inflammatory complexes that cause many chronic inflammatory diseases.

Dosage: 90,000–120,000 IU 1–2 times daily between meals.

Hyaluronic acid (HA) provides a structural framework in joints and affects the ability of the cartilage to hold water. By 70 years of age, HA content has dropped by 80% in most people, predisposing them to a decrease in connective tissue integrity, especially in the skin and joints.

Dosage: 100–200 mg daily.

Diet and Lifestyle Tips for Osteoarthritis

Dietary changes are absolutely essential for reducing pain and chronic inflammation. Research has shown that foods rich in anti-inflammatory omega-3 fatty acids, such as wild salmon and other cold water fish, freshly ground flaxseeds, and walnuts may help reduce inflammation. Increasing antioxidant-rich foods may also reduce tissue and collagen damage from chronic inflammation.

Always include a rainbow of fresh, local, and preferably organic fruits and vegetables in your daily diet. Certain spices and herbs such as turmeric, ginger, rosemary, and hops contain naturally occurring compounds that also combat inflammation.

Avoid foods that actually cause inflammation and destroy collagen, including the following:

- Sugar – Refined carbohydrates rapidly increase your blood sugar, which in turn causes your body to create large amounts of insulin. This will often result in a pro-inflammatory response.

- **Red meat** – Too much red meat (i.e., eating red meat more than twice per week) will increase a pro-inflammatory fat called arachidonic acid. The human body needs some arachidonic acid, but too much can be toxic and can lead to chronic inflammation.

- **Hydrogenated oils** – These oils are found in many processed foods, and their effect is pretty obvious! Pastries, convenience foods, trans fats, margarines, and fried foods all promote inflammation.

- **Dairy** – Dairy is considered a common food allergy that can put more stress on the immune system, and increase the pro-inflammatory fat arachidonic acid.

- **Gluten** – Gluten is a common food allergen that can result in an immediate inflammatory response for many when it enters the body.

- **Coffee and alcohol** – Reduce consumption of both!

- **Vegetables from the nightshade family** – Some individuals experience increased inflammation from members of the nightshade family such as tomatoes, potatoes, peppers, and eggplant. For those individuals who are consuming any of the above in excess, consider reducing or eliminating these foods.

Irritable Bowel Syndrome

Irritable bowel syndrome (IBS) is the most common gastrointestinal disorder and represents 30–50% of all referrals to gastroenterologists. It is difficult to determine the exact frequency of IBS in populations, as many sufferers never seek medical attention. However, it has been estimated that approximately 15% of the population complains of IBS, with twice as many women as men experiencing symptoms.

Gender Differences in IBS

As mentioned above, statistics indicate that women suffer from IBS twice as often as men. Researchers have identified a number of reasons that could explain why females experience IBS more often than males, including anatomy, physiology, and the environment of women. Women's digestive systems seem to contain a larger amount of immune, nerve, and hormonal cells than the rest of the body, and therefore the gut is much more receptive. Women are more sensitive to symptoms, which results in signalling to the brain that there is an inflammatory response in the gastrointestinal (GI) tract.

Sex hormones, and in particular estrogen and progesterone, also influence IBS. Receptors for these hormones have been found on gastrointestinal cells, which suggests that the gastrointestinal tract is designed to sense and react to them. There is also evidence that such reactions do indeed occur. Women with and without IBS tend to experience systematic changes in gastrointestinal symptoms at the times in their menstrual cycle when the amounts of these hormones in the blood change the most. Symptoms such as stomach pain, diarrhea, nausea, and bloating are generally greatest during menses, when estrogen and progesterone drop down to the lowest levels in the body. Bloating is the only IBS-type symptom, which also seems to be worse during the second half of the cycle (the luteal phase) before the beginning of menses. Although GI symptoms related to the menstrual cycle are common in women in general, those who have IBS are significantly more likely to report an exacerbation of bowel symptoms during menses. Interestingly, women who have IBS-type symptoms also appear to experience worse menstrual symptoms, such as water retention and concentration difficulties, compared to other women.

It is unclear how changes in sex hormones cause GI symptoms to change, however balloon distention studies have shown that women who suffer from IBS are more sensitive to discomfort in the intestines during menses. This suggests that heightened pain sensitivity in the gut might play a role in the increase in symptoms due to these hormone changes. Epidemiological data also suggests that IBS in women becomes less common after menopause. It was found that the frequency of IBS decreases after 45 years of age in women, but remains unchanged in men. The decrease in IBS after menopause indicates again that sex hormone fluctuations play a part in producing the symptoms, because such fluctuations stop after menopause.

It is widely recognized that stress has a negative influence on IBS. The adrenal hormone cortisol is central to producing many of the physical effects that emotional stress causes in the body. Researchers report that cortisol is unusually high in women with IBS, although it is unclear whether the increase is the result of greater psychological stress levels of women with the disorder, or whether the higher hormone level is independent of mental stress.

Signs and Symptoms of IBS

Signs and symptoms of IBS are characterized by some combination of the following:

- Abdominal pain or distention (bloating)
- Altered bowel function, constipation, or diarrhea
- Hypersecretion of mucus in bowels
- Gas, belching, nausea, or loss of weight
- Varying degrees of anxiety or depression

Possible Causes of IBS

IBS is a functional disorder of digestion that is the result of interplay of gut inflammation (leaky gut), bacterial flora (dysbiosis), food allergies, and dietary factors (see below and *Chapter 2* for more detail).

Gut and inflammation – What is leaky gut?

For decades, alternative medical practitioners have referred to the unofficial diagnosis of "leaky gut syndrome" to describe a combination of poor digestion, microbiota imbalance, and inflammatory disease. However, Western medicine, at least in the past, has called the concept of abnormal intestinal permeability (leaky gut) unproven. While this is still fairly standard thinking in the majority of the conventional medical world, this opinion seems to fly in the face of medical research. Emerging information suggests leaky gut syndrome is indeed quite real and is a strong contributor to diseases such as diabetes, obesity, insulin resistance syndrome, gastrointestinal disorders, and mood disorders. (Refer to *Chapter 2* for more information on leaky gut.)

Many people with bloating, abdominal pain, constipation, or diarrhea are diagnosed with IBS but never get adequate responses to treatment. Others are given no diagnosis at all for their suffering, which leads to even less chance of recovery. Many of these people suffer from intestinal microbial overgrowth. In addition, the inflammation that is characteristic of Crohn's disease and ulcerative colitis – types of inflammatory bowel disease – are a result of dysregulated immune interactions and imbalances of candida and other intestinal bacterial overgrowth.

Food allergies

The importance of food allergies in IBS has been recognized since the early 1900s. Later studies have further documented these findings. According to a double-blind challenge, approximately two-thirds of patients with IBS have at least one food intolerance, and most have multiple intolerances. Foods rich in carbohydrates, as well as fatty food, coffee, alcohol, and hot spices, are most frequently reported to cause symptoms. The most common allergens are dairy products (40–44%) and grains (40–60%). Many people notice a marked improvement with the use of elimination diets. (Refer to *Chapter 2* for more information on gut supportive lifestyle and diet.)

Dietary FODMAPs

A group of short-chain carbohydrates are poorly absorbed in the small intestine and thus are likely to be fermented by intestinal bacteria, producing large amounts of gas that can cause abdominal bloating. These carbohydrates include fermented oligosaccharides, disaccharides, monosaccharides, and polyols (FODMAPs for short). Recent studies have identified these short-chain carbohydrates as important triggers of functional gut symptoms such as IBS.

Open studies have suggested that three out of four people with IBS will see decrease in symptoms when they restrict their intake of FODMAPs.

FODMAP diet

Try to avoid high FODMAP foods and focus primarily on the foods containing low FODMAPs. For a more detailed outline of a FODMAP diet, please see **ibsdiet.org**.

HIGH FODMAP			
VEGETABLES	**FRUIT**	**GRAINS**	**MILKS**
Garlic	Apples	Barley	Cow
Onions	Apricots	Bran	Goat
Asparagus	Avocado	Couscous	Sheep
Beans (e.g., black, broad, kidney	Blackberries	Granola	Soy (made from soy bean)
	Grapefruit	Rye	
Cauliflower	Mango	Semolina	Rice
Cabbage, savoy	Peaches	Spelt	**DAIRY**
Celery (less than 5 cm stalk)	Pears	All wheat products (e.g., cereals, pasta)	Buttermilk
	Plums		Cream
Mange tout	Raisins	**NUTS**	Custard
Mushrooms	Watermelon	Cashews	Greek yogourt

HIGH FODMAP cont.			
VEGETABLES	**FRUIT**	**NUTS**	**CHEESES**
Peas	Nectarines	Pistachios	Cream cheese
Scallions (white part)	Prunes		Ricotta
Artichoke	Cherries		

LOW FODMAP			
VEGETABLES	**FRUIT**	**GRAINS**	**MILKS**
Bamboo shoots	Bananas	Oats	Almond
Bean sprouts	Blueberries	Quinoa	Coconut
Green beans	Melon (e.g., honey-dew, cantaloupe)	Gluten-free products	Hemp
Celery (less than 5 cm stalk)			Oat
	Cranberries	Buckwheat	Lactose free
Chick peas (¼ cup max)	Clementines	Corn, popcorn	Soy
	Grapes	Rice (brown, white)	**CHEESES**
Corn (½ cob max)	Kiwifruit	**NUTS AND SEEDS**	Brie
Cucumber	Lemons	Almonds (max of 15)	Camembert
Eggplant	Oranges	Chestnuts	Camembert
Green peppers	Pineapples	Chia seeds	Cheddar
Kale	Raspberries	Hazelnuts	Cottage cheese
Lettuce (e.g., butter, iceberg, rocket)	Rhubarb	Macadamia nuts	Feta
	Strawberries	Peanuts	Mozzarella
Parsnip	Limes	Pecans (max of 15)	Parmesan
Potato	Passion fruit	Poppy seeds	Swiss
Pumpkin	Papaya	Pumpkin seeds	**DAIRY**
Red peppers		Sesame seeds	Butter
Scallions/spring onions (green part)		Sunflower seeds	Margarine
		Brazil nuts	Tofu
Squash		Walnuts	Tempeh
Sweet potato			
Tomatoes			

Small intestine bacterial overgrowth – SIBO

Sometimes the bacteria that are part of the normal flora in the large intestine are able to invade and set up shop in the small intestine. Because the bacteria do not belong in the small intestine, they can wreak havoc and cause many different symptoms, including the following:

- Flatulence and belching
- Bloating and gas
- Abdominal pain or cramps
- Constipation, diarrhea, or both
- Nausea
- Malabsorption
- Headache
- Fatigue
- Joint/muscle pain

IBS affects 20% of the population and SIBO is a common cause. In fact, it is involved in over half the cases of IBS. Eradication of this overgrowth leads to a 75% reduction in IBS symptoms.

Other conditions that can be associated with SIBO include hypothyroidism, lactose intolerance, gallstones, Crohn's disease, celiac disease, chronic pancreatitis, diverticulitis, diabetes, fibromyalgia and chronic regional pain syndrome, interstitial cystitis, restless leg syndrome, and acne rosacea.

Possible causes of SIBO include the following:

- Sometimes the ileocecal value (IC) is not functioning properly and allows a reflux of bacteria from the large intestine into the small intestine. The IC valve is between the large and small intestine.

- Bile and hydrochloric acid are bacteriostatic, so when the gallbladder, pancreas, or stomach enzymes are not adequate there is a greater risk of SIBO.

- Moderate and heavy drinking is associated with a greater risk of SIBO.

- The use of proton pump inhibitors encourages overgrowth.

Hydrogen/methane breath testing is the most widely used diagnostic method for this condition. Stool analysis is commonly used to diagnose dysbiosis/leaky gut, but has no value in diagnosing SIBO. Both tests are available from your health care practitioner. Because many of the symptoms of dysbiosis and SIBO are similar, lab testing can help with a more specific diagnosis.

Testing and Diagnosis

The diagnosis of IBS is often made by exclusion and after ruling out other conditions that can often mimic IBS. These conditions include:

- Infection caused by giardiasis, or other parasites and bacteria
- Intestinal candidiasis
- Disturbed bacterial microflora as a result of antibiotic or antacid usage
- Laxative abuse

- Lactose intolerance
- Inflammatory bowel disease (Crohn's disease and ulcerative colitis)
- Celiac disease
- Diverticular disease
- Cancer
- Fecal impaction
- Excessive consumption of coffee, tea, carbonated beverages, and simple sugars

what we know works

Support for IBS

ReliefBiotic™ contains probiotics, which appear to be a key component in a comprehensive approach to treating IBS. Each capsule contains the four unique clinically researched strains of probiotic: *Lactobacillus helveticus, Lactobacillus rhamnosus, Bacillus subtilis,* and *Enterococcus faecium.*

Dosage: 1 capsule daily.

GISense™ contains powerful anti-inflammatory herbs including boswellia, chamomile, and curcumin, in addition to ashwagandha and bacopa to support stress-induced inflammation. Inflammation is one of the main causes of IBS. Chamomile has anti-spasmodic properties and is known for its calming effect on smooth muscle tissue, making it an effective remedy for gastrointestinal spasms as well as GI tension resulting from stress.

Dosage: 3 capsules daily.

AdrenaSense® includes several adaptogenic herbs that have been studied extensively and have proven very effective during times of increased demands and stress. Stress is certainly an important factor to consider in treating IBS. Greater intestinal motility during exposure to stressful situations has been shown to occur in both normal subjects and people suffering from IBS.

Dosage: 2–3 capsules daily (2 with breakfast and 1 midday).

Treatment for SIBO

Step 1 – Using the Elemental Diet in place of all other food sources for 2–3 weeks has shown a success rate of 80–85% in the treatment of IBS and other gastrointestinal conditions. It is a powdered mix of free-form amino acids, fat, vitamins, and minerals, as well as rapidly absorbed carbohydrates. The concept behind this treatment is that the nutrients will be absorbed before reaching the bacterial organisms, thus feeding the patient but starving the flora. Elemental diets are not protein powders or typical detoxification formulas. The Elemental Diet puts the small intestine to sleep and helps put people out of their misery. It is also very important to address the dysbiosis in the large intestine in order to prevent relapse following the SIBO treatment in Step 1.

SIBOSense™ is an elemental diet that contains proteins in the form of amino acids, carbohydrates, fats, and oils as well as vitamins and minerals. It supplies complete nutritional support during the SIBO elimination program.

Step 2 – The next step in treating SIBO involves following a low carbohydrate diet, and using prokinetics, antimicrobials, and probiotics to reduce and balance the bacteria in both the small and large intestines.

Diet Plan – Once you have completed your Elemental Diet, you are ready to incorporate a diet plan. Bacteria use sugars and carbohydrates as their source of energy for fermentation and growth, so the goal is to reduce the food source for the bacteria. There are two diet plan options:

- **Option 1** – Those with chronic IBS, diagnosed SIBO, or more severe gastrointestinal symptoms should follow the FODMAP diet. This diet greatly reduces fermentable levels of carbohydrate-containing foods and has a success rate of 76% in IBS. The diet should be followed for a minimum of 4 weeks, but many practitioners recommend up to 3 months to prevent the relapse of SIBO.

- **Option 2** – The dysbiosis protocol outlined in *Chapter 2* can be used by those who have mild to moderate gastrointestinal symptoms. Follow this diet and program for at least 6–8 weeks. Most people today have some degree of microbial imbalance and would benefit from a dysbiosis program. Using the Elemental Diet for 3–5 days gives the digestive system a rest in preparation for the dysbiosis program and can provide additional benefit. If you start feeling better you may be inclined to continue for longer.

Prokinetics – A key underlying cause of SIBO is thought to be deficient activity of the migrating motor complex (MMC), or in simple terms, motility. The MMC moves debris and bacteria down into the large intestine during fasting at night and between meals, and prokinetics stimulate the MMC. Ginger *(Zingiber officinale)* has been used to treat a number of medical conditions, including GI disorders such as dyspepsia, flatulence, nausea, and abdominal pain. Studies have also reported that ginger enhances gastrointestinal motility, making it a useful prokinetic for the treatment of SIBO.

Dosage: 1-2 1000 mg capsules before meals.

Antibacterial herbs – The herbs listed below all have antimicrobial properties and could prove effective in in the treatment of SIBO. For those who would prefer not to use antibiotics, choose one of the herbs listed below and take it daily for 4–6 weeks.

Garlic *(Allium sativum)* is rich in allicin, which has antibacterial properties.

Dosage: 450 mg 2–3 times daily.

Berberine *(Berberis vulgaris)* is also a very effective antimicrobial and has recently been proven effective against group B streptococcus and antibiotic-resistant *Staphylococcus aureus* infections.

Dosage: 500 mg 2 times daily.

Peppermint oil has been used for centuries as a remedy for nausea, indigestion, abdominal bloating, and many other GI symptoms. Studies have also confirmed the benefit of peppermint oil for IBS, dyspepsia, and spasms of the gastrointestinal tract.

Dosage: 1–2 100 mg capsules 20 minutes before meals.

A breath test can be repeated to see if the natural antimicrobial was effective. If it was not, then antibiotics may be necessary.

Antibiotics – The most studied and successful prescription antibiotic for SIBO is rifaximin. It has a broad spectrum of activity and acts locally, and it is therefore less likely to cause systemic side effects common to other antibiotics. Rifaximin has up to a 91% success rate when prescribed at 550 mg 3 times daily for 14 days. Rifaximin purportedly does not cause yeast overgrowth and antibiotic resistance does not develop, making it effective for repeat treatments when necessary. Conventional medical treatment involves the use of the Elemental Diet as well as antibiotics.

Probiotics – Probiotics as well as yogourt and fermented vegetables have shown good results in people with SIBO. However, it is important to avoid the prebiotics that are added to some brands of probiotics because they are fermentable food for bacteria and can make symptoms worse. Common prebiotics found in probiotic supplements include FOS (fructooligosaccharide), inulin, AG (arabinogalactan), MOS (mannose-oligosaccharide), and GOS (galactooligosaccharide).

ReliefBiotic™ contains probiotics, which appear to be a key component in a comprehensive approach to treating IBS and other inflammatory gastrointestinal disorders.

Dosage: 1 capsule daily.

Diet and Lifestyle Tips for IBS

IBS represents a health condition caused by many interrelated factors and therefore the best approach is often to address the following:

- Increase dietary fibre
- Eliminate foods to which there is an allergy or intolerance (see above discussion regarding food allergies)
- Eliminate refined sugars
- Reduce dietary FODMAPs (see above)
- Treat dysbiosis (refer to *Chapter 2* for dietary recommendations)
- Address the psychological components, especially stress

If IBS is caused by SIBO, follow the treatment recommendations above.

Dietary fibre

An increase in dietary fibre has a long history of success with IBS. Increasing dietary fibre from fruits and vegetables rather than grain sources may offer more benefit to some individuals. Psyllium seed husks are a popular bulk-forming supportive for healthy bowel function, as well as guar gum, ground flax, chia, and hemp hearts.

Food allergies

As mentioned earlier, identifying possible food allergies is an important treatment strategy for IBS. The most common food allergies include dairy, wheat/gluten, eggs, corn, soy, citrus, and peanuts.

Stress management

Mental and emotional problems – anxiety, fatigue, depression, and sleep disturbances – are all reported by the vast majority of patients with IBS. Stress is certainly an important factor to consider. Greater intestinal motility during exposure to stressful situations has been shown to occur in people suffering from IBS. Stress management techniques such as psychotherapy, counselling, massage, deep breathing, meditation, acupuncture, and exercise are useful tools to help reduce symptom frequency and severity of IBS.

Celiac Disease

Celiac disease, also known as non-tropical sprue, gluten-sensitive enteropathy, or celiac sprue, is characterized by symptoms of varying severity. Symptoms range from very mild gastrointestinal discomfort to serious malabsorption (e.g., diarrhea, gas, abdominal bloating, and increased amounts of fat and undigested food particles in the stool). It is also characterized by abnormalities in small-intestine structure that revert to normal with removal of gluten, and more specifically its smaller derivative, gliadin, found primarily in wheat, barley, and rye grains. Symptoms most commonly appear during the first three years of life after gluten-containing foods are introduced into the diet. However, a second peak incidence occurs during early adulthood. While celiac disease used to be thought of as a disease diagnosed early in life, more diagnoses are being made in adulthood than in childhood.

Gender Differences in Celiac Disease

As with many other autoimmune diseases, celiac disease is more common in women, with a female to male ratio of 2:1–3:1. Some genetic loci are gender-influenced and immunoregulation is subject to hormones, which may explain these differences. By contrast, patients over 60 years of age who are diagnosed as having celiac disease are more frequently males.

Men and women who have celiac disease tend to show different symptoms. Women may have infertility or problems with their menstrual cycle as their first sign of celiac disease. They may also have thyroid disorders, weak bones, or anemia. In fact, women may actually not have any obvious digestive symptoms, such as diarrhea, abdominal pain, or bloating, or if they do have them, their digestive issues are not severe. Men, on the other hand, are more likely to have the "classic" celiac symptoms of diarrhea and weight loss when they are first diagnosed with the condition, but this may be because they are more likely to wait to see a doctor. Men with celiac disease are also more likely than women to be underweight, to have reflux, and to have the itchy gluten-caused rash called dermatitis herpetiformis (DH).

Signs and Symptoms of Celiac Disease

Most patients with celiac disease have gastrointestinal symptoms, though not necessarily the classical symptoms of diarrhea, constipation, abdominal pain and bloating, or weight loss. However, some patients do not have gastrointestinal symptoms, and in these "silent" cases the disease may not be detected until the patient presents with low iron, low vitamin B12, osteoporosis, or infertility.

Other symptoms/conditions that can be associated with celiac disease include:

- Chronic fatigue
- Headaches
- Anemia – iron or vitamin B12 deficiency
- Itchy, blistery skin rash (DH)
- Mouth ulcers
- Osteopenia/osteoporosis
- Nervous system injury, including numbness and tingling in the feet and hands, possible problems with balance, and cognitive impairment
- Joint pain

- Acid reflux and heartburn
- Neurological disorders
- Liver disease
- Infertility
- Arthritis
- Asthma
- Psoriasis
- Hair loss
- Chronic hives
- Erythema nodosum
- Lowered immune system
- Dental anomalies

Possible Causes of Celiac Disease

Celiac disease tends to be more common in people who have:

- A family member with celiac disease or DH
- Type 1 diabetes
- Down syndrome or Turner syndrome
- Autoimmune thyroid disease (Hashimoto's or Graves' disease)
- Microscopic colitis
- Addison's disease
- Rheumatoid arthritis
- SIBO

Celiac disease occurs from an interaction between genes, eating foods with gluten, and other environmental factors. Infant feeding practices, gastrointestinal infections, and gut bacteria may also all contribute to developing celiac disease. Sometimes celiac disease is triggered – or becomes active for the first time – after a stressful event such as surgery, childbirth or pregnancy, viral infection, or severe emotional stress.

When the body's immune system overreacts to gluten in food, the reaction that occurs damages the tiny, hair-like projections (villi) that line the small intestine. Villi absorb vitamins, minerals, and other nutrients from the food you eat. If your villi are damaged, you cannot get enough nutrients to fuel your body and prevent illness.

Testing and Diagnosis

The most reliable diagnostic test for celiac disease is the villous atrophy or small-intestine biopsy. Two different blood tests (IgA antiendomysial anti-bodies [EMA] and tissue transglutaminase antibodies [tTG]) are also used to diagnose or screen for the disease.

Combining antibody testing with specific genetic marker testing known as HLA-B8 and DRw3 that appear on the surface of cells may enhance the sensitivity of the testing. For example, the HLA-B8 marker has been found in 85–90% of celiac patients, as compared with 20–25% of normal patients.

what we know works

··

Support for Celiac Disease

ReliefBiotic™ contains probiotics, which appear to be a key component in a comprehensive approach to treating celiac disease. Among the most commonly used and studied are lactobacillus and bifidobacterium. Each capsule contains the four unique clinically researched strains: *Lactobacillus helveticus, Lactobacillus rhamnosus, Bacillus subtilis*, and *Enterococcus faecium*.

Dosage: 1 capsule daily.

GISense™ contains powerful anti-inflammatory herbs including boswellia, chamomile, and curcumin, in addition to ashwagandha and bacopa, to support stress-induced inflammation. Inflammation is one of the underlying factors of celiac disease. Chamomile has anti-spasmodic properties and is known for its calming effect on smooth muscle tissue, making it an effective remedy for gastrointestinal spasms as well as GI tension resulting from stress.

Dosage: 3 capsules daily.

AdrenaSense® supports the stress response to allow the gut to function more efficiently by reducing inflammation and spasms. Stress is certainly an important factor to consider in all gastrointestinal conditions, including celiac disease.

Dosage: 2–3 capsules daily (2 with breakfast and 1 midday).

Pancreatic enzymes enhance the benefit of a gluten-free diet during the first 30 days after initial diagnosis. Lipase, the key ingredient in pancreatic enzymes, helps the body absorb fat and it can naturally help major digestive disorders like IBS and celiac disease. Lipase is often taken in combination with the two other vital enzymes: protease and amylase. Protease processes proteins and amylase takes care of carbohydrates.

Dosage: varies depending on the supplement you choose. Standard lipase dosage for adults is 6000 LU (Lipase Activity Units) or 1–2 capsules 3 times daily 30 minutes before meals on an empty stomach.

Diet and Lifestyle Tips for Celiac Disease

Once the diagnosis of celiac disease has been established, a gluten-free diet is absolutely indicated. This diet does not contain any wheat, kamut, rye, barley, triticale, spelt, or oats (unless gluten-free). Buckwheat and millet are often excluded as well. Although buckwheat is not in the grass family and millet appears to be more closely related to rice and corn, buckwheat and millet contain compounds known as prolamins with activity similar to that of gluten.

Grains that can be used to replace gluten-containing grains include:

- Amaranth
- Sorghum flour
- Quinoa
- Pure oats or oat flour
- Corn (ensure it is non-GMO and consume in moderation)
- Rice (brown, red, black, and wild)

It is also recommended that newly diagnosed celiac patients eliminate milk and milk products until they redevelop an intestinal structure and function.

Although many gluten-free products are available in grocery and health food stores, make sure to read the labels carefully. Just because it says "wheat free" doesn't necessarily mean that it is necessarily gluten free. For example, gluten is often added to baked goods to improve their quality.

Other sources of hidden gluten-containing foods include:

- Soy sauce (unless wheat free)
- Beer (unless gluten free)
- Wheat bread, pasta, crackers, cereal
- Wheat bran
- Some sausages or deli meats
- Some soups and gravy sauces
- Batter fried foods

Gluten-containing ingredients may also be listed on labels as flour, graham, wheat germ, wheat bran, wheat starch, gluten, modified food starch, vegetable starch, or vegetable gum.

Chapter 15

Chronic Fatigue Syndrome and Fibromyalgia

Defining Chronic Fatigue Syndrome and Fibromyalgia

Chronic fatigue syndrome, also referred to as myalgic encephalomyelitis, and fibromyalgia represent a complex, multisystem group of afflictions, adversely affecting the brain, heart, neuro-endocrine, immune, and musculoskeletal, and circulatory systems in the body. At times, this leads to symptoms being confused with the symptoms for other conditions such as multiple chemical sensitivities, depressive disorder, myofacial pain syndrome, and chronic mononucleosis.

The US Centers for Disease Control and Prevention (CDC) first defined chronic fatigue syndrome in 1988. Since then, definitions have multiplied, and now the conditions have also been given a new name: systemic exertion intolerance disease (SEID), the latest name proposed in a report in 2015 by the US Institute of Medicine (USIM). With the name change and establishment of diagnostic criteria, the USIM report hopes to raise awareness and encourage doctors to recognize this condition as a real and "serious, complex, multisystem disease", rather than saying it is a psychological problem or just a figment of people's imagination. For simplicity, we will refer to this complex condition as chronic fatigue syndrome (CFS), or its painful cousin fibromyalgia (FM), throughout this chapter.

Even though CFS was defined in 1988 by the CDC and more than 3,000 research studies have been done in this field, there is still some debate about the existence of this syndrome. The uncertainty about its existence and the lack of a specific laboratory test or marker to identify it, associated with hesitancy about making a diagnosis without knowing exactly how to treat it, all act as barriers to the diagnosis and treatment of CFS. Evaluating and treating chronic fatigue is a challenging situation for physicians, as it is a challenging and difficult condition for patients.

Gender Differences in CFS and FM

Between 836,000 and 2.5 million Americans and approximately 350,000 Canadians are estimated to have CFS, but only 20% are diagnosed due to lack of awareness. This illness strikes more people in the United States than multiple sclerosis, lupus, and many forms of cancer.

Epidemiological studies have found that CFS is four times more prevalent in women than in men. FM may affect as much as 3–6% of the US population. Although it is more common in women than in men, the reasons for this difference are unclear. Researchers are examining hormones, immune system differences, brain chemistry, and genetics, among other areas, to shed light on the gender differences.

Due to the fact that CFS is a chronic condition that predominantly affects women, few epidemiologic studies have been done with men. In a recent study of 1,309 CFS patients, 9.1% were men and the study found the mean age of the onset of symptoms was lower in men than women. The most common trigger factor in both sexes is an infection. Men suffering from CFS experience less pain and less muscle and immune symptoms, and a better quality of life in general. Widespread pain, muscle spasms, dizziness, sexual dysfunction, Raynaud's phenomenon, morning stiffness, migratory arthritic pain, drug and metals allergy, and facial edema are more frequent in women than in men.

Signs and Symptoms of CFS

CFS is characterized by profound, debilitating fatigue and a combination of other symptoms resulting in substantial reduction in occupational, personal, social, and educational status. Unfortunately, the causes are not well under-stood. Table 15.1 indicates the CDC's primary and secondary symptoms of CFS. The second column indicates the survey results from Chronic Fatigue Syndrome: A Treatment Guide. The third column shows the results of a single survey of symptoms of adrenal fatigue (AF) from **adrenaladvice.com**.

Table 15.1 Primary and Secondary Symptoms of CFS and AF

PRIMARY SYMPTOMS	CFS %	AF %
Exhaustion/sickness after physical or mental exertion	95–100	81.4
Sleep problems	65–100	61.0
Cognitive problems and brain fog	80–90	92.6
Muscle pain	65–95	63.6
Joint pain	65–95	71.9
Headaches	50	58.1
Tender lymph nodes (neck, armpit)	50–80	38.8
Sore throat	50–90	39.8
SECONDARY SYMPTOMS	CFS %	AF %
Dizziness on standing/fainting	60–90	61.7
Irritable bowel	50–90	63.0
Sensitivity to light, visual disturbances	45–55	74.2
Chills or night sweats	60–90	67.7
Depression, anxiety, mood swings	70–90	93.8

People with CFS experience sympathetic dominance (part of the nervous system that is more active during stress) for years before experiencing the main symptoms for CFS. They are essentially on the edge of the fight-or-flight stress response at all times: "wired but tired". This is essentially the same as Stage 2 adrenal fatigue as described in General Adaptation Syndrome (GAS) defined by Dr. Hans Selye (refer to *Chapter 3* for more information on GAS). We are able to adapt to elevated stress at least for a while, but over time our stress adaptive system starts to fail. Stage 3, the last stage of GAS, is called "Exhaustion" – the same name as the primary symptom of CFS.

Signs and Symptoms of FM

FM is a chronic, diffuse musculoskeletal pain syndrome of unknown etiology characterized by chronic widespread pain, heightened pain sensitivity, chronic fatigue, sleep disorders, and emotional distress or depression. There appears to be more diagnostic variability in FM relative to other coexisting syndromes that have overlapping symptoms, therefore it is often difficult to diagnose FM separately from CFS. Primary symptoms of FM include:

- Sleep problems
- Sensitivity to touch
- Difficulty with concentration
- Widespread pain
- Migraines
- Intolerant to exercise

- Grinding or clenching of teeth
- Irritable bowel syndrome
- Multiple chemical and food sensitivities
- History of depression and anxiety
- Irritable bladder

Possible Causes of CFS and FM

The gut connection

CFS, a disease of many names, is in your gut, not your head. In June 2016, Cornell University researchers reported that they have identified biological markers of the disease in gut bacteria and inflammatory microbial agents in the blood. The study was published in the journal *Microbiome*, and the team claim they correctly diagnosed ME/CFS in 83% of patients through stool samples and blood work. This new finding offers a non-invasive diagnosis and a step toward a greater understanding of one of the possible causes of the disease.

The researchers found that imbalances in the gut microbiome cause inflammatory symptoms. Overall, the diversity of types of bacteria was greatly reduced and there were fewer bacterial species known to be anti-inflammatory in CFS patients compared with healthy people, an observation also seen in people with Crohn's disease and ulcerative colitis. At the same time, the researchers discovered specific markers of inflammation in the blood, likely due to leaky gut problems that allow bacteria to enter the blood. Bacteria in the blood will trigger an immune response, which could worsen overall symptoms.

Functional gastrointestinal disorders are found in the majority of FM patients, with one study citing 98%, compared with 39% of controls. Studies have demonstrated that patients with IBS alone or in combination with FM have hypersensitivity to pain.

A total of 95% of the body's serotonin is produced in the gut and can be depleted due to imbalances in the gut microbiome. Decreased serotonin levels have been associated with functional changes such as constipation and diarrhea. Clinicians could consider changing diets and using prebiotics such as dietary fibres or probiotics to help treat the disease. Most people with FM and/ or CFS have some degree of SIBO and dysbiosis and should consider being tested for SIBO. They should also follow the dysbiosis protocol as outlined in *Chapter 2* or the SIBO protocol outlined in *Chapter 14*.

The immune system connection

Researchers have identified distinct immune changes in patients diagnosed with CFS and FM. These immune signatures represent the physical evidence that it is a biological illness as opposed to a psychological disorder. Remember that long-term stress causes deficiencies in the immune system.

Because some symptoms of CFS resemble those of a viral illness, many researchers have focused on the possibility that a virus or some other infection is the cause in some cases. Although experts have long been divided on whether infections play any role in this disorder, both viral-related and non-viral CFS may exist. The theory that CFS has a viral cause is based on the following:

- In 2009, researchers reported that a retrovirus – xenotropic murine leukemia virus-related virus (XMRV) – was present in a large percentage of patients with CFS. Errors in the research were later identified and the researchers retracted their publication.

- Some CFS patients have higher levels of antibodies to viruses and other infections that may cause fatigue and other CFS symptoms. These infections include herpesvirus type 6 (HHV-6), human T-cell lymphotropic virus (HTLV), Epstein-Barr, measles, coxsackie B, cytomegalovirus, and parvovirus. Many of these viruses are very common, however none has emerged as a clear cause of CFS.

- In up to 80% of cases, CFS starts suddenly with a flu-like condition. However, there is no evidence that CFS is spread through casual contact, such as shaking hands or coughing.

- Adolescents who have had mononucleosis have an increased risk of developing chronic fatigue that lasts for a year or more after the illness.

- Researchers have recently found that CFS is linked to a dysfunction in calcium immune cell receptors. This study documents an actual pathology and adds to the evidence that CFS stems from the body rather than the mind only.

Allergies

Allergies are caused by stress and immune compromise, and some studies have reported that a majority of CFS patients have allergies to foods, pollen, metals (such as nickel or mercury), or other substances. One theory is that allergens, like viral infections, may trigger a cascade of immune abnormalities that lead to CFS. However, most allergic people do not have CFS.

Stress and adrenal fatigue

Naturopathic and alternative medicine doctors have recognized many possible causes and supportive treatments for these debilitating conditions. An article in the journal *American Family Physician* sums up the current understanding of CFS by conventional medicine as follows: "The etiology (cause) of CFS is unclear, is likely complex, and may involve dysfunction of the immune or adrenal systems, an association with certain genetic markers, or a history of childhood trauma." Immune system issues are a major component of CFS, and stress is a major cause of immune system deficiencies.

Those who have experienced childhood trauma are more "wired" and experience hypervigilance due to sympathetic nervous system dominance. They often cause an increased startle response common in both CFS and adrenal fatigue. People with FM have also been found to have dysregulation of the hypothalamus-pituitary-adrenal (HPA) axis.

More and more health care practitioners are becoming aware of adrenal fatigue in general, and perhaps this is one reason why the number of people with adrenal fatigue are increasing and CFS decreasing. Most of the symptoms of CFS and adrenal fatigue are identical. Some researchers believe stress is the cause of CFS.

Adrenal stress hormones

The HPA axis controls important functions, including sleep, the stress response, and depression. Of particular interest to CFS researchers are certain chemicals and other factors controlled by the HPA axis. For example:

- Some patients with CFS have abnormally high levels of serotonin, a chemical messenger in the brain (neurotransmitter), deficiencies of dopamine, an important neurotransmitter associated with feelings of reward, or imbalances between the neurotransmitters norepinephrine and dopamine.

- CFS patients appear to have lower levels of cortisol, a stress hormone produced in the adrenal glands. Cortisol deficiency causes an impaired response to psychological or physical stresses. Low-dose cortisol improves symptoms in some patients.

- Stress and adrenal fatigue can also cause imbalances in the sleep-wake cycle. The circadian clock – a group of nerve cells in the brain –

regulates this cycle. A mentally or physically stressful event may disrupt natural circadian rhythms. An interruption in these rhythms can lead to constantly disrupted sleep.

Overall, people with CFS have hypofunction of the adrenal glands, as well as the entire HPA axis in general. Don't forget the intimate relationship between adrenal fatigue and thyroid problems.

The thyroid connection

The CDC explains that before a patient is diagnosed with CFS, other conditions that may explain the chronic fatigue should be ruled out. The very first such example that is listed is untreated hypothyroidism. In other words, patients with symptoms of chronic fatigue might actually be suffering from low thyroid function.

Thyroid and adrenal function are necessary for normal immune function. Thyroid hormones play a role in the maintenance of lymphocytes and natural killer T-cells, and play a role in modulating the inflammation response to pathogens such as bacteria, viruses, moulds, or yeasts. Having adrenal fatigue, which is all-too-common with hypothyroidism, compounds the problem. When a person has a viral or bacterial intruder, cortisol is needed to balance out the initial inflammatory response by the immune system in its attack on the intruder. In the later stages of adrenal fatigue, cortisol levels are too low, which causes increased inflammation. (Refer to *Chapter 4* for more information on thyroid.)

Wilson's thyroid syndrome is very commonly found in people who have CFS or FM. It is a thyroid disorder that occurs when there is a low temperature and an excess of reverse T3 (RT3) because the liver is unable to convert T4 to T3. The enzyme responsible for this conversion is dependent on selenium and zinc, vitamin B12, and the amino acid cysteine. Heavy metals such as mercury, cadmium, and lead will also block this conversion in the liver. Adrenal stress and adrenal fatigue are also culprits in Wilson's temperature syndrome, and as a result adrenal function should be assessed if levels of RT3 are high.

The inflammation connection

Neuroinflammation, the inflammation of nerve cells, has also been thought to be a causative factor in CFS. In a study published in *The Journal of Nuclear Medicine,* researchers found that the levels of markers for neuroinflammation are elevated in CFS patients compared to the healthy controls. Researchers used positron emission tomography (PET) scans and a questionnaire describing levels of fatigue, cognitive impairment, pain, and depression. Inflammation in certain areas of the brain was elevated in a way that correlated with the symptoms in those with CFS. For example, those people who reported impaired cognition tended to demonstrate neuroinflammation in the amygdala, which is the area of the brain known to be involved in cognition.

Studies also suggest that heavy metal-induced inflammation is an important risk factor in patients with FM. The most frequent reactions are to nickel, followed by inorganic mercury, cadmium, and lead. In addition, there is evidence that FM may be associated with immune dysregulation of circulatory levels of pro-inflammatory cytokines, causing symptoms such as fatigue, fever, sleep, pain, and myalgia, all of which usually develop in FM patients.

Mitochondrial dysfunction

Mitochondrial disease or mitochondrial dysfunction occurs when mitochondria of the cell fail to produce enough energy for cell or organ function due to genetic or environmental factors. The mitochondria's main role is to transform food and oxygen that enter the cells. They are responsible for creating more than 90% of the energy needed by the body to sustain life. The organs in the body that require the most energy are the brain, muscles, liver, kidneys, gastrointestinal tract, heart, and lungs. Mitochondrial dysfunction is prevalent in FM. Muscle pain is in part due to the buildup of lactic acid, implying a lack of oxygenation to the muscle tissue.

In addition to mitochondrial dysfunction, oxidative stress and inflammation have been implicated in the development of FM. People with CFS also have altered mitochondrial function, specifically the function of mitochondria in producing adenosine triphosphate (ATP), the energy currency for all body functions.

Clinical trials have shown that supplements such as l-carnitine, alpha-lipoic acid, coenzyme Q10, nicotinamide adenine dinucleotide (NADH), and phospholipids can reduce the fatigue and other symptoms associated with chronic disease and can naturally restore mitochondrial function, even in long-term patients. Studies also suggest that the use of B vitamins, magnesium, and malic acid are helpful in mild-to-moderate fatigue and widespread pain. (Refer to *Chapter 14* for more information on inflammation.)

Low blood pressure

Some people with symptoms of CFS also have symptoms of a condition known as neurally mediated hypotension (NMH). NMH causes a dramatic drop in blood pressure when a person stands up. Its immediate effects can be light-headedness, nausea, and fainting.

The gluten intolerance connection

Many people with CFS and FM experience symptoms of brain fog or brain drain. Evidence of neurological symptoms in patients with established celiac disease has been reported since 1966. However, it was not until 30 years later that gluten sensitivity was first shown to lead to neurological dysfunction. Gluten sensitivity, also referred to as non-celiac gluten sensitivity (NCGS), may be even more of a cause of psychiatric illness than overt celiac disease. Gluten sensitivity occurs at six times the rate of celiac disease and causes inflammation throughout the body, including the brain.

Gluten intolerance is a growing problem worldwide, but especially in North America and Europe. Gluten is relatively new to our diet; humans did not frequently consume it over the last two million years. When we eat a diet high in foods that contain gluten, it causes inflammation, which is now being recognized as the cornerstone of most chronic disease.

Experts estimate that 1 in 100 people have celiac disease, and this number does not include those with undiagnosed celiac disease. Only 1 in 4,700 who suffer from celiac disease have actually been diagnosed; the number is even higher when undiagnosed cases of NCGS are included. The estimated number of people suffering from gluten problems is closer to 1 in 30. NCGS has profound effects on FM.

Testing and Diagnosis

Diagnosing CFS

A CFS diagnosis is made by excluding many diseases that have chronic fatigue as a major or frequent symptom. Unfortunately, there are no physical signs or diagnostic tests that definitively identify CFS. The diagnosis is primarily made by fitting the two major criteria set out by a group of CFS research experts:

1. The patient must have severe chronic fatigue that persists for more than six months and is accompanied by fatigue, which is often profound, is of new or definite onset, is not the result of ongoing excessive exertion, and is not substantially alleviated by rest.

2. The patient must have four or more of the following symptoms that either occurred at the same time or after the severe chronic fatigue:

- Substantial impairment in short-term memory or concentration
- Sore throat
- Tender lymph nodes
- Muscle pain
- Multi-joint pain without swelling or redness
- Headaches of a new type, pattern or severity
- Unrefreshing sleep
- Post-exertion malaise lasting more than 24 hours

The scale on the following page is a useful and sensitive measure of the level of activity and ability to function of patients with CFS.

Diagnosing FM

Previously, in order to receive a diagnosis of FM, a patient must have experienced widespread pain in all four quadrants of the body for a minimum duration of three months and experienced tenderness or pain in at least 11 of the 18 specified tender points when pressure was applied. New criteria recognize the multisystem involvement that was neglected in the previous diagnostic criteria. Again, as in the CFS, physical exam and labs are used to rule out other conditions.

Aside from predominantly affecting women, there are several risk factors for FM, including the following:

- **Age** – The condition usually occurs in people 20–60 years of age, although cases have been reported in children and elderly people.

- **Family history** – Studies have shown that having a relative with FM may put you at higher risk for developing the disorder.

- **Other rheumatic diseases** – People with other rheumatic diseases, including rheumatoid arthritis and lupus, may be more likely to develop FM.

- **Stress** – Although controversial, certain studies suggest that people who have had difficult or stressful past experiences may be at risk of developing FM.

As in CFS, FM is a diagnosis of exclusion and may be challenging to treat due to multisystem involvement. Biochemical and functional changes are exacerbated by a lack of sleep and chronic pain, leading to a variety of symptoms and many of the possible causes of FM are the same as CFS.

THE BELL CFS ABILITY SCALE
(0 IS THE MOST SEVERE)

0   Severe symptoms on a continuous basis; bedridden constantly; unable to care for self.

1   Severe symptoms at rest; bedridden the majority of the time. No travel outside of the house. Marked cognitive symptoms preventing concentration.

2   Moderate-to-severe symptoms at rest. Unable to perform strenuous activity. Overall activity 30–50% of expected. Unable to leave house except rarely. Confined to bed most of the day. Unable to concentrate for more than 1 hour per day.

3   Moderate-to-severe symptoms at rest. Severe symptoms with any exercise; overall activity level reduced to 50% of expected. Usually confined to house. Unable to perform any strenuous tasks. Able to perform desk work 2–3 hours per day, but requires rest periods.

4   Moderate symptoms at rest. Moderate-to-severe symptoms with exercise or activity; overall activity level reduced to 50–70% of expected. Able to go out once or twice per week. Unable to perform strenuous duties. Able to work sitting down at home 3–4 hours per day, but requires rest periods.

5   Moderate symptoms at rest. Moderate-to-severe symptoms with exercise or activity; overall activity level reduced to 70% of expected. Unable to perform strenuous duties, but able to perform light duty or desk work 4–5 hours per day, but requires rest periods.

6   Mild-to-moderate symptoms at rest. Daily activity limitation clearly noted. Overall functioning 70–90%. Unable to work full-time in jobs requiring physical labour (including just standing), but able to work full-time in light activity (sitting) if hours flexible.

7   Mild symptoms at rest; some daily activity limitation clearly noted. Overall functioning close to 90% of expected except for activities requiring exertion. Able to work full-time with difficulty.

8   Mild symptoms at rest. Symptoms worsened by exertion. Minimal activity restriction noted for activities requiring exertion only. Able to work full-time with difficulty in jobs requiring exertion.

9   No symptoms at rest; mild symptoms with activity; normal overall activity level; able to work full-time without difficulty.

10 No symptoms at rest or with exercise; normal overall activity level; able to work or do house/home work full-time without difficulty.

Lab tests for FM and CFS

No one blood, urine, or other laboratory test can diagnose FM or CFS. However, the following lab tests can assist in ruling out other conditions as well as provide information for treatment. The following tests are typically recommended to rule out other conditions that can cause persistent fatigue:

- Complete blood count (CBC)
- Gluten sensitivity
- Allergy testing
- C-reactive protein (inflammatory marker)
- Liver function
- Blood sugar (glucose)
- Serum calcium and magnesium
- Serum creatinine
- Hemoglobin and ferritin levels
- B12
- Homocysteine
- Thyroid hormones
- 24-hour salivary cortisol levels

Allergy testing: Allergy versus food sensitivity/intolerance

Food intolerance, also known as non-IgE-mediated food hypersensitivity or non-allergic food hypersensitivity, refers to difficulty in digesting certain foods. It is important to note that food intolerance is different from food allergy. Food allergy triggers the immune system, while food intolerance does not. An allergen is a protein that causes a food allergy. Food intolerance is usually due to an enzyme deficiency, meaning that a substance in the food is not digested properly. Food intolerance reactions can be severe and extremely unpleasant, but are rarely life-threatening. However, in some cases of food allergy, there can be a severe and life-threatening allergic reaction (anaphylaxis) to certain foods.

As those with food allergies know, food sensitivities and allergies can have a profound effect on the brain and cognitive function, as well as the gut and overall energy levels.

Conventionally accepted medical approaches for allergy assessment include skin scratch tests in which small punctures are made on the skin with needles containing tiny amounts of allergens. This test is limited because it only tests IgE (immediate) reactions. A blood test called enzyme-linked immunosorbent assay (ELISA) is used to test both IgE and IgG reactions, providing a more comprehensive analysis to determine both immediate and delayed food and environmental allergies. It is important for people with FM and CFS to eliminate any allergies and/or food intolerances from their diet.

what we know works

Support for CFS and FM

The goals for CFS and FM are the same: to improve sleep, improve the immune system, reduce pain and inflammation, normalize HPA axis, address gut health, increase tissue oxygenation, and improve energy and overall vitality.

AdrenaSense® is a herbal adaptogen formulation providing a whole-system approach to restoring HPA axis dysfunction. AdrenaSense contains therapeutic levels of rhodiola, ashwagandha, Siberian ginseng (known as eleuthero in the US), schisandra, and suma. Adrenal regulation is necessary to stop the vicious cycle of stress and insomnia. Stress hormones can keep you wired even though you are exhausted from lack of sleep. Insomniacs and those who feel "tired but wired" should take most supplements – including adrenal support – in the morning. (Refer to *Chapter 3* for more information on stress and stress support.)

Dosage: 2–3 capsules daily, 2 in the morning and 1 at lunch.

MagSense™ (magnesium bisglycinate) is necessary for the function of an enzyme that releases energy from adenosine triphosphate (ATP). Most patients with CFS have low intracellular magnesium levels, and it is an essential mineral in human nutrition with a wide range of biological functions. Magnesium is involved in over 300 metabolic reactions, many of which involve the functioning of the immune system. An activated immune system uses magnesium and zinc at rapid rates. It has been shown that CFS patients in particular have lower levels of intracellular magnesium than healthy controls. MagSense contains magnesium glycinate, allowing for faster and more efficient absorption, as well as taurine, glycine, vitamin B6, malic acid, and other muscle supportive ingredients. Malic acid has been shown to provide improvement in symptoms of FM and is involved in the production of energy in the mitochondria.

Dosage: 1–2 scoops daily.

CalmBiotic™ offers a beneficial defence against inflammation as well as enhancing the body's innate immunity. A total of 70–80% of our entire immune system resides within the gut. CalmBiotic contains *Bifidobacterium longum* and *Lactobacillus helveticus*, which have been proven to reduce symptoms of stress, a main cause of inflammation not only in the gut, but also in the rest of the body.

Dosage: 1 capsule daily.

Brilliant Mind™ (known as Higher Thoughts in the US) contains the phospholipids phosphatidylserine (PS) and phosphatidylcholine (PC), green tea extract, and omega-3 fatty acids to help provide additional benefit to those with CFS. The use of phospholipids to repair mitochondrial membranes damaged by oxidative stress has proven to be very effective at increasing mitochondrial function and reducing fatigue. PS has been shown to decrease cortisol associated with stress and may be helpful for patients experiencing insomnia associated with elevated nighttime cortisol. However, CFS patients are at various stages of adrenal dysfunction and 24-hour cortisol testing is indicated.

Dosage: 2 capsules twice daily.

Liver MD™ helps support the liver and remove heavy metals from the body. Heavy metals and environmental toxins continue to increase in our lives and have been shown to be a cause of many problems in people with CFS. Liver MD contains alpha-lipoic acid (ALA) and N-acetyl-L-cysteine (NAC), two very critical nutrients proven to increase the synthesis of glutathione within the body, as well as powerful antioxidants such as vitamin C, selenomethionine, zinc, broccoli powder, and vitamin B12 to support detoxification pathways and bind free radicals. It also contains hepatoprotective herbs such as milk thistle and curcumin. (Refer to *Chapter 2* for more information on the liver and individual ingredients.)

Dosage: 2 capsules twice daily.

NADH and **CoQ10** work to improve fatigue. NADH is a coenzyme that can stimulate energy production by replenishing depleted cellular stores of ATP. CoQ10 has been shown to be a biological marker of mitochondrial dysfunction, and deficiencies have been well documented in CFS and FM. An eight-week, randomized, double-blind, placebo-controlled trial was conducted to evaluate the benefits of oral CoQ10 plus NADH supplementation on fatigue and biochemical parameters including immune activation, inflammation, dysfunctional mitochondria, lowered antioxidant status, and leaky gut. A significant improvement of fatigue and a recovery of the biochemical parameters were reported in the treated group versus placebo.

Dosage: CoQ10: 200 mg daily; NADH: 20 mg daily.

Acetyl-L-carnitine is essential for mitochondrial energy production, and disturbances in mitochondrial function may contribute to the fatigue in people with CFS. Previous investigations have reported decreased carnitine levels in CFS. L-carnitine is also effective in treating the fatigue seen in a number of chronic neurological diseases. It has been proven to be a safe and very well-tolerated medicine that improves the symptoms in people with CFS.

Dosage: 500 mg twice daily.

Low-dose naltrexone (LDN) was shown to significantly reduce baseline pain compared to the placebo group in a small, double-blind, randomized, placebo-controlled trial where participants took 4.5 mg LDN. Secondary outcomes included general satisfaction with life, positive mood, and some improvement in sleep quality and fatigue.

Dosage: up to 4.5 mg daily. LDN must be prescribed by an ND or MD and is formulated through compounding pharmacies.

what we know works
Inflammation Support

GISense™ combines bacopa, ashwagandha, curcumin, boswellia, and chamomile to support cognition, prevent and treat inflammation, and support the body during times of stress. (Refer to *Chapter 9* for more information on the anti-inflammatory properties of GISense.)

Dosage: 2 capsules twice daily.

Omega-3 fatty acids are as effective as NSAIDs at reducing inflammatory pain, and they are a much safer alternative. Clinical studies show that an imbalance in the dietary intake of fatty acids is linked to impaired brain performance and disease. When choosing an omega-3 product, ensure it is free from heavy metals such as lead and mercury, pesticides, and other contaminants. Look for a combined product that contains at least 1000 mg of eicosapentaenoic acid (EPA) and docosahexaenoic acid (DHA).

Dosage: 1000 mg daily for general health; 3000 mg daily for inflammatory conditions.

what we know works
Sleep Support

In order for people with CFS to heal, it is absolutely essential to restore normal sleep patterns. Hypothalamic-pituitary-adrenal (HPA) dysfunction causing elevated cortisol and melatonin dysregulation is a key player in sleep disturbance.

SleepSense™ contains melatonin, which has been shown to be effective in improving sleep, as well as decreasing tender point number and pain level in FM.

Dosage: 2–3 3 mg tablets at bedtime.

Restful Sleep™ (known as The Best-Sleep in the US) contains passionflower, California poppy, skullcap, and linden flower to help ensure a good night's sleep. (Refer to *Chapter 12* for more information on sleep disorders.)

Dosage: 2–4 capsules one hour before bed.

....

Additional support for CFS and FM

Pantothenic acid (B5) can down-regulate hypersecretion of cortisol due to high stress conditions and is important for energy production by helping convert glucose into energy.

Dosage: 500 mg 3 times daily.

Vitamin B6 is a necessary cofactor for the formation of several important neurotransmitters such as GABA, serotonin, and dopamine, which are commonly associated with stress and CFS.

Dosage: 100–250 mg daily.

Vitamin B12 is thought to have an effect on helping to reset healthy secretion of cortisol during periods of stress, thus improving the stress response and quality of sleep, which are very important for people with CFS and FM. Increased homocysteine levels have been found in people with FM and CFS, and B12/folic acid has been found to be effective nutritional support.

Dosage: 1000–5000 mcg daily in the form of methylcobalamin.

Vitamin C is very important because it is used in the formation of adrenal hormones such as cortisol. During times of stress, the body's requirement for vitamin C can increase 10–20 fold.

Dosage: 2000–4000 mg daily (or until you begin to experience loose stools).

Support for anxiety and depression related to CFS

Many people with CFS also experience depression and/or anxiety, but no one knows for sure which comes first. Many natural support remedies have proven beneficial in the treatment of depression and anxiety. (Refer to *Chapter 11* for more information and treatment suggestions.)

Prescription medication

Common medications for treating FM pain include analgesics (including NSAIDs or nonsteroidal anti-inflammatory drugs), muscle relaxants, and anti-seizure drugs. Medications for FM and CFS patients to ease sleep disturbances include antidepressants and short-term use of sleeping pills. Some health care practitioners recommend combining medication with therapy to help patients learn the techniques to cope with stress, which can exacerbate or trigger pain symptoms of FM or fatigue symptoms in CFS.

Diet and Lifestyle Tips for CFS and FM

Medications come with side effects, especially in people who have hypersensitive nervous systems as in those with CFS and FM. Many have found relief through alternative treatments including acupuncture, massage therapy, tai chi, yoga, medication, and natural supplements.

Meditation

Different types of meditation have been shown to result in psychological and biological changes that are associated with improved health. Meditation has been found to reduce blood pressure and heart rate, alter levels of melatonin and serotonin, suppress stress hormones, boost the immune system, and have a favourable influence on overall and spiritual quality of life in late-stage disease.

More than eight in ten North Americans think prayer or meditation can augment medical treatment, according to a survey released by the sponsor of Harvard Medical School's Spirituality and Healing in Medicine seminars. Just as we need physical exercise and good whole foods to keep our physical body healthy, we need daily spiritual exercises (e.g., contemplation, prayer, or meditation) to keep our minds and emotions balanced. Life is moving so quickly today that a meditative practice is more necessary than ever before.

Massage therapy

Studies have shown that massage therapy can decrease cortisol and increase serotonin and dopamine levels. The research reviewed studies on depression, pain syndrome, autoimmune conditions, immune disorders, stress on the job, stress of aging, and pregnancy stress. The results show that massage therapy led to an average decrease in cortisol of 31%, and average increases in the neurotransmitters serotonin and dopamine.

Exercise as able

Too much exercise in those people with CFS will result in what is called post-exertional fatigue, where a person may end up bedridden the next day. However, not enough exercise will result in poor physical conditioning, which is

SECTION 4 – MORE GENDER DIFFERENCES IN COMMON DISEASES

almost as bad. Begin with a simple walking program where you feel tired after, but not to the point of exhaustion. Try to increase the walk by 50–100 steps a day as tolerated. By increasing exercise tolerance gradually, physical energy will increase as well.

Anti-inflammatory diet

An anti-inflammatory diet, such as the Mediterranean diet (which consists of foods containing omega-3 fatty acids such as fish, walnuts, and flaxseed oil), can help prevent inflammation. (Refer to *Chapter 19* for details on the Mediterranean diet.)

Chapter 16

Diabetes and Metabolic Syndrome

Blood Glucose Regulation – An Overview

When we eat, our bodies break carbohydrates down into glucose (sugar), which is the main energy source for the body. Under normal conditions, the body maintains a very narrow range of blood glucose despite wide variations in food intake and energy demands. This balance is regulated by two hormones produced in the pancreas – insulin and glucagon – which have opposite effects. High blood glucose stimulates the secretion of insulin, which results in the cellular uptake of glucose and lowering of blood sugar. Conversely, low levels of glucose stimulate the secretion of glucagon, which stimulates a rise in blood glucose.

The adrenal glands also play an important role in blood glucose regulation. The adrenal stress hormone epinephrine stimulates the breakdown of the glucose stored in the liver (glycogen), and cortisol promotes glucose production (gluconeogenesis). Stress causes the adrenal glands to secrete more cortisol, which helps raise blood sugar levels for more energy in response to the stressor. In turn, the increased blood sugar puts extra demands on the pancreas to secrete more insulin. When this demand on the pancreas is too great, the cells become resistant to insulin. Insulin resistance occurs when the cell has a weakened or delayed response to insulin, resulting in the inability of the cell to absorb sufficient glucose from the blood.

The primary cause of the poor insulin cell receptor response is the chronic overproduction of insulin due to stress and a diet high in sugars, refined carbo-hydrate foods, or foods with a high-glycemic index (GI). The GI measures how quickly blood sugar increases after eating a particular food: the higher the GI, the faster the rise and more rapid lowering of blood sugar. Foods with a high GI, such as refined sugars, white flour products, and other sources of simple carbohydrates and sugars, are quickly absorbed into the bloodstream. (See the Support for Diabetes and Metabolic Syndrome section for more information on how to choose low-GI foods.)

Diabetes

Diabetes is a condition in which the body cannot properly store or use fuel for energy. To use glucose, the body's main fuel source, insulin, is required. Insulin is made by the pancreas and allows glucose to leave the blood and enter the cells for energy. Diabetes develops when the pancreas cannot make enough insulin or when the cells become resistant and do not respond to insulin, resulting in high levels of glucose in the blood.

There are three main types of diabetes:

- **Type 1 diabetes,** previously known as insulin-dependent diabetes mellitus (IDDM) or juvenile diabetes, typically strikes before the age of 30. The pancreas is not able to produce insulin. The immune system or environmental factors are believed to trigger type 1, which accounts for 5–10% of cases of diabetes.

- **Type 2 diabetes** is the most common diabetes diagnosis, and is dis-cussed in more detail below. Previously known as noninsulin-dependent diabetes mellitus (NIDDM) or adult onset diabetes, type 2 diabetes affects over 90% of people with diabetes. About 30% of people over age 70 have type 2 diabetes.

- **Type 3 diabetes** or gestational diabetes is the rarest form of diabetes, affecting 2–5% of pregnancies. Those who develop gestational diabetes have a greater risk of developing type 2 diabetes later in life.

In 2016, 11 million (29%) of Canadians had prediabetes or diabetes, and by the year 2026 it is estimated that this will increase to 41%. It is also estimated that

700,000 people have diabetes and do not know it. This is shocking, particularly when, in most cases, diabetes can be prevented with diet and lifestyle changes. When diabetes is controlled, there is a reduced risk of coexisting diseases including hypertension, hyperlipidemia, coronary artery disease (CAD), cerebral vascular accidents, chronic kidney disease, retinopathy, and neuropathy.

Gender Differences in Diabetes

Women with diabetes have it worse, on average, than men with diabetes. This inequality was revealed in a study that found that, between 1971 and 2000, death rates fell for men with diabetes, while rates for women with the disease stayed the same. Why the disparity? It is most likely a combination of factors, according to the 2007 study in *Annals of Internal Medicine*. Differences in physiology are involved, and research suggests that, as a group, doctors treat men and women differently. That gap in care leads to poorer outcomes for women and can even be downright deadly.

The risk for heart disease is six times higher for women with diabetes than those without, while in men, diabetes increases the risk for heart disease two to threefold. Women with diabetes are also more likely to have poor blood glucose control, be obese, and have high blood pressure and unhealthy cholesterol levels. A 2007 study published in the *European Heart Journal* found that the association between diabetes and death by heart failure is stronger for women than it is for men. Another study found that heart attacks are more often fatal for women with diabetes than they are for men with diabetes. This greater risk may be due in part to how women and men experience heart attacks. For men, the most common warning sign of a heart attack is chest pain or discomfort in the upper body. However, women are more likely than men to experience only nausea, shortness of breath, and back or jaw pain during a heart attack. If a woman experiences these but does not recognize them as heart attack warning signs, she may not seek treatment, lowering her chances of recovery.

The gender bias was also apparent in a *2005 Diabetes Care* study. It found that women with diabetes are less likely than men to receive medication for heart disease risk factors, and in general women tend to be treated less aggressively than men for cardiovascular risk factors.

Another diabetes complication, kidney disease, is also worse for women than men with diabetes. Other research has shown that women with depression have a higher risk for diabetes, and those with both conditions are twice as likely to die early as women who have neither diabetes nor depression. Depression and diabetes are associated in women, but not in men.

Statins increase diabetes in older women

New research indicates that statin therapy increases the risk of new-onset diabetes in elderly women, ranging from a low of 17% with the lowest doses of statin to a high of 51% for those taking the highest doses. These findings are based on a new analysis of the *Australian Longitudinal Study on Women's Health*, which included 8372 women aged 76–82 years who were followed for 10 years. The research strongly suggests that elderly women should not be exposed to higher doses of statins, and in many cases it may be wiser to stop statins altogether. It is also critical for practitioners to conduct ongoing risk assessment to ensure optimal health outcomes in elderly women.

Signs and Symptoms of Diabetes

The signs and symptoms of diabetes include:

- Unquenchable thirst
- Frequent urination
- Weight changes (gain or loss)
- Fatigue or lack of energy, especially after eating
- Blurred vision
- Frequent bladder or yeast infections
- Male impotence (erectile dysfunction)
- Slow healing of cuts or sores

People with diabetes are at a greater risk for problems that involve damage to the small blood vessels and nerves, as well as for the development of hardening of the arteries (atherosclerosis), which can result in heart attacks, strokes, and poor blood flow to extremities and the brain (vascular dementia). Damage to the small blood vessels affects the eyes, specifically the retina. This is called diabetic retinopathy and is the leading cause of blindness. Damage to the kidneys – called diabetic nephropathy – leads to kidney failure and the need for dialysis. Damage to the nerves that supply the arms, legs, and gastrointestinal tract is called neuropathy. Peripheral neuropathy results in poor blood flow wherein the legs may eventually need to be amputated.

Complications of diabetes are associated with increased risk of the following:

- **Premature death** – It is estimated that one in ten deaths in Canadian adults is attributable to diabetes.

- **Hospitalization** – People with diabetes are three times more likely to be hospitalized with cardiovascular disease, 12 times more likely to be hospitalized with end-stage renal disease, and 20 times more likely to be hospitalized for a non-traumatic lower limb amputation.

- **Depression** – 30% of those diagnosed with diabetes have clinically relevant depressive symptoms, and individuals with depression have an approximately 60% increased risk of developing type 2 diabetes.

- **Foot ulceration** – 15–25% of people with diabetes are affected by foot ulceration.

In addition, 57% of Canadians with diabetes report they cannot adhere to prescribed treatment due to the cost of needed medications, devices, and supplies. As a result of stigma or fear of stigma, 37% of Canadians with type 2 diabetes do not feel comfortable disclosing their diabetes.

As you can see, this is not a pretty picture, and what makes it more difficult to accept is that diabetes, in most cases, is preventable through diet and exercise.

Metabolic Syndrome/Insulin Resistance

Metabolic syndrome is a group of risk factors that increase the risk of diabetes, coronary heart disease (CHD), and stroke. In general, signs include abdominal obesity, dyslipidemia (high triglycerides and low HDL cholesterol), elevated blood pressure, and blood sugar irregularities (insulin resistance). Metabolic syndrome increases the risk of type 2 diabetes anywhere from 9–30 times over the normal population, and the risk of heart disease 2–4 times the normal population. It is also associated with fatty liver, kidney damage, sleep apnea, polycystic ovary syndrome (PCOS), and increased risk for dementia. Statistics indicate that more than 40% of individuals older than 50 years of age may be at risk for insulin resistance, however it can affect anyone at any age.

Signs and Symptoms of Metabolic Syndrome

The signs and symptoms of metabolic syndrome include:

- Craving for sugars and carbohydrates

- Nighttime awakening due to cortisol dysregulation

- Shaky without food, better after eating

- Anxiety and depression

- Weight gain, fat storage, and difficulty losing weight (for most people, excess weight is from high-fat storage; the fat in insulin resistance is generally stored in and around abdominal organs in both males and females; it currently is suspected that hormones produced in fat cells are a precipitating cause of insulin resistance)

- High blood sugar and increased blood triglyceride levels
- Increased blood pressure (many people with hypertension are either diabetic or pre-diabetic and have elevated insulin levels due to insulin resistance; one of insulin's effects is to control arterial wall tension throughout the body)
- Increased inflammation
- Skin tags

Diabetes and Metabolic Syndrome

Possible Causes of Diabetes and Metabolic Syndrome

Risk factors for type 2 diabetes include:
- Advanced age
- Being overweight
- Family history of diabetes
- Developed gestational diabetes during pregnancy
- Having high blood pressure and/or high cholesterol
- Highly refined carbohydrate diet
- Sedentary lifestyle

Risk factors for metabolic syndrome/insulin resistance include:
- Being overweight, especially excess fat in the abdominal region
- Sedentary lifestyle
- Family history of type 2 diabetes, high blood pressure, cardiovascular disease
- Elevated cortisol
- History of glucose intolerance or gestational diabetes
- A diagnosis of elevated triglycerides/low HDL, acute pancreatitis, polycystic ovary syndrome, chronic kidney disease, cardiovascular disease

Possible causes of metabolic syndrome/insulin resistance include:
- Genetic factors
- Insulin resistance

- Inflammation
- Aging
- Obesity and overweight (BMI >25)
- Lifestyle factors such as diet, lack of exercise, alcohol consumption

Statins and diabetes risk in the general population

A new population-based study concluded that statin therapy appears to increase the risk for type 2 diabetes by 46%, even after adjustment for confounding factors. This new information suggests a higher risk for diabetes with statins in the general population than has previously been reported, which was a 10–22% increased risk. The researchers found that the risk for diabetes was dose-dependent.

Statin supporters argue that even if statin treatment is increasing the risk of diabetes, statins are still very effective in reducing cardiovascular risk. However, all of the research strongly suggests that diabetes is one of the leading risk factors for CVD, so it is uncertain how this argument can support statin use in people with or at risk for diabetes. What the statin supporters do agree on is that people who are at the higher risk, such as those who are obese or have a history of diabetes in the family, should lower their statin dose because high-dose statin treatment increases the risk for diabetes.

Obesity and overweight

Obesity is one of the main risk factors for diabetes and metabolic syndrome. Obesity rates in Canada have tripled since 1985, according to new research from Memorial University in Newfoundland. It is expected that about 21% of Canadian adults will be obese by 2019, according to a study published in the *Canadian Medical Association Journal*. Analyzing data from Canadian health surveys conducted between 1985 and 2011, researchers found that the overall obesity rate increased from 6–18% over the 26-year period, although numbers varied by province.

According to the American Heart and Stroke Foundation, 154.7 million Americans 20 years old and older were overweight or obese in 2013, with a body mass index (BMI) of 25.0 and higher. Of these, 78.4 million were obese (BMI of 30.0 and higher). The obesity epidemic in children 12–19 years of age continues to grow: 24.9 million are overweight and 12.8 million of these are obese.

BMI and waist circumference

A blood pressure of 130/85 or more and a waist circumference greater than 102 cm in Caucasian men (89 cm in Asian men) or 89 cm in Caucasian women (79 cm in Asian women) can be indicative of metabolic syndrome.

TO CALCULATE BMI,
use the following equation:

BMI in kilograms =
weight in kilograms ÷ [height in centimetres × height in centimetres]
× 10,000

Example: 54 kg ÷ (165 cm × 165 cm) × 10,000 = 19.83

Weight Status BMI

Underweight: Below 18.5   Overweight: 25.0–29.9

Normal: 18.5–24.9   Obese: 30.0 and above

Obesity has been defined as a BMI greater than or equal to 30.0 in World Health Organization (WHO) classification, but it does not take into account the morbidity and mortality associated with milder degrees of overweight. A significant increase in risk of death from cardiovascular disease was found for all BMIs of greater than 25.0 in women and 26.5 in men. There is a direct relationship between a BMI up to 30.0 and the relative risk of several chronic conditions caused by excess body fat, such as type 2 diabetes, hypertension, coronary artery disease, and gallstones.

Testing and Diagnosis

Your health care practitioner will take a medical history and run some blood and urine lab tests. A common finding in the diagnosis of diabetes is evidence of both protein and sugar in the urine. Increased fasting glucose and elevated triglycerides are also common. For example, if a fasting glucose is 7.0 mmol/L (126 mg/dL) or higher, a diagnosis of diabetes is made. If the fasting blood glucose is between 6.1–6.9 mmol/L (110–125 mg/dL), the person has as a higher risk for diabetes down the road.

However, many people are in the pre-diabetic state and blood sugar levels will still be in what is considered the "normal" range. The main goal of diabetes management is to maintain blood glucose levels within the normal range. Weight control, diet, and exercise are extremely important.

If metabolic syndrome is suspected, a thorough medical history and physical exam along with lab tests should be done. Early detection is very important in preventing the more chronic diseases associated with metabolic syndrome.

Lab tests for diabetes and metabolic syndrome

A number of lab tests can be done to help diagnose diabetes and metabolic syndrome, including:

- Fasting blood sugar and a post-meal two- and four-hour glucose challenge or a two-hour glucose challenge
- Fasting insulin
- Lipid panel: low-density-lipoproteins (LDL), high-density-lipoprotein (HDL), triglycerides, total cholesterol
- Hemoglobin A1c
- Cortisol levels (saliva testing)

Other tests should include blood pressure and calculation of BMI.

what we know works
Support for Diabetes and Metabolic Syndrome

Chromium deficiency causes hyperglycemia and impaired glucose tolerance. A large meta-analysis found that reduced HbA1c and FBS levels were achieved with chromium supplementation with a combination therapy of 600 mcg chromium picolinate and 2 mg of biotin. Biotin is a B vitamin that enhances chromium absorption and is involved with intracellular metabolism of glucose. Biotin administration of 9–16 mg daily improved glucose tolerance and decreased mean FBS by 45%. It has been shown to augment the action of insulin, thereby reducing insulin requirements in those people taking insulin.

Dosage: 200–600 mcg daily.

Note: Higher doses may be required for insulin resistance: 1000–5000 mcg daily of chromium and 2–5 mg of biotin, according to Jonathan Wright, MD.

PolyGlycopleX® (PGX®) is a completely new and unique fibre matrix. The effectiveness of any fibre for reducing appetite, regulating blood sugar, and lowering cholesterol is based on the amount of water the fibre is able to absorb.

The health benefits linked to soluble dietary fibre, including stabilizing blood sugar levels, are significantly magnified with PGX. Detailed published clinical studies indicate that PGX has the following benefits:

- Stabilizes blood sugar in overweight and obese persons
- Reduces appetite and promotes weight loss, even in the morbidly obese

- Increases insulin sensitivity and decreases blood insulin levels
- Improves diabetes control
- Lowers blood cholesterol and triglycerides

Dosage: 750–1500 mg before each meal.

For weight loss: 2500–5000 mg before meals (start with 750–1000 mg and work your way up to the full dosage over the course of two weeks).

Ultimate™ Probiotic helps regulate the natural flora in the gut. Digestive health is important in the treatment of blood sugar irregularities. Inflammatory cytokines in the gut can blunt the insulin response and probiotic help maintain a healthy gut microflora and prevent inflammation.

Dosage: 1 capsule 2–3 times daily.

AdrenaSense® is the foundation of the prevention and treatment of hypoglycemia, metabolic syndrome, and diabetes. AdrenaSense helps the body adapt to stress and regulates the stress hormones.

Dosage: 2–3 capsules daily (2 with breakfast and 1 midday).

Vitamin D deficiency has been associated with IR and diabetes.

Dosage: 5000 IU daily. Higher doses may be taken as recommended by a health care practitioner.

GlucoSense® provides diabetic support by normalizing blood sugar, decreasing cortisol levels, and reducing cholesterol. The important ingredients to control blood sugar include ALA, berberine, bitter melon, chromium, biotin, Chinese cinnamon, mission cactus powder, and bilberry extract. Refer below for more information about individual ingredients.

Dosage: 1 capsule daily.

> **Cinnamon** *(Cinnamomum cassia)* has been used for thousands of years in traditional Chinese medicine to treat type 2 diabetes. The herb activates insulin receptors and increases glycogen synthesis. Five clinical trials evaluated doses of 1–6 g daily and saw decreases in fasting blood glucose levels of 18–29%.
>
> **Berberine** is a compound found in goldenseal, Oregon grape, barberry, and other plants. Compared with metformin, berberine exhibits an identical effect in the regulation of glucose metabolism such as HbA1c, FBG, fasting blood glucose, blood sugar after eating, fasting insulin, and insulin levels after eating. In the regulation of lipid metabolism, berberine activity is better than metformin. By week 13, triglycerides and total cholesterol in

the berberine group had decreased and were significantly lower than in the metformin group.

Bitter melon *(Momordica charantia)* is a plant native to India and Asia. It has been used medicinally for over 600 years. Evidence has shown positive effects on glucose levels, glucose uptake, glycogen synthesis, and glucose oxidation.

Alpha-lipoic acid (ALA) is a potent antioxidant that is an approved drug in Germany for the treatment of diabetic neuropathy at a dosage of 400–600 mg daily. It is also thought to improve blood glucose metabolism, improve blood flow to peripheral nerves, and actually stimulate the regeneration of nerve fibres.

Gymnema sylvestre is used in Ayurvedic medicine to treat type 2 diabetes, high cholesterol, and obesity. Improvements in FBS and HbA1c levels were obtained using *Gymnema sylvestre.*

Dosage: 200–800 mg daily.

Medication

For many people, following a healthy diet and exercise program may be all that is required to help control glucose levels. For others, this may not be enough, and medications may need to be taken in order to sustain glucose in a normal range. Medications for type 2 diabetes are taken by mouth or injection. There are several types of oral diabetes medications, so talk to your health care practitioner about what medication would best suit you.

Diet and Lifestyle Tips for Diabetes and Metabolic Syndrome

Overall risks for diabetes and metabolic syndrome can be lowered by reducing excess weight, increasing physical activity, and improving lipid levels and blood pressure. In addition and equally important are diet and lifestyle. Nutritional and dietary treatment of metabolic syndrome and type 2 diabetes are very similar.

Diet

As mentioned earlier, foods with a high GI are quickly absorbed into the bloodstream and lead to chronic over-production of insulin. As a result, it is important to avoid junk food and pay more attention to the GI of the food you eat by choosing foods in the low-to-medium GI categories. Table 16.1 shows the GI of a variety of common foods.

Table 16.1 Glycemic Index of Foods

FRUIT AND VEGETABLES

LOW	MEDIUM	HIGH
Green vegetables	Yams/sweet potatoes	Potatoes
Brassica family	Raw carrots	Beets
Tomatoes	Blueberries	Parsnips
Apples	Grapes	Dried fruit
Pears	Orange juice	Pineapples
Cherries		Bananas
Grapefruit		Raisins
Peaches		Mangoes
Beans (lentils, black, mung, pinto, black-eyed, chickpeas)		

GRAINS

LOW	MEDIUM	HIGH
Pearl barley	Corn	Couscous
Rice bran	Brown rice	English muffin
Whole rye	Oat bran/oatmeal	French baguette
Wheat bran	Wild rice	Bread
Quinoa	Pumpernickel	Millet
Slow Oats		Crackers
		Taco shells
		Corn flakes
		Rice krispies
		Shredded wheat

Other diet tips include the following:

- Limit foods with high sugar content, especially on an empty stomach.
- Refer to GI sources and keep 80–90% of food intake in the low-to-moderate GI range.
- Eliminate as much as possible refined carbohydrates (white breads, pasta, pizza, dessert, soda pop, etc.).

- Eat small frequent meals and snacks high in protein.
- Eat a diet high in fibre, fresh vegetables and fruits, good quality protein, and good oils such as flaxseed and olive oil.
- Carry some juice or dried fruit for when you feel your blood sugar drop.
- If you are overweight, find a program that can help you lose weight.
- Losing even 2–5 kg (5–10 lbs) can help regulate glucose.

Consuming raw fats such as sesame, coconut, avocado, flaxseed, and olive oil help reduce HbA1c. A low-carb Mediterranean diet effectively reduces HbA1c, achieves diabetes remission, and delays the need for medications. Eating a diet that contains lots of good fat is more effective in slowing the progression of type 2 diabetes than a low-fat diet. The key factor in the Mediterranean diet is that more than 30% of daily calories are from fat. Olive oil is high in oleic acid and monounsaturated content, providing antioxidant and anti-inflammatory properties. (Refer to *Chapter 19* for more information on the Mediterranean diet.)

Exercise

Exercise is a very important aspect of a healthy lifestyle to both prevent and help with the treatment of blood sugar problems such as insulin resistance and diabetes. The average adult spends over 90% of his or her waking hours sitting. This "Society of Sitters" goes from the breakfast table, to the car, to the desk, back to the table, and then to the couch to read or watch TV. Only 1–5% of waking hours are spent performing moderate to physical activity, with only 0.5% of this activity being sustained for at least 10 minutes. It has been found that each two-hour increase in sitting time is associated with a 5–23% increase in the risk of obesity and 7–14% increase in the risk of type 2 diabetes, as well as an increased probability of metabolic syndrome and ovarian cancer. According to a recent study, prolonged sitting is a "health hazard".

> Start kicking the sitting habit now and take five minutes of every hour to get out of your chair and stretch, stand, or walk.

How do you conquer the negative effects of prolonged sitting when you have a desk job? Yes, exercise helps, but it is only part of the solution. Researchers evaluated the health of men and women who reported exercising five days a week for 30 minutes, a standard that is considered active enough to have health benefits. The results were surprising – waist size, blood pressure, and cholesterol levels were still all negatively affected by the amount of time spent sitting, and these results were more pronounced in women than in men. The researchers labelled the people who sit all day but still find time to exercise "active couch potatoes". So, what can you do if regular exercise does not counteract the ill effects of sitting?

Get up and move! Often! Simple activities like standing to answer the phone, getting up to fill your water glass, taking the stairs, walking, and moving whenever you can will all contribute to a more healthy you. Researchers found that people who took frequent breaks during long periods of sedentary activity had a waist circumference that, on average, was 5 cm less than that of people who did not get out of their chair.

Chapter 17

Cardiovascular Disease

Cardiovascular Disease – An Overview

Cardiovascular disease (CVD) is the term used to include all the diseases of the heart and circulation, including coronary heart disease (CHD), angina, heart attack, congenital heart disease, and stroke. According to the World Health Organization (WHO), it is estimated that 30% of all deaths globally each year (approximately 18 million people) are caused by cardiovascular disease. Stroke is the third-leading cause of death in Canada, and approximately 300,000 Canadians are currently living with the long-term effects of stroke.

In January 2010, the Heart and Stroke Foundation designated young adults as the newest at-risk group for heart disease in Canada. In the span of just a decade, rates of high blood pressure among Canadians have jumped by 77%, diabetes by 45%, and obesity by 18%. These factors are all risks for heart disease and are becoming more prevalent among young adults. More than 250,000 Canadians 20–30 years of age have high blood pressure. In the 35–49 age group, high blood pressure has increased by a staggering 127%, diabetes by 64% and obesity by 20%. Very alarming statistics indeed.

Not All Cholesterol Is Created Equal

Cholesterol is an essential component of our cell membranes:

- It acts as an antioxidant.

- It is a precursor for the synthesis of vitamins D, E, and K, as well as for the production of steroid hormones such as cortisol and other adrenal hormones such as estrogen, progesterone, and testosterone.

- It is a precursor for calcitriol, which regulates calcium and is used in brain/nerve communication.

- It repairs lesions in the membranes of arteries and veins.

Fats are insoluble in water, therefore cholesterol cannot be transported in the blood on its own. The body's solution is to bind cholesterol to transport vehicles called lipoproteins. Two types of lipoproteins carry most of the cholesterol: low-density-lipoproteins (LDL) and high-density-lipoprotein (HDL). HDL is the garbage collector of waste materials, including excess LDL. HDL carries the garbage back to the liver for processing. Therefore, higher levels of HDL are beneficial.

We have been told that elevated LDL is risk factor when it comes to CVD. However, some forms of LDL are relatively safe, while other forms are more dangerous, and treating them all as one and the same is overly simplistic. More important than the level of LDL is the type of LDL a person has. LDL comes in four basic forms: a big, fluffy form known as large LDL, and three increasingly dense forms known as medium, small, and very small LDL. Lumping all forms of LDL cholesterol together, as labs currently do, does not identify how much LDL is small and how much is large. People can have mostly large LDL or mostly small LDL in their overall total LDL, depending upon a host of genetic, lifestyle, and environmental factors. Large fluffy LDL is primarily benign.

Lipoproteins are comprised of proteins (apolipoproteins), phospholipids, triglycerides, and cholesterol. The lipoproteins vary in the major lipoprotein content. Lipoproteins such as very low-density lipoprotein (VLDL) or lipoprotein(a) contain apolipoprotein B (ApoB) and several studies have shown that ApoB may be a better predictor of cardiovascular disease risk than LDL-C. Furthermore, it has been shown that ApoB may be elevated despite normal or low concentrations of LDL-C.

According to current information, which is constantly changing when it comes to dangers of various cholesterols, Apo B containing lipoproteins are the ones that are most likely to enter the wall of the arteries. They are capable of trafficking cholesterol into the artery wall, and if present in increased numbers may be the main initiating factor in atherosclerosis. Lp(a)s, another LDL troublemaker, inflames the blood and makes it sticky – making it more prone to clotting. Most doctors now routinely test ApoB levels in those people at higher risk for CVD, however Lp(a) is not usually tested.

The cholesterol hypothesis links cholesterol levels to CVD. Because cholesterol is considered a risk factor for atherosclerosis, many believe that lowering cholesterol in the blood is the best way to prevent CVD. However, examination of the original Framingham Heart Study data (as an example) indicates that the cholesterol levels and development of CVD was only a factor when total cholesterol levels were either very high or very low. Cholesterol may be associated with CVD, but this does not prove causation.

Despite the fact that high triglycerides and low HDL have long been associated with CVD, studies designed to raise HDL or lower triglycerides have failed to reduce mortality. Similarly, cholesterol should not automatically become a treatment target. It may be a leap of faith to assume that lowering cholesterol with statins is the best way to prevent CVD.

Gender Differences in CVD

Many people are aware that CVD is the primary cause of death in men, but most people, including many health care practitioners, are unaware that heart disease is the main cause of death in women 50 years of age and older. Women tend to develop heart disease about 10 years later in life, and risk begins to equal that of men when women reach their mid-70s. The absolute number of women living with and dying of CVD and stroke exceed those of men, and women constitute a larger proportion of the elderly population in which the prevalence of CVD is the greatest.

Data over the past decade have shown that women have higher 30-day mortality after a myocardial infarction. The difference may be explained by delay in women seeking care, health care practitioner delay in recognition and treatment, underlying differences in the disease process, or older age at time of presentation among women compared with men.

In addition, more women than men suffer a stroke each year. Although many of the risk factors for stroke are the same for men and women, including a family history of stroke, high blood pressure, and high cholesterol, some risk factors are unique to women, including birth control pills, pregnancy, hormone replacement therapy, frequent migraine headaches, a waist larger than 89 cm (particularly in postmenopausal women), and high triglyceride levels.

Alarming statistics among younger women 35–44 years of age show that CVD mortality rates have increased an average of 1.3% annually between 1997 and 2002, a statistically significant trend.

Gender differences in risk factors and treatment

Research is identifying gender differences in heart disease that may help fine-tune prevention, diagnosis, and treatment in women. Here are some examples.

- **Blood lipids** – Before menopause, a woman's own estrogen helps protect her from heart disease by increasing HDL (good) cholesterol and decreasing LDL (bad) cholesterol. After menopause, women have higher concentrations of total cholesterol than men do. But this alone does not explain the sudden rise in heart disease risk after menopause. Elevated triglycerides are an especially powerful contributor to cardiovascular risk in women. *Low HDL and high triglycerides appear to be the only factors that increase the risk of death from heart disease in women over age 65.*

- **Diabetes** – Diabetes increases the risk of heart disease in women more than it does in men, perhaps because women with diabetes more often have added risk factors, such as obesity, hypertension, and high cholesterol. Although women usually develop heart disease about 10 years later than men, diabetes erases that advantage. In women who have already had a heart attack, diabetes doubles the risk for a second heart attack, and increases the risk for heart failure.

- **Metabolic syndrome** – Metabolic syndrome includes a group of risk factors, including large waist size, elevated blood pressure, glucose intolerance, low HDL cholesterol, and high triglycerides. These risks increase the chance of developing heart disease, stroke, and diabetes. Research out of Harvard Medical School suggests that metabolic syndrome is the most important risk factor for heart attacks in women at an unusually early age. (Refer to *Chapter 16* for more information on metabolic syndrome.)

- **Smoking** – Women who smoke are twice as likely to have a heart attack as male smokers.

- **Symptoms** – Many women do not experience the crushing chest pain that is a classic symptom of a heart attack in men. Some feel extremely tired or short of breath. Other atypical symptoms include nausea and abdominal, neck, and shoulder pain. During a heart attack, only about one in eight women reported chest pain; even then, they described it as pressure, aching, or tightness rather than pain.

- **Diagnosis and treatment** – Women have smaller and lighter coronary arteries than men do. This makes angiography, angioplasty, and coronary bypass surgery more difficult to do, thereby reducing a woman's chance of receiving a proper diagnosis. Women's responses to standard exercise stress tests are also different from men's, so it is difficult to interpret the results. Fortunately, these problems are diminishing due to a better understanding of heart disease in women.

- **Clinical trials** – Even though CVD is the leading cause of death in women, only one-third of cardiovascular clinical trial subjects are female and only 31% of cardiovascular clinical trials that include women report results by sex.

Gender differences in response to statins

Cholesterol may not play the same role in heart disease in women as in men and should not be the end point of the risk goal. Women can have high cholesterol and have a low risk of heart disease. Women have been under-represented in clinical trials of statins, even though they represent more than half of the population. As a result, evidence on the benefits and risks for women is limited. Studies have found that healthy women who took statins to prevent CVD did experience fewer episodes of chest pain and fewer stents and bypass surgeries. However, most importantly, statins did not prevent healthy women from having their first heart attacks and statins did not save lives. In a review of some trials where women with pre-existing heart disease were represented, cardiac events were reduced by only 0.8% per year for a five-year period and there was no decline in overall death rates.

The Jupiter trial, which included 6,801 women 60 years of age and older, found a significantly lower risk of hospitalizations for unstable angina in women taking statins. However, there was no significant reduction in heart attacks, strokes, and deaths among these women. By contrast, male participants on statins had significantly fewer heart attacks and strokes. Women who are healthy derive little if any benefit from statins, and even those women who have established heart disease derive only half the benefit men do.

In addition, an overview in the medical journal *The Lancet* (2007) emphasized that there has never been a single clinical trial showing that statin therapy is beneficial for women who don't already have heart disease or diabetes. They question the evidence base for promoting statin use for this large population of women (75% of women statin users do not have heart disease), which is based on research extrapolated from men.

Researchers at Women and Health Protection recently reviewed the effectiveness and safety of statin medications for women in Canada. They were looking for the evidence base for use of this widely-prescribed class of drugs. What they found was evidence for caution. To view the full report, *Evidence for Caution,* go to the Women and Health Protection website at **whp-apsf.ca.**

The debate on how to treat women who have some of the common risk factors for CVD has taken on urgency due to the questionable benefits as well as the risks associated with taking statins. Some of the common side effects are muscle pain, liver and kidney damage, and cognitive effects such as memory loss and confusion. The most common side effect is diabetes. For example, a study published in 2012 showed that postmenopausal women who participated in the Women's Health Initiative were much more likely to develop diabetes if they took statins. Diabetes is a significant independent risk factor for heart disease.

Despite the lack of data supporting the benefits of statins for women as well as the significant risk of side effects, women remain heavy users of statins.

Gender differences in response to aspirin

Another good example of the different effects of medication on women compared to men is the study done on aspirin to prevent CVD in both men and women. A meta-analysis of randomized controlled trials of aspirin available in 1997 supported the use of low-dose aspirin to prevent CVD in both high-risk men and women. The first large-scale clinical trial was the Physicians Health Study of men without CHD; aspirin reduced the incidence of MI, but had no effect on stroke risk.

In contrast, the Women's Health Study (WHS) showed that aspirin had no overall effect on CVD, although a reduction in ischemic stroke was observed. In women over 65 years of age, there was a significant reduction in the risk of ischemic stroke and a small reduction in risk of MI; among women under 65 years of age, there was no MI benefit and a small benefit in reduction of stroke risk. Overall, the risk of hemorrhagic stroke and gastrointestinal bleeding appeared to mitigate much of the beneficial effects of aspirin in the WHS.

The US Preventive Services Task Force recommends that aspirin use be encouraged only among women when the potential benefit of reduction in ischemic stroke outweighs the potential harm of an increase in gastrointestinal hemorrhage, a situation difficult to define. The gender differences in benefits associated with aspirin may be associated several factors including the following:

- The later onset of CVD in women
- The greater proportion of ischemic strokes among women in general compared with men
- The relatively small incidence of MI among women and stroke among men
- Gender differences in aspirin metabolism
- The fact that aspirin resistance is more common in women than men

But whatever the reason, all of these possibilities confirm that there is a significant gender difference in disease and how drugs are metabolized by each sex.

Signs and Symptoms of CVD

It is important to recognize the warning signs of a heart attack to ensure prompt medical treatment. Women's symptoms may be different from men's. For example, while chest pain is considered the most common heart attack warning sign, many women have heart attacks without chest pain. Some less familiar symptoms are more common in women than in men. Table 16.2 shows a list of the leading symptoms for women before and during a heart attack.

Table 16.2 Heart Attack Symptoms in Women

One month before a heart attack	During a heart attack
Unusual fatigue (71%)	Shortness of breath (58%)
Sleep disturbance (48%)	Weakness (55%)
Shortness of breath (42%)	Unusual fatigue (43%)
Indigestion (39%)	Cold sweat (39%)
Anxiety (36%)	Dizziness (39%)
Heart racing (27%)	Nausea (36%)
Arms weak/heavy (25%)	Arms weak/heavy (35%)

Source: *Circulation* 2003, Vol. 108, p. 2621.

Possible Causes of and Risk Factors for CVD

A number of risk factors are associated with developing CHD, including the following:

- **Increasing age** – over 83% of people who die of CHD are 65 or older.
- **Heredity and race** – Children of parents with heart disease are more likely to develop it themselves. African-Americans, Mexican-Americans

and First Nations peoples are at higher risk, partly due to higher rates of obesity and diabetes.

- **Smoking** – A smoker's risk of developing CHD is 2–4 times that of non-smokers.

- **Cholesterol** – It is important to maintain a high level of HDL and a low level of LDL, particularly ApoB and Lipoprotein (a).

- **High blood pressure** – Elevated blood pressure indicates the heart's workload, causing the heart to thicken and become stiffer.

- **Physical inactivity** – Regular moderate exercise helps prevent heart disease.

- **C-reactive protein (CRP) levels** – People with elevated CRP levels, a marker for inflammation, are at higher risk.

- **Obesity and overweight** – People who have excess body fat are more likely to develop heart disease and stroke even if they have no other risk factors.

- **Diabetes and metabolic syndrome** – Both of these significantly increase the risk of developing heart disease.

- **Stress** – Stress and the inflammatory response caused by increased stress hormones are known to be a significant risk for heart disease.

- **Excess alcohol** – Excess consumption of alcohol can cause increased blood pressure, contribute to elevated triglycerides, and increase risk of obesity and heart disease as well as many other alcohol-related diseases. The risk of heart disease in moderate drinkers (one drink for women, two for men per day) is lower than in non-drinkers.

- **Age** – Young adults are the new at-risk group for heart disease in Canada.

Other factors involved in CVD

Vitamin D

Vitamin D insufficiency is very common in the Canada and worldwide. Several recent epidemiologic studies have demonstrated a strong association between vitamin D insufficiency and risk of CVD, diabetes, and metabolic syndrome. Other studies have suggested that vitamin D deficiency predisposes individuals to increased risk of hypertension, ischemic heart disease, sudden cardiac death, or heart failure. For the general population, increasing vitamin D status with a daily supplement containing at least 2000 IU may be sufficient. Vitamin D deficiency is implicated in so many chronic diseases that we would encourage people to have a baseline vitamin D level done. The results may surprise you.

Vitamin C and lysine

Two-time Nobel Prize winner, Linus Pauling, discovered a breakthrough in how to treat heart disease. He proposed that heart disease could be prevented or treated by taking vitamin C and lysine. Pauling based this theory on a couple of findings: He found that plaque deposits are made up of a form of cholesterol called lipoprotein (a) and that plaque buildup only forms in areas of the artery that are inflamed. The inflammation in the walls of the arteries would expose strands of the amino acid lysine (another important component of collagen) to attract Lp(a), causing plaque buildup. Collagen is an important structural component in the arterial walls and vitamin C is a key player in the production of collagen throughout the body, especially for healthy blood vessels.

Another important observation by Pauling was that CVD does not occur in any of the animals that are able to manufacture their own vitamin C. Humans, however, as well as apes and guinea pigs, have lost the ability to produce our own vitamin C. We therefore must get it through our diets or through supplementation. When vitamin C levels are reduced, collagen production is decreased.

Magnesium

Unfortunately, many Canadians are not getting enough of magnesium, an essential mineral. A recent study by Health Canada showed that more than 34% of Canadians have a magnesium intake that is below the estimated average requirement. This means that more than one-third of Canadians have insufficient magnesium levels, and are therefore at risk for various health problems associated with low magnesium levels. A chronic low magnesium state has been associated with a number of chronic diseases, including diabetes, hypertension, CHD, myocardial infarction, asthma, and osteoporosis.

Magnesium has important effects on the cardiovascular system, affecting cardiac electrical activity, myocardial contractility, and vascular tone. The relationship between magnesium deficiency and cardiac arrhythmias associated with acute myocardial infarction is well known. There is also a substantial body of epidemiological and experimental evidence linking magnesium deficiency and atherosclerotic cardiovascular disease.

Experimental magnesium deficiency is characterized by increased triglycerides, cholesterol, VLDL, LDL, apolipoprotein B, and triglyceride-rich lipoproteins, and a reduced HDL. Magnesium supplementation of hyperlipidemic subjects has been shown to cause a reduction in total and LDL cholesterol and apolipoprotein B, and an increase in HDL. In several studies, magnesium supplementation was associated with a significant decrease in blood pressure.

Emotional stress and inflammation

Emotions associated with stress are important risk factors for cardiovascular disease. The Mayo Clinic reported that the strongest risk factor for future cardiac event among individuals with existing coronary artery disease (CAD) is psychological – stressful emotions like anger, anxiety, and worry dramatically increased the risk.

At least half, with some sources claiming as high as 75%, of all heart attacks occur in people without any traditional risk factors. People who are prone to anger, hostility, and depressive symptoms respond to stress with increased production of the stress hormones that activate the inflammatory arm of the immune system, triggering chronic inflammation, characterized by high levels of C-reactive protein (CRP.) The study showed that those people prone to anger had 2–3 times higher CRP levels than their calmer counterparts. The more pronounced their negative moods, the higher the CRP.

Inflammation and atherosclerosis

Abnormal lipid levels (dyslipidemia) paired with inflammation cause a vicious circle in the development of atherosclerosis. Dyslipidemia triggers an inflammatory process and inflammation elicits dyslipidemia. As a result, fatty deposits in the inner walls of arteries can develop. This narrows the arteries and increases the risk they will become blocked. Atherosclerosis is derived from the Greek words "athero" meaning paste and "sclerosis", which means hardening.

The inflammation occurs in response to stimulus arising from substances (e.g., pathogens, damaged cells, toxins, irritants) that pose threats to the survival of the cells.

Atherosclerosis develops due to factors including failure of the immune system to counteract or destroy harmful agents detected by the system as foreign. As a result, the artery becomes inflamed, thus encouraging the deposition of plaque containing lipids. These two factors cause a heightened state of cardiovascular activity, resulting in damage to blood vessels and the production of cytokines and other inflammatory mediators, all of which promote the inflammatory process and the deposition of plaque. These atherosclerotic lesions can remain asymptomatic for years or progress into disease stages where clinical manifestations such as angina, heart attack, or stroke.

Nonsteroidal Anti-inflammatory Drugs

Nonsteroidal anti-inflammatory drugs (NSAIDs) are a class of drugs that reduce or relieve pain and inflammation. A meta-analysis published in the *British Journal of Medicine* in May 2017 found that all NSAIDs, including naproxen, are associated with an increased risk of acute myocardial infarction. This meta-analysis involved 61,460 cases in 446,763 individuals, and is the largest investigation of its type.

Stress hormones

Adrenal stress hormones called glucocorticoids are powerful anti-inflammatory agents initially, but in chronic stress, a problem can occur in the feedback loop of the HPA. Eventually this causes cells in the immune system to release cytokines, which are molecules that promote inflammation. In several studies, activation of the HPA axis, with increased cortisol, has been associated with higher plasma glucose, triglycerides, blood pressure, obesity, insulin resistance, glucose intolerance, dyslipidemia, and hypertension.

Stress also causes blood to become thicker (increased viscosity). The combination of a narrowing of the arteries due to plaque and increased viscosity of the blood puts considerable stress on the heart and blood vessels. This can cause increases in blood pressure, and plaque can often become dislodged and travel in the blood stream, becoming a ticking time bomb. If it gets stuck in one of the heart's arteries, it triggers a heart attack. Or if it is trapped in a blood vessel in the brain, it can cause a stroke. Abnormalities in the HPA have been described in several chronic inflammatory disorders. It is clear that stress can create significant damage to the cardiovascular system.

Thyroid disorders and CVD

The cardiovascular signs and symptoms of thyroid disease are some of the most profound and clinically relevant findings that accompany both hyperthyroidism and hypothyroidism. Scientists have identified a previously unknown group of nerve cells that develop in the brain with the aid of thyroid hormone, which is produced in the thyroid gland. Individuals who produce too much or too little thyroid hormone risk developing problems with these nerve cells. This, in turn, has an effect on the function of the heart, leading to cardiovascular disease.

It is well known that patients with untreated hyperthyroidism or hypothyroidism often develop heart problems as a result of thyroid hormone affecting the heart directly. However, this new research shows that thyroid hormone also affects the heart indirectly, through the newly discovered neurons in the brain.

Hypothyroidism and CVD

The most common cardiovascular signs and symptoms of hypothyroidism include blood pressure changes, alterations in lipid metabolism, decreased cardiac contractility, decreased cardiac output, accelerated atherosclerosis and coronary artery disease, and increased stroke risk. Although subclinical hypothyroidism is often considered to be asymptomatic, many people have symptoms in the early stages of thyroid hormone deficiency. Lipid metabolism is altered and cholesterol levels appear to rise in parallel with thyroid-stimulating hormone (TSH) in hypothyroidism. C-reactive protein, a risk factor for heart disease, is also commonly increased in subclinical hypothyroidism. In addition, atherosclerosis, coronary heart disease, and myocardial infarction risk are increased in women with subclinical hypothyroidism. (Refer to *Chapter 4* for more information about thyroid testing and lab values to determine optimal thyroid function.)

Hyperthyroidism and CVD

Hyperthyroidism and thyrotoxicosis, conditions that result from excess thyroid hormone, are associated with palpitations, tachycardia, exercise intolerance, shortness of breath on exertion, and sometimes atrial fibrillation. Cardiac contractility is enhanced, and resting heart rate and cardiac output are increased. Recent studies now indicate that elevated T4 levels are a risk factor for atherosclerotic disease and myocardial infarction in middle-aged and elderly adults.

Subclinical hyperthyroidism is characterized by a low or undetectable serum TSH concentration in the presence of normal levels of serum T4 and T3. There may be no clinical signs or symptoms, however studies show that individuals are at risk for many of the cardiovascular manifestations associated with overt hyperthyroidism. The prevalence of subclinical hyperthyroidism appears to increase with advancing age. In a 10-year cohort study of older patients, a low TSH was associated with increased risk for cardiovascular mortality and atrial fibrillation.

Primary pulmonary hypertension is a progressive disease that leads to right-sided heart failure and premature death, and is often of unknown origin. Recently, a link to thyroid disease has been identified. In one study of 40 patients with primary pulmonary hypertension, more than 22% of patients were determined to have hypothyroidism. Some evidence exists that autoimmune disease may play a role in both hypothyroid- and hyperthyroid-linked cases of primary pulmonary hypertension. Thyroid disease should be considered in the differential diagnosis of primary pulmonary hypertension.

Testing and Diagnosis

Heart disease is often called the "silent killer" because all tests may be in the normal range. Many people may have few or no symptoms, and do not even know that they have it. Your health care practitioner may want to run a number of tests to assess your risks for cardiovascular disease, including the following:

- **Triglycerides** – Triglycerides are an important risk factor in insulin resistance as risk for heart disease.

- **LDL/HDL ratio** – It is important to maintain a higher level of HDL.

- **Apolipoprotein B (ApoB)** – ApoB is the primary apolipoprotein of the LDL (bad cholesterol) and is responsible for carrying cholesterol to the tissues. High levels of ApoB can lead to plaque that causes vascular disease (atherosclerosis) and has been found to be a better predictor of heart disease than LDL.

- **Lipoprotein (a)** – Lipoprotein (a) is a strong risk factor for CAD, cerebrovascular disease, atherosclerosis, thrombosis, and stroke.

Lipoprotein (a) levels are only slightly affected by diet, exercise, and other environmental factors, and commonly prescribed lipid-reducing drugs have little or no effect. High Lp(a) predicts risk of early atherosclerosis similar to LDL. However, in advanced atherosclerosis, Lp(a) is an independent risk factor, not dependent on LDL. In cases of elevated lipoprotein (a), aspirin has been shown to lower levels up to 80%.

- **CRP** – CPR is a general marker for infection and inflammation. Ask for the high-sensitivity CRP (hs-CRP).

- **Homocysteine** – This common amino acid is related to early development of heart and blood vessel disease. A high level of homocysteine causes inflammation in the blood vessels, and even slightly elevated levels can significantly increase risk factors. It has been correlated with the occurrence of blood clots, heart attacks, and strokes.

- **Fibrinogen** – This protein produced by the liver is essential for blood clot formation. The test is used as part of an investigation of a possible or inappropriate blood clot formation (thrombotic episode).

- **Lipoprotein particle testing (LPP)** – Approximately 50% of people who suffer from heart attacks have "normal" cholesterol numbers. Advanced cholesterol testing is now offered by specialized labs, which accurately measure both the density and number of lipoprotein particles. This may be a more accurate assessment of cardiovascular risk.

- **Ferritin** – High levels of this storage form of iron can also be a marker for inflammation and a predictor for heart disease.

- **Fasting blood sugars, HbA1c, and insulin** – Diabetes, metabolic syndrome, and insulin resistance can all increase the risk of developing heart disease.

- **Oxidata™ test** – This test is usually performed by a naturopathic doctor and assesses free-radical burden in the body, which can lead to chronic inflammation and increased risk of cardiovascular disease.

- **Pulse** – A pulse rate of more than 76 beats per minute represents a higher risk for heart disease.

- **High blood pressure** – High blood pressure increases risk for CAD.

- **25-hydroxy vitamin D** – Low vitamin D status can be an increased risk for cardiovascular disease.

- **Salivary cortisol** – Assessment of stress hormone levels throughout the day is important.

- **Lp-PLA2 -(PLAC Test)** – This test measures an enzyme that promotes inflammation inside the arteries, leading to the formation of unstable, rupture-prone plaques. It is different from standard tests for inflammation because Lp-PLA2 is a specific cardiovascular risk factor that provides unique information about the stability of arterial plaques. Unstable arterial plaques can rupture, leading to CHD and ischemic stroke.

The pulse test

In an era of high-tech medicinal wonders, medical researchers have recently found a free and easy way to predict a woman's risk of future heart attack: take her pulse. It was found that those women with the highest resting pulse – greater than 76 beats per minute – were more likely to suffer a heart attack or die from CHD than women with the lowest – 62 beats per minute or less. Doctors have known for years that heart rate predicts heart attack risk in men, and the higher a man's resting pulse, the greater the risk. Until recently, there was no good evidence the same held true for women.

HAIR GIVES A HEADS-UP ON HEART ATTACK RISK

A study published in the journal *Stress* found that the stress hormone cortisol can be measured in hair, providing the first long-term record of chronic stress. In this study, high levels of cortisol in the hair were associated with heart attacks. This test may be used to identify people at risk for cardiovascular disease. *Journal of Clinical Endocrinology and Metabolism,* May 2013.

what we know works

Support for CVD

AdrenaSense® helps regulate stress hormones related to cardiovascular disease. In several studies, elevated cortisol has been associated with higher plasma glucose, triglycerides, blood pressure, obesity, insulin resistance, glucose intolerance, dyslipidemia, and hypertension.

Dosage: 2–3 capsules daily (2 with breakfast and 1 midday).

Note: Siberian ginseng (known as eleuthero in the US) in AdrenaSense is an adaptogenic herb that regulates blood pressure, as opposed to *Panax ginseng* that has been known to elevate blood pressure in some people. If you have hypertension, start with 1 capsule of AdrenaSense a day and slowly increase, and monitor your blood pressure.

MagSense™ (magnesium bisglycinate) is an easy-to-take powder that provides an ideal dose in an efficiently absorbed and well-tolerated form of magnesium. MagSense also includes other important minerals, vitamins, and nutrients that are involved in the biochemical reactions and metabolism in the body.

All of these are essential factors in the body and work with magnesium to promote optimal functioning of the heart, nerves, muscles, and other systems throughout the body.

Dosage: 1 scoop daily.

CardioSense® contains hawthorn, grapeseed extract, berberine, boswellia, chamomile, beet, and ganoderma to support the causes of CVD, including inflammation, antioxidant deficiency, lipids, and stress. It is an important supplement for both prevention and support of CVD. Refer below for more information on individual ingredients.

Dosage: 2 capsules 1–2 times daily.

Hawthorn *(Crataegus oxyacantha)* increases coronary blood flow, thus improving the use of oxygen by the heart. The berries, leaves, and flowers of hawthorn have been used traditionally as cardiac tonics in a variety of heart disorders. The cardioprotective ingredient comes from its flavonoid content, specifically the proanthocyanidin, which gives the herb significant antioxidant activity. In addition, it is effective for hypertension, reducing cholesterol (LDL and triglycerides), and preventing atherosclerosis and heart disease.

Grape seed extract *(Vitis vinifera)* contains proanthocyanidins (PC), a class of antioxidants found in foods such as grape seeds, barley, chocolate, red wine, rose hips, apples, and berries. PC has been shown to help prevent cardiovascular disease and improve blood circulation, and reduce platelet aggregation, a common cause of stroke. Grape seed extract is available in supplement form and is a good source of PCs.

Berberine *(Berberis vulgaris)* has been show to significantly reduce LDL-C and triglycerides. In addition, berberine also has antihypertensive and antiarrhythmic properties and has proven to be a useful treatment of CVD. Diabetes is a contributing factor in CVD and studies show that berberine is effective in regulating blood sugar in people with insulin resistance and diabetes type 2.

Boswellia *(Boswellia serrate)* is a very effective anti-inflammatory herb. Chronic inflammation is intimately involved in all stages of atherosclerosis, the process that leads to cholesterol-clogged arteries and that sets the stage for heart attacks, most strokes, peripheral artery disease, and even vascular dementia, a common cause of memory loss. It is very important to address the inflammatory cause of CVD.

Reishi mushrooms *(Ganoderma lucidum)* have been proven to increase resistance to stress and improve mental and physical fatigue. Reishi mushrooms also provide antioxidant to help prevent inflammation, a common cause of heart disease.

Beet *(Beta vulgaris* root) is effective in dilating blood vessels to decrease blood pressure. Researchers suggest that it works by reducing overstimulation of the sympathetic nervous system that occurs with heart disease and are exploring the use of beet juice as a treatment option for people with cardiovascular disease.

Chamomile *(Chamomilla recutita)* is effective in the treatment of gut inflammation which has been shown to be a factor in cardiovascular disease.

Coenzyme Q10 (CoQ10) deficiency has been identified in 50–75% of heart tissue biopsies in patients with various heart conditions. Many studies show its effectiveness in the treatment of high blood pressure, atherosclerosis, angina, congestive heart failure, and cardiomyopathy. It seems to work better when taken with vitamin E.

Dosage: 50–150 mg daily or 2 mg for each kg of body weight. Some experts say the sicker the cardiac patient, the higher the CoQ10 levels need to be.

Note: Be aware that medications for hypertension and high cholesterol (i.e., statins) deplete CoQ10.

Omega-3 fatty acids have special anti-inflammatory properties and have been proven beneficial for hypertension and other symptoms of CVD. Canadian researchers examined the effects of daily ingestion of ground flaxseed on systolic (SBP) and diastolic blood pressure (DBP) in patients with peripheral artery disease. Individuals with a baseline SBP greater than 140 mm Hg who consumed 30 g of flaxseed daily for six months obtained an average reduction of 15 mm Hg in SBP and 7 mm Hg in DBP, while those with normal BP showed no effect. This study shows that the simple addition of flaxseed to the diet produces a potent blood pressure-lowering action in people with high BP. It can be added to the diet in the form of flaxseed oil, pumpkin seed oil, or mixed blends containing omega-3 and omega-6 fatty acids. Some people prefer capsules in the form of fish oils.

Dosage: 1000–3000 mg daily.

Medi-C Plus™ contains vitamin C and lysine. Vitamin C is a powerful antioxidant that prevents oxidation of LDL, raises HDL, and lowers triglycerides. Vitamin C is an essential part of any health program and may help prevent atherosclerosis. As discussed earlier, the combination of vitamin C and lysine helps reduce the formation of bad cholesterol and hardening of the arteries, and promotes healthy collagen, thus preventing heart disease.

Dosage: 1–3 scoops daily mixed in water.

Sytrinol® is derived from natural citrus and palm fruit extracts. It is a powerful antioxidant, reduces arterial plaque, improves glycemic control, reduces blood platelet aggregation, and improves overall cardiovascular health. Studies show that the combination of the ingredients found in Sytrinol work independently of diet. This is great news if you are just starting to evolve your diet toward a more heart-healthy way of eating.

Dosage: 1 capsule daily.

Additional support for CVD

Folic acid, B6, and **B12** enable our bodies to recycle homocysteine back to methionine or change it to a helpful cysteine. Homocysteine, as mentioned earlier, is a marker for heart disease and chronic inflammation in the body. Insufficient levels of B12, folic acid, and vitamin B6, cause homocysteine levels to rise, which leads to increased risk of CHD, stroke, and peripheral vascular disease.

Dosage: Folic acid: 0.4–3 mg daily; Vitamin B12: 400–1000 mcg daily; Vitamin B6: 25–100 mg daily.

Garlic improves circulation and has been shown to reduce blood pressure. Use liberally in foods or take as a supplement.

Dosage: 1000–3000 mg daily.

Vitamin E with mixed tocopherols is an antioxidant that improves blood flow and reduces fatty plaques.

Dosage: 200–400 IU daily.

Note: Do not take with blood thinners such as Warfarin.

Alpha-lipoic acid (ALA) is a powerful antioxidant that prevents free-radical formation, thereby protecting the cardiovascular system. It is both fat- and water-soluble, and is easily transported to all tissues and cells of the body, as well as crossing the blood-brain barrier. ALA protects against LDL oxidation and reduces inflammation, thereby helping to prevent atherosclerosis and other cardiovascular disease.

Dosage: 50–150 mg daily (up to 500 mg daily can be taken without side effects).

Vitamin D deficiency is very common in people suffering from atherosclerosis and heart disease. There is a strong inverse relationship between vitamin D levels and artery calcification. The more vitamin D in the blood, the less calcification. Artery cells have vitamin D receptors which, when stimulated by vitamin D, inhibit the deposit of calcium.

Dosage: 3000–5000 IU daily.

Medications

Information for women who take statins

The low cholesterol levels related to statin use have frequently been associated with an increased risk of cancer. Most statin trials are terminated within 2–5 years, a period too short to see most cancers develop. Nevertheless, some studies have shown a greater incidence of cancer in people who take statins, and one long-term study demonstrated a dramatic increase in the incidence of breast cancer among women who had used statins for more than 10 years.

Reports out of Britain have revealed that leaders in health care and research, including the editor in chief of the *British Medical Journal* and the chair of Britain's Commons Health Select Committee, have called for drug companies to release all of their records involving undisclosed adverse effects of statins in their clinical trials.

Statins and vitamin D

One common side effect of statin use is muscle stiffness, pain, or cramping, called myalgia. The mechanism for statin-related myalgia is not fully understood, but vitamin D has been speculated to play a role. Vitamin D deficiency itself is associated with symptoms of myalgia that resemble those caused by statins. There has been speculation that statins themselves might affect vitamin D levels. Because low-density lipoprotein (LDL) cholesterol is a vitamin D carrier and statins reduce LDL cholesterol, it has been proposed that statins could decrease vitamin D levels. This could be one of the reasons we are seeing so many people, particularly the aging, with low vitamin D status. Doctors are told to prescribe statins to everyone over 50 to lower LDL. Statin-treated patients with lower vitamin D levels had increased odds of myalgia compared with non-statin users; however, statin users with higher vitamin D levels did not have an increased risk for myalgia compared with non-statin users.

RELATIVE RISK VERSUS ABSOLUTE RISK

At this point it is important to provide more information on the way results and statistics from clinical trials are presented in terms of absolute risk reduction versus relative risk reduction:

- Absolute risk reduction is the decrease in risk of a treatment in relation to a control treatment.

- Relative risk reduction is calculated by dividing the absolute risk reduction by the control event rate.

Most drug companies that are the stakeholders in clinical trials present results in terms of relative risk reduction. However, the way the results of a study are presented make a huge difference in our understanding of the findings.

For example, suppose that in a study of 200 women to examine the risk of disease X, half of them take a drug and half take a placebo.

After five years, two women in the drug group develop disease X, compared to four who took the placebo. This data could lead to either of the following statements and both would be correct:

- New miracle drug cuts disease X risk by 50%!

- New drug results in 2% drop in disease X risk!

The headlines represent two different ways to express the same data. The first headline expresses the relative risk reduction – the two women who took the drug (subjects) and developed disease X equal half the number (50%) of the four women who took the placebo (controls) and developed disease X. The second headline expresses the absolute risk reduction – 2% of the subjects (2 out of 100) who took the drug developed disease X and 4% of the controls (4 out of 100) who took the placebo developed disease X – an absolute difference of 2% (4% minus 2%). Now you can see why clinical trials, especially those funded by drug companies, cite relative risk reductions rather than absolute risk reductions: Relative risk tells you nothing about the actual risk.

Not all experts agree on the benefits of statins. Some researchers have found that statins, the cholesterol-lowering drugs prescribed to prevent heart attacks, are not as effective nor are as safe as we have been led to believe. Statins do produce a reduction in cholesterol levels, but have failed to substantially prevent strokes, heart attacks, and heart disease-related deaths and the "statistical deception" has been used to inflate claims about their effectiveness.

The exaggeration of beneficial effects of statin treatment was illustrated in some of the bigger clinical trials, including the Jupiter trial, the Anglo-Scandinavian Cardiac Outcomes Trial Lipid Lowering Arm (ASCOT-LLA), and the British Heart Protection Study. For example, in the Jupiter trial, the public and health care workers were informed of a 54% reduction in heart attacks, when the actual reduction of coronary events was less than 1%.

The statin debate is ongoing based on differences in the interpretation of data and other stakeholder factors. Early statin trials reported significant mortality benefits, yet serious concerns have been raised in some studies regarding biased results, premature trial terminations, under reporting of adverse events, high numbers of patients lost to follow-up and oversight by the pharmaceutical company sponsor. For example, since 2004, researchers at the University of California in San Diego have been compiling information on statin-related problems. Their research has estimated that, while clinical trials may report 1–7% of patients experience adverse drug reactions, the number of adverse reactions with statin use may be closer to 15%.

The exaggerated claims in terms of relative risk and absolute risk are not isolated to the statin statistics in the portrayal of benefits and minimized risks.

Low-dose aspirin, CVD, and diabetes

Low-dose aspirin does not prevent cardiovascular events in patients with type 2 diabetes and, as mentioned earlier, aspirin provides no benefit to women in preventing CVD with the exception of stroke. The new data come from The Japanese Primary Prevention of Atherosclerosis with Aspirin for Diabetes (JPAD), a long-term randomized study involving 2,500 patients with type 2 diabetes who were randomly assigned to low-dose aspirin or no aspirin. The initial findings showed no effect of aspirin on sudden death, heart disease, stroke, or peripheral artery disease. In Europe, the guidelines do not recommend aspirin for primary prevention of cardiovascular events in patients with type 2 diabetes except in high-risk cases. It may be time for the North American guidelines to be revisited and changed.

Diet and Lifestyle Tips for CVD

What is the Mediterranean diet?

The Mediterranean diet is a nutritional model inspired by traditional dietary patterns of the countries of the Mediterranean basin, particularly Italy, Greece, and Spain. It is based primarily on the following:

- Olive oil (primary fat)
- High vegetable/fruit intake
- Whole grains
- Moderate fish intake

- Moderate dairy intake
- Moderate wine consumption
- Limited red meat and saturated fats

Refer to *Chapter 19* for more information on the Mediterranean diet.

Epidemiological studies demonstrate that the Mediterranean diet reduces the incidence of CHD. In particular, the antioxidant effects of olive oil may contribute to these protective effects by preventing the oxidation of LDL. There is also a reduced incidence of hypertension in populations that consume the Mediterranean diet. Several studies have demonstrated the anti-hypertensive properties of olive oil. It is suggested that the mechanism for blood pressure reduction is that olive oil is a calcium channel antagonist closely related to the common calcium channel blocker drugs.

"Let Food be Your Medicine and Medicine Your Food."
– Hippocrates

The effect of barley on lipids

There has been recent interest in barley as a therapeutic food owing to its high content of beta-glucan, a viscous soluble fibre recognized for its cholesterol-lowering properties. A meta-analysis was done on randomized controlled trials that investigated the cholesterol-lowering potential of barley beta-glucan on low-density lipoprotein cholesterol (LDL-C), non-high-density lipoprotein cholesterol (non-HDL-C), and apolipoprotein B (apoB) for CVD risk reduction. Results of the analysis show that barley beta-glucan has a lowering effect on LDL-C and non-HDL-C.

FISH INTAKE, CONTAMINANTS, AND HUMAN HEALTH:
Evaluating the Risk and Benefits

- Even modest consumption of fish reduces risk of coronary death by 36% and total mortality by 17%.

- Avoidance of seafood consumption due to perceived health risks could result in thousands of needless deaths per year due to CHD and suboptimal neurodevelopment in children.

- Recommendation: consumers should vary the species of fish in their diets.

(*JAMA*, October 18, 2006)

Other health tips to decrease your risk factors for CVD

- **Exercise** – A lack of exercise has been found to be a primary factor in increasing the risk of heart disease, diabetes, and obesity. Even walking 30 minutes three times per week decreases your risk of heart attack by 30%. Gentle jogging or increased walking speed can reduce risk up to 60%. A recent study in the *Journal of the American Medical Association* found that leisure time and physical activity decreased heart disease by 50%.

- **Water, water, water** – Keeping well-hydrated can help maintain healthy blood flow. As little as five or six glasses of water daily can cut your risk of heart disease in half.

- **Quit smoking** – Quit smoking, or at the very least, reduce it.

- **Change your diet** – A diet high in fruits and vegetables, fish (a good source of essential fatty acids) and lean meats such as the Mediterranean diet can considerably reduce the risk of heart disease as well as other chronic diseases.

- **Rest and relaxation** – Make sure to get adequate sleep and find ways to reduce your stress, such as exercise or meditation. Sleep deprivation increases the risk of obesity, diabetes, and hypertension. There are several interesting studies showing the positive effects of meditation for the management of stress-related disorders such as hypertension and other risk factors for heart disease. The physiological effects of meditation include decreased heart rate, reduced respiratory rate, reduced blood pressure, lower cortisol levels, and reduced free radicals.

- **Eliminate refined carbohydrates** – Refined carbohydrates stimulate the release of insulin, which has many harmful effects on the body. Through a series of steps throughout the body, high insulin levels promote fat storage, increase blood pressure, shut off fat-burning path ways, and turn on pathways that produce fat and triglycerides. Arterial damage and plaque formation (atherosclerosis) is also increased.

- **Emotional state** – Studies at Harvard Medical School show that negative emotions such as anger, depression, worry, or anxiety are linked to an increased risk of heart disease. In older adults, it has been found that depression is associated with a greater than 50% risk of heart failure.

- **Consumption of fats and oils** – Do not get caught up in the "fat phobia". Good fats do not promote heart disease or cholesterol problems. Instead of hydrogenated and heated oils such as margarines, deep fried foods, and processed oils, use essential fatty acids (omega-3 and omega-6) from flaxseed, pumpkin seed, and fish oils. Olive oil is also good for the heart. Animal fats are not the bad guys – heated, refined oils are.

Chapter **18**

Dementia

Memory Disorders – An Overview

Alzheimer's disease is the leading form of dementia, representing 63% of all dementias. Vascular dementia is second, representing 20% of all dementias. In 2011, 15% of Canadians 65 or older were living with cognitive impairment, including dementia. This year alone, more than 100,000 Canadians will be diagnosed with dementia – that is one person every five minutes.

Tau is a protein found inside brain cells. Its role is to provide a structure to help the cells clear any accumulation of unwanted and toxic proteins. Fewer plaques accumulate outside the brain cells when tau is functioning. Plaques are an accumulation of sticky proteins called beta-amyloid. The death of brain cells begins when tau fails to function properly. When tau is abnormal, these proteins, which include beta-amyloid, accumulate inside the neurons. Essentially, the proteins begin to exert toxic effects inside the cell, so the cells do their best to spit out the proteins into the extracellular space. The beta-amyloid protein fragments are sticky, so they begin to clump together into plaque.

The protein that cannot be spit out and remains inside the neurons is what destroys them – not the plaques building up on the outside of the cells. The cell cannot remove the garbage, and this garbage includes beta-amyloid as well as tau. Meanwhile, the beta-amyloid released from the dead neuron sticks to the plaque and adds to its bulk. Researchers have found that without interaction of toxic beta-amyloids with tau, the Alzheimer's cascade cannot begin. People who suffer from Alzheimer's show plaques and tangles (twisted strands of tau) inside the brain.

Lewy bodies are clumps of protein similar to beta-amyloid plaques, but which contain a different protein. These form in the cortex of the brain, not the hippocampus as in Alzheimer's.

Types of Dementia

Vascular dementia

Vascular dementia is a general term describing problems with reasoning, planning, judgment, memory, and other thought processes. It is caused by brain damage from impaired blood flow from the brain. Vascular dementia can occur after a stroke blocks an artery in the brain, but strokes do not always cause vascular dementia. Whether a stroke affects thinking and reasoning depends on its severity and where it occurs in the brain. Vascular dementia can also be caused by other conditions or treatments that damage blood vessels and reduce circulation, depriving your brain of vital oxygen and nutrients.

Alzheimer's

There are three types of Alzheimer's:

- **Early-onset Alzheimer's** – This rare form of Alzheimer's affects people before 65 years of age. Less than 10% of the people with Alzheimer's have this form of the disease. Early-onset Alzheimer's appears to be linked with a genetic defect, whereas late-onset Alzheimer's is not.

• **Late-onset Alzheimer's** – This is the most common form of Alzheimer's, accounting for about 90% of all cases. It usually occurs after 65 years of age. The neuronal loss and atrophy occurs principally in the frontal cortex and temporal lobe, which houses the hippocampus. Several studies have demonstrated that pro-inflammatory substances accompany the deposition of plaque called beta-amyloid proteins, which is the signature of Alzheimer's.

• **Familial Alzheimer's** – This form of Alzheimer's is entirely inherited. It is very rare and accounts for less than 1% of all cases. Familial Alzheimer's can occur as early as the late thirties or early forties.

Gender Differences in Dementia

Women represent 72% of the cases in Alzheimer's and 47% of vascular dementias. More women than men get Alzheimer's, in part because women tend to live longer than men and the chances of developing Alzheimer's increases with age. But new research suggests there may be genetic reasons as well.

Researchers at Stanford University School of Medicine reported that women who carry the apolipoprotein E type 4 allele (APOE-e4) gene, which increases the risk for Alzheimer's, are more likely to develop the disease than men who have the same gene. While only about 15% of the general population carries the APOE-e4 gene, almost half of those with Alzheimer's have the gene. Everyone carries some version of the APOE gene, which plays a role in how cholesterol and fats are shuttled throughout the body. But only people who carry the APOE-e4 variant are at increased risk.

Signs and Symptoms of Dementia

People developing dementia may exhibit the following symptoms:

• Memory loss affecting day-to-day function, such as forgetting phone numbers (even your own), appointments, a colleague's name, etc.

• Difficulty performing familiar tasks such as preparing a meal, or becoming so distracted that you forget to turn off the stove.

• Problems with language such as finding the right words – even simple words – and making substitutions that do not make sense.

- Disorientation of time and place, such as becoming lost in a familiar area and not knowing how to get home, or not knowing what month it is.

- Poor judgment, such as wearing cold-weather clothing on a warm day, or not recognizing a condition that needs medical attention.

- Problems with abstract thinking, such as balancing a chequebook or being able to pay bills.

- Misplacing things on a regular basis, or putting things in inappropriate places, such as the phone in the freezer.

- Changes in mood, behaviour, or personality (e.g., going from tears to anger for no apparent reason, feelings of confusion or suspicion, being withdrawn and apathetic, feeling extremely fearful over nothing); people with Alzheimer's seem to have more dramatic personality changes and anger outbursts than people with vascular dementia.

Possible Causes of Dementia

Although there is a connection between family history and genetics for some people, many other factors have been linked to the development of dementia, including Alzheimer's.

Metabolism – diabetes and insulin resistance

Multiple clinical observations have demonstrated that dementia in general, and Alzheimer's in particular, are associated with type 2 diabetes and obesity. Moreover, type 2 diabetes is considered an independent risk factor for dementia, with the prevalence of dementia in diabetic populations double that of healthy patient populations.

Researchers have shown that individuals with Alzheimer's have a lower concentration of insulin in their cerebrospinal fluid and a higher concentration in their blood than controls, both of which indicate impaired insulin metabolism in the brain. Based on the results of these studies, Alzheimer's could be considered as a metabolic disease, with progressive impairment of the brain's capacity to use glucose and respond to insulin. Insulin treatment improves memory and attention span and lowers the concentrations of the amyloid precursor protein. This protein has been implicated in the development of Alzheimer's, which is now being referred to as type 3 diabetes.

Metabolic syndrome is an important factor in the development of mild cognitive impairment, vascular dementia, and Alzheimer's. Stress hormones, inflammation, and oxidative stress contribute to an insulin-resistant brain state, causing decreased glucose metabolism and the formation of beta-amyloid and tau proteins, both signatures of Alzheimer's.

Inflammation

Inflammation is the cornerstone of Alzheimer's, Parkinson's disease, multiple sclerosis, and other autoimmune disorders. Researchers have found that systemic inflammation leads to the production of pro-inflammatory cytokines in the hippocampus region of the brain. This region is involved in memory and learning.

A UK study published in the *Journal of Biological Psychiatry* in 2010 suggests inflammation in the brain may accelerate the progress of dementia. The research team found that just one episode of systemic inflammation (whole body inflammation) could be sufficient to trigger a more rapid decline in neurological function. The researchers found that systemic inflammation leads to the production of a pro-inflammatory cytokine by the brain's immune cells in the hippocampus region of the brain. This region is involved in memory and learning.

Alzheimer's and generalized cognitive decline are marked by age-related brain changes, such as disturbed immune function and increased oxidative stress, which contribute to inflammation. These factors are influenced by diet and the gut microbiota. In addition, brain-derived neurotrophic factor (BDNF), which protects and encourages the survival of healthy brain cells and whose production is influenced by gut bacteria, is shown to be decreased in people with Alzheimer's.

Head and heart connection

Growing evidence suggests that the health of the brain is closely linked to the overall health of the heart and blood vessels. A healthy heart helps ensure that enough blood is pumped through these blood vessels to the brain, and healthy blood vessels help ensure that the brain is supplied with the oxygen and nutrient-rich blood it needs to function normally.

Vascular dementia is associated with decreased blood flow to the brain. Cerebral blood flow is automatically regulated, allowing maintenance of a constant blood supply over a wide range of blood pressure. This regulatory mechanism shifts in the elderly, which can allow for rapid changes in blood pressure. Hypertension (increase in blood pressure) has been recognized as a risk factor for vascular dementia, but more recent studies show that lesions in the brain and cognitive decline can also be caused by a rapid fall in blood pressure.

New evidence suggests a strong link between dementias and heart disease, and there also seem to be many similarities between the two diseases. Research has shown that the same risk factors that result in cardiovascular disease, such as high blood pressure, cholesterol, and obesity, put people at higher risk for dementias, including Alzheimer's. These risk factors lead to atherosclerosis, a process where deposits of cholesterol and other substances (plaques) buildup in the arteries and narrow the blood vessels. Researchers have found that this process not only occurs in the cardiovascular system, but also in the brain.

Atherosclerosis can lead to heart attack causing blood clots, and may also lead to dementias by reducing the flow of blood that nourishes the brain. Inflammation is at the root of atherosclerosis.

Free-radical damage

Excessive free-radical damage is now thought to be a major player not only in brain aging and traumatic brain injury, but also in degenerative conditions like Alzheimer's and in mild cognitive impairment. As cognitive function begins to decline, markers for free-radical damage correlate directly with the degree of mental impairment.

Traumatic brain injury

Traumatic brain injury (TBI) is the disruption of normal brain function caused by a blow or jolt to the head or penetration of the skull by a foreign object. Moderate TBI is associated with twice the risk of developing Alzheimer's and other dementias compared with no head injuries, and severe TBI is associated with 4.5 times the risk.

Gluten intolerance and the brain

Gluten, which is in most carbohydrates such as breads, pastas, and cereals, might cause inflammation in the brain. Grains also cause an increase in blood sugar, and even slight elevations in blood sugar can increase the risk of developing dementia.

Dr. David Permutter, well-known neurologist and author of *Grain Brain*, says: "The biggest issue by far is that carbohydrates are absolutely at the cornerstone of all of our major degenerative conditions". He adds, "That includes things like Alzheimer's, heart disease, and even cancers. What we know is that even mild elevations in blood sugar are strongly related to developing Alzheimer's.

Even mild elevations in blood sugar compromise brain structure and lead to shrinkage of the brain. That's what our most well-respected, peer-reviewed journals are telling us." In addition to gluten, other food intolerances or allergies can affect brain function and memory.

Stress

Stress hormones appear to rapidly exacerbate the formation of brain lesions and the progression of dementias, including Alzheimer's. Management of both physical and psychological stress is crucial in the prevention and treatment of this devastating disease. The hippocampus is the primary area of degeneration in Alzheimer's. Stress hormones are toxic to the nerve cells, and stress-mediated glucocorticoids, whether too high or too low, reduce the size and plasticity of the hippocampus.

Researchers showed that when animals were injected for just seven days with stress hormones, the levels of the different proteins in the brain increased by 60%. These proteins, called beta-amyloids, form plaques or tangles in the brain, which is another signature of Alzheimer's. However, so far the drugs that remove these proteins have not succeeded in arresting the steady decline of thinking and memory.

Gut microbiota imbalances

In addition to the stress factor, neurodegenerative diseases such as Alzheimer's and generalized cognitive decline are marked by age-related brain changes, disturbed immune function, and increased oxidative stress, which are influenced by diet and abnormal gut microbiota. The imbalance in the microbiota interferes with the production of BDNF that protects and encourages survival of healthy brain cells. This BDNF is decreased in people with Alzheimer's. We know that depression and dementia are closely connected, so it is notable that the unhealthy dietary patterns that negatively influence the gut microbiota are also risk factors for depression.

Pesticides

New evidence published in March 2014 in *JAMA Neurology* suggests that pesticides and Alzheimer's could be intricately linked. The research showed that 74 out of the 86 Alzheimer's patients studied had blood levels of DDE (a toxic chemical compound) almost four times higher than those of the 79 people in the control group who did not have Alzheimer's. Patients with a version of APOE gene apolipoprotein E (ApoE4), which greatly increases the risk of developing Alzheimer's, along with high blood levels of DDE, exhibited even more severe cognitive impairment than the patients without the risk gene. Epidemiological studies also show evidence that DDT/DDE affect pathways associated with the development of beta-amyloid plaques, a hallmark of Alzheimer's. Other contaminants such as heavy metals (aluminum) and chemicals in the water, soil, or air are also thought to be involved in dementias.

Telomeres

Each time a cell replicates, a small piece of the DNA is removed from each chromosome. As these telomeres shorten, it affects genetic expression, resulting in degenerative conditions such as Alzheimer's. Curcumin has been shown to prevent the shortening of telomeres.

Depression

Early Alzheimer's and depression share many symptoms, so it can be hard to distinguish between the disorders. In addition, approximately 45% of people with Alzheimer's also are depressed. Similar symptoms include loss of interest in once-enjoyable activities and hobbies, social withdrawal, memory problems, sleeping too much or too little, and impaired concentration. People who have both Alzheimer's and depression may find it easier to cope with the changes caused by Alzheimer's when they feel less depressed, so it is important that the depression be addressed. It is interesting to note that inflammation has been proven to be one of the causes of both depression and Alzheimer's.

Elevated homocysteine levels

Elevated homocysteine levels occur in approximately one-third of people over 61 years of age. This risk factor is estimated to account for 22% of the instances of Alzheimer's. The rate of brain atrophy is associated with elevated levels of homocysteine, an essential amino acid that regulates phospholipid metabolism. Elevated homocysteine inhibits this process and, as a result, less omega-3 fatty acids are incorporated into phosphatidylcholine (PC). Decreased omega-3 content of PC has been linked to Alzheimer's.

B vitamins, particularly B6, B12, and folic acid, reduce levels of homocysteine and one study showed a nine-fold reduction in brain shrinkage and a substantial reduction in rate of memory loss with the addition of these vitamins. In subjects with above average omega-3 levels, B vitamins reduced brain atrophy rates by 40% and improved Hopkins Verbal Learning Test (HVLT) scores. The HVLT assesses verbal learning and memory.

Patrick Holford is an expert in nutrition who specializes in mental health and memory disorders. He stresses the importance of nutrition and supplementation for optimal brain function. His foundation, Food for the Brain (foodforthebrain.org), promotes awareness of the connection between learning, behaviour, mental health, and nutrition.

Thyroid disorders

A clinically detectable over- or underactive thyroid has long been recognized as a cause of cognitive (thinking, learning, and memory) impairment. Research shows that older women who have high or low levels of TSH have more than twice the risk of developing Alzheimer's than those with more moderate thyroid hormone levels. Thyroid hormone function is intricately linked to the central nervous system: adults with hypothyroidism are more prone to depression, whereas those with hyperthyroidism are subject to confusion. Recent studies have also related thyroid dysfunction to an increased risk for irreversible dementia. (Refer to *Chapter 4* for more information on thyroid.)

Other possible causes

Apart from neurodegenerative disease like dementias or neurological diseases, other medical conditions may also lead to an impairment of memory. Diabetes, insomnia, obesity, thyroid disorders, obstructive sleep apnea, and hormonal changes are examples of non-dementia conditions that can cause memory impairment.

Brain atrophy has been associated with diabetes, and hypoglycemia due to insulin therapy may also lead to memory impairments. TBI survivors often suffer from long-term memory impairment as a consequence, and mood disorders such as depression are often accompanied by cognitive deficits not related to dementias.

However, depressive patients also suffer from structural abnormalities, such as reduced hippocampus volume, which may be reversible during remission. Many people, particularly the aging, are taking a mix of pharmaceuticals that can contribute to memory disorders. A broad range of medications may cause or increase memory impairment, including benzodiazepines, antipsychotics, opioids, anticonvulsants, glucocorticoids (steroids), some antidepressants, analgesics (pain medications and anticholinergics (statins), pointing to the importance of a detailed drug history in patients who complain of memory deficits.

Testing and Diagnosis

While there may not be a definitive test for most brain disorders, a range of tests can help identify possible risk factors, allowing for early intervention and treatment. Tests for inflammation, diabetes, and cardiovascular disease should be considered as risk factors for cognitive decline, including the following:

- C-reactive protein (CRP)
- Homocysteine
- Heavy metal testing
- Fating blood sugar and insulin
- Hemoglobin A1c

- ApoE4
- Positron emission tomography (PET) scan
- Blood pressure monitoring
- Thyroid hormones

Refer to *Chapter 17* on cardiovascular disease for details on these tests that could help save your brain.

More specific tests for dementias include the following:

- The "smell test" maintains that when you lose the ability to sense certain smells, like lemon, leather, natural gas, or strawberry, you are at a much greater risk for Alzheimer's. This loss of ability means the neurons in the olfactory (smell) centres are dying. Smell identification tests may be available from your health care practitioner.

- Canadian researchers have developed a simple saliva test for the diagnosis of Alzheimer's, and also to identify individuals at high risk of developing the condition in future. The test is based on detecting levels of amyloid-beta 42 (Aβ42), a part of amyloid-beta protein precursor common in Alzheimer's. Research shows that Aβ42 is continuously being generated throughout the body and is secreted into the saliva as well as other tissues and bodily fluids. They found that patients with Alzheimer's had levels at least twice as high as controls.

These measures will not guarantee that you will not get dementia or forms of memory loss, but they will certainly lower the risk. According to one study from the Veterans Affairs Hospital in San Francisco, preventing the diseases associated with Alzheimer's decreases the incidence by 50%.

Preventing conditions associated with Alzheimer's

For many people, it may be possible to prevent Alzheimer's by doing what you can to prevent the conditions associated with it. For example, insulin resistance, diabetes, hypertension, and heart disease all increase the risks. In most cases, these conditions are preventable and/or treatable. In addition, if dementia is a concern due to family history, chronic stress, toxic exposure, or medical history, review the supplements that can help prevent inflammation and provide nutritional support for the brain.

what we know works

Support for Memory Disorders

Memory Boost™ combines important memory support supplements such as N-acetyl-L-cysteine (NAC), ALA, ginkgo, vinpocetine, phosphatidylserine (PS), phosphatidylcholine (PC), phosphatidylethanolamine (PE), and huperzia. Refer below for more information on individual ingredients.

Dosage: 4 capsules daily.

Huperzine A *(Huperzia serrata)* can significantly improve the cognitive function in patients with mild-to-moderate vascular dementia. A randomized, double-blind, placebo-controlled study was done with Huperzine A in vascular dementia patients. After 12 weeks of treatment, the test assessment scores significantly improved in the Huperzine A group, whereas the placebo group did not show any improvement.

ALA plays a therapeutic role in supporting cognitive functions. Oxidative stress plays a crucial role in age-related neurodegenerative disorders. One study with mice examined alpha-lipoic acid (ALA) and NAC in animals with cognitive deficits. Administration of either LA or NAC improved cognition.

NAC has been shown to be effective in the treatment of Alzheimer's and some other brain disorders. This effect may be directly associated with the inflammatory pathway and/or working through oxidative processes associated with inflammation. In addition to the effects on oxidative balance, alterations in cysteine levels have also been shown to modulate neurotransmitter pathways, including glutamate.

PS can slow, halt, or reverse the decline of memory and mental function due to aging. With the increasing aging population and cognitive and memory problems in general, the work of Dr. Thomas Crook, internationally recognized memory expert, is important to consider. In a double-blind trial, Dr. Crook and his team found that administering 300 mg of PS daily could restore up to 12 years' worth of lost mental function. Studies using PET scanning to investigate brain glucose use in Alzheimer's patients noted increased glucose use in PS-supplemented patients. PS may also protect cells from damage produced by free radicals. Elderly patients showed significant improvements in behavioural alterations (loss of motivation, initiative, interest in the environment, and socialization), memory, and learning in the PS group compared to placebo. At least a dozen other studies note similar significant improvements in learning, memory, concentration, and recall.

Acetyl-L-carnitine increases synaptic connections in the brain and consequently improves learning capacity. It is able to travel through the blood-brain barrier, where it then helps protect brain cells from free-radical damage and is a precursor for the synthesis of the neurotransmitter acetylcholine.

Vinpocetine (periwinkle) increases blood circulation and glucose metabolism, and reduces brain impairment after ischemic stroke. Studies have shown improved cognitive effects even in patients who have had multiple cerebral blockages, leading researchers to conclude that vinpocetine is effective in the treatment of vascular dementia.

Dosage: 5–10 mg 3 times daily.

Ginkgo biloba, a powerful antioxidant, is often associated with increased cerebral blood flow and enhanced memory. Catechins, procyanidins, and flavonoids are important components of standardized extracts of ginkgo. These active components were found to be potent inhibitors of beta-amyloid aggregation, and are able to destabilize the exiting plaques.

Dosage: 150–250 mg daily of a standardized extract.

Note: Contraindicated in people taking blood thinners such as Coumadin.

In addition to taking a supplement providing the ingredients mentioned above, it is important to prevent and/or treat the inflammation that is the cause of many memory disorders.

Brain Defence™ (known as Brain Fix in the US) combines therapeutic levels of bacopa, ashwagandha, curcumin, boswellia, and chamomile to support cognition, and to prevent and treat inflammation in brain disorders and depression. Refer below for more information on individual ingredients.

Dosage: 2 capsules twice daily.

Curcumin *(Curcuma longa)* is a potent anti-inflammatory that can prevent and help treat the inflammatory cause of Alzheimer's. It also has antioxidant, lipophilic, and metal chelation effects. It plays a significant role in the treatment of dementias, including Alzheimer's, as well as other brain disorders such as depression, and symptoms related to traumatic brain injuries. Another protective effect of curcumin may be its effect on telomerase expression. In a study published in the *Journal of Alzheimer's Disease,* curcumin demonstrated the ability to enter the brain, bind, and destroy the beta-amyloid plaques present in Alzheimer's, with reduced toxicity.

Boswellia *(Boswellia serrata)* has been used as an anti-inflammatory agent for centuries. Many studies have shown that it is as effective as nonsteroidal anti-inflammatory drugs, which are the most common treatment for inflammatory conditions.

Ashwagandha *(Withania somnifera)* can be used for anxiety, cognitive and neurological disorders, brain injuries, inflammation, and neurodegenerative diseases such as dementia and Alzheimer's. Ashwagandha has been shown to regenerate brain cells, and preliminary research has found that it also inhibits the formation of beta-amyloid plaques. It does not alter brain chemistry, but rather boosts a protein in the liver that clears amyloid from the brain.

Bacopa *(Bacopa monnieri)* supports the nervous system and the adrenals, the stress adaptive organs. It has been used historically to strengthen the immune response and increase the ability to cope with physical and mental stress. It provides antioxidant protection for memory centres and reduces the effects of stress on the brain. Bacopa improves cognitive performance, anxiety, and depression, and reduces amyloid deposits in the brain.

Chamomile *(Chamomilla recutita)* has been referred to as "herbal aspirin" due to its powerful anti-inflammatory properties Recent research has shown it is also effective in the treatment of anxiety and depression.

MoodSense™ contains important nutrients for depressive disorders experienced by many people with dementias, including lavender, saffron, 5-hydroxytryptophan (5-HTP), magnesium, and B6. Saffron also has been proven to be both safe and effective in treating mild-to-moderate Alzheimer's.

Dosage: 1 capsules 3 times daily.

Brilliant Mind™ (known as Higher Thoughts in the US) contains omega-3 fatty acids, phosphatidylserine, phosphatidylcholine, alpha-glycerophosphorylcholine (Alpha-GPC), and green tea for added support for the aging brain. Refer below for more information on individual ingredients.

Dosage: 2 capsules twice daily.

Alpha-GPC has been shown to be effective in reducing the loss of neuro-connecting fibres and brain cells. GPC is an extremely bioavailable source of choline, which is a building block of acetylcholine, which decreases with age. GPC has been linked with helping memory loss due to low acetylcholine levels. Studies have shown significant improvement in memory and overall function in patients with dementias.

Omega-3 fatty acids protect the brain from damages related to oxidative stress (free-radical damage). A number of studies have shown that reduced intake of omega-3 fatty acids is associated with increased risk of age-related cognitive decline or dementia, including Alzheimer's. Scientists believe the omega-3 fatty acid docosahexaenoic acid (DHA) is protective against Alzheimer's and dementia. It is thought that DHA might enhance cognitive abilities by facilitating synaptic plasticity and/or enhancing synaptic membrane fluidity; it might also act through its effects on metabolism, as DHA stimulates glucose use and mitochondrial function, reducing oxidative stress.

It is also important to treat the depression commonly found in people with dementias.

Additional support for memory disorders

B12 and **folic acid** help maintain normal homocysteine levels for healthy cognitive function. B12 promotes normal memory, concentration, and verbal function. Older people may not produce enough stomach acid to process the vitamin B12. People with vitamin B12 deficiency are more likely to score lower on cognitive tests, as well as have a smaller total brain volume, which suggests a lack of the vitamin may lead to brain shrinkage. Studies have shown that those with the lowest B12 levels had a six-fold greater rate of brain volume loss compared with those who had the highest levels. Interestingly, none of the participants were actually deficient in vitamin B12 – they just had low levels within a normal range. This goes to show that normal is not necessarily the same as optimal. One of the researchers stated, "Our results suggest that rather than maintaining one's B12 at a level that is just above the cut-off for deficiency, it might be prudent to aim to keep it higher up than normal range". Symptoms of vitamin B12 deficiency include numbness and tingling of the extremities, especially the legs; difficulty walking; concentration problems; memory loss; disorientation; and dementia that may or may not be accompanied by mood changes.

Dosage: B12: 1000–2000 mcg daily; folic acid: 1–2 mg daily.

Vitamin E has been shown to reduce the problems of memory loss and learning in the aging population. A study in the January 1, 2014 issue of the *Journal of the American Medical Association* showed that 2000 IU of vitamin E significantly delayed clinical progression in patients with mild-to-moderate Alzheimer's.

Dosage: 400–800 IU daily.

Pyrroloquinoline quinone (PQQ) is a vitamin-like compound found in plant foods that has shown a wide range of benefits. It is an extremely powerful antioxidant that provides defence against decay as well as growth of new mitochondria, the cell's energy producers. Mitochondrial dysfunction is a key biomarker of aging and is definitively linked to the development of virtually all diseases of aging, from Alzheimer's, Parkinson's, and type 2 diabetes, to heart failure. PQQ protects brain cells against oxidative stress and neurotoxicity induced by other powerful toxins, and protects nerve cells from the damaging effects of the beta-amyloid protein linked with Alzheimer's. Overall, it protects against memory and cognition decline.

Dosage: 20 mg daily.

Diet and Lifestyle Tips for Memory Disorders

Mediterranean diet

New research suggests that adherence to the Mediterranean diet may prevent brain atrophy and thereby preserve cognition in the elderly. Participants who adhered more to a Mediterranean diet had larger brain volumes both in grey matter and white matter, associated with the higher intake of fish and lower intake of meat.

Potential mechanisms include anti-inflammatory and/or antioxidative effects, as well as potential slowing of the accumulation of beta-amyloid or tau proteins. Dr. David Knopman, professor of neurology at the Mayo Clinic College of Medicine in Rochester, Minnesota, said the finding that diet may influence brain volume is novel and adds a "dimension of biology" to the hypothesis that diet and brain health are linked. (Refer to *Chapter 19* for more information on the Mediterranean diet.)

Water

Water is essential for optimal brain function. Water prevents dehydration, increases blood circulation, aids in the removal of toxins, and keeps the brain from overheating – all factors that contribute to cognitive decline and even nerve cell damage. Dehydration can lead to fatigue, dizziness, poor concentration, and reduced cognitive abilities. Even mild levels of dehydration affect mental performance.

Exercise

Studies have shown significant increases in brain volume in both grey and white matter regions of the brain in older adults who participated in aerobic fitness training, but not for those who participated in stretching and toning (non-aerobic). No significant changes in either grey or white matter volume were detected for younger participants. This study strongly suggests a positive role for aerobic fitness in maintaining and enhancing brain health and cognitive functioning in older adults.

New studies are providing even more evidence that regular aerobic exercise not only prevents problems with memory that come with aging, but can actually help turn back the clock on brain aging. Researchers at the Mayo Clinic found that moderate exercise in mid-life is associated with a 39% reduced chance of developing cognitive impairment. Furthermore, moderate exercise in late life is associated with a 32% reduction in the odds of mental decline. Moderate exercise includes exercise such as brisk walking, aerobics, yoga, strength training, and swimming. Try incorporating one or more of these activities into your regular routine four times per week for 20–30 minutes. A growing body of literature supports the benefits of a physically active lifestyle in general, but also on the brain. Exercise decreases inflammation and increases healthy gut bacteria – both factors that have positive benefits on brain health.

Karen Jensen, ND

I read a Dutch study that said, "Backward locomotion appears to be a very powerful trigger to mobilize cognitive resources". Because my grandmother, my mother, and my aunt all had varying degrees of dementia, I want to do all I can to prevent it from happening to me. One day, as I was walking up a hill backward, a truck stopped and the driver asked what I was doing. I said, "I am trying to prevent Alzheimer's". The driver then said, "Sorry to tell you but you are too late lady!" Well, whether walking backwards will prevent Alzheimer's or not, it is a great way to use muscles you don't know you have, and it's good for a few laughs, too!

Brain games – use it or lose it

Several different brain training or brain games promote neuroplasticity and help with optimal performance. Brain fitness requires variety and curiosity. Most of us like familiarity, but when anything you do becomes rote or second nature, then you need to make a change. Try something new! Take a new route to work, go to a different grocery store, or try a new type of exercise.

Brain fitness games are also a good way to challenge your brain. Sudoku, crossword puzzles, Internet or electronic games, and card games like bridge can all exercise your brain. These games rely on logic, word skills, math, and more. Try to find 15–20 minutes a day to exercise your brain.

Memory loss and cognitive impairment are not part of the normal aging process. While cognitive decline may be caused by brain lesions associated with Alzheimer's, these changes are not inevitable and it is entirely possible to prevent damage from occurring in the first place. (Refer to *Chapter 19* for information on dietary guidelines for brain and optimal health.)

For more information on brain health, refer to the book *Three Brains: How the Heart, Brain, and Gut Influence Mental Health and Identity* by Karen Jensen, ND.

DIET AND LIFESTYLE GUIDE

"The doctor of the future will give no medicine, but will interest his patients in the care of the human frame, in diet, and in the cause and prevention of disease." – **Thomas Edison (1847–1931)**

Chapter 19

Eating for the Health of It

Creating Optimal Health

What are the basic steps required to create overall optimal health? The first step is to know what optimal health is. Optimal health is definitely more than the absence of disease. When you are experiencing optimal health, you enjoy a vibrant sense of well-being on all levels: physical, emotional, mental, and spiritual. You are in a state that promotes optimal function, regeneration, and repair of the body's cells, tissues, and organ systems.

In the field of health, as in any area of life, it is crucial to understand what it is you are trying to achieve. Then you will be in a position to more readily assess the ability of different medical approaches to meet individual needs, based as they are on distinct medical philosophies. You will also be able to make more informed choices regarding health promotion and disease prevention and management.

The next step in achieving optimal health is to start taking more responsibility for your own health. Too often people turn that responsibility over to someone else, and frequently that someone is a medical doctor. When we ask our patients why they are taking a certain prescription medication, most do not know; they are simply following their health care practitioner's orders. Frequently, however, doing what you are told to do without understanding why you are doing it does little to provide any level of knowledge or understanding. Instead, ask questions, know your options, and make sure you are comfortable with your decision. After reading the information in the previous chapters on the gender differences in many common diseases and treatments, you can see that it becomes even more important for women to ask questions and stay informed.

Adverse drug reactions (ADRs) are one of the leading causes of morbidity and mortality in health care. The Institute of Medicine reported in January 2000 that more than 2 million serious ADRs cause over 106,000 deaths annually. These statistics make ADRs the fourth leading cause of death. ADRs represent a significant public health problem that is, for the most part, preventable. Today, more and more people are becoming aware of these statistics and want more information on various health care choices available to them. They want more information on how to achieve and maintain optimal health through safe, effective medicines. Often physicians are questioned about diets and nutritional supplements as patients look for instruction and guidance in this area. Limited by time constraints, medical politics, and a lack of education in the area of diet and natural supplements, physicians become frustrated and patients become disillusioned.

An Integrated Approach to Health Care

No one system of medicine has all the answers! Naturopathic and allopathic medicine are two of the world's medical philosophies and systems. There are many ways of understanding the language of the body, and each approach has its strengths and limitations.

We would encourage you to try to prevent problems through healthy diet and lifestyle choices, and next, to seek to understand the underlying cause of any health condition. Whenever possible, treat the condition with appropriate non-invasive, non-toxic therapies. However, when symptoms are debilitating or life threatening and more immediate symptom treatment or aggressive therapies are called for, conventional medicine can provide excellent intervention.

Make sure not to stop with only the symptomatic treatment – address the cause as well. If the underlying cause is not addressed, then the body will react in a similar way again or manifest deeper symptoms. For example, if your red oil light comes on in your car and you simply tape a piece of paper over the light and continue to drive, what happens? You end up with much bigger problems down the road. The same is true of our physical vehicle, the body. If you ignore your symptoms by covering them up with symptomatic treatment, there will be much bigger problems later on.

Diet and lifestyle, as well as natural health supplements, are an important part of treating most health conditions. Remember, when choosing supplements look for the ISURA seal.

What is ISURA™?

Not all supplements are created equal. Natural health products that have passed the most rigorous testing in the world are granted the ISURA seal of approval. This seal guarantees that the products are safe, clean, effective, GMO-free, and properly labelled. When purchasing supplements, look for the Isura seal of approval on product labels. For more information, go to **isura.ca**

Food Factors That Affect Optimal Health

Fats and Oils – to Eat or Not to Eat?

Contrary to popular belief, optimal health depends largely on having appropriate amounts of fat in our diet – but it must be the right types of fat. Most people today have become "fat-phobic"; they have come to believe that all fats are the same and cause disease, especially cardiovascular conditions.

Fats and oils come in many forms: short-chain, long-chain, saturated, unsaturated, monounsaturated, polyunsaturated, and essential and non-essential fatty acids. Rather than go into great detail about the various compositions of these fats, we will simply highlight their key characteristics so you can better understand why some fats are better for health than others.

Essential fatty acids: The "good" fats

Essential fatty acids (EFAs) are important to health and have many roles in the body. They are the only fatty acids not manufactured by our bodies, so they must be supplied by our diet. There are two categories of EFAs: omega-3 and omega-6 fatty acids, also called alpha-linolenic and linoleic acid, respectively.

> "People are beginning to realize that it is cheaper and more advantageous to prevent disease rather than to cure it."
>
> – Henry Lindlahr
>
> (1862–1924), author of cornerstone text of naturopathic medicine, *Nature Cure*
>
> (This wise statement was written in 1913. To think that even in 1913 we knew this to be true.)

Alpha-linolenic acid (omega-3) is primarily found in fish oils such as herring, salmon, mackerel, sardines, and halibut, and in flaxseed oil, soybeans, walnuts, and green leafy vegetables. Deficiency symptoms include inflammatory conditions, water retention, dry skin, high blood pressure, platelet aggregation or stickiness associated with heart disease (platelets are the blood cells involved in blood clotting), low metabolism, growth retardation and poor brain development, learning disability and behavioural changes, and vision impairment.

The EFAs are ideally ingested in a particular ratio. Western diets are typically overabundant in omega-6 fatty acids, which are pro-inflammatory. It is estimated that the average diet in the west contains more than ten times the amount of omega-6 fatty acids that are required for health. It has been proposed that in adults, the ideal intake of EFAs is four parts omega-6 fatty acids for every one part omega-3 fatty acids.

Saturated fatty acids

Short-chain saturated fatty acids (SFAs) are usually liquid at room temperature, partly soluble in water, and easy to digest, making them readily available for energy production in the body. Sources of short-chain SFAs include butter and coconut oil. Refined sugars and starches are converted to short-chain SFAs in the body. Long-chain SFAs are solid at room temperature and insoluble in water and are referred to as unsaturated fatty acids. They are not the "bad guys" when it comes to cardiovascular health.

Unsaturated fatty acids

Included in this group are monounsaturated fatty acids (MUFAs) and polyunsaturated fatty acids (PUFAs). These substances are liquid at room temperature. The most commonly ingested MUFA is the oleic acid found in olive oil, almonds, and other seed oils, and in the fat of most land animals. It stimulates the flow of bile; people with a diet high in olive oil have lower levels of cholesterol and lower blood pressure than those eating margarine and large quantities of butter. Olive oil fits into the "no harm" category, but does not provide many of the EFAs.

The processing of oils

Most commercially available oils are highly processed. The most harmful stage of oil processing is hydrogenation, a means of making oils into solids.

Oil is saturated with hydrogen atoms by mixing it with a metal catalyst and subjecting it to extremely high temperatures, as high as 196 °C. The molecular structure of the hydrogenated oil changes into substances the body finds unrecognizable and unusable – trans-fatty acids, potentially carcinogenic and disruptive of the normal metabolism of EFAs.

In North America, some "food" goods are estimated to have a trans-fatty acid content as high as 60%. Hydrogenated oils are commonly used in margarines, shortenings, ice cream, candy, and snack foods. In Holland, trans-fatty acids have been banned. The production of other oils uses temperatures of 95–260 °C, temperatures that destroy nutrients and create trans-fatty acids. Do not be fooled by the commercially produced oils that are labelled "cold pressed"; even these oils are subjected to high heat from friction generated by giant oil presses. Because no external heat has been applied, however, these products can legally be called cold pressed. Buyer beware.

The big fat lies about low-fat diets

"And the circle we go round and round… on the carousel of time…": on the topic of low-fat versus low-carb diets.

Before 1920, coronary heart disease was rare in North America. However, today heart disease is the leading cause of all deaths. What has changed? It is not the consumption of animal products. In fact, since the 1950s and the popularization of the theory that increased fat consumption causes an increased risk for heart disease, the consumption of animal products such as red meat and butter has decreased. The proportion of animal fat declined from 83% to 62% and butter consumption fell from 8 kg to 1.8 kg per person per year, while the consumption of sugar and processed foods increased about 60%.

The obesity epidemic started in the 1980s when the "medical experts" started advocating low-fat diets to prevent heart disease and obesity. This exclusive focus on the adverse effects of fat has contributed to the obesity epidemic and the increase in heart disease. Type 2 diabetes, the most common form of the disease, also increased significantly during this period. Low-fat weight loss diets fail in clinical trials and in real life. Fast food consumption also increased in the 1970s and 1980s, but not at the pace at which obesity surged. Also around this time, oil refineries with high heat and chemical extraction methods replaced the oil press. These new extraction methods cause the formation of free radicals, which in turn damage cells, including heart tissue, and encourage the deposition of cholesterol.

With the "fat phobia" in full swing, people started substituting breads, pastas, and other refined carbohydrates, thinking this was the "right" thing to do for heart health. It is not working. High levels of insulin and glucose, the result of eating a diet high in refined carbohydrates, is resulting in higher rates of heart disease, hypertension, obesity, diabetes, and cancer.

Choosing healthy fats

Oils

For optimal health, choose expeller-pressed, unprocessed oils. Extra-virgin olive oil is also safe, since it can be extracted from olives without high heat being generated in the process. One way to offset the damaging effects of trans-fatty acids is to consume high levels of the beneficial fatty acids found in flaxseed, sesame, evening primrose, olive, and fish oils.

If oils are dangerous when heated, how can we safely cook with them? Some oils offer more heat stability than others. Avocado oil has the safest higher heat tolerance, and you can use sesame oil, olive oil, cocoa butter, or butter when cooking at low heats. If the oil becomes black or brown during cooking, discard it.

Sources of omega-3 fatty acids (alpha-linolenic acid) include:

- Fish oils (herring, salmon, Poppy seed oil mackerel, sardines, tuna, halibut)
- Soy oil
- Pumpkin seed oil
- Flaxseed oil
- Walnuts

Sources of omega-6 fatty acids (linoleic acid) include:

- Almond oil
- Peanut oil
- Brazil nut oil
- Pecan oil
- Evening primrose oil
- Pumpkin seed oil
- Flaxseed oil
- Safflower oil
- Grape seed oil
- Sesame seed oil

- Hazelnut oil
- Sunflower seed oil

- Coconut oil
- Walnut oil

Butter versus margarine

It is not logical to presume that butter, a saturated fat that humans have been consuming for hundreds of years, has caused the abrupt rise in the incidence of heart disease since the 1900s. There is, however, a correlation between the rise of heart disease and the replacement of the butter churn, olive press, and expeller-pressed oils with industrial oil refineries.

Margarine is hydrogenated oil and contains many toxic chemicals; no "health" margarine is available and it does not matter whether the label says it is polyunsaturated or not. A natural, polyunsaturated fat that is solid at room temperature does not exist – any margarine has to have been chemically altered by hydrogenation and totally denatured to get that way. Butter, on the other hand, is a saturated fat in its natural state and contains healthy fatty acids, vitamins, and minerals.

In summary:

- Choose butter over margarine
- Avoid refined heated oils, fried and deep-fried oils, margarines, shortenings, and partially hydrogenated oils
- Moderate your intake of saturated fats from pork, beef, mutton, and dairy products

Guilt-Free Butter

Mix together:
250 mL of butter
(at room temperature)
250 mL of flaxseed
or olive oil

Store in the refrigerator.

This recipe helps you get more of the EFAs and at the same time reduces your intake of saturated fats. Use this combination on popcorn, baked potatoes, toast, cooked corn, etc. It tastes great!

Additives

Some artificial food additives like aspartame and monosodium glutamate (MSG) trigger inflammatory responses, especially in people who are already suffering from inflammatory conditions. Only packaged foods contain artificial food additives. If you need to buy them, read the labels carefully and weigh your risks. If you order Chinese take-out food, make sure you have the option to ask for no MSG. Otherwise, look elsewhere. In addition to limiting the consumption of processed foods, use anti-inflammatory herbs or spices, or natural sweeteners to add flavour to your dishes instead of relying on food additives.

Genetically Modified Organisms

According to an article by the David Suzuki Foundation, the first genetically modified crop was approved by the United States Food and Drug Administration (FDA) in 1994. Since then, genetically modified corn, soy, sugar beets, and canola have become common local crops in Canada. In addition, genetically modified varieties of cottonseed oil, papaya, squash, and milk products are imported from the United States into Canada. These crops – called Roundup Ready crops – have had their DNA altered to allow them to withstand the herbicide glyphosate (the active ingredient of Monsanto's herbicide Roundup). They are also known as glyphosate-tolerant crops. In only 20 years, genetically modified organisms (GMOs) have made their way into most of the processed foods available in Canadian grocery stores. Genetically modified apples, potatoes, and wheat are currently in the lineup for approval.

The safety of genetically modified foods is unproven, and a growing body of research connects these foods with several negative health effects, primarily the production of new allergens, antibiotic resistance, increased toxicity, decreased nutrition, and gluten-related disorders, including celiac disease, an autoimmune disorder. Canadian researchers have also found the presence of pesticides associated with genetically modified foods in maternal, fetal, and non-pregnant women's blood.

Allergies and Food Intolerances

Many people are sensitive to certain foods, but they are not aware of it.

Unlike food allergies where symptoms are obvious, symptoms caused by food intolerance may be subtle and take longer to manifest. Common symptoms of food sensitivities may include digestive upsets, brain fog and difficulty concentrating, joint pains, headaches, behavioural problems in the young, dark circles under the eyes, fatigue, and a general sense of not feeling well. Long-term exposure to food sensitivities can cause inflammation and lead to chronic disease.

Common food allergens are gluten (whether celiac or simply gluten sensitive), milk, nuts, eggs, and nightshade vegetables. Contrary to common belief, it is possible to develop an allergy to the foods that you eat often. If you suspect a particular food may be responsible for some of your symptoms, try avoiding it completely for at least two weeks and monitor your reaction. At the end of the abstinence period, re-introduce the food back into your diet. You should be able to notice the difference in how you feel.

Foods That Contribute to Inflammation

Besides adding anti-inflammatory foods to your diet, you will also want to avoid the following pro-inflammatory dietary culprits as much as possible.

Trans fats

You will find trans fats in any product that has partially hydrogenated vegetable oil, which is prominent in margarine and commercially prepared baked goods and snacks. Trans fatty acids increase the levels of "bad" cholesterol while lowering levels of "good" cholesterol. They have also been found to promote inflammation, obesity, and resistance to insulin, laying the ground for de-generative illnesses to take place. Deep-fried foods, fast foods, commercially baked goods, and those prepared with partially hydrogenated oil, margarine, and/or vegetable shortening also contain trans fats.

Grains

Most grains we eat are refined. They are devoid of fibre and B vitamins com-pared to unrefined grains, and they can be considered empty calorie foods – like sugar. Like refined sugars, refined grains have a higher glycemic index than unprocessed grains. Products made from refined grains are almost everywhere. The most common include white rice, white flour, white bread, noodles, pasta, biscuits, and pastries. Refined grains are often loaded with excess sugar, salt, artificial flavours, and/or partially hydrogenated oil in the process. Choose unprocessed or minimally processed grains if you are not gluten intolerant or allergic to grains.

Protein

Proteins alone are not anti- or pro-inflammatory. Rather, it is the source of the protein that makes the difference. Choose proteins from lean meats and fish to be sure you get enough complete protein without any accompanying pro-inflam-matory fats. You can also get sufficient protein by eating a variety of legumes, non-GMO organic fermented soy products (if tolerated), and vegetables.

Commercially produced meats are fed with grains like soy beans and corn, a diet that is high in inflammatory omega-6 fatty acids, but low in anti-inflammatory omega-3 fats. Due to the small and tight living environment, these animals also gain excess fat and end up with high-saturated fats. Organic free-range animals that are fed a natural diet such as grasses instead of grains and hormones contain more omega-3 fats. Having more room to roam freely, they are also leaner and contain fewer saturated fats. Remember that no amount of processed meat is safe. Replace the bulk of your red meat with organic vegetables, organic or free-range poultry, fish, and red meat 1–2 times per week. When you do eat red meat, remember to choose organic or grass-fed animals.

Sugar

Sugar has been linked to increased risks of obesity, inflammation, and chronic diseases such as metabolic syndrome and type 2 diabetes. Sugar-sweetened beverages like soft drinks and fruit drinks are major sources of dietary sugars. Other sugar-laden foods to avoid include pastries, most desserts, candies, and ice cream. When looking for sugar in the ingredients list, note that sugar comes in many disguises, including corn syrup, dextrose, fructose, golden syrup, maltose, sorghum syrup, and sucrose.

Natural sweeteners like stevia, honey, blackstrap molasses, or agave can be used in moderation. Natural sugars that are found in fresh or dried fruits are also great choices. Not only do they give you the sweetness you crave, fruits also supply you with vitamins, antioxidants, and fibres that you will not find in refined sugary foods and drinks.

Dairy

As much as 60% of the world's population cannot digest milk, and humans are the only mammals that drink milk after they are weaned. Milk is also a common allergen that can trigger inflammatory responses, such as stomach distress, constipation, diarrhea, skin rashes, acne, hives, and breathing difficulties in susceptible people. In addition, food allergens are linked to brain disorders.

Apart from obvious milk products like butter and cheese, foods with hidden dairy content include breads, cookies, crackers, cakes, cream sauces, and boxed cereals. Fermented dairy products like kefirs and unsweetened yogourt are acceptable in moderation for those who are not allergic to milk. They are easier on the stomach as the lactose and proteins in the milk have already been broken down. Sheep and goat's milk and cheese are also good alternatives.

Optimal Health Guidelines

Tips to Eliminate Xenoestrogens – Optimizing Hormonal Health

Include foods in the diet designed to enhance liver function and the elimination of harmful estrogens (xenoestrogens) – many are mentioned above, but as a recap, liver-friendly foods to include in the diet are broccoli, kale, cabbage, artichokes, garlic, parsley, celery, beets and beet greens, dandelion greens, and turmeric.

High fibre foods help support a healthy intestinal tract as well as an optimal balance of "good" to "bad" bacteria. Ensuring an adequate amount of good bacteria flora in the digestive tract helps metabolize excess bad estrogens and prevents the recycling of these estrogens back throughout the body.

Heavy metals such as lead, mercury, cadmium, and aluminum can increase a toxic burden on the liver, which can impede healthy liver detoxification and metabolism of "bad" estrogens. Eliminate plastic containers, pesticides, PVC, and cosmetics containing phthalates and parabens, along with toxic metals, from your environment.

The Mediterranean Diet

The traditional Mediterranean diet has shown tremendous benefit in fighting and preventing inflammation, heart disease, and cancer, as well as diabetes. The Mediterranean diet focuses on the following guidelines:

- Use olive oil as the principal source of fat.
- Eat an abundance of plant-based foods, including fruit, vegetables, breads, pasta, potatoes, beans, nuts, and seeds.
- Ensure foods are minimally processed and focus on seasonally fresh and locally grown food.
- Eat fresh fruit as a daily dessert, and consume sweets containing concentrated sugars or honey a few times per week at the most.
- Consume dairy products daily (e.g., cheese and yogourt) in low-to-moderate amounts and in low-fat varieties.
- Eat fish on a regular basis.
- Consume poultry and eggs in moderate amounts, about 1–4 times weekly, or not at all.

- Eat red meat in small, infrequent amounts.
- Drink wine in low-to-moderate amounts, normally with meals.

Reduce Inflammation

The Mediterranean diet has been shown to reduce inflammation in as little as six weeks. The link between a wide variety of common health problems – from obesity and diabetes to heart disease and cancer – is chronic inflammation. The key to reducing chronic inflammation in your body starts with your diet, and being liberal with your use of high-quality herbs and spices. It is important to realize that dietary components can either prevent or trigger inflammation from taking root in your body.

Top anti-inflammatory foods include the following:

- **Omega-3 fats** – Found in fatty fish like wild Alaskan salmon, krill, mackerel, sardines, and black cod, as well as in fish oil and krill oil, these fats help fight inflammation and are particularly important for brain health.

- **Leafy greens** – Dark leafy greens such as kale, spinach, collard greens, and Swiss chard contain powerful antioxidants, flavonoids, carotenoids, and vitamin C, all of which help protect against cellular damage. Ideally, opt for organic locally grown veggies that are in season, and consider eating some of them raw, particularly in the summer months. Juicing is an excellent way to get more greens into your diet.

- **Blueberries** – Blueberries are a good source of antioxidants compared to other fruit and vegetables. They are also lower in sugar than many other fruit.

- **Tea** – Matcha tea is the most nutrient-rich green tea. It comes in the form of a stone-ground unfermented powder and has up to 17 times the antioxidants of wild blueberries.

- **Fermented vegetables and traditionally cultured foods** – These foods help optimize your gut flora, which is important for a well-functioning immune system. They also help ward off chronic inflammation. In fact, the majority of inflammatory diseases start in your gut as the result of an imbalanced microbiome. Fermented foods such as kefir, kimchee, miso, tempeh, pickles, sauerkraut, and other fermented vegetables, help recolonize the gut with beneficial bacteria. Fermented foods can also help your body rid itself of harmful toxins such as heavy metals and pesticides that promote inflammation.

- **Shiitake mushrooms** – These mushrooms contain strong compounds with the natural ability to discourage inflammation and inhibit oxidative stress.

- **Garlic and onions** – Garlic has been shown to work similarly to nonsteroidal anti-inflammatory pain medications (like ibuprofen), shutting off the pathways that lead to inflammation. Onions contain similar anti-inflammatory chemicals, including the phytonutrient quercetin and the compound allicin, which break down to produce free-radical-fighting sulfenic acid.

- **Nuts and seeds** – Nuts and seeds help fight inflammation, particularly almonds, which are rich in fibre, calcium, and vitamin E, and walnuts, which have high amounts of alpha-linolenic acid, a type of omega-3 fat. All nuts contain high levels of antioxidants, which can help your body fight off and repair the damage caused by inflammation.

- **Olive oil** – The Mediterranean diet's many health benefits may be largely due to its liberal use of olive oil, especially the extra-virgin kind. The compound oleocanthal, which gives olive oil its taste, has been shown to have a similar effect to nonsteroidal anti-inflammatory painkillers in the body.

- **Berries** – All fruit can help fight inflammation because they are low in fat and calories and high in antioxidants. Berries in particular have been shown to have anti-inflammatory properties, possibly because of anthocyanins (antioxidants), the powerful chemicals that give them their rich colour. Animal studies have shown that red raspberry extract helps arthritis, and blueberries can help protect against intestinal inflammation and ulcerative colitis. Women who eat more strawberries have lower levels of C-reactive protein.

- **Tart cherries (sour cherries)** – Oregon Health & Science University researchers suggest that tart cherries have the highest anti-inflammatory content of any food. Studies have found that tart cherry juice can reduce the inflammation in blood vessels by up to 50%, and it has been shown to reduce people's use of anti-inflammatory pain medication. Experts recommend eating 355 g (1.5 cups) of tart cherries, or drinking 235 mL (about 1 cup) of tart cherry juice daily to see similar benefits. Sweet cherries do not seem to have the same effects.

- **Avocado** – This creamy fruit is considered the most perfect food in the world. It is loaded with fibre and vitamins, and is an excellent source of healthy fats. Dr. Perlmutter, a neurologist and author of the book *Grain*, considers the avocado part of his "anti-Alzheimer's trio", along with coconut oil and grass-fed beef.

The Importance of Water

Nearly 70% of the human body is made of water – and nearly every bodily function, from the transportation of nutrients to the elimination of toxins, is done through this medium. Ingesting adequate amounts of water (2.5 L daily) is critical for optimal health. Conditions linked to inadequate water intake include inflammatory conditions such allergies, arthritis, cardiovascular diseases, chronic pain, dyspeptic conditions (e.g., gastritis, heartburn, ulcers), and obesity. People often reach for tea, coffee, soft drinks, or juice, which do not have the ability to help flush toxins from the body. In fact, these drinks add to the burden.

Over the years, our natural water supplies have become contaminated by acid rain, chemical leaching, and industrial waste, as well as two very toxic chemicals that are often added to municipal water supplies: chlorine and fluoride. Fluoride is certified rat poison and is toxic at any level. Yet, many people ingest large amounts from water, foods, and beverages made with fluoridated water, toothpaste, and mouth wash. There are varieties of water filtration systems available all at different prices – at the very least, use a basic filtration system.

Summary of Nutritional Tips

- Avoid all non-foods.
- Replace non-foods with organically grown, fibre-rich whole grains and fresh fruits and vegetables, and hormone- and chemical-free animal products.
- Limit consumption of refined carbohydrates (e.g., sugar, white breads, pasta) and increase consumption of complex carbohydrates such as whole grains and legumes. Use concentrated carbohydrates such as honey, dried fruits, and fruit juices in moderation.
- Avoid saturated fats, heated oils and margarines, fried foods, and processed cooking oils. Increase consumption of the essential fatty acids.

- Increase protein intake from vegetarian sources such as legumes and nuts and seeds.

- Increase intake of green leafy vegetables.

- Decrease intake of milk and dairy products, chocolate, and chocolate-containing foods.

- Decrease salt intake.

- Drink only unfluoridated, unchlorinated water, and drink a minimum of 2.5 L of water daily!

- Minimize or eliminate the consumption of soft drinks; drink beer and wine in moderation, and spirits sparingly, if at all. Coffee and tea can be taken in moderation, 1–2 cups daily at the most, because they are diuretics and flush much-needed fluids from your body.

Cleansing and Detoxification

In the past 150 years, there has been incredible progress in medicine, science, and industry. However, as we have discussed, these developments have come with a tremendously high price; the side effects of our chemical-dependent technology are the contamination of our atmosphere, water, and food, and depletion of our soil. Although the human body has an incredible ability to adapt, these contaminants are accumulating faster than our bodies are able to handle them. In many people, the toxic burden is resulting in altered metabolism, enzyme dysfunction, nutritional deficiencies, hormonal imbalances, and the development of chronic physical and mental disorders.

Why Is Detoxification Important?

We know that drugs, preservatives, pesticides, and other pollutants can remain stored in the body long after the initial exposure. For example, the residues of the pesticide DDT (DDE and DDD) have a half-life of 20–50 years in the fat tissues of humans. Indeed, the predominant storage site for most chemicals is in fatty tissues. From these tissues, toxins re-enter the bloodstream during illness, exercise, and periods of fasting, emotional stress, or excessive heat. When these chemicals enter the bloodstream, every organ in the body is continually exposed at low levels. Remember, it is not any one single agent that causes serious problems – it is the total load. Remember, too, that while the effects of many individual chemicals have been studied, little is known about how the many chemicals potentially in circulation within our bodies interact with one another to affect us.

These toxic chemicals find their way into our bodies through the air we breathe, the food we eat, and the water we drink. Although the body has systems in place to eliminate toxins, it cannot always handle the overload that is present in today's environment. The result is a variety of diseases.

Before the outbreak of serious disease, the body will often warn of a toxic overload with a number of possible symptoms: allergies, back pain, bowel problems, headaches, insomnia, joint pain, mood changes, respiratory problems, sinus congestion, or skin eruptions such as psoriasis and acne. These conditions indicate a need for cleansing.

In response to such symptoms, many naturopathic doctors and related health care practitioners recommend a variety of "detoxification" programs. These programs aim to improve bowel and liver health so that toxins circulating in the bloodstream due to poor functioning of these two organs can be eliminated from the body. These programs also move toxins out of their storage sites in the fatty tissue, support the liver's ability to break them down, and support the functioning of the other major organs of elimination: the skin, the lungs, the kidneys, and the gastrointestinal tract. The step-by-step program described below will detoxify the body and strengthen the organs of elimination.

The Overall Cleanse

We now know how to cleanse our colon and support the adrenal glands and liver through the use of botanical medicines and nutrition. Given the current state of our environment, it is usually important to take another step in the detoxification of our bodies. Short overall internal cleanses give our digestive system and stress-response organs a much-needed rest, and the opportunity to do some "house cleaning" and rebuilding. After a cleanse, nutrient assimilation also usually improves.

Traditionally, fasting has been used to rid the body of toxins and to facilitate healing. There are typically two types of fasts: those that allow water only, and those that include freshly made juices. The cleansing program outlined here is less severe, as it starts with a cleansing diet for the first seven days and then moves into a 3–7 day juice fast.

Most people currently carry such a heavy load of toxins that as the body begins to cleanse, it requires more supportive nutrients than are supplied by traditional fasts to aid the organs of elimination in their work. Otherwise, they may become overwhelmed. As the body eliminates toxins, some people may experience uncomfortable side effects. These effects are temporary and may include constipation due to loss of fluids and lack of fibre, headaches, inability to concentrate, nausea, or rashes or skin outbreaks. These symptoms usually occur within the first 48 hours of the cleanse. They should not last longer than 3–4 days, although in some people they may continue for up to seven days. If you are concerned or symptoms persist, consult your naturopathic doctor or natural health care practitioner.

To keep toxins moving outwards at all levels, it is very important to ensure that your bowels continue eliminating regularly, and remember to drink the required amount of water during a cleanse, a minimum of 2.5 L daily. You can add lemon juice to give your liver extra help.

10–12-Day Detoxification and Cleansing Program

General guidelines: Do each one of the things on this list daily throughout your cleanse:

- Drink at least 2.5–3 L of purified water.
- Make sure you have 2–3 substantial bowel movements. If you have difficulty achieving this, use buckthorn or cascara sagrada.
- Exercise moderately on at least five of the seven initial days of the cleanse.
- Reduce personal obligations and rest more.
- Sleep for at least eight hours each night.
- Have regular detoxification baths (described below) and, if available, sauna sessions.
- Throughout the day, take a moment here or there to visualize your body, mind, and spirit as healthy. Know that you are healthy!

Cleansing program diet

Your diet during the first seven days is restricted to whole grains, lean organic protein, vegetables, and small amounts of fruit, condiments, and oil.

- Choose 2–3 grains for the week from the following list: brown rice, brown basmati rice, quinoa, millet, oats, hulled barley, and buckwheat. You may have 2–3 moderate servings daily.

- Eat as much as you like of the following: steamed vegetables, raw vegetables, and vegetable juices. Have a minimum of three servings of vegetables and two 250 mL glasses of fresh vegetable juice daily. Vegetable juice recipes are provided below.

- Eat fruit sparingly, no more than three pieces daily, and eat any fruit at least 30 minutes before or two hours after your other meals.

- Healthy, lean, organic proteins include free-range chicken and turkey, wild fish, legumes, and nuts and seeds.

Cleansing juices

Drink these juices right after they are made so that nutrients are not lost. If you do not have a juicer and cannot buy one, most health food stores or restaurants will sell you freshly made vegetable juices.

Carrot, Beet, and Garlic or Ginger Juice

Juice 4–5 carrots, 1 small beet, and 1–2 fresh cloves of garlic or a small piece of ginger.

Carrot-Apple Delight Juice

Juice half an apple, 4–5 carrots, and a small piece of ginger (optional).

Green Vitality Juice

Juice 3–4 kale leaves, 1 bunch of parsley, 1 cucumber, 2–3 celery stalks, and 3–4 carrots.

Foods and substances to avoid completely during a cleanse

This list is based on our years of clinical experience:

- Alcohol
- Tobacco
- Coffee and caffeinated tea
- Sugar of any kind, including honey, molasses, corn syrup, maple syrup, barley or rice malt, and table syrup
- Table salt
- Dairy products
- Eggs
- Beef and lamb
- Butter and margarine
- Heated oils
- Soy
- Gluten
- Corn
- Shellfish

Substitutions for non-permitted foods and substances include:

- Herbal teas
- Fresh herbs for flavour
- Sea salt used sparingly, herbal salt substitutes (ground herbs), and sea vegetables (e.g., wakame, hijiki, dulse)
- Ground flaxseed and flaxseed oil or olive oil, in moderation
- Stevia

The next step

"Yard by yard, life is hard; inch by inch, life's a cinch."

If you feel ready to take the next step – or the next yard – we recommend embarking on a juice-only cleanse for 2–3 days after the initial seven-day detoxification. Trust your intuition. You may need to wait to take this step until you have done more to buildup your overall health. The juice cleanse portion may not work for everyone, so listen to your body and act accordingly. If you find it difficult, stop and wait 4–6 months, then start again with the seven-day restricted diet. This time, you will likely feel ready to move on to the juice cleanse.

Days 8–10 or 12

During this period, drink only fresh vegetable juices of your choice. Have at least 6–8 glasses of juice daily and drink 2.5–3 L of water daily as well, with the juice of 1–2 lemons. Make sure you have regular bowel elimination and continue to follow the general guidelines outlined at the beginning of this cleansing protocol.

After the juice cleanse, slowly begin to eat again. For the first three days, follow the dietary suggestions outlined for Days 1–7, then slowly introduce legumes, beans, tofu, and raw nuts and seeds over the next few days. By the end of five days, re-introduce hormone-free animal proteins such as fish, chicken, turkey, eggs, veal, and the like.

During your cleanse, give your eliminative organs as much support as possible by using various detoxification aids often. For instance, during a cleanse, we suggest three detoxification baths (described below) each week. Experiment with the other aids and use your intuition to guide you in determining how frequently you use each one. These techniques are valuable between cleanses as well to lower the accumulated internal toxins.

Detoxification Baths

Detoxification baths use hot water to increase blood flow to the skin's surface and open the pores, thereby encouraging perspiration and toxin elimination. Start the baths slowly, as some people experience symptoms, especially if the toxic load is great. If you experience dizziness, headaches, fatigue, nausea, or weakness during a bath, stop, and next time, bathe for a shorter period.

A detoxification bath involves the following steps:

- Filter the water supply into your tub and shower with filters to remove as much chlorine and other chemicals as possible. These are all absorbed into the body through the skin during a bath, and will counteract the bath's cleansing power.
- Wash thoroughly with a gentle natural soap of your choice and scrub with a skin brush or coarse washcloth to remove oils and skin creams.
- Rinse thoroughly.
- Fill the tub with water as hot as is tolerable and begin with a five-minute soak. Gradually increase your time in the detoxification bath to 30 minutes if you are not experiencing any symptoms.
- After soaking, shower and scrub thoroughly with soap to rinse off toxins that have accumulated on the skin.
- Drink at least 2–3 glasses of water before, during, and after your bath.

Epsom salt baths

Epsom salt baths help eliminate toxins by increasing the blood supply to the skin, and by drawing from the body water and, with it, toxins. Epsom salts also contain sulphur, which is well-known for its medicinal and detoxification properties.

Add 250 mL Epsom salts to a regular bath and gradually increase the amount to 0.5 kg (1 lb) per tub. Stay in an Epsom salts bath no longer than 30 minutes.

You can add other substances to the bath to help detoxification, including:

- Apple cider vinegar, which works similarly to Epsom salts. Add 250 mL to your bath, gradually increasing to 500 mL per tub.
- Baking soda baths used to be a common household remedy for colds, flus, and skin irritations. Baking soda (sodium bicarbonate) balances the pH and is good for cleansing. Use 250 mL baking soda per tub.
- Clay draws out toxins. Use 125–250 mL clay per tub. Bentonite clay or green clay are most commonly used for this purpose.

Dry brushing

Dry brushing the skin prior to a sauna, detoxification bath, or shower removes dead skin and improves circulation to the skin, helping to open the pores for elimination of toxins. Use a special brush made for this purpose, available from many health food stores. Do up to five minutes of long strokes over every area of the body, always moving toward the heart.

Lymphatic drainage

The lymphatic system circulates lymph fluid throughout the body. In lymph fluid, toxic wastes and bacteria are carried to lymph nodes, where these materials are engulfed and destroyed by large cells called macrophages. Clearly, it is always important, and especially so during cleansing, that the lymphatic system remain uncongested. Lymphatic massage can be done daily to help facilitate detoxification.

what we know works

Support for Detoxification

Take liver drainage herbs as well as blood and kidney support herbs during the cleanse. These organs need extra support during a cleanse due to the increased load of toxins they have to process. Drainage herbs for the liver include dandelion, curcumin, and artichoke. Burdock helps cleanse the blood as well as the liver, and support for the kidneys includes parsley, corn silk, celery seed, bearberry, and dandelion.

Liver MD™ is designed to provide support for heavy metal detoxification as well as antioxidant protection from free radicals caused by other environmental stressors and toxins. Alpha-lipoic acid (ALA) and N-acetyl-L-cysteine (NAC) are two very critical nutrients proven to increase the synthesis of glutathione within the body. Glutathione is a very powerful antioxidant and key nutrient for detoxification that is often depleted by environmental toxins such as heavy metals. Liver MD also contains powerful antioxidants such as vitamin C, selenomethionine, zinc, broccoli powder, and vitamin B12 to support detoxification pathways, as well as hepatoprotective herbs such as milk thistle and curcumin.

Dosage: 2 capsules twice daily.

In Summary

Undertaking a 1–2 week detoxifying program at least once per year, and making regular use of detoxification aids while simultaneously taking action to support and strengthen the intestines, liver, and adrenal glands, are key steps in recovering from many symptoms and conditions. This will start you down the road to optimal health.

The Spiritual Side of Optimal Health

At this point we have covered many of the physical aspects of optimal health and touched on many of the mental and emotional aspects. There is a third aspect of health that has been largely ignored or overlooked: the spiritual. Historically speaking, be it in the traditional practices of Buddhism, Christianity, Islam, or other religions, the power of prayer, contemplation, or meditation has been seen as an integral part of health and healing. Prayer is a special form of meditation and may therefore convey all the health benefits that have been associated with meditation. Different types of meditation have been shown to result in psychological and biological changes that are associated with improved health.

Meditation has been found to have a number of benefits, including:

- Reducing blood pressure and heart rate
- Altering levels of melatonin and serotonin
- Suppressing stress hormones
- Boosting the immune system
- Promoting positive mood states
- Reducing anxiety and pain
- Enhancing self-esteem

In addition, meditation has a favourable influence on the overall and spiritual quality of life in late-stage disease.

More than eight in ten Americans think prayer or meditation can augment medical treatment, according to a survey released by the sponsor of Harvard Medical School's Spirituality and Healing in Medicine seminars.

Just as we need physical exercise and good whole foods to keep our physical body healthy, we need daily spiritual exercises (i.e., contemplation, prayer, or meditation) to keep our mental/emotional bodies balanced.

Life is moving so quickly that spiritual practice is more necessary than ever before, and it is easy to lose balance if spiritual exercises are not done every day. The pace of life today is like that of a treadmill with the speed turned up to ten, and the fitness level (physical, mental/emotional, and spiritual) at around five. Further, the treadmill shows no signs of slowing its movement and instead is gaining greater and greater speed. There are going to be more and more casualties as the speed increases unless people start to take responsibility for strengthening themselves on all levels.

The various forms of spiritual exercises are ways of communicating with something greater than ourselves. Each religion or philosophy has its own terms that refer to this universal energy and love available to all.

Communicating with the divine power is the same thing as opening the heart to love; becoming acquainted with the love, the "god-like" qualities within yourself and others.

However you perceive the spiritual side of your life, whether it is a walk in nature, going to your church, quiet contemplation or meditation, or simply listening to beautiful music, we urge you to choose to regularly access this part of yourself. It is through awareness and understanding ourselves that we can heal and make changes so as to prevent illness from occurring again.

THE ATTITUDE OF GRATITUDE – REMEMBER TO SAY THANK YOU!

New research conducted by Robert A. Emmons, PhD, of the University of California, and Michael E. McCullough, of the University of Miami, shows that the "attitude of gratitude" has been linked to better health, sounder sleep, less anxiety and depression, higher long-term satisfaction with life, and kinder behaviour toward others.

In the study, people kept a brief "gratitude journal" – just one sentence for each of five things that they were grateful for, done once a week. There were significant effects after only two months. Compared with a control group, the people keeping the gratitude journal were more optimistic and felt happier. They reported fewer physical problems and spent more time working out.

"If you want to sleep more soundly, count blessings, not sheep", Dr. Emmons advises in *Thanks!*, his book on gratitude research.

A Women's Health
Bill of Rights
and Responsibilities

1   I have a right to be treated as an equal human being.

2   I have a right to be listened to and have my problems taken seriously.

3   I have a right to an explanation that I can understand in my native language (using a translator if necessary) on any questions concerning my health care.

4   I have a right to know the choices I face in getting treated for any health problem, and to have the possible side effects of any drugs or surgical treatments clearly explained.

5   I have a right to choose the types of treatment I prefer from among the options offered to me by my doctor.

6   I have a right for normal events in my life, such as pregnancy and menopause, not to be treated as diseases requiring treatment.

7   I have a right to choose natural therapies and not be ridiculed for doing so.

8   I have a right to request a second opinion on any major surgery or health decision.

9   I have a right to refuse any drug or surgical treatment.

10 I have a responsibility to become knowledgeable about my body and how it works.

11 I have a responsibility to learn as much as possible about my health problems so I can make informed choices.

12 I have a responsibility to look after my diet, reduce stress, exercise and relax on a regular basis.

13 I have a responsibility to avoid pressuring my doctor to giving me drugs when I don't need them.

14 I have a responsibility to prepare my questions for my doctor beforehand and schedule adequate appointment time to discuss them.

15 I am ultimately responsible for my own healthcare, using my doctor as a resource rather than an authority.

Source: *Take Charge of Your Body: Women's Health.* Carolyn DeMarco, MD

References

Introduction

Correa-de-Araujo R. Serious gaps: How the lack of sex/ gender-based research impairs health. *J Women's Health.* 2007; 15(10):1116-22.

Dagres N, Nieuwlaat R, Vardas PE, et al. Gender-related differences in presentation, treatment, and outcome of patients with atrial fibrillation in Europe: A report from the Euro Heart Survey on Atrial Fibrillation. *J Am Coll Cardiol.* 2007; 49:572-7.

Holdcroft A. Gender bias in research: How does it affect evidence based medicine? *J R Soc Med.* 2007; 100(1):2-3.

Kim AM, Tingen CM, Woodruff, TK. Sex bias in trials and treatment must end. *Nature.* 2010; 465(7299):688-9.

Kim ESH, Carrigan TP, Menon V. Enrollment of women in national heart, lung, and blood institute-funded cardiovascular randomized controlled trials fails to meet current federal mandates for inclusion. *J Am Coll Cardiol.* 2008; 52(8):672-3.

Liu LY, Schaub MA, Sirota M, et al. Sex differences in disease risk from reported genome-wide association study findings. *Hum Genet.* 2012; 131(3):353-64.

Lloyd-Jones D, Adams RJ, Brown TM, et al. Heart disease and stroke statistics–2010 update. *Circulation.* 2010; 121(7):e46-e215.

Mazure, CM, Jone, DP. Twenty years and still counting: including women as participants and studying sex and gender in biomedical research. *BMC Womens Health.* 2015; 15:94.

Regitz-Zagrosek V. Sex and gender differences in health. *EMBO Rep.* 2012; 13(7):596-603.

Regitz-Zagrosek V. Sex and gender differences in symptoms of myocardial ischaemia. *Eur Heart J.* 2011; 32(24): 3064-6.

Regitz-Zagrosek V, Oertelt-Prigione S, Seeland U, et al. Sex and gender differences in myocardial hypertrophy and heart failure. *J Circ.* 2010; 74(7):1265-73.

Regitz-Zagrosek V. Therapeutic implications of the gender-specific aspects of cardiovascular disease. *Nat Rev Drug Discov.* 2006; 5(5):425-38.

Weinberger AH, McKee SA, Mazure CM. Inclusion of women and gender-specific analyses in randomized clinical trials of treatments for depression. *J Womens Health.* 2010; 19(9):1727-32.

Yang X, Schadt EE, Wang S, et al. Tissue-specific expression and regulation of sexually dimorphic genes in mice. *Genome Res.* 2006; 16(8):995-1004.

Section 1 – The Hormonic Orchestra

Chapter 2 – The Liver and Gut Microbiome in Hormonal Balance

Aremu DA, Madejczyk MS, Ballatori, N. N-Acetylcysteine as a potential antidote and biomonitoring agent of methylmercury exposure. *Environ Health Perspect.* 2008; 116(1):26-31.

Bhatnagar R, Abou-Issa H, Curley RW, et al. Growth suppression of human breast carcinoma cells in culture by N-(4-hydroxyphenyl) retinamide and its glucuronide and through synergism with glucarate. *Biochem Pharmacol.* 1991; 41:1471-1477.

Braundmeier AG, Lenz KM, Inman KS, et al. Individualized medicine and the microbiome in reproductive tract. *Front Physiol.* 2015; 6:97.

Clarke G, Stilling RM, Kennedy PJ, et al. Minireview: gut microbiota: the neglected endocrine organ. *Mol Endocrinol.* 2014; 28(8):1221-38.

Galland L. The gut microbiome and the brain. *J Med Food.* 2014; 17(12):1261-72.

Kelly JR, Kennedy PJ, Cryan JF, et al. Breaking down the barriers: the gut microbiome, intestinal permeability and stress-related psychiatric disorders. *Front Cell Neurosci.* 2015; 9:392.

Le HT, Schaldach CM, Firestone GL, et al. Plant-derived 3,3'-diindolylmethane Is a Strong Androgen Antagonist in Human Prostate Cancer Cells. *J Biol Chem.* 2003 Jun 6;278(23):21136-45.

Michnovicz JJ, Adlercreutz H, Bradlow HL. Changes in levels of urinary estrogen metabolites after oral indole-3-carbinol treatment in humans. *J Natl Cancer Inst.* 1997; 89(10):718-23.

Mulcrow C, Lawrence V, Jacobs B, et al. Milk thistle: effects on liver disease and cirrhosis and clinical adverse effects. *Evid Rep Technol Assess (Summ).* 2000; (21):1-3.

Rajora S, Suriano R, Parmar PS, et al. .3,3'-diindolylmethane Modulates Estrogen Metabolism in Patients with Thyroid Proliferative Disease: A Pilot Study. *Thyroid.* 2011, Mar 21(13): 299-304.

River-Espinoza Y, Muriel P. Pharmacological actions of curcumin in liver diseases or damage. *Liver Int.* 2009; 29(10):1457-66.

Schmitt B, Vincenzi M, Garrel C, et al. Effects of N-acetylcysteine, oral glutathione (GSH) and a novel sublingual form of GSH on oxidative stress markers: A comparative crossover study. *Redox Biol.* 2015; 6:198-205.

Selkirk JK, Cohen GM, Macleod MC. Glucuronic acid conjugation in the metabolism of chemical carcinogens by rodent cells. *Arch Toxico Suppl.* 1980; 3:171-8.

Walaszek Z, Hanausek-Walaszek M. D-Glucono-1, 4-Lactone: its excretion in the bile and urine and effect on biliary excretion of beta-glucuronidase after oral administration in rats. *Hepatology.* 1988; 9(4):552-6.

Walaszek Z, Szemraj J, Narog M, et al. Metabolism, uptake, and excretion of a D-glucaric acid salt and its potential use in cancer prevention. *Cancer Detect Prev.* 1997; 21(2):178-90.

Winnie-Pui-Pui Liew, Jia-Sin Ong, Chee-Yuan Gan, et al. Gut microbiome and stress. Beneficial microorganisms in medical and health applications. *Microbiol Monogr.* 2015; 28:223-55.

Chapter 3 – The Adrenal Glands and the Hormone Connection

Archana R, Namasivayam A. Antistressor effect of *Withania somnifera*. *J Ethnopharmacol.* 1999; 64(1):91-3.

Dhuley JN. Effect of ashwagandha on lipid peroxidation in stress-induced animals. *J Ethnopharmacol.* 1998; 60(2): 173-8.

Emmons RA. *Thanks! How the new science of gratitude can make you happier.* Houghton Mifflin Harcourt Publishing Company; 2008.

Farnsworth NR, Kinghorn AD, Soejarto, DD, et al. Siberian ginseng *(Eleutherococcus senticosus)*: Current status as an adaptogen. *Economic and Medicinal Plant Research.* 1985; 1:156-215.

Head KA, Kelly GS. Nutrients and botanicals for treatment of stress: Adrenal fatigue, neurotransmitter imbalance, anxiety, and restless sleep. *Altern Med Rev.* 2009; 14(2):114-40.

Chapter 4 – The Thyroid and the Hormone Connection

Bokkenheuser VD, Winter J. Biotransformation of steroid hormones by gut bacteria. *Am J Clin Nutr,* 1980; 33(11 Suppl):2502-6.

Campbell, AW. Autoimmunity and the gut. *Autoimmune Dis.* 2014; 2014:152428.

Dunn JT. Seven deadly sins in confronting endemic iodine deficiency, and how to avoid them. *J Clin Endocrinol Metab.* 1996; 81(4):1332-5.

Fuge R. Iodine deficiency: an ancient problem in a modern world. *Ambio.* 2007; 36(1):70-2.

Gaby, AR. "Sub-laboratory" hypothyroidism and the empirical use of armour thyroid. *Altern Med Rev.* 2004; 9(2): 157-79.

Kelly GS. Peripheral metabolism of thyroid hormones: a review. *Altern Med Rev.* 2000; 5(4):306-33.

Morganti S, Ceda GP, Saccani M, et al. Thyroid disease in the elderly: sex-related differences in clinical expression. *J Endocrinol Invest.* 2005; 28(11 Suppl Proceedings):101-4.

O'Hara AM, Shanahan F. The gut flora as a forgotten organ. Review Article. *EMBO Rep.* 2006; 7(7):688-93.

Walter KN, Corwin EJ, Ulbrecht J, et al. Elevated thyroid stimulating hormone is associated with elevated cortisol in healthy young men and women. *Thyroid Res.* 2012; 5(1):13

Section 2 – For Women and The Men In Their Life

Chapter 5 – Perimenopause and Menopause

Bolton JL, Shen L. p-Quinone methides are the major decomposition products of catechol estrogen o-quinones. *Carcinogenesis.* 1996; 17(5):925-9.

Chen I, Wollman Y, Chernichovsky T, et al. Effect of oral administration of high-dose nitric oxide donor L-arginine in men with organic erectile dysfunction: results of a double-blind, randomized placebo-controlled study. *BJU Int.* 1999; 83(3):269-73.

Colditz GA, Hankinson SE, Hunter DJ, et al. The use of estrogens and progestins and the risk of breast cancer in postmenopausal women. *N Engl J Med.* 1995; 332(24):1589-93.

Klotz, T, Mathers MJ, Braun M, et al. Effectiveness of oral L-arginine in first-line treatment of erectile dysfunction in a controlled crossover study. *Urol Int.* 1999; 63(4):220-3.

Philp HA. Hot flashes – a review of the literature on alternative and complementary treatment approaches. *Altern Med Rev.* 2003; 8(3):284-302.

Shen L, Qiu S, Chen Y, et al. Alkylation of 2'-deoxynucleosides and DNA by the Premarin metabolite 4-hydroxyequilenin semiquinone radical. *Chem Res Toxicol.* 1998; 11(2):94-101.

Toda N, Ayajiki K, Okamura T. Nitric oxide and penile erectile function, *Pharmacol Ther.* 2005; 106(2):233-66.

Writing Group for the PEPI Trial. Effects of estrogen or estrogen/progestin regimens on heart disease risk factors in postmenopausal women: The postmenopausal estro-gen/progestin interventions (PEPI) trial. *JAMA*. 1995; 273(3):199-208.

Zieve, L. Conditional deficiencies of ornithine or arginine. *J Am Coll Nutr.* 1986; 5(2):167-76.

Chapter 6 – Estrogen-Dominant Conditions

Cutler W. *Hysterectomy: Before and after.* New York: Harper and Row, NY, 1998 Paperback update issued March 1990.

Meeker JD, Stapleton HM. House dust concentrations of organophosphate flame retardants in relation to hormone levels and semen quality parameters. *Environ Health Perspect.* 2010; 118(3):318-23.

Meeker JD, Barr DB, Hauser R. Human semen quality and sperm DNA damage in relation to urinary metabolites of pyrethroid insecticides. *Hum Reprod.* 2008; 23(8), 1932-40.

National Institute for Occupational Safety and Health. RTECS: 4-Isothiazolin-3-one, 5-chloro-2-methyl-. 2003. Available from: www.cdc.gov/niosh/rtecs/nx7c76b2. html.

National Institute for Occupational Safety and Health. RTECS: Ammonium, ethyl (4-(p-(ethyl(m-sulfobenzyl) amino)-alpha-(o-sulfophenyl)benzylidene)-2,5-cyclo-hexadien-1-ylidene)(m-sulfobenzyl), hydroxide, inner salt, disodium salt. 2000. Available from: www.cdc.gov/ niosh/rtecs/bq481908.html.4

National Institute for Occupational Safety and Health. RTECS: Benzoic acid, p-hydroxy-, methyl ester. 2003. Available from: www.cdc.gov/niosh/rtecs/dh256250. html.

National Institute for Occupational Safety and Health. RTECS: Glycerol. 2003. Available from: www.cdc.gov/ niosh/rtecs/ma7ad550.html.

Parker WH, Broder MS, Chang E, et al. Ovarian conserva-tion at the time of hysterectomy and long-term health outcomes in the nurses' health study. *Obstet Gynecol.* 2009; 113(5):1027-37.

Saldeen P, Saldeen T. Women and omega-3 fatty acids. *Obstet Gynecol Surv.* 2004; 59(10):722-30.

U.S. EPA. Office of Prevention, Pesticides, and Toxic Substances. 2004. Response to Freedom of Information Act request of October 19, 2004. Washington, D.C. Response dated November 17.

U.S. EPA. Office of Prevention, Pesticides, and Toxic Substances. 1997. Reregistration eligibility decision (RED): 3-Iodo-2-propynyl butylcarbamate (IPBC). Available from: www.epa.gov/pesticides. p.7.

Chapter 7 – Common Hormone Imbalances

Abraham G. Nutritional factors in the etiology of the premenstrual tension syndromes. *J Reprod Med.* 1983; 28(7):446-64.

Atmaca M, Kumru S, Tezcan E. Fluoxetine versus Vitex agnus castus extract in the treatment of premenstrual dys-phoric disorder. *Hum Psychopharmacol.* 2003; 18(3):191-5.

Chen J, Tominaga K, Sato Y, et al. Maitake mushroom *(Grifola frondosa)* extract induces ovulation in patients with polycystic ovary syndrome: a possible montotherapy and a combination therapy after failure with first-line comi-phene citrate. *J Altern Complem Med.* 2010; 12(12):1295-9.

Head, KA. Premenstrual syndrome: nutritional and alterna-tive approaches. *Altern Med Rev.* 1997; 2:12-25.

Lydic M, McNurlan M, Bembo S, et al. Chromium pico-linate improves insulin sensitivity in obese subjects with polycystic ovary syndrome. *Fertil Steril.* 2006; 86(1): 243-6.

Marshall K. Polycystic ovary syndrome: conical consider-ations. *Altern Med Rev.* 2001; 6(3):272-92..

Pasquali R, Gambineri A. Cortisol and the polycystic ovary syndrome. *Expert Rev Endocrinol Metab.* 2012; 7(5): 555-66.

Thys-Jacobs S, Donovan D, Papadopoulos A, et al. Vitamin D and calcium dysregulation in the polycystic ovarian syndrome. *Steroids.* 1999; 64(6):430-5.

Chapter 8 – Breast Disease

Arcidiacono B, Iiritano S, Nocera A, et al. Insulin resistance and cancer risk: an overview of the pathogenetic mecha-nisms. *Exp Diabetes Res.* 2012; 2012:789174.

Bhatnagar R, Abou-Issa H, Curley RW, et al. Growth suppression of human breast carcinoma cells in culture by N-(4-hydroxyphenyl) retinamide and its glucuronide and through synergism with glucarate. *Biochem Pharmacol.* 1991; 41:1471-77.

Bucher HC, Weinbacher M, Gyr K. Influence of method of reporting study results on decision of physicians to prescribe drugs to lower cholesterol concentration. *BMJ.* 1994; 309(6957):761-4.

Chao C, Studts JL, Abell T, et al. Adjuvant chemotherapy for breast cancer: how presentation of recurrence risk influences decision-making. *J Clin Oncol.* 2003; 21(23): 4299-305.

References

Curley RW Jr, Humphries KA, Koolemans-Beynan A, et al. Activity of D-glucarate analogues: synergistic antiproliferative effect in cultured human mammary tumor cells appear to specifically require the D-glucarate structure. *Life Sci.* 1994; 54(18):1299-1303.

Gøtzsche PC, Jørgensen KJ. Screening for breast cancer with mammography. *Cochrane Database Syst Rev.* 2013; (6): CD001877.

Kaur M, Agarwal C, Agarwal R. Anticancer and cancer chemopreventive potential of grape seed extract and other grape-based products. *J Nutr.* 2009; 139(9):1806S-1812S.

Kawaiiri H, Takashima T, Onoda N, et al. Efficacy and feasibility of neoadjuvant chemotherapy with FEC 100 followed by weekly paclitaxel for operable breast cancer. *Oncol Lett.* 2012; 4(4):612-6.

Lissoni P, Barni S, Meregalli S, et al. Modulation of cancer endocrine therapy by melatonin: a phase II study of tamoxifen plus melatonin in metastatic breast cancer patients progressing under tamoxifen alone. *Br J Cancer.* 1995; 71(4):854-6.

Liu D, Chen Z. Effect of curcumin on breast cancer cells. *J Breast Cancer.* 2013; 16(2):133-7.

Miller, AB, Wall C, Baines CJ, et al. Twenty-five year follow-up for breast cancer incidence and mortality of the

Canadian National Breast Screening Study: randomized screening trial. *BMJ.* 2014; 348:g366.

Morgan G, Ward R, Barton M. The contribution of cytotoxic chemotherapy to 5-year survival in adult malignancies. *Clin Oncol (R Coll Radiol).* 2004; 16(8):549-60.

National Cancer Institute. Milk Thistle (PDQ®)-Health Professional Version. *PDQ Integrative, Alternative, and Complementary Therapies Editorial Board.* Published online: July 20, 2016.

Orgel E, Mittelman SD. The links between insulin resistance, diabetes, and cancer. *Curr Diab Rep.* 2013; 13(2): 213-22.

Segelov, E. The emperor's new clothes – can chemotherapy survive? *Australian Prescriber.* 2006; 29(1):2-3.

Siegel AB, Stebbing J. Milk thistle: early seeds of potential. *Lancet Oncol.* 2013; 14(10):929-30.

Wadhwa R, Singh R, Gao R, et al. Water extract of ashwagandha leaves has anticancer activity: identification of an active component and its mechanism of action. *PLoS One.* 2013; 8(11):10.1371.

Wolford C, McConoughey SJ, Jalgaonkar SP, et al. Transcription factor ATF3 links host adaptive response to breast cancer metastasis. *J Clin Invest.* 2013; 123(7): 2893-906.

Section 3 – Gender Differences in Common Diseases

Chapter 9 – Urinary Tract Infections, Interstitial Cystitis, and Urinary Incontinence

Gomelsky A, Dmochowski RR. Urinary incontinence in the aging female. *Aging Health.* 2011; 7(1):79-88.

Ho MH, Bhatia NN, Bhasin S. Anabolic effects of androgens on muscles of female pelvic floor and lower urinary tract. *Curr Opin Obstet Gynecol.* 2004; 16(5):405-9.

Kaplan SA, Dmochowski R, Cash BD, et al. Systematic review of the relationship between bladder and bowel function: implications for patient management. *Int J Clin Pract.* 2013; 67(3):205-16.

Molander U, Sundh V, Steen B. Urinary incontinence and related symptoms in older men and women studied longitudinally between 70 and 97 years of age. A population study. *Arch Gerontol Geriatr.* 2002; 35(3):237-44.

Nicolle LE. Cranberry for the prevention of urinary tract infections? Time to move on. *JAMA.* 2016; 316(18):1873-4.

Nishimura M, Ohkawara T, Sato H, et al. Pumpkin seed oil extracted from *Cucurbita maxima* improves urinary disorder in human overactive bladder. *J Tradit Complement Med.* 2014; 4(1):72-4.

Sammon JD, Sharma P, Rahbar H, et al. Predictors of admission in patients presenting to the emergency department with urinary tract infection. *World J Urol.* 2014; 32(3):813-9.

Yanagisawa E. Study of effectiveness of mixed processed food containing Cucurbita pepo seed extract and soybean seed extract on stress urinary incontinence in women. *Jpn J Med Pharm Sci.* 2003; 14(3):313-22.

Chapter 10 – Infertility

Aksoy Y, Aksoy H, Altinkaynak K, et al. Sperm fatty acid composition in subfertile men. *Prostaglandins Leukot Essent Fatty Acids.* 2006; 75(2):75-9.

Ambiye VR, Langade D, Dongre S, et al. Clinical evaluation of the spermatogenic activity of the root extract of ashwagandha *(Withania somnifera)* in oligospermic males: a pilot study. *Evid Based Complement Alternat Med.* 2013; 2013:571420.

Andersson AM, Jørgensen N, Main KM, et al. Adverse trends in male reproductive health: we may have reached a crucial 'tipping point'. *Int J Androl.* 2008; 31(2):74-80.

Barbieri RL, Makris A, Randall RW, et al. Insulin stimulates androgen accumulation in incubations of ovarian stroma obtained from women with hyperandrogenism. *J Clin Endocrinol Metab.* 1986; 62(5):904-10.

Chen J, Wollman T, Chernichovsky A, et al. Effect of oral administration of high-dose nitric oxide donor l-arginine in men with organic erectile dysfunction: results of a double-blind, randomized, placebo-controlled study. *BJU International.* 1999; 83(3):269-73.

Cicero AF, Bandieri E, Arletti R. *Lepidium meyenii Walp* improves sexual behaviour in male rats independently from its action on spontaneous locomotor activity. *J Ethnopharmacol.* 2001; 75(2-3):225-9.

Desai N, Sabanegh E Jr, Kim T, et al. Free radical theory of aging: implications in male infertility. *Urology.* 2010; 75(1):14-9.

Goyal A, Chopra M, Lwaleed BA, et al. The effects of dietary lycopene supplementation on human seminal plasma. *BJU Int.* 2007; 99(6):1456-60.

Greco E, Romano S, Iacobelli M, et al. ICSI in cases of sperm DNA damage: beneficial effect of oral antioxidant treatment. *Hum Reprod.* 2005; 20(9):2590-4.

Hunt CD, Johnson PE, Herbel J, et al. Effects of dietary zinc depletion on seminal volume and zinc loss, serum testosterone concentrations, and sperm morphology in young men. *Am J Clin Nutr.* 1992; 56(1):148-57.

Ibrahim HA, Zhu Y, Wu C, et al. Selenium-enriched probiotics improves murine male fertility compromised by high fat diet. *Biol Trace Elem Res.* 2012; 147(1-3):251-60.

Jørgensen N, Joensen UN, Jensen TK, et al. Human semen quality in the new millennium: a prospective cross-sectional population-based study of 4867 men. *BMJ Open.* 2012; 2:e000990.

Merzenich H, Zeeb H, Blettner M. Decreasing sperm quality: a global problem? *BMC Public Health.* 2010; 10:24.

Morgante G, Scolaro V, Tosti C, et al. Treatment with carnitine, acetyl carnitine, L-arginine and ginseng improves sperm motility and sexual health in men with asthenopermia. *Minerva Urol Nefrol.* 2010; 62(3):213-8. [Article in Italian]

Omu AE, Dashti H, Al-Othman S. Treatment of asthenozoospermia with zinc sulphate: andrological, immunological and obstetric outcome. *Eur J Obstet Gynecol Reprod Biol.* 1998; 79(2):179-84.

Paffoni A, Ferrari S, Viganò P, et al. Vitamin D deficiency and infertility: insights from in vitro fertilization cycles. *J Clin Endocrinol Metab.* 2014; 99(11):E2372-6.

Safarinejad MR, Hosseini SY, Dadkhah F, et al. Relationship of omega-3 and omega-6 fatty acids with semen characteristics, and anti-oxidant status of seminal plasma: a comparison between fertile and infertile men. *Clin Nutr.* 2010; 29(1):100-5.

Safarinejad MR, Safarinejad S. Efficacy of selenium and/or N-acetyl-cysteine for improving semen parameters in infertile men: a double-blind, placebo controlled, randomized study. *J Urol.* 2009; 181(2):741-51.

Saldeen P, Saldeen T. Women and omega-3 fatty acids. *Obstet Gynecol Surv.* 2004; 59(10):722-30.

Talevi R, Barbato V, Fiorentino I, et al. Protective effects of in vitro treatment with zinc, d-aspartate and coenzyme q10 on human sperm motility, lipid peroxidation and DNA fragmentation. *Reprod Biol Endocrinol.* 2013; 11:81.

Wathes DC, Abayasekara DR, Aitken RJ. Polyunsaturated fatty acids in male and female reproduction. *Biol Reprod.* 2007; 77(2):190-201.

Chapter 11 – Mood Disorders – Depression and Anxiety

Abdou AM, Higashiguchi S, Horie K, et al. Relaxation and immunity enhancement effects of gamma-aminobutyric acid (GABA) administration in humans. *BioFactors.* 2006; 26(3):201-8.

Akhondzadeh S, Tahmacebi-Pour N, Noorbala AA, et al. Crocus sativus L. in the treatment of mild to moderate depression: a double-blind, randomized and placebo controlled trial. *Phytother Res.* 2005; 19(2):148-51.

Avena NM, Rada P, Hoebel BG. Evidence for sugar addiction: behavioral and neurochemical effects of intermittent, excessive sugar intake. *Neurosci Biobehav Rev.* 2008; 32(1):20-39.

Beckmann H, Athen D, Olteanu M, et al. Dl-phenylalanine versus imipramine: a double-blind controlled study. *Eur Arch Psychiatry Clin Neurosci.* 1979; 227(1):49-58.

Bell IR, Edman JS, Morrow FD, et al. B complex vitamin patterns in geriatric and young adult inpatients with major depression. *J Am Geriatr Soc.* 1991; 39(3):252-7.

Blumenthal M, Busse WR, Goldberg A, et al. (eds). *The complete german commission monographs: therapeutic guide to herbal medicines.* Austin: American Botanical Council and Boston: Integrative Medicine Communications; 1998.

Bottiglieri T. Folate, vitamin B12, and neuropsychiatric disorders. *Nutr Rev.* 1996; 54(12):382-90.

Brodie HKH, Sack R, Siever L. *Clinical studies of L-5-hydroxytryptophan in depression.* In: Barchas J and Usdin E, editors. Serotonin and behavior. New York: Academic Press; 1973.

Buydens-Branchey L, Branchey M, Hibbeln JR. Associations between increases in plasma n-3 polyunsaturated fatty acids following supplementation and decreases in anger and anxiety in substance abusers. *Prog Neuropsychopharmacol Biol Psychiatry.* 2008; 32(2):568-75.

Byerley WF, Judd LL, Reimherr FW, et al. 5-hydroxytryptophan: a review of its antidepressant efficacy and adverse effects. *J Clin Psychopharmacol.* 1987; 7(3):127-37.

Calabrese C, Gregory WL, Leo M, et al. Effects of a standardized *Bacopa monnieri* extract on cognitive performance, anxiety, and depression in the elderly: a randomized, double-blind, placebo-controlled trial. *J Altern Complement Med.* 2008; 14(6):707-13.

References

Chandrasekhar KA, Kapoor J, Anishetty S. A prospective, randomized double-blind, placebo-controlled study of safety and efficacy of a high concentration full-spectrum extract of Ashwagandha root in reducing stress and anxiety in adults. *Indian J Psychol Med*. 2012; 34(3):255-62.

Chiu CC, Liu JP, Su KP. The use of omega-3 fatty acids in treatment of depression. *Psychiatric Times*. 2008; 25(9):76-80.

Coppen A, Bolander-Gouaille C. Treatment of depression: time to consider folic acid and vitamin B12. *J Psychopharmacol*. 2005; 19(1):59-65.

Eschenauer G, Sweet BV. Pharmacology and therapeutic uses of theanine. *Am J Health Syst Pharm*. 2006; 63(1):26, 28-30.

Fournier JC, DeRubeis RJ, Hollon SD, et al. Antidepressant drug effects and depression severity: a patient-level meta-analysis. *JAMA*. 2010; 303(1):47-53.

Freeman MP, Rapaport MH. Omega-3 fatty acids and depression: from cellular mechanisms to clinical care. *J Clin Psychiatry*. 2011; 72(2):258-9.

Gilbody S, Lightfoot T, Sheldon T. Is low folate a risk factor for depression? A meta-analysis and exploration of heterogeneity. *J Epidemiol Community Health*. 2007; 61(7):631-7.

Hasler G, vander Veen JW, Tumonins T, et al. Reduced prefrontal glutamate/glutamine and gamma-aminobutyric acid levels in major depression determined using proton magnetic resonance spectroscopy. *Arch Gen Psychiatry*. 2007; 64(2):193-200.

Hoes MJ. L-tryptophan in depression and strain. *J Orthomol Med*. 1982; 11(4):231-42.

Jacka FN, O'Neil A, Opie R, et al. A randomised controlled trial of dietary improvement for adults with major depression (the 'SMILES' trial). *BMC Medicine*. 2017; 15:23.

Kerr DCR, Zava DT, Piper WT, et al. Associations between vitamin D levels and depressive symptoms in healthy young adult women. *Psychiatry Res*. 2015; 227(1):46-51.

Kiecolt-Glasera JK, Belury MA, Andridge R, et al. Omega-3 supplementation lowers inflammation and anxiety in medical students: a randomized controlled trial. *Brain, Behav Immun*. 2011; 25(8):1725-34.

Lakhan SE, Vieira KF. Nutritional therapies for mental disorders. *Nutr J*. 2008; 7(2):1-8.

Lenze EJ, Mantella RC, Shi P, et al. Elevated cortisol in older adults with generalized anxiety disorder is reduced by treatment: a placebo-controlled evaluation of escitalopram. *Am J Geriatr Psychiatry*. 2011; 19(5):482-90.

Leonard BE. The role of noradrenaline in depression: a review. *J Psychopharmacol*. 1997; 11(Suppl 4):39-47.

Levine J, Barak Y, Gonzalves M, et al. Double-blind, controlled trial of inositol treatment of depression. *Am J Psychiatry*. 1995; 152(5):792-4.

Lichtman JH, Biggrt JT, Blumenthal, JA. Depression and coronary heart disease. *Circulation*. 2008; 118(17):1768-75.

Lopresti AL, Maes M, Meddens MJ, et al. Curcumin and major depression: a randomised, double-blind, placebo

controlled trial investigating the potential of peripheral biomarkers to predict treatment response and antidepressant mechanisms of change. *Eur Neuropsychopharmacol*. 2015; 25(1):38-50.

McLean A, Rubinsztein JS, Robbins TW, et al. The effects of tyrosine depletion in normal healthy volunteers: implications for unipolar depression. *Psychopharmacol (Berl)*. 2004; 171(3):286-97.

Merete C, Falcon LM, Tucker KL. Vitamin B6 is associated with depressive symptomatology in Massachusetts elders. *J Am Coll Nutr*. 2008; 27(3):421-7.

Möller HJ. Is there evidence for negative effects of antidepressants on suicidality in depressive patients? A systematic review. *Eur Arch Psychiatry Clin Neurosci*. 2006; 256(8):476-96.

Mukai T, Kishi T, Matsuda Y, et al. A meta-analysis of inositol for depression and anxiety disorders. *Hum Psychopharmacol*. 2014; 29(1):55-63.

Nieper HA. The clinical applications of lithium orotate. A two years study. *Agressologie*. 1973; 14(6):407-11.

Noorbala AA, Akhondzadeh S, Tamacebi-Pour N, et al. Hydro-alcoholic extract of Crocus sativus L. versus fluoxetine, in the treatment of mild to moderate depression: a double-blind, randomized pilot trial. *J Ethnopharmacol*. 2005; 97(2):281-4.

O'Donnell T, Rotzinger S, Ulrich M, et al. Effects of chronic lithium and sodium valproate on concentrations of brain amino acids. *Eur Neuropsychopharmacol*. 2003; 13(4):220-7.

Petty F. GABA and mood disorders: a brief review and hypothesis. *J Affect Disord*. 1995; 34(4):275-81.

Setiawan E, Wilson AA, Mizrahi R, et al. Role of translocator protein density, a marker of neuroinflammation, in the brain during major depressive episodes. *JAMA Psychiatry*. 2015; 72(3):268-75.

Shevtsov VA, Zholus BI, Shervarly VI, et al. A randomized trial of two different doses of a SHR-5 *Rhodiola rosea* extract versus placebo and control of capacity for mental work. *Phytomedicine*. 2003; 10(2-3):95-105.

Stetler C, Miller GE. Blunted cortisol response to awakening in mild to moderate depression: regulatory influences of sleep patterns and social contacts. *J Abnorm Psychol*. 2005; 114(4):697-705.

Tafet GE, Idoyaga-Vargas VP, Abulafia DP, et al. Correlation between cortisol level and serotonin uptake in patients with chronic stress and depression. *Cogn Affect Behav Neurosci*. 2001; 1: 388-93.

Tombaugh, TC, Yang SH, Swanson RA, et al. Glucocorticoids exacerbate hypoxic and hypoglycemic hippocampal injury in vitro: biochemical correlates and a role for astrocytes. *J Neurochem*. 1992; 59(1):137-46.

Volz, HP, Kieser, M. Kava-kava extract WS 1490 versus placebo in anxiety disorders: a randomized placebo-controlled 25-week outpatient trial. *Pharmacopsychiatry*. 1997; 30(1):1-5.

Vreeburg, SA, Hoogendijk RH, DeRijk RH, et al. Salivary cortisol levels and the 2-year course of depressive and anxiety disorders. *Psychoneuroendocrinology.* 2013; 38(9): 1494-502.

Watson AW, Haskell-Ramsay CF, Kennedy DO, et al. Acute supplementation with blackcurrant extracts modulates

cognitive functioning and inhibits monoamine oxidase-B in healthy young adults. *J Funct Foods*, 2015: 17:524-39.

Wium-Andersen MK, Ørsten DD, Nielsen SF, et al. Elevated C-reactive protein levels, psychological distress, and depression in 73,131 individuals. *JAMA Psychiatry.* 2013; 70(2):176-84.

Chapter 12 – Sleep Disorders

Aguirre-Hernández E, Martinez AL, Gonzalez-Trujano ME, et al. Pharmacological evaluation of the anxiolytic and sedative effects of *Tilia americana* L. var. *mexicana* in mice. *J Ethnopharmacol.* 2007; 109(1):140-5.

Akhondzadeh S, Naghavi HR, Vazirian M, et al. Passionflower in the treatment of generalized anxiety: a pilot double-blind randomized controlled trial with oxazepam. *J Clin Pharm Ther.* 2001; 26(5):363-7.

Appel K, Rose T, Fiebich B, et al. Modulation of the γ-aminobutyric acid (GABA) system by *Passiflora incarnate* L. *Phytother Res.* 2011; 25(6):838-43.

Awad R, Arnason JT, Trudeau V, et al. Phytochemical and biological analysis of skullcap (*Scutellaria lateriflora* L.): a medicinal plant with anxiolytic properties. *Phytomedicine.* 2003; 10(8):640-9.

Balbo M, Leproult R, Van Cauter E. Impact of sleep and its disturbances on hypothalamo-pituitary-adrenal axis activity. *Int J Endocrinol.* 2010; 2010:759234.

Basta M, Chrousos GP, Vela-Bueno A, et al. Chronic insomnia and stress system. *Sleep Med Clin.* 2007; 2(2):279-91.

Blumenthal M, Goldberg A, Brinckmann J. *Herbal medicine: expanded Commission E monographs.* Newton, MA: Integrative Medicine Communications; 2000.

Buscemi N, Vandermeer B, Pandya R, et al. Melatonin for treatment of sleep disorders: summary. Agency for Healthcare Research and Quality. Publication Number 05-E002-1. 2004. Available from: http://archive.ahrq.gov/ clinic/epcsums/melatsum.htm.

Cauffield JS, Forbes HJ. Dietary supplements used in the treatment of depression, anxiety, and sleep disorders. *Lippincotts Prim Care Pract.* 1999; 3(3):290-304.

Elsas SM, Rossi DJ, Rabera J, et al. *Passiflora incarnata* L. (Passionflower) extracts elicit GABA currents in hippocampal neurons in vitro, and show anxiogenic and anticonvulsant effects in vivo, varying with extraction method. *Phytomedicine.* 2010; 17(12):940-9.

Gafner S, Dietz BM, McPhail KL, et al. Alkaloids from *Eschscholzia californica* and their capacity to inhibit binding of [3H]8-hydroxy-2-(di-N-propylamino)tetralin to 5-HT1A receptors in Vitro. *J Nat Prod.* 2006; 69(3):432-5.

Gottesmann C. GABA mechanisms and sleep. *Neuroscience.* 2002; 111(2):231-9.

Hanus M, Lafon J, Mathieu M. Double-blind, randomised, placebo-controlled study to evaluate the efficacy and safety of a fixed combination containing two plant extracts (*Crataegus oxyacantha* and *Eschscholtzia californica*) and magnesium in mild-to-moderate anxiety disorders. *Curr*

Med Res Opin. 2004; 20(1):63-71.

Lewis JG. Steroid analysis in saliva: an overview. *Clin Biochem Rev.* 2006; 27(3):139-46.

Medina JH, Viola H, Wolfman C, et al. Flavonoids: a new family of benzodiazepine receptor ligands. *Neurochem Res.* 1997; 22:419-25.

National institutes of health office of dietary supplements. Valerian: fact sheet for health professionals. March 2013. Available from: https://ods.od.nih.gov/factsheets/ Valerian-HealthProfessional/.

Ngan A, Conduit R. A double-blind, placebo-controlled investigation of the effects of *Passiflora incarnate* (passionflower) herbal tea on subjective sleep quality. *Phytother Res.* 2011; 25(8):1153-9.

Rolland A, Fleurentin J, Lanhers MC, et al. Behavioural effects of the American traditional plant *Eschscholzia californica:* sedative and anxiolytic properties. *Planta Med.* 1991; 57(3):212-6.

Rolland A, Fleurentin J, Lanhers MC, et al. Neurophysiological effects of an extract of *Eschscholzia californica* Cham. (Papaveraceae). *Phytother Res.* 2001; 15(5):377-81.

Shinomiya K, Inoue T, Utsu Y, et al. Hypnotic activities of chamomile and passiflora extracts in sleep disturbed rats. *Biol Pharm Bull.* 2005; 28(5):808-10.

Soulairac A, Lambinet H. Effect of 5-hydroxytryptophan, a serotonin precursor, on sleep disorders. *Ann Med Psychol* (Paris). 1977; 1(5):792-8.

Törnhage CJ. Salivary cortisol for assessment of hypothalamic-pituitary-adrenal axis function. *Neuroimmunomodulation.* 2009; 16(5):284-9.

Van Cauter E, Knutson K, Leproult R, et al. The impact of sleep deprivation on hormones and metabolism. *Neurology.* 2005; 7(1). Available from: http://www.medscape.org/ viewarticle/502825.

Wolfson P, Hoffmann DL. An investigation into the efficacy of *Scutellaria lateriflora* in healthy volunteers. *Altern Ther Health Med.* 2003; 9(2):74-8.

Zhdanova IV, Wurtman RJ, Regan MM, et al. Melatonin treatment for age-related insomnia. *J Clin Endocrinol Metab.* 2001; 86(10):4727-30.

Ziegler G, Ploch M, Miettinen-Baumann A, et al. Efficacy and tolerability of valerian extract LI 156 compared with oxazepam in the treatment of non-organic insomnia – a randomized, double-blind, comparative clinical study. *Eur J Med Res.* 2002; 7(11):480-6.

Chapter 13 – Osteoporosis

Agnusdei D, Bufalino L. Efficacy of ipriflavone in established osteoporosis and long-term safety. *Calcif Tissue Int.* 1997; 61 Suppl 1:S23-7.

Bischoff-Ferrari HA, Willett WC, Wong JB, et al. Fracture prevention with vitamin D supplementation: meta-analysis of randomized controlled trials. *JAMA.* 2005; 293(18):2257-64.

Feskanich, D, Willett WC, Stampfer MJ, et al. Milk, dietary calcium, and bone fractures in women: a 12-year prospective study. *Am J Public Health.* 1997; 87(6):992-7.

Holick MF, Siris ES, Binkley N, et al. Prevalence of vitamin D inadequacy among postmenopausal North American women receiving osteoporosis therapy. *J Clin Endocrinol Metab.* 2005; 90(6):3215-24.

Jugdaohsingh R. Silicon and bone health. *J Nutr Health Aging.* 2007; 11(2):99-110.

McCabe LR, Irwin R, Schaefer L, et al. Probiotic use decreases intestinal inflammation and increases bone density in healthy male but not female mice. *J. Cell Physiol.* 2013; 228(8):1793-8.

Newnham RE. Essentiality of boron for healthy bones and joints. *Environ Health Perspect.* 1994; 102 Suppl 7:83-5.

O'Connor DJ. Understanding osteoporosis and clinical strategies to assess, arrest and restore bone loss. *Altern Med Rev.* 1997; 2(1):3647.

Patrick, L. Comparative absorption of calcium sources and calcium citrate malate for the prevention of osteoporosis. *Altern Med Rev.* 1999; 4(2):74-85.

Weinsier RL, Krumdieck CL. Dairy foods and bone health: examination of the evidence. *Am J Clin Nutr.* 2000; 72(3): 681-9.

Section 4 – More Gender Differences in Common Diseases

Chapter 14 – The Inflammation Factor in Osteoarthritis and Gastrointestinal Disorders

Drossman DA, Li ZM, Andruzzi E, et al. U.S. householder survey of functional gastrointestinal disorders – Prevalence, sociodemography, and health impact. *Digest Dis Sci.* 1993; 38(9):1569-80.

Green PHR, Stavropoulos SN, Panagi SG, et al. Characteristics of adult celiac disease in the USA: results of a national survey. *Am J Gastroenterol.* 2001; 96(1):126-31.

Heitkemper MM, Jarrett M, Cain KC, et al. Gastrointestinal symptoms in women with and without a diagnosis of IBS. *Dig Dis Sci.* 1995; 40(7):1511-9.

Heitkemper MM, Jarrett M. Pattern of gastrointestinal and somatic symptoms across the menstrual cycle. *Gastroenterology.* 1992; 102(2):505-13.

Houghton LA, Lea R, Jackson N, et al. The menstrual cycle affects rectal sensitivity in patients with irritable bowel syndrome but not healthy volunteers. *Gut.* 2002; 50(4):471-4.

Jacobson DL, Gange SJ, Rose NR, et al. Epidemiology and estimated population burden of selected autoimmune diseases in the United States. *Clin Immunol Immunopathol.* 1997; 84(3): 223-43.

Lawrence RC, Helmick CG, Arnett RC, et al. Estimates of the prevalence of arthritis and selected musculoskeletal

disorders in the United States. *Arthritis Rheum.* 1998; 41(5):778-99.

Lee OY, Mayer EA, Schmulson M, et al. Gender-related differences in IBS symptoms. *Am J Gastroenterol.* 2001; 96(7):2184-93.

Lee SY, Kim JH, Sung IK, et al. Irritable bowel syndrome is more common in women regardless of the menstrual phase: a Rome II-based survey. *Can J Gastroenterol.* 2012; 26(5): 252-6.

Longstreth GF, Wolde-Tsadik G. Irritable bowel-type symptoms in HMO examinees. Prevalence, demographics, and clinical correlates. *Diges Dis Sci.* 1993; 38(9):1581-9.

Megiorni F1, Mora B, Bonamico M, et al. HLA-DQ and susceptibility to celiac disease: evidence for gender differences and parent-of-origin effects. *Am J Gastroenterol.* 2008; 103(4):997-1003.

Singh GB, Atal CK. Pharmacology of an extract of salai guggal ex-Boswellia serrate, a new non-steroidal anti-inflammatory agent. *Agents Actions.* 1986; 18(3-4):407-12.

Triadafilopoulos G, Finlayson M, Grellet C. Bowel dysfunction in postmenopausal women. *Women Health.* 1998; 27(4):55-66.

Zhang Y, Jordan JM. Epidemiology of osteoarthritis. *Clin Geriatr Med.* 2010; 26(3):355-69.

Chapter 15 – Chronic Fatigue Syndrome and Fibromyalgia

Adams D, Wu T, Yang X, etal. Traditional Chinese herbs for the treatment of idiopathic chronic fatigue and chronic fatigue syndrome. *Cochrane Database Syst Rev.* 2009; 4: CD006348.

Castro-Marrero J, Cordero MD, Segundo MJ, et al. Does oral coenzyme Q10 plus NADH supplementation improve fatigue and biochemical parameters in chronic fatigue syndrome? *Antioxid Redox Signal.* 201510; 22(8):679-85.

Engleberg NC. *Chronic fatigue syndrome*. In: Mandell GL, Bennett JE, Dolin R, editors. *Principles and practice of infectious diseases*. 7th ed. Philadelphia, Pa: Elsevier Churchill Livingstone; 2009. Chapter 131.

Fuller-Thomson E, Nimigon J. Factors associated with depression among individuals with chronic fatigue syndrome: findings from a nationally representative survey. *Fam Pract*. 2008; 25(6):414-22.

Giloteaux L, Goodrich JK, Walters WA, et al. Reduced diversity and altered composition of the gut microbiome in individuals with myalgic encephalomyelitis/chronic fatigue syndrome. *Microbiome*. 2016; 4(1):30.

Heim C, Nater UM, Maloney E, et al. Childhood trauma and risk for chronic fatigue syndrome: association with neuroendocrine dysfunction. *Arch Gen Psychiatry*. 2009; 66(1):72-80.

Hornig M, Montoya JG, Klimas NG, et al. Distinct plasma immune signatures in ME/CFS are present early in the course of illness. *Sci Adv*. 2015; (1). pii : e1400121.

Katz BZ, Shiraishi Y, Mears CJ, et al. Chronic fatigue syndrome after infectious mononucleosis in adolescents. *Pediatrics*. 2009; 124(1):189-93.

Kerr JR. Gene profiling of patients with chronic fatigue syndrome/myalgic encephalomyelitis. *Curr Rheumatol Rep*. 2008; 10(6):482-91.

Lombardi VC, Ruscetti FW, Das Gupta J, et al. Detection of an infectious retrovirus, XMRV, in blood cells of patients with chronic fatigue syndrome. *Science*. 2009; 326(5952):585-9.

Myhill S, Booth NE, McLaren-Howard J. Chronic fatigue syndrome and mitochondrial dysfunction. *Int J Clin Exp Med*. 2009; 2(1):1-16.

Nicolson GL. Mitochondrial dysfunction and chronic disease: treatment with natural supplements. *Altern Ther. Winter* 2014; 20(Suppl. 1):18-25.

Plioplys AV, Plioplys S. Amantadine and L-carnitine treatment of chronic fatigue syndrome. *Neuropsychobiology*. 1997; 35(1):16-23.

Price JR, Mitchell E, Tidy E, et al. Cognitive behaviour therapy for chronic fatigue syndrome in adults. *Cochrane Database Syst Rev*. 2008; (3):CD001027.

Regland B, Anderson M, Abrahamsson L, et al. Increased concentrations of homocysteine in the cerebrospinal fluid in patients with fibromyalgia and chronic fatigue syndrome. *Scand J Rheumatol*. 1997; 26(4):301-7.

Regland B, Forsmark S, Halaouate L, et al. Response to vitamin B12 and folic acid in myalgic encephalomyelitis and fibromyalgia. *PLoS One*. 2015 ; 10(4):e0124648.

Santhouse A, Hotopf M, David AS. Chronic fatigue syndrome. *BMJ*. 2010; 340:c738.

Shiomi, K. Yamaguti, M. Inaba, H. et al. Neuroinflammation in patients with chronic fatigue syndrome/myalgic encephalomyelitis: An 11C-(R)-PK11195 PET study. *J Nucl Med*. 2014; 55(6):945-50.

Spector TD, Calomme MR, Anderson SH, et al. Choline-stabilized orthosilicic acid supplementation as an adjunct to calcium/vitamin D3 stimulates markers of bone formation in osteopenic females: a randomized, placebo-controlled trial. *BMC Musculoskelet Disord*. 2008; 9:85.

Stejskal V, Ockert K, Bjørklund G. Metal-induced inflammation triggers fibromyalgia in metal-allergic patients. *Neuro Endocrinol Lett*. 2013; 34(6):559-65.

Chapter 16 – Diabetes and Metabolic Syndrome

Adam TC, Hasson RE, Ventura EE, et al. Cortisol is negatively associated with insulin sensitivity in over-weight Latino youth. *J Clin Endocrinol Metab*. 2010; 95(10):4729-35.

Björntorp P, Rosmond R. Obesity and cortisol. *Nutrition*. 2000; 16(10):924-36.

Brand-Miller JC, Atkinson FS, Gahler RJ, et al. Effects of PGX®, a novel functional fibre, on acute and delayed post-prandial glycaemia. *Eur J Clin Nutr*. 2010; 64(12):1488-93.

Cassoobhoy A. Morning report: Type 2 diabetes, aspirin, & CVD, PPIs & stroke, psilocybin (magic mushrooms) for depression. *Medscape* . 2016.

Dale AC, Nilsen TI, Vatten L, et al. Diabetes mellitus and risk of fatal ischaemic heart disease by gender: 18 years follow-up of 74 914 individuals in the HUNT 1 Study. *Eur Heart J*. 2007; 28(23):2924-9.

Demmer RT, Gelb S, Suglia SF, et al. Sex differences in the association between depression, anxiety, and type 2 diabetes mellitus. *Psychosom Med*. 2015; 77(4):467-77.

Fernàndez-Real JM, Ricart W, Casamitjana R. Lower cortisol levels after oral glucose in subjects with insulin resistance and abdominal obesity. *Clin Endocrinol (Oxf)*. 1997; 47(5):583-8.

Gale EA, Bingley PJ, Emmett CL, et al. European Nicotinamide Diabetes Intervention Trial (ENDIT): a randomised controlled trial of intervention before the onset of type 1 diabetes. *Lancet*. 2004; 363(9413):925-31.

Gregg EW, Gu Q, Cheng YJ, et al. Mortality trends in men and women with diabetes, 1971 to 2000. *Ann Intern Med*. 2007; 147(3):149-55.

Kahn R, Buse J, Ferrannini E, et al. The metabolic syndrome: time for a critical appraisal. Joint statement from the American Diabetes Association and the European Association for the Study of Diabetes. *Diabetes Care*. 2005; 28(9):2289-304.

Lotta LA, Sharp SJ, Burgess S, et al. Association between low-density lipoprotein cholesterol-lowering genetic variants and risk of type 2 diabetes: A meta-analysis. *JAMA*. 2016; 316(13):1383-91.

References

Mino D, Amato D, Cuevas ML, et al. Relationship of insulin resistance and overweight with cortisol and de-hydroepiandrosterone-sulfate levels. *Arch Med Res.* 2002; 33(6):524-30.

Owen N, Healy GN, Matthews CE, et al. Too much sitting: the population health science of sedentary behavior. *Exerc Sport Sci Rev.* 2010; 38(3):105-13.

Pan A, Lucas M, Sun Q, et al. Bidirectional association between depression and type 2 diabetes mellitus in women. *Arch Intern Med.* 2010; 170(21):1884-91.

Rabe K, Lehrke M, Parhofer KG, et al. Adipokines and insulin resistance. *Mol Med.* 2008; 14(11-12):741-51.

Rizza RA, Mandarino LJ, Gerich JE. Cortisol-induced insulin resistance in man: impaired suppression of glucose production and stimulation of glucose utilization due to a postreceptor detect of insulin action. *J Clin Endocrinol Metab.* 1982; 54(1):131-8.

Vuksan V, Sievenpiper JL, Owen R, et al. Beneficial effects of viscous dietary fiber from Konjac-mannan in subjects with the insulin resistance syndrome: results of a controlled metabolic trial. *Diabetes Care.* 2000; 23(1):9-14.

Chapter 17 – Cardiovascular Disease

Buring JE, Hennekens CH. The Women's Health Study: summary of the study design. *J Myocardial Ischemia.* 1992; 4:27-9.

Clifford T, Howatson G, West DJ, et al. The Potential Benefits of Red Beetroot Supplementation in Health and Disease. *Nutrients.* 2015 Apr; 7(4): 2801-2822.

Crook NR, Cole ST, Buring JE. Aspirin in the primary prevention of cardiovascular disease in the Women's Health Study: Effect of noncompliance. *Eur J Epidemiol.* 2012; 27(6):431-8.

Culver AL, Ockene IS, Balasubramanian R, et al. Statin use and risk of diabetes mellitus in postmenopausal women in the Women's Health Initiative. *Arch Intern Med.* 2012; 172(2):144-52.

Diamond DM, Ravnskov U. How statistical deception created the appearance that statins are safe and effective in primary and secondary prevention of cardiovascular disease. *Expert Rev Clin Pharmacol.* 2015; ;8(2):201-10.

Doggrell, SA. Berberine – a novel approach to cholesterol lowering. *Expert Opin Investig Drugs.* 2005; 14(5):683-5.

Facchinetti F, Neri I, Tarabusi M. *Eleutherococcus senticosus* reduces cardiovascular response in healthy subjects: a randomized, placebo-controlled trial. *Stress Health.* 2002; 18:11-7.

Hayden M, Pignone M, Phillips C, et al. Aspirin for the primary prevention of cardiovascular events: a summary of the evidence for the US Preventive Services Task Force. *Ann Intern Med.* 2002; 136(2):161-72.

Ho HV, Sievenpiper JL, Zurbau A, et al. A systematic review and meta-analysis of randomized controlled trials of the effect of barley β-glucan on LDL-C, non-HDL-C and apoB for cardiovascular disease risk reduction. *Eur J Clin Nutr.* 2016; 70(11):1239-45.

Kaczorowski E. Exploring statins: What does the evidence say? *Women's Health Activist.* National Women's Health Network; 2007 May/June. Available from: http://www. womenshealthnetwork.org.

Kim LK, Looser P, Swaminathan RV, et al. Sex-based disparities in incidence, treatment, and outcomes of cardiac arrest in the United States, 2003-2012. *JAHA.* 2016; 5(6): pii: e003704.

Lairon D. Intervention studies on Mediterranean diet and cardiovascular risk. *Mol Nutr Food Res.* 2007; 51(10): 1209-14.

Levin RI. The puzzle of aspirin and sex. *N Engl J Med.* 2005; 352(13):1366-8.

Mozaffarian D, Rimm EB. Fish intake, contaminants, and human health: evaluating the risks and the benefits. *JAMA.* 2006; 296(15):1885-99.

Notay K, Incognito AV, Millar PJ. Acute beetroot juice supplementation on sympathetic nerve activity: a randomized, double-blind, placebo-controlled proof-of-concept study. *American Journal of Physiology - Heart and Circulatory Physiology.* 2017; 313(1).

Ravnskov U, Diamond DM, Hama R, et al. Lack of an association or an inverse association between low-density-lipoprotein cholesterol and mortality in the elderly: a systematic review. *BMJ Open.* 2016; 6(6):e010401.

Rexrode KM, Lee IM, Cook NR, et al. Baseline characteristics of participants in the Women's Health Study. *J Womens Health Gend Based Med.* 2000; 9(1):19-27.

Ridker PM. Rosuvastatin in the primary prevention of cardiovascular disease among patients with low levels of low-density lipoprotein cholesterol and elevated high-sensitivity C-reactive protein: rationale and design of the JUPITER trial. *Circulation.* 2003; 108(19):2292-7.

Ridker PM, Buring JE, the Women's Health Study Research Group. A randomized trial of low-dose aspirin in the primary prevention of cardiovascular disease in 39,876 women. The Women's Health Study. Program and abstracts of the American College of Cardiology Annual Scientific Session; 2005 March 6-9. Orlando, Florida. Late Breaking Clinical Trials 1.

Ridker PM, Cook MR, Lee I-M, et al. A randomized trial of low-dose aspirin in the primary prevention of cardiovascular disease in women. *N Engl J Med.* 2005; 352:1293-1304.

Roeters van Lennep JE, Westerveld HT, Erkelens DW, et al. Risk factors for coronary heart disease: implications of gender. *Cardiovasc Res.* 2002; 53(3):538-49.

Seshasai SR, Wijesuriya S, Sivakumaran R, et al. Effect of aspirin on vascular and nonvascular outcomes: meta-analysis of randomized controlled trials. *Arch Intern Med.* 2012; 172(3):209-16.

Steering Committee of the Physicians' Health Study Research Group. Final report on the aspirin component of the ongoing Physicians' Health Study. *N Engl J Med.* 1989; 321:129-35.

Tang W, Gao Y, Chen G, et al. A Randomized, Double-Blind and Placebo-Controlled Study of a *Ganoderma lucidum* Polysaccharide Extract in Neurasthenia. *Journal of Medicinal Food.* April 2005, 8(1): 53-58.

Tawakol A, Ishai A, Takx R, et al. Relation between resting amygdalar activity and cardiovascular events: a long-

itudinal and cohort study. *The Lancet.* 2017; pii: S0140-6736(16)31714-7.

Taylor F, Huffman MD, Macedo AF, et al. Statins for the primary prevention of cardiovascular disease. *Cochrane Database Syst Rev.* 2013; (1):CD004816.

Wong KL, Chao HH, Chan P, et al. Antioxidant activity of Ganoderma lucidum in acute ethanol-induced heart toxicity. Phytother Res. 2004 Dec; 18(12):1024-6.

Wright, J, Abramson JM. Are lipid-lowering guidelines evidence based? *Lancet.* 2007; 369(9557):168-9.

Chapter 18 – Dementias

Arnsten, AF. Stress signalling pathways that impair prefrontal cortex structure and function. *Nat Rev Neurosci.* 2009; 10(6):410-22.

Balestreri R, Fontana L, Astengo F. A double-blind placebo controlled evaluation of the safety and efficacy of vinpocetine in the treatment of patients with chronic vascular senile cerebral dysfunction. *J Am Geriatr Soc.* 1987; 35(5):425-30.

Barcelos RCS, Benvegnu DM, Boufleur N, et al. Effects of omega-3 essential fatty acids (omega-3 EFAs) on motor disorders and memory dysfunction typical neurolepticin-duced: behavioral and biochemical parameter. *Neurotox Res.* 2010; 17(3):228-37.

Bavarsad Shahripour R, Harrigan MR, Alexandrov AV. N-acetylcysteine (NAC) in neurological disorders: mechanisms of action and therapeutic opportunities. *Brain Behav.* 2014; 4(2):108-22.

Bégin ME, Langlois MF, Lorrain D, et al. Thyroid function and cognition during aging. *Curr Gerontol Geriatr Res.* 2008; 2008:1-11.

Bermejo-Pareja F, Antequera D, Vargas T, et al. Saliva levels of Abeta1-42 as potential biomarker of Alzheimer's disease: a pilot study. *BMC Neurol.* 2010; 10:108.

Bremner JD. Traumatic stress: effects on the brain. *Dialogues Clin Neurosci.* 2006; 8(4):445-61.

Brüning JC, Gautam D, Burks DJ, et al. Role of brain insulin receptor in control of body weight and reproduction. *Science.* 2000; 289(5487):2122-5.

Collet TH, Gussekloo J, Bauer DC, et al. Subclinical hyperthyroidism and the risk of coronary heart disease and mortality. *JAMA Internal Medicine.* 2012; 172(10): 799-809.

Conrad CD. Chronic stress-induced hippocampal vulnerability: the glucocorticoid vulnerability hypothesis. *Rev Neurosci.* 2008; 19(6):395-411.

Cooper C, Sommerlad A, Lyketsos CG, et al. Modifiable predictors of dementia in mild cognitive impairment: a systematic review and meta-analysis. *Am J Psychiatry.* 2015; 172(4):323-34.

Davison K, Berry NM, Misan G, et al. Dose-related effects of flavanol-rich cocoa on blood pressure. *J Hum Hypertens.* 2010; 24(9):568-76.

De Jager CA, Oulhai A, Jacoby R, et al. Cognitive and clinical outcomes of homocysteine-lowering B-vitamin treatment in mild cognitive impairment: a randomized controlled trial. *Int J Geriatr Psychiatry.* 2012; 27(6):592-600.

Dean O, Giorlando F, Berk M. N-acetylcysteine in psychiatry: current therapeutic evidence and potential mechanisms of action. *J Psychiatry Neurosci.* 2011; 36(2):78-86.

Dobos N, Korf J, Luiten PG, et al. Neuroinflammation in Alzheimer's disease and major depression. *J Psychiatry Neurosci.* 2010; 67(6):503-4.

Dong H, Csernansky JG. Effects of stress and stress hormones on amyloid-b protein and plaque deposition. *J Alzheimers Dis.* 2009; 18(2):459-69.

Farr SA, Poon HF, Dogrukol-Ak D, et al. The antioxidants alpha-lipoic acid and N-acetylcysteine reverse memory impairment and brain oxidative stress in aged SAMP8 mice. *J Neurochem.* 2003; 84(5):1173-83.

Feher G, Koltai K, Kesmarky G, et al. Effect of parenteral or oral vinpocetine on the hemorheological parameters of patients with chronic cerebrovascular diseases. *Phyto-medicine.* 2009; 16(2-3):111-7.

Figlewicz DP, Szot P, Chavez M, et al. Intraventricular insulin increases dopamine transporter mRNA in rat VTA/substantia nigra. Brain Res. 1994; 644(2):331-4.

Havrankova J, Roth J, Brownstein M. Insulin receptors are widely distributed in the central nervous system of the rat. *Nature.* 1978; 272(5656):827-9.

Javed H, Khan A, Vaibhav K, et al. Taurine ameliorates neurobehavioral, neurochemical and immunohistochemical changes in sporadic dementia of Alzheimer's type (SDAT) caused by intracerebroventricular treptozotocin in rats. *Neurol Sci.* 2013; 34(12):2181-92.

Jernerén F, Elshorbagy AK, Oulhaj A, et al. Brain atrophy in cognitively impaired elderly: the importance of long-chain omega-3 fatty acids and B vitamin status in a randomized controlled trial. *Am J Clin Nutr.* 2015; 102(1):215-21.

Kanai M, Otsuka Y, Otsuka K, et al. A phase I study investigating the safety and pharmacokinetics of highly bioavailable curcumin (Theracurmin) in cancer patients. *Cancer Chemother Pharmacol.* 2013; 71(6):1521-30.

References

Kemény V, Molnar S, Andrejkovics M, et al. Acute and chronic effects of vinpocetine on cerebral hemodynamics and neuropsychological performance in multi-infarct patients. *J Clin Pharmacol.* 2005; 45(9):1048-54.

Kobayashi S, Iwamoto M, Kon K, et al. Acetyl-L-carnitine improves aged brain function. *Geriatr Gerontol Int.* 2010; 10Suppl 1:S99-S106.

Könner AC, Hess S, Tovar S, et al. Role for insulin signaling in catecholaminergic neurons in control of energy homeostasis. *Cell Metab.* 2011; 13(6):720-8.

Koch, S. Walking backwards may sharpen thinking. *Psychol Sci.* 2009; 20:549-50.

Lonskaya I, Hebron M, Chen W, et al. Tau deletion impairs intra cellular b-amyloid-42 clearance and leads to more extracellular plaque deposition in gene transfer models. *Mol Neurodegener.* 2014; 9:46.

Louzada PR, Paula Lima AC, Mendonca-Silva DL, et al. Taurine prevents the neurotoxicity of beta-amyloid and glutamate receptor agonists: activation of GABA receptors and possible implications for Alzheimer's disease and other neurological disorders. *FASEB J.* 2004; 18(3):511-8.

Lupien SJ, de Leon M, de Santi S, et al. Cortisol levels during human aging predict hippocampal atrophy and memory deficits. *Nat Neurosci.* 1998; 1(1):69-73.

Mishra S, Palanivelu K. The effect of curcumin (turmeric) on Alzheimer's disease: an overview. *Ann Indian Acad Neurol.* 2008; 11(1):13-9.

Moretti R, Torre P, Antonello RM, et al. Risk factors for vascular dementia: hypotension as a key point. *Vasc Health Risk Manag.* 2008; 4(2):395-402.

Ng TP, Chiam P-C, Lee T, et al. Curry consumption and cognitive function the elderly. *Am J Epidemiol.* 2006; 164(9):898-906.

Nussbaum JM, Schilling S, Cynis H, et al. Prion-like behavior and tau-dependent cytotoxicity of pyroglutamylated amyloid-β. *Nature.* 2012; 485(7400):651-5.

Ohwada K, Takeda H, Yamazaki M, et al. Pyrroloquinoline quinone (PQQ) prevents cognitive deficit caused by oxidative stress in rats. *J Clin Biochem Nutr.* 2008; 42(1):29-34.

Sun QQ, Xu SS, Pan JL, et al. Huperzine-A capsules enhance memory and learning performance in 34 pairs of matched adolescent students. *Zhongguo Yao Li Xue Bao.* 1999; 20(7):601-3.

Szilágyi G, Nazy Z, Balkay L, et al. Effects of vinpocetine on the redistribution of cerebral blood flow and glucose metabolism in chronic ischemic stroke patients: a PET study. *J Neurol Sci.* 2005; 229-230:275-84.

Tan ZS, Beiser A, Vasan RS, et al. Thyroid function and the risk of Alzheimer disease. *Arch Intern Med.* 2008; 168(14):1514-20.

Whiley L, Sen A, Heaton J, et al. Evidence of altered phosphatidylcholine metabolism in Alzheimer's disease. *Neurobiol Aging.* 2014; 35(2):271-8.

Witte AV, Kerti L, Hermannstädter HM, et al. Long-chain omega-3 fatty acids improve brain function and structure in older adults. *Cereb Cortex.* 2014; 24(11):3059-68.

Xiao Z, Zhang A, Lin J, et al. Telomerase: a target for therapeutic effects of curcumin and a curcumin derivative in ab1-42 insult in vitro. *PLoS One.* 2014; 9(7):e101251.

Xie H, Wang JR, Yau LF, et al. Catechins and procyanidins of Ginkgo biloba show potent activities towards the inhibition of b-amyloid peptide aggregation and destabilization of preformed fibrils. *Molecules.* 2014; 19(4):5119-34.

Xu ZQ, Ling XM, Juan-Wu L, et al. Treatment with huperzine A improves cognition in vascular dementia patients. *Cell Biochem Biophys.* 2012; 62(1):55-8.

Yang G, Want Y, Tian J, et al. Huperzine A for Alzheimer's disease: a systematic review and meta-analysis of randomized clinical trials. *PLoS One.* 2013; 8(9):e74916.

Yarchoan M, Arnold SE. Repurposing diabetes drugs for brain insulin resistance in Alzheimer disease. *Diabetes.* 2014; 63(7):2253-61.

Zandi PP, Anthony JC, Khachaturian AS, et al. Reduced risk of Alzheimer disease in users of antioxidant vitamin supplements: the Cache County Study. *Arch Neurol.* 2004; 61(1):82-8.

Zhang L, Fiala M, Cashman J, et al. Curcuminoids enhance amyloid-beta uptake by macrophages of Alzheimer's disease patients. *J Alzheimers Dis.* 2006; 10(1):1-7.